The Product Development Challenge

The Harvard Business Review Book Series

The Product Development Challenge

Competing through Speed, Quality, and Creativity

Edited with
an Introduction by
**Kim B. Clark and
Steven C. Wheelwright**

A Harvard Business Review Book

The *Harvard Business Review* articles in this collection are available as
individual reprints. Discounts apply to quantity purchases. For information
and ordering contact Customer Service, Harvard Business School
Publishing, Boston, MA 02163. Telephone: (617) 495-6192, 9 a.m. to
5 p.m. Eastern Time, Monday through Friday. Fax: (617) 495-6985,
24 hours a day.

The paper used in this publication meets the requirements of the American
National Standard for Permanence of Paper for Printed Library Materials
Z39.48-1984

Library of Congress Cataloging-in-Publication Data

The product development challenge : competing through speed, quality,
    and creativity / edited with an introduction by Kim B. Clark and
    Steven C. Wheelwright.
        p.   cm.—(A Harvard business review book)
    Includes index.
    ISBN 0-87584-609-2
    1. Industrial management.   2. Product management.   3. Quality of
    products.   4. New products.   5. Quality function deployment.
    I. Clark, Kim B.   II. Wheelwright, Steven C., 1943–   .
    III. Series: Harvard business review book series.
    HD31.P763   1995
    658.5'6—dc20   94-44895
                                                                CIP

Contents

Part II   Managing the Creation of New Technologies

computer companies that developed a similar product in the 1980s suggests that "system-focused" companies achieve the best product improvements at the lowest cost.

stay just ahead of the pack, Edward R. McCracken,
CEO of Silicon Graphics, Inc., asserts that the key to
competitive advantage is to produce the chaos by
being an innovation leader.

Introduction

Kim B. Clark
Steven C. Wheelwright

The articles in this collection address one of the most powerful but difficult activities in business—the development of new products. The power of new product development derives from the character of technology and markets in the closing years of the twentieth century. These are years of change in technology, customer requirements, channels of distribution, competitors, and the very structure of industry. This is a dynamic time when new technical concepts create new opportunities and new threats, when new demands emerge in the market, when competitors make new and unexpected moves, and when new ways of competing emerge.

The dynamics of change and their impact on competition have worked their way into every sector of the economy. We see their effects in consumer packaged goods, food products, diesel engines, financial services, health care, pharmaceuticals, medical instruments and devices, entertainment, computers, transportation, telecommunications, chemicals and engineered plastics, and automobiles. In all of these industries—and in many others we could mention—the dynamics of technology, markets, and competition place a premium on outstanding performance in the development of new products.

Take, for example, the case of the world auto industry. In the decade from 1985 to 1995, the character of that industry and the fortunes of individual enterprises in it changed dramatically. In only a few short years, the entry of Japanese firms into the luxury segment turned that market inside out. In the late 1980s, outstanding new products from Toyota, Nissan, and Honda redefined the value relationship in that segment and established new benchmarks for quality. The entry of these Japanese firms into the luxury segment seemed to foreshadow their dominance of the entire industry. Building from strength in small and medium-sized cars, they successfully developed a position in the high end of the market. Yet a mere three years later, U.S. and European automakers mounted a vigorous competitive response. Nowhere is this more evident than in the case of Chrysler. Once the laughing stock of the industry, saved from bankruptcy only by government loan guarantees, and seemingly mired in a tradition of boring, boxy products, Chrysler emerged in the early to mid-nineties as a company on a roll. It dramatically increased its market share in the United States, established strong export markets in Europe and Japan, and generated significant cash flow and profitability to boot. Meanwhile, at the high end of the market, the likes of Mercedes and BMW moved aggressively to recapture market share, to expand the breadth of their product lines, and to reposition their international manufacturing network to compete more effectively in the world market.

At the heart of the Japanese firms' success in the 1980s, and of the resurgence of firms such as Chrysler and BMW, lies creative, rapid, high-performance product development. What matters in the world auto industry and what matters in every other dynamic industry is not the single successful product, but the continuous development of outstanding products—products that hit the market with great quality, compelling customer value and extraordinary efficiency. Chrysler survived the 1980s because it created a great product in the minivan. And it sustained and grew its market share in the mid-90s by moving quickly and efficiently to bring out the LH Series, the Jeep Grand Cherokee, the T300 truck, the Neon, the Cirrus, and other outstanding products.

The dynamic, intense competitive environment that characterizes our times places a premium on speed, efficiency, and quality in product development. The enterprise with consistent excellence in its product development wields great power. Yet actually achieving consistent excellence is no simple task. This is the challenge of product development: to build capabilities in technology, marketing, product design, engineering, and manufacturing; to overcome uncertainty and make decisions; to link initiatives in new products to business strategy; to integrate functional expertise into a coherent whole; and to do so time after time after time.

Exceptional product development is difficult because it cuts across every aspect of the enterprise. It involves the varied skills of many people who must work effectively together on the details. And these details must be integrated into a coherent package that customers in an uncertain future will find compelling. The need to do all this with speed, efficiency, and high quality underscores the magnitude of the challenge.

Over the last several years, as firms throughout the world have struggled to meet this challenge, practitioners and academics have sought to understand the principles that drive outstanding product development performance. In doing so they have created a number of powerful new concepts, frameworks, tools, and methodologies. Much of this work has been published in the *Harvard Business Review*, and in this collection we have tried to capture the ideas that really make a difference. The themes we emphasize here reflect our view of what matters most in meeting the challenge of new product development.

The first part of the collection focuses on managing what we call the front end of the development process, explored in Part I, "Competing through New Product Development"; Part II, "Managing the Creation of New Technologies"; and Part III, "Creating a Development Strategy." While much of the historical literature in this field has focused on the management of individual projects, we have found that what goes on before the individual projects ever start is often decisive in determining their subsequent speed, efficiency, and quality. Three activities are crucial at the front end of the process. The first is laying a strong foundation of capability, particularly in the creation, acquisition, and application of new knowledge. The second is aligning the set of new product development projects to the firm's business strategy, and vice versa. It is often the case in business that the processes behind the creation of business plans and "how we do business" and the processes that "generate ideas for new projects" are quite different and unconnected. The result is a set of projects that reflect neither the realities of the business nor the strategic intent of the organization. And further, senior management's involvement is often ad hoc and downright unhelpful. What is missing is a set of frameworks and activities that allow senior management to effectively link the strategy of the business to the generation of new concepts and the creation of an attractive project portfolio that will lead to a stream of effective new products.

With a foundation of capabilities and with a process that links strategy to projects, the third front-end activity is the process of matching projects to capacity. Simply put, most companies have too many projects. This lack of focus leads to congestion in the execution of projects, poor allocation of resources, a lack of discipline and on-schedule delivery, and a haphazard flurry expediting and scrambling to meet market deadlines.

Articles in Parts I and II by Hirotaka Takeuchi and Ikujiro Nonaka,

Joseph Bower and Thomas Hout, Ralph Gomory, Fumio Kodama, Marco Iansiti, Rebecca Henderson, and members of the Manufacturing Vision Group[1] highlight the importance of linking capabilities and strategy and committing the entire enterprise to common goals. Examples from the computer and pharmaceutical industries, in particular, illustrate the power derived from aligning these elements. The articles in Part III, by Frederick Gluck and Richard Foster, Steven Wheelwright and W. Earl Sasser, James Hodder and Henry Riggs, and Steven Wheelwright and Kim Clark, offer practical tools for improving project planning, evaluation, and resource allocation.

Getting the front end right sets the stage for the second theme: achieving effective execution of development projects. The articles in Part IV, "Building High-Performance Teams," and Part V, "Executing Development Projects," emphasize the power of teams, the importance of integration across functions and disciplines, and the critical role of structured methodologies in achieving speed, efficiency, and high quality. To execute a project successfully the firm must accomplish two basic tasks. It must achieve depth of expertise in the various disciplines and functional areas that contribute to developing the product. But it must also bring those areas of expertise together into a coherent system. Research on high-performance product development has shown quite clearly that problems in lead time and in productivity generally revolve around the challenge of integration. The typical problem is that important connections between functional activities are not made in either a timely or an effective way. The result is that difficulties with the product as a system crop up late in the development cycle, resulting in significant delays, redesigns, and poor quality.

Making quick and effective connections between functional activities entails more than simply increasing communication or establishing good working relationships. These, of course, are important. But the kind of integration that leads to rapid, high-quality, efficient development must go much deeper. In this context, teams play a crucial role. They become a way to achieve shared understanding of the objectives and purposes of the project across functions, and a mechanism that allows that shared understanding to drive changes in the way problems get posed and solved, and tasks get defined and organized in carrying out the basic development work. The power of teams lies in their ability to take hold of the project, shape it, and influence how actual work gets done in the organization. The articles in Part IV by Jon Katzenbach and Douglas Smith, Charles House and Raymond

Price, Christopher Meyer, Kim Clark and Takahiro Fujimoto, and members of the Manufacturing Vision Group illustrate the power of cross-functional teams in action.

Teams are most effective when they work in a context that supports that deep integration. Structured methodologies such as design for manufacturing (DFM) or quality function deployment (QFD) provide a powerful context for teamwork and, of course, help generate technical insight. But they also facilitate integration by recasting narrow functional problems in terms of their consequences for system performance. This recasting makes evident the interactions between functions and thus the deeper issues in the development of the product. They create a language system that allows people with different jargon to communicate. And they provide mechanisms for teams to redefine tasks, reshape processes, and integrate work. In Part V, John Hauser and Don Clausing, Daniel Whitney, David Burt and William Soukup, and James Dean and Gerald Susman explore the processes and systems required to support teamwork and execute viable projects that link design and manufacturing capabilities.

If we step back from our look at the front end of product development and the actual execution of projects, it becomes clear that a central aspect of success in meeting the challenge of new products is strengthening leadership. This third and final theme of the collection is illustrated in Part VI, "Creating a Competitive Advantage," which features articles by T. Michael Nevens, Gregory Summe, and Bro Uttal and by the Manufacturing Vision Group, as well as an interview with Silicon Graphics' Ed McCracken. Leadership must come from senior management. Senior managers have a unique perspective on the business as a whole and on the role that new products must play in it. The people running the business, including the general manager and the heads of the major functions, have a responsibility to articulate direction in the organization, pull together the expertise and knowledge resident in the enterprise, and integrate the strategy for the business with the plans for projects and new products.

But leadership is also crucial at the level of individual projects. Much of the power of what we call "heavyweight" teams derives from the leadership of the heavyweight project leader. Indeed, the leader of the heavyweight team plays a general management role. Once again, that individual sees the whole, helps to make connections between the parts and the whole, and takes responsibility for effectively integrating all of the elements of the project into a coherent system that not only functions effectively as a product, but delivers to customers outstanding and compelling value. This is what we mean by product integrity, and product integrity is what effective team leaders deliver.

A close look at the role played by the heavyweight project leader compared to the work done by senior management in the front end of the process reveals a powerful symmetry in their respective roles and activities. Indeed, we have argued that projects are in fact the school for leaders. The way an organization both develops outstanding products and creates the leaders required for that purpose is to make projects a focus of the enterprise—of the systems and procedures, and the concepts and principles that govern it. In this way, senior managers set the pattern that guides action throughout the firm. They make product development a central focus of the enterprise, manage the front end of that process through effectively linking strategy with the project portfolio, and create processes in the organization to support effective teamwork and effective project execution. In so doing they create an environment that nurtures the development of leaders for projects and ultimately for the enterprise as a whole.

These then are the themes that characterize this collection of articles—managing the front end (by building capability, linking strategy to projects, and shaping the project portfolio), achieving effective project execution (through deep integration across functions and disciplines, teamwork, and structured methods) and strengthening leadership (of senior management and project leaders). We hope you find the articles stimulating and useful, and that you also see them as part of a larger work in process. We have learned a great deal about meeting the challenge of new product development, but there is much more to learn and much work to be done.

Note

1. The Manufacturing Vision Group was a unique collaborative effort between academics from engineering and management disciplines in four universities—Stanford, Purdue, MIT, and Harvard—and senior executives from five companies—Kodak, DEC, HP, Chaparral Steel, and Ford. The group conducted research in the companies, met frequently to digest the results, and produced teaching materials, articles, and a book. Three articles in this collection were written by members of the Group: H. Kent Bowen, Kim B. Clark, Charles A. Holloway, Dorothy Leonard-Barton, and Steven C. Wheelwright.

The Product Development Challenge

PART

I

Competing through New Product Development

1
Development Projects: The Engine of Renewal

H. Kent Bowen, Kim B. Clark, Charles A. Holloway, and Steven C. Wheelwright

Digital Equipment's effort in the 1980s to develop high-density disk drives is an outstanding example of how a company can use a development project to create not only a new product or process but also a competitively important expertise. The undertaking, known as the RA90 hard-disk-drive project, also demonstrates a critical truth about development projects that managers often miss: the resulting capability can be and often is more important than the product itself. Indeed, by many measures, the RA90 project was anything but a total success. However, the capability gained laid the foundation for a generation of products that significantly enhanced DEC's competitiveness.

At the end of the 1970s, Digital, the world's second largest computer maker, found itself in a serious predicament: it was about ten years behind the state of the art in a key computer component, magnetic storage systems. Senior managers felt this area would be increasingly important for the company to retain its leadership position. Some executives spotted the emergence of two dramatically new technologies on the competitive landscape: thin-film magnetic storage media and thin-film heads for reading and writing the media. If DEC could master these technologies, they believed, the company could leapfrog the existing leaders in the field and become a major force in hard-disk-drive systems. By the early 1980s, DEC had progressed enough with the technology that it could launch a major effort. The result was the ambitious RA90 project, one of the largest development efforts in the company's history.

The project's success required four significant breakthrough innovations: the thin-film media and the process to manufacture it; the thin-film head and its process; a new electromechanical drive system; and a new process for assembling the components into the final system. Based on R&D estimates of where leading competitors might be in three to five years, senior managers set highly ambitious cost and performance targets for the product. They marshaled a phenomenal amount of resources in terms of money and talent, recruiting people from both inside and outside the company to work on the project.

The original specs called for a 9-inch drive with a storage density of 30 million bits per square inch. But after two of its engineers visited Japan and found Fujitsu planning to develop a drive with a density of 45 million bits per square inch, DEC upped its goal to the same level. Development of parts of the drive, notably the read/write heads, was already proving difficult, and the more ambitious density target created undue risk, frustration, and delays. DEC finally shipped the RA90 in 1988, two years late. The final product cost, originally targeted at $2,500, had risen to $5,000. Even more traumatic for the company was the fact that the industry was moving to smaller drives by this time, so the 9-inch drive would soon be obsolete.

DEC also never achieved the 45-million-bit mark and had to settle for 40 million bits. But Fujitsu had also failed to reach the 45-million-bit mark, and the state of the art for the rest of the industry by 1988 had risen to only 30 million bits.

If DEC executives had not panicked after the visit to Japan and set a course for 40 million bits, they could have saved significant time and expense. In hindsight, they also could have done a better job integrating the efforts involved in developing the drive's major subsystems. But the project nonetheless succeeded in achieving an important strategic goal. It gave DEC what it needed to become a leader in disk drives: state-of-the-art capabilities for making thin-film media and heads and designing and assembling high-performance disk-drive systems. The RA90 effort shows how a manufacturing company can build new capabilities by consciously using development projects as agents of change.

Learn through Development

There are several reasons why development projects provide the best opportunities for a manufacturing company to renew itself constantly so that it can attain and then retain a leadership position. The most obvious reason is because development projects are where new products and processes are created. But, equally important, a company, by wisely selecting the projects it undertakes, can use them to develop new skills, new knowledge, and new systems.

Why is a development project such a good place for this? A development project is a microcosm of the whole organization. A project team is made up of people from many areas of the company. A team's success is determined by the integrated outcome of everyone's work. The teams must also interact with suppliers and customers. Moreover, because development projects typically are conducted under intense time and budget pressures, they usually magnify the strengths and weaknesses of a company, including its people, systems, and culture. Development projects provide a comprehensive, real-time test of the systems, structures, and values of the whole organization. And most projects are sufficiently limited in duration and scope to enable a company to use them to experiment without incurring major risk.

If employees are taught that every project has two dimensions—that what matters is not just the resulting product or process but how the result is achieved—they will take to heart the idea that learning is a primary goal for everyone in the organization. Without exception, the most successful projects that the Manufacturing Vision Group examined were those in which the teams operated in a learning environment (see Exhibit I). People learned from previous projects, advanced their skills during the course of their project, and applied what they learned to renew the company's capabilities. Conversely, the unsuccessful projects typically operated in an atmosphere that did not emphasize learning. Two efforts at Ford—to develop an air-conditioner compressor for automobiles and to create the 1989 Thunderbird—demonstrate how effective corporate learning occurs in development projects only if management makes the learning of specific things an explicit project goal.

Ford decided in 1986 to develop an air-conditioner compressor in-house for the first time after it was stung by Nippondenso. Shortly after Ford paid Nippondenso to license compressor technology, the Japanese components supplier unveiled an improved compressor that it was making available to other carmakers. Outraged, executives at Ford decided to give the company's climate-control division the challenge of creating its own compressor-design capability.

In setting the goals for the project, the division's managers decided

Exhibit I.

Members of the Manufacturing Vision Group

Chaparral Steel Company
David Fournie
Gordon E. Forward

Ford Motor Company
Richard Billington
Max Jurosek

Massachusetts Institute of Technology
H. Kent Bowen
Thomas W. Eagar
George Stephanopoulos

Digital Equipment Corporation
Douglas Braithwaite
William Hanson
Michael Titelbaum

Harvard University
Kim B. Clark
Marco Iansiti
Dorothy Leonard-Barton
Gil Preuss
Steven C. Wheelwright

Purdue University
Ferdinand Leimkuhler
James Solberg
Carolyn Woo

Eastman Kodak Company
C. (Robin) Farran
David Groff
Rohn Harmer
John Owen
Jack Rittler

Hewlett-Packard Company
Sara Beckman
Harold Edmondson

Stanford University
Philip Barkan
Charles A. Holloway

to shoot high. Their goals were to develop a compressor that would outperform but cost less than Nippondenso's; to develop it very quickly (in two years); and to put designers, manufacturing engineers, machining specialists, and assemblers from the division on the same team and in the same place. Getting these 17 people together was a revolutionary concept at Ford, where people in different functions, particularly those in design and manufacturing, normally worked at arm's length. Ford managers had two reasons for setting this last goal. First, they thought there was no other way to create the compressor so quickly. And second, they saw the project as a laboratory where the group could figure out how to integrate design and manufacturing functions, thereby producing a new development capability for the company.

By several measures, the project was a success. The resulting FX15 compressor performed better than Nippondenso's, was less expensive, and was much easier to manufacture, proving the value of integrating design and manufacturing. While the development process used was far from perfect, it laid the foundation for a new process that Ford could use in other projects. The climate-control division continually improved the integrated cross-functional approach in other endeavors. Ultimately, the approach enabled Ford to reduce the time and money required to develop new products.

In contrast, during development of the 1989 Thunderbird, Ford missed a golden opportunity to create an increasingly important capability in the automobile business: integrating the work of research and advanced-technology development directly and effectively with commercial automotive products. Traditionally, groups that do research and create advanced technology for U.S. carmakers have lived in their own world. A team would develop new knowledge about components or materials and put it on a shelf along with an array of other insights and technologies. The engine- or car-development teams would then occasionally search through them, shopping for solutions to specific problems. But not everyone would shop, and not everything on the shelf was useful. Moreover, those who found something with potential often discovered that the new technologies could solve commercial problems only after a lot more time-consuming, expensive work. While it is important to have critical advanced technologies fully or partially developed before major product-development efforts proceed, this approach has usually resulted in neither fast nor effective product introductions.

As Ford realized after the fact, it could have used the Thunderbird project to break out of this rut by figuring out a way to link research and advanced technology more effectively with the development of a new component—in this instance, a new supercharged engine—that fit a new car model's specific needs. But senior managers failed both to make this an explicit project goal and to think through how the project should be organized in order to achieve the necessary coordination.

Besides calling for a new engine design, the Thunderbird required a new car platform. Following standard practice, Ford managers treated the engine, including the development of the supercharger, as a separate project and spread the detailed work for the rest of the project (all of the car except the engine) among traditional functional groups. About halfway through the project, Ford put a new manager in charge of the entire project. Even so, the separate teams were not closely integrated.

The lack of integration between the engine work and development of the rest of the vehicle created significant problems for the project. Late in the timetable, the supercharged engine had to be redesigned because it ran into unexpected durability and performance problems due to the supercharger. These problems probably could have been avoided had the engine group been plugged into the advanced-technology-development group that had been conducting research on supercharging, but it was not. Eventually, Ford did get a supercharged Thunderbird. But the process it had used—with its multiple, unplanned design iterations, long delays, and substantial weight and cost overruns—was not one it would ever want to repeat.

When the Manufacturing Vision Group reviewed the project, it discovered that the supercharger episode had surprised a number of executives at Ford. They were surprised because Ford had formed cross-functional planning groups of senior managers and senior staffers to think about future technology needs. One reason for forming the groups was to provide guidance for research work, which they did. But the executives wrongly assumed that the groups would also naturally serve as a link between research and the operating engine-development groups, thereby making sure the latter would tap the former's knowledge. But those links never materialized at the working level. By managing the project as they did, Ford executives ensured that the project was not the powerful agent of change for the company that it could have been.

Projects Studied by the Manufacturing Vision Group

Chaparral Steel

Digital Pulpit Controls. This project was initiated in 1987 to upgrade the company's furnace control systems. Both electric-arc furnaces used by Chaparral to melt scrap were controlled with analog instrumentation. To improve efficiency, the project team developed the world's first digital furnace control system in 1988. Digital electronics facilitated precision control of the movement of the carbon electrodes in the electric-arc furnaces.

Electric-Arc Saw. This project was Chaparral's attempt in the mid-1980s to develop the industry's first electric-arc saw for cutting large volumes of steel. Electric-arc saws had never been used before on the scale or throughput required for semicontinuous mass production. The lesson of this project was that management must carefully consider whether it is asking a project to make too great a leap.

Horizontal Caster. The goal of this project was to develop a new casting process for making high-grade steel. In the mid-1980s, all carbon steelmakers were using a vertical casting process. A horizontal caster would enable Chaparral, a minimill, to compete with the large, integrated steelmakers in the manufacture of selected carbon steel and low-alloy, forging-quality steels. The project resulted in the first horizontal steel caster in the world in 1990.

Microtuff 10 Steel. With this project, Chaparral sought to move into a new market in the late 1980s: high-quality alloy steels for forging. By meeting strict quality standards, Microtuff helped enhance Chaparral's image as a high-tech innovator.

Digital Equipment

CDA Software. As DEC's line of office workstations expanded, the company perceived a need in the late 1980s to develop an overreaching computer architecture to link its desktop-publishing products. Compound-document-architecture (CDA) software was the solution that DEC pursued. DEC's goal was to make it a standard for desktop publishing. The project showed how DEC overcame integration difficulties and illustrated the company's different approaches to hardware and software development.

DECstation 3100. Facing competitive pressures in the late 1980s, DEC launched this project to develop a new workstation based on a UNIX operating system and RISC architecture (instead of the company's standard VMS system). Completed in record time, the project was a technical success, but the workstation did not meet its sales targets because of a lack of applications software.

LAN Bridge 200. This communications network product serves as the traffic-control node to link several computer networks and is a follow-on to an earlier successful product. The product-development team, which consisted of members from different DEC sites and functions, carried out the work in an integrated fashion during 1987 to 1989. But the project revealed two areas in which the company was weak: identifying customer needs and including less dominant functions in critical decision making.

RA90 Disk Drive. This project, launched in 1981 and completed in 1987, had two goals: to develop a high-density disk drive for computers and to give DEC the state-of-the-art capabilities it needed to be a leader in the field. The project was divided into three subprojects that were carried out in parallel. The RA90 product goals required DEC to make major technical breakthroughs in thin-film storage media, thin-film heads, automated clean-room assembly, and electromechanical-drive-systems design.

Eastman Kodak

Antistatic Film Coating. The purpose of this project, begun in 1985, was to develop a clear, antistatic coating for microfilm that would prevent it from attracting dust without compromising the perceived sharpness of its image. With a clear idea of what customers wanted and applying Kodak's technical strengths, the coating made use of off-the-shelf but state-of-the-art technology. The project was fully executed under MAP, Kodak's new companywide system for managing development projects.

"Factory of the Future." Kodak initiated this project in 1986 to upgrade and expand the capacity of its factories that cut, perforate, wind, and package 35mm consumer films. The project quickly became the vehicle for trying to incorporate many experimental production technologies. Kodak began it in the days when the company was beginning its conversion from a functional to a line-of-business structure.

FunSaver Camera. Kodak launched this project in 1987 to design and produce a "single-use" camera. The concept was to package film in a simple, inexpensive plastic camera body. After the pictures were taken, the consumer would hand the whole assembly to a photofinisher. The film would then be processed and the body discarded or recycled. The design drew on existing design knowledge but was executed on a unique CAD/CAM system that enhanced integration and shortened the lead time from design to production.

Panda Printer. Panda was a thermal printer that could produce large-format, color images of extremely high quality from digital data. Such a product was needed in the late 1980s by the U.S. Department of Defense and top-of-the-line industrial and professional companies. This project was one of Kodak's first attempts to integrate divisions from different lines of business and to merge both government and consumer product specifications.

Ford

Crown Victoria/Grand Marquis (EN53). This 1991 model was built on an existing platform. It was the second vehicle to use a new modular engine and the first project to use Ford's total concept-to-customer (CTC) development process.

FX15 Air-Conditioner Compressor. This project, begun in 1986, represented the first time that Ford tried designing a compressor for an automobile's air-conditioning system. The compressor was developed by Ford's climate-control division, which was run as a separate company and did not use the CTC process. However, the climate-control division did try several new methods for product development, including concurrent engineering.

Lincoln Continental (FN9). This automobile was Ford's first attempt to build a luxury car on the Taurus platform. It required major suspension-system modifications and was the first time the company used a 3.8-liter engine in a transverse configuration in a car. The 1988 Continental was begun in the "old Ford," in which projects were organized by function. By the time the car was finished, the company had adopted the CTC process.

Thunderbird/Cougar (MN 12). This 1989 model was built on a new car platform that included a novel supercharged engine. Launched in 1984, the project was the first in which Ford used codified lessons from the Taurus program. The company completed the project using the new CTC system.

Hewlett-Packard

DeskJet Printer. In 1985, HP set out to design a new class of low-cost computer printers based on ink-jet print technology. The development effort to get the products to market quickly and at low cost was unprecedented in the company. This was one of HP's early attempts to integrate manufacturing, marketing, and R&D.

Hornet Spectrum Analyzer. This project, which was undertaken in the mid-1980s, developed a less expensive version of a standard instrument to test and analyze radio-frequency and microwave signals. Like the Logic Analyzer, described below, the Hornet was a product for electronics engineers, and HP could take advantage of its own in-house customers as well as its strong industrial customer base in defining the project's objectives. HP wanted to use the Hornet to ward off competitors in the low end of the market. The project required breaking some well-entrenched product-development practices.

HP 150 Computer. Begun in 1981, the HP 150 was the company's first formal attempt to enter the personal computer market. The development team tried to design a machine that would function as both a stand-alone PC and as a terminal for a central computer. This project revealed clearly the difficulties of integrating a development effort involving a diverse set of autonomous corporate divisions.

Logic Analyzer. This project was an attempt by HP to beat out a competitor in the newly emerging digital oscilloscope market. The Logic Analyzer was developed in the early 1970s, when HP, like most engineering companies of the day, was organized along functional lines.

Seven Elements for Breakthrough Learning

As the Ford and Digital examples demonstrate, development projects can be designed and managed so that they continually generate powerful, distinctive capabilities as well as winning products or processes. The Manufacturing Vision Group found seven key elements, which, when applied holistically, optimized development, fostered learning, and initiated change throughout an organization. Without exception, the most successful projects masterfully combined all these elements; inevitably, those that failed were lacking in one or more.

CORE CAPABILITIES. The attributes of a company that enable it to serve customers in a unique way, distinguishing it from its competitors, are its core capabilities. These include knowledge and skills, managerial systems, manufacturing processes, and values—the attitudes, behaviors, and norms that dominate in an organization. In the best-managed companies, core capabilities naturally grow stronger with each development project and are leveraged in a way that enables a company to do things its competitors cannot. But there is a dark side of core capabilities that managers often overlook: if a company fails to update or replace core capabilities as its industry evolves, they can become *core rigidities* that can thwart needed change.

GUIDING VISION. A clear picture of the future, a light at the end of the tunnel that serves as a focal point for daily work, is the guiding vision of a company. Such a vision is not a specific goal but a general destination that describes what must be accomplished and why, and leaves room for individuals to determine how to get there. A company needs integrated or synergistic guiding visions for products, projects, and each line of business in order to create products (or processes) that fulfill an intended set of customer expectations, build enduring capabilities, and support the business strategy.

ORGANIZATION AND LEADERSHIP. Companies need a customized system for promoting teamwork and supplying managers to head projects who have a clear concept of what a given product should be, can provide direction, and have decision-making authority. No one organizational structure or type of leadership is best for all projects; a company needs to develop a range of approaches and have a system for matching each project with the approach that best suits its goals and competitive environment.

OWNERSHIP AND COMMITMENT. A sense of devotion that team members feel toward a project defines their ownership and commitment. Skillful managers and good company practices can bolster ownership and commitment among employees.

"PUSHING THE ENVELOPE." The practice of constantly making improvements to a company's products, processes, and capabilities on a broad front is called pushing the envelope. This practice creates a tension in carrying out work that is necessary for reaching ever higher levels of performance.

PROTOTYPES. Models, mock-ups, and computer simulations of the product or process created at strategic junctures in development projects are called prototypes. They help employees solve problems and learn faster and better, and they help create a common language that knits a team together.

INTEGRATION. To optimize work, companies need a system to promote joint decision making among all functional units and divisions involved in the project. Integration is much more than coordination; it redefines work content and individual tasks to maximize the efficiency of the whole development team.

The careful attention that Chaparral Steel paid to all of these elements explains why its horizontal caster project was so successful. From nothing when it was founded in 1975, Chaparral, a minimill located in Midlothian, Texas, has mushroomed into the nation's thirteenth-largest steelmaker. How did Chaparral achieve its breathtaking growth? First, Chaparral managers have always believed that there is no limit to how much conventional processes and equipment can be improved. As a result, Chaparral has repeatedly shattered the conventional industry wisdom about how much a given piece of equipment can produce or the tolerances that it can achieve. And second, Chaparral has disproved the presumption that minimills can produce only low-grade commodity steel.

Chaparral's development of the industry's first horizontal caster shows how nothing is impossible if the seven elements are married to a deep knowledge of process and product technology. Minimills consist of three basic parts: an electric-arc furnace, a caster that converts the liquid metal to solid billets, and a rolling mill to create the final shapes. Like all other minimills, Chaparral used a vertical caster, which imposed a ceiling on the quality of the steel it could produce. In the early 1980s, Chaparral executives decided that the company was constraining itself by defining growth to mean producing more of the same low-grade products. Determined to make more high-grade, higher-margin products and expand the areas in which the company competed with the big, vertically integrated steelmakers, the executives said, "If the vertical caster is the obstacle, then let's remove it."

Chaparral's deep understanding of the vertical casting process led it to the elegant conclusion that casting horizontally would be the ticket to making new high-grade products. When its managers learned that earlier experiments with the horizontal casting of steel had failed, they looked outside their industry and discovered a half-dozen sites around the world where aluminum and copper (metals that are much easier to cast) were being horizontally cast.

In 1984, the executives formed a project team, including line operators, to visit all these casting sites. Afterward, combining what they saw with the knowledge they already had about steel casting, the team members came up with a radically new concept for a horizontal caster, which, they thought, just might work. At first, Chaparral contracted an engineering company to build a prototype caster at the latter's own site. But managers soon realized that their company wouldn't gain the insights it needed to make the caster work unless they put the prototype on the shop floor where employees could constantly experiment with it.

By mid-1985, five Chaparral shop-floor operators had tinkered enough with the caster that it occasionally produced billets successfully. Over the next two years, the company purchased and modified pieces of equipment and eventually built a pilot production line. By mid-1988, Chaparral had built a full-fledged production line, which employees ran and refined continually into the next year.

Even then, when the caster seemed ready for full-scale, commercial production, the Chaparral team did not give up its quest for learning. "With what we know now, we might be able to learn more from the casters that we examined originally," the team members decided. So they revisited all the sites and found they were indeed able to refine their caster further. After the caster was operating fully, Chaparral continued to press for ways to improve it and ended up investing in new mechanical drives and controls. In 1990, thanks to the horizontal caster, Chaparral produced 300,000 tons of steel whose quality was even higher than the company had hoped at the project's outset. It was an amazing technical feat for any steelmaker, let alone a minimill with fewer than 1,000 employees.

The horizontal caster project leveraged several of Chaparral's core capabilities. These included its ingenuity in taking existing manufacturing equipment (in this case, from other industries) and getting it to do something that had never been done before and its exceptional ability to train and broaden the knowledge of people at every level of the company. In other words, the project's scope and technical challenges were aligned with one of Chaparral's core strengths: continuously advancing the art and science of casting steel products.

There was also a compelling harmony between this project's goals and the company's overarching vision, which was to be the leading international low-cost supplier of high-quality steel products. No one on the team ever had any doubts about the project's ultimate goal. And even though it was a breakthrough project, the undertaking was totally consistent with Chaparral's view of life: that a company must relentlessly push the envelope to be a leader, a passion that obviously infected the team. The knowledge that they could make a tremendous difference and that they would ultimately operate the caster infused team members with a sense of ownership and reality that indisputably contributed to the caster's great technical and commercial success. The fact that the team members, like everyone at Chaparral, were stockholders gave them even more of a stake in the project's outcome.

The fact that the team leader had a lot of experience heading development projects at Chaparral and had deep technical knowledge of casters certainly did not hurt. This was not simply the luck of the draw. At Chaparral, virtually everyone is involved in a development or improvement project at any moment in time. People may lead one team and then be members of another, an approach that has produced a broad array of people who know exactly how to lead a given project or how to make effective contributions as team members. And at Chaparral, unlike many other companies, careful thought goes into choosing both the leader and the members of every project and into how the project is organized. For example, Chaparral classified the horizontal caster as an "advanced development project" and accordingly assigned it to one of its seven general foremen who reported directly to the vice president for manufacturing. That step ensured that the horizontal caster would be integrated into the manufacturing process.

The way the caster project evolved seamlessly from idea to crude concept to prototype to pilot to full-scale production was no accident. This smooth evolution was the result of the masterful way the team members integrated their work. Besides sharing the vision, everyone on the team had worked in a variety of functions, which was not unusual at Chaparral, where functional fiefdoms are verboten. The team's rigorous use of prototypes, starting with a small primitive one and then moving steadily toward a preproduction version, also helped team members understand how each person's contribution affected and meshed with everyone else's. And because each person knew that at some point he or she would be responsible for running the actual machine, everyone focused on the whole, not on the parts.

Learning from Post-Project Reviews

As the leaders of Chaparral understand, the key to becoming and remaining a leader is not just getting it right one time but developing a system for applying what was learned in one project to subsequent projects. Companies that excel in doing this create an atmosphere in which everyone recognizes that learning is the ultimate goal and the most effective way to push the company forward. This requires systematic planning for each project or series of projects that includes establishing realistic goals and conducting a "learning audit" of projects after they have been completed.

Kodak's attempt to build a "factory of the future" for cutting, perforating, winding onto spools, and packaging 35mm film demonstrates the perils of poor planning. In 1984, Kodak saw the need to add substantial finishing capacity and in 1986 initiated a project to fulfill this goal. Kodak put two managers, one from manufacturing and one from engineering, in charge. They agreed that they could use the project both to add the required capacity and to develop a process that had lower operating costs and greater quality control.

But the teams went overboard. Knowing that revolutionary projects like this one don't come along very often, they tried to cram all sorts of experimental production technologies into the project. The project soon became bloated, and major delays occurred several times. Trying to do everything at once, the teams had lost sight of the primary goal of adding enough capacity so that the company would be able to meet increased demand. Eventually, Kodak executives had to kill the endeavor.

Of the five companies that the Manufacturing Vision Group studied, Chaparral best exemplified how a manufacturing company can use development projects to learn (see Exhibit II). One of the tenets of its culture—if all employees learn, then the organization will learn—has been instrumental in Chaparral's strong growth.

Chaparral does three things that serve as a model for all companies. First, it requires every development project to advance the company's capabilities. Second, it carefully plans which series of projects to undertake and how to carry them out so that altogether they will strengthen the company's overall set of capabilities. And third, after each project has been completed, Chaparral analyzes it to find out what it achieved or failed to achieve so the operational lessons—not flow charts and organizational structures but the way people actually worked best together—can be passed on to subsequent projects.

During their careers, the members of the Manufacturing Vision Group have collectively studied or participated in hundreds of development projects at numerous companies in a range of industries. Of those companies, many have gone a lot farther in installing effective planning systems for development projects than in installing effective auditing systems. Indeed, only a handful have any kind of auditing system, and often the purpose of those audits is to ensure that the project is complying with bureaucratic procedures rather than to analyze both the positive and negative aspects of the project so the company can learn.

Some of the 20 projects that the group studied were audited after their completion, but the review was not systematic. Sometimes the reviewers were reluctant to highlight problems, fearful that doing so would embarrass people and appear unfair. But companies must strive to change this perception. Otherwise, project after project will experience the same mistakes. For any organization to learn, someone has

Exhibit II.

Performance of Projects

Company and Project	Met schedule	Initial market acceptance	Met technical objectives	Met business objectives
Chaparral Steel				
Digital pulpit controls for arc furnace	2	5	5	5
Electric-arc saw	2	NA	1	1
Horizontal caster for high-grade steel	3	4	5	4
Microtuff 10 – new forging steel	4	4	4	5
Digital Equipment				
CDA – desktop publishing software	3	4	4	4
DECstation 3100 – UNIX workstation	5	2	5	3
LAN Bridge 200 – local area network	2	4	3	4
RA90 – high-density disk drive	2	3	3	4
Eastman Kodak				
Antistatic film coating (Chem. 181)	5	5	5	5
"Factory of the Future" – 35mm film	1	NA	2	2
FunSaver – "single-use" camera	5	4	5	4
Panda – large-format printer	1	4	4	3
Ford Motor				
1991 Crown Victoria/Grand Marquis (EN53)	2	3	5	4
FX15 Air-conditioner compressor	4	2	3	3
1988 Lincoln Continental (FN9)	2	4	4	2
1989 Thunderbird/Cougar (MN12)	4	3	4	2
Hewlett-Packard				
DeskJet – ink-jet printer	4	5	5	5
Hornet – spectrum analyzer	4	5	5	5
HP 150 – computer to use as a:				
terminal	4	4	4	2
personal computer	4	2	4	2
Logic analyzer – digital oscilloscope	3	4	4	5

Degree of Success in Meeting Objectives

Relative Success Ratings 5 = very high 4 = high 3 = medium 2 = low 1 = very low NA = not applicable

to step back and ask what a given development team, and the company in support of that team, did right and wrong. Then management must find a way to implement the needed changes in the next project.

Aside from Chaparral, Ford is one of the few companies to have realized this. Recognizing the need to institutionalize learning, in 1985, Ford established a special team of people who were experienced in development. It gave them the mission to develop new concepts, guidelines, and milestones for product development that became known as the concept-to-customer process (CTC). Learning by assessing projects was an important part of the CTC team's work. Each time a project ended, the CTC team reviewed it and involved the members of the project's core team in the process, thereby teaching people how to learn from their experience. The process has evolved into what Ford considers an excellent approach. But this doesn't mean Ford is satisfied. Even though a large number of people involved in development now know how to assess projects effectively, the CTC team continues to strive to improve the process even more.

Pitfalls to Avoid

Apparently, one reason that so few companies audit their projects is the extra expense; this is shortsighted. The fact is, it takes extra time, effort, and money to use development projects to learn. Many people on the projects that the Manufacturing Vision Group studied pointed to things they could have learned had they been given enough time or resources. And careful analysis showed that this was not just typical grumbling. In several instances, the narrow financial perspective of senior managers, an overemphasis on holding down costs, blocked companies from using projects to develop new capabilities that over time would have yielded a handsome return on a relatively minor investment. In other instances, financial myopia interfered with the development of the product itself. The 1988 Lincoln Continental is a case in point.

A classic U.S. luxury car, the Continental had been a strong seller for years. But by the mid-1980s, the luxury models of the Big Three automakers were losing ground to Japanese and European cars that were just as plush but smaller, more fuel efficient, and easier to handle. To counter this competitive threat, Ford executives sought to introduce the concept of "contemporary luxury" with its 1988 Continental.

Ford's plan called for an extensive redesign of the Continental. Realizing that integrated teamwork was critical to the project's success, managers placed design, manufacturing, and marketing people on the same team. Even so, there were many starts and stops in the initial stages due to disagreements over styling. Moreover, numerous changes in engineering specifications were issued late in the design phase, and serious problems surfaced in the manufacturing system during the buildup to full production. Many of these complications could have been avoided if the team had been able to build more, and better, prototypes earlier in the process. But penny-foolish senior managers said no. Prototypes would have surfaced problems early and reduced the changes in engineering specifications. And production would have begun much more smoothly had full-system prototypes been made sooner so that the team could test the tooling. The first fully representative prototypes were delivered only 20 months before mass production was due to begin. In hindsight, the eventual delays cost the company much more than the prototypes would have. They hurt the product's profitability and, more important, they prevented Ford from learning how to integrate the design, marketing, and manufacturing functions. With the CTC process it now has in place, Ford is unlikely to experience such pitfalls again.

Contrast Ford's attitude in this project with Chaparral's. Chaparral had a loss in one particular poor year that happened to equal the amount it had spent on development projects that year. Chaparral executives could have taken the view that if the company hadn't pursued the development projects, it would have broken even. But Chaparral managers knew that if they wanted to attain the competitive position they sought two years down the road, they had to pursue projects now that would expand the company's capabilities. So they justified the projects on a strategic basis, not a financial one.

Another common management foible that the Manufacturing Vision Group spotted was a tendency to establish some kind of "learning SWAT team." The problem with this approach is it can make employees look at learning as "that group's job, not mine."

Senior managers often try to take another shortcut. They assign someone else to figure out what was learned from Project X and how to apply it to Project Y. The trouble is, that approach sends the message that management doesn't place a premium on learning. In the companies that most effectively utilize development projects to expand their capabilities, senior managers strive to be leaders in learning. They know they must learn firsthand about the detailed workings of the company before they can help others do the same. They believe that they cannot delegate this responsibility because it requires knowledge of the entire corporation and an understanding of how a change in one area affects other areas.

Still another common failing among companies is the lack of a reward system that adequately encourages learning and project leadership. At most companies, employees are rewarded for concrete results, not for learning. And few career paths encourage managers to take on project leadership. An important part of the job of a project leader is to push the team and the company to change. Since most people resist change, project leaders often end up with a lot of arrows in their backs. It's no coincidence that project leaders who are effective in project after project tend to be those who have the visible support of senior managers.

Development projects are the place to start changing the priorities and goals of all employees, to create a corporate environment in which line operators, managers, and executives continually seek to advance their own knowledge and that of the whole company. These projects are invaluable catalysts for cultivating managers who can be leaders in learning. But this requires a certain mind-set. Meetings to review proposals for new development projects will no longer be dominated only by issues about product concept, market plans, budgets, and the like. Senior managers will also ask a project's advocates to outline the learning objectives. "What lessons learned in previous projects can we apply to this one?" they will inquire. "What new management or engineering processes will we test? What new organization or team structures will we develop? What new skills will employees learn? What new capabilities will the company gain? And, equally important, do we have core capabilities that have outlived their usefulness, that might prevent the project from achieving its goals?"

The last question in particular is asked all too rarely. Many managers presume that core capabilities are eternal. They fail to recognize that even a capability that has been a pillar of a company's success for decades can become a liability unless the company constantly tests and shapes it.

2
The New New Product Development Game

Hirotaka Takeuchi and Ikujiro Nonaka

The rules of the game in new product development are changing. Many companies have discovered that it takes more than the accepted basics of high quality, low cost, and differentiation to excel in today's competitive market. It also takes speed and flexibility.

This change is reflected in the emphasis companies are placing on new products as a source of new sales and profits. At 3M, for example, products less than five years old account for 25% of sales. A 1981 survey of 700 U.S. companies indicated that new products would account for one-third of all profits in the 1980s, an increase from one-fifth in the 1970s.[1]

This new emphasis on speed and flexibility calls for a different approach for managing new product development. The traditional sequential or "relay race" approach to product development—exemplified by the National Aeronautics and Space Administration's phased program planning (PPP) system—may conflict with the goals of maximum speed and flexibility. Instead, a holistic or "rugby" approach—where a team tries to go the distance as a unit, passing the ball back and forth—may better serve today's competitive requirements.

Authors' note: We acknowledge the contribution of Ken-ichi Imai in the development of this article. An earlier version of this article was coauthored by Ken-ichi Imai, Ikujiro Nonaka, and Hirotaka Takeuchi. It was entitled "Managing the New Product Development Process: How Japanese Companies Learn and Unlearn" and was presented at the seventy-fifth anniversary Colloquium on Productivity and Technology, Harvard Business School, March 28 and 29, 1984.

Under the old approach, a product development process moved like a relay race, with one group of functional specialists passing the baton to the next group. The project went sequentially from phase to phase: concept development, feasibility testing, product design, development process, pilot production, and final production. Under this method, functions were specialized and segmented: the marketing people examined customer needs and perceptions in developing product concepts; the R&D engineers selected the appropriate design; the production engineers put it into shape; and other functional specialists carried the baton at different stages of the race.

Under the rugby approach, the product development process emerges from the constant interaction of a hand-picked, multidisciplinary team whose members work together from start to finish. Rather than moving in defined, highly structured stages, the process is born out of the team members' interplay (see Exhibit I). A group of engineers, for example, may start to design the product (phase three) before all the results of the feasibility tests (phase two) are in. Or, the team may be forced to reconsider a decision as a result of later information. The team does not stop then, but engages in iterative experimentation. This goes on in even the latest phases of the development process.

Exhibit I illustrates the difference between the traditional, linear approach to product development and the rugby approach. The sequential approach, labeled A, is typified by the NASA-type PPP system. The overlap approach is represented by type B, where the overlying occurs only at the border of adjacent phases, and type C, where the overlap extends across several phases. We observed a type B overlap at Fuji-Xerox and a type C overlap at Honda and Canon.

This approach is essential for companies seeking to develop new products quickly and flexibly. The shift from a linear to an integrated approach encourages trial and error and challenges the status quo. It stimulates new kinds of learning and thinking within the organization at different levels and functions. Just as important, this strategy for product development can act as an agent of change for the larger organization. The energy and motivation the effort produces can spread throughout the big company and begin to break down some of the rigidities that have set in over time.

In this article, we highlight companies both in Japan and in the United States that have taken a new approach to managing the product development process. Our research examined such multinational

Exhibit I. Sequential (A) vs. overlapping (B and C) phases of development

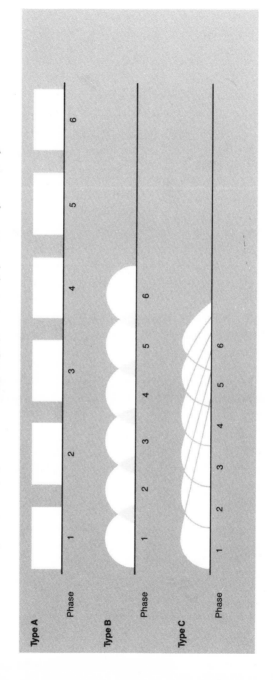

The Sport of Rugby

One of the charms of the Rugby Union game is the infinite variety of its possible tactics. Whatever tactics a team aims to adopt, the first essential is a strong and skilful [sic] pack of forwards capable of winning initial possession from the set pieces. For, with the ball in its hands, a team is in a position to dictate tactics which will make the best use of its own particular talents, at the same time probing for and exposing weaknesses in the opposing team. The ideal team has fast and clever half-backs and three-quarters who, with running, passing, and shrewd kicking, will make sure that the possession won by the forwards is employed to the maximum embarrassment of the opposing team.

From *The Oxford Companion to World Sports and Games* ed. John Arlott (London: Oxford University Press, 1975) by permission of Oxford University Press.

---

companies as Fuji-Xerox, Canon, Honda, NEC, Epson, Brother, 3M, Xerox, and Hewlett-Packard. We then analyzed the development process of six specific products:

FX-3500 medium-sized copier (introduced by Fuji-Xerox in 1978)

PC-10 personal use copier (Canon, 1982)

City car with a 1200 cc engine (Honda, 1981)

PC 8000 personal computer (NEC, 1979)

AE-1 single-lens reflex camera (Canon, 1976)

Auto Boy, known as the Sure Shot in the United States, lens shutter camera (Canon, 1979)

We selected each product on the basis of its impact, its visibility within the company as part of a "breakthrough" development process, the novelty of the product features at the time, the market success of the product, and the access to and availability of data on each product.

Moving the Scrum Downfield

From interviews with organization members from the CEO to young engineers, we learned that leading companies show six characteristics in managing their new product development processes:

1. Built-in instability
2. Self-organizing project teams
3. Overlapping development phases
4. "Multilearning"
5. Subtle control
6. Organizational transfer of learning

These characteristics are like pieces of a jigsaw puzzle. Each element, by itself, does not bring about speed and flexibility. But taken as a whole, the characteristics can produce a powerful new set of dynamics that will make a difference.

BUILT-IN INSTABILITY

Top management kicks off the development process by signaling a broad goal or a general strategic direction. It rarely hands out a clear-cut new product concept or a specific work plan. But it both offers a project team a wide measure of freedom and also establishes extremely challenging goals. For example, Fuji-Xerox's top management asked for a radically different copier and gave the FX-3500 project team two years to come up with a machine that could be produced at half the cost of its high-end line and still perform as well.

Top management creates an element of tension in the project team by giving it great freedom to carry out a project of strategic importance to the company and by setting very challenging requirements. An executive in charge of development at Honda remarked, "It's like putting the team members on the second floor, removing the ladder, and telling them to jump or else. I believe creativity is born by pushing people against the wall and pressuring them almost to the extreme."

SELF-ORGANIZING PROJECT TEAMS

A project team takes on a self-organizing character as it is driven to a state of "zero information"—where prior knowledge does not apply. Ambiguity and fluctuation abound in this state. Left to stew, the process begins to create its own dynamic order.[2] The project team begins to operate like a start-up company—it takes initiatives and risks, and develops an independent agenda. At some point, the team begins to create its own concept.

A group possesses a self-organizing capability when it exhibits three conditions: autonomy, self-transcendence, and cross-fertilization. In our study of the various new product development teams, we found all these conditions.

AUTONOMY. Headquarters' involvement is limited to providing guidance, money, and moral support at the outset. On a day-to-day basis, top management seldom intervenes; the team is free to set its own direction. In a way, top management acts as a venture capitalist. Or as one executive said, "We open up our purse but keep our mouth closed."

This kind of autonomy was evident when IBM developed its personal computer. A small group of engineers began working on the machine in a converted warehouse in remote Boca Raton, Florida. Except for quarterly corporate reviews, headquarters in Armonk, New York allowed the Boca Raton group to operate on its own. The group got the go-ahead to take unconventional steps such as selecting outside suppliers for its microprocessor and software package.

We observed other examples of autonomy in our case studies:

> The Honda City project team, whose members' average age was 27, had these instructions from management: to develop "the kind of car that the youth segment would like to drive." An engineer said, "It's incredible how the company called in young engineers like ourselves to design a car with a totally new concept and gave us the freedom to do it our way."

> A small group of sales engineers who originally sold microprocessors built the PC 8000 at NEC. The group started with no knowledge about personal computers. "We were given the go-ahead from top management to proceed with the project, provided we would develop the product by ourselves and also be responsible for manufacturing, selling, and servicing it on our own," remarked the project's head.

SELF-TRANSCENDENCE. The project teams appear to be absorbed in a never-ending quest for "the limit." Starting with the guidelines set forth by top management, they begin to establish their own goals and keep on elevating them throughout the development process. By pursuing what appear at first to be contradictory goals, they devise ways to override the status quo and make the big discovery.

We observed many examples of self-transcendence in our field work. The Canon AE-1 project team came up with new ideas to meet the challenging parameters set forth by top management. The company asked the team to develop a high-quality, automatic exposure camera that had to be compact, lightweight, easy to use, and priced 30% lower than the prevailing price of single-lens cameras. To reach this ambitious target, the project team achieved several firsts in camera design and production: an electronic brain consisting of integrated circuits custom-made by Texas Instruments; modularized production, which made automation and mass production possible; and reduction in the number of parts by 30% to 40%. "It was a struggle because we had to deny our traditional way of thinking," recalled the head of the AE-1 team. "But we do that every day in the ongoing parts of our business," responded another Canon executive. The entire organization makes daily, incremental improvements to strengthen what the president calls "the fundamentals": R&D, production technology, selling prowess, and corporate culture.

The Honda City project team also achieved a breakthrough by transcending the status quo. The team was asked to develop a car with two competitive features for the youth segment: efficiency in resources and fuel, and uncompromising quality at a low price. The team's natural instinct was to develop a scaled-down version of Honda's best-selling Civic model. But after much debate, the team decided to develop a car with a totally new concept. It challenged the prevailing idea that a car should be long and low and designed a "short and tall" car. Convinced that an evolution toward a "machine minimum, man maximum" concept was inevitable, the team was willing to risk going against the industry norm.

CROSS-FERTILIZATION. A project team consisting of members with varying functional specializations, thought processes, and behavior patterns carries out new product development. The Honda team, for example, consisted of hand-picked members from R&D, production, and sales. The company went a step further by placing a wide variety of personalities on the team. Such diversity fostered new ideas and concepts.

While selecting a diverse team is crucial, it isn't until the members start to interact that cross-fertilization actually takes place. Fuji-Xerox located the multifunctional team building the FX-3500—consisting of members from the planning, design, production, sales, distribution, and evaluation departments—in one large room. A project member gave the following rationale for this step: "When all the team members are located in one large room, someone's information becomes yours, without even trying. You then start thinking in terms of what's best or second best for the group at large and not only about where you stand. If everyone understands the other person's position, then each of us is more willing to give in, or at least to try to talk to each other. Initiatives emerge as a result."

OVERLAPPING DEVELOPMENT PHASES

The self-organizing character of the team produces a unique dynamic or rhythm. Although the team members start the project with different time horizons—with R&D people having the longest time horizon and production people the shortest—they all must work toward synchronizing their pace to meet deadlines. Also, while the project team starts from "zero information," each member soon begins to share knowledge about the marketplace and the technical community. As a result, the team begins to work as a unit. At some point, the individual and the whole become inseparable. The individual's rhythm and the group's rhythm begin to overlap, creating a whole new pulse. This pulse serves as the driving force and moves the team forward.

But the quickness of the pulse varies in different phases of development. The beat seems to be most vigorous in the early phases and tapers off toward the end. A member of Canon's PC-10 development team described this rhythm as follows: "When we are debating about what kind of concept to create, our minds go off in different directions and list alternatives. But when we are trying to come to grips with achieving both low cost and high reliability, our minds work to integrate the various points of view. Conflict tends to occur when some are trying to differentiate and others are trying to integrate. The knack lies in creating this rhythm and knowing when to move from one state to the other."

Under the sequential or relay race approach, a project goes through several phases in a step-by-step fashion, moving from one phase to the next only after all the requirements of the preceding phase are satisfied. These checkpoints control risk. But at the same time, this approach leaves little room for integration. A bottleneck in one phase can slow or even halt the entire development process.

Under the holistic or rugby approach, the phases overlap considerably, which enables the group to absorb the vibration or "noise" generated throughout the development process. When a bottleneck appears, the level of noise obviously increases. But the process does not come to a sudden halt; the team manages to push itself forward.

Fuji-Xerox inherited the PPP system (see type A in Exhibit I) from its parent company, but revised it in two ways. First, it reduced the number of phases from six to four by redefining some of the phases and aggregating them differently. Second, it changed the linear, sequential system into the so-called "sashimi" system. Sashimi is slices of raw fish arranged on a plate, one slice overlapping the other (see Exhibit II).

The sashimi system requires extensive interaction not only among project members but also with suppliers. The FX-3500 team invited them to join the project at the very start (they eventually produced 90% of the parts for the model). Each side regularly visited the other's plants and kept the information channel open at all times. This kind of exchange and openness—both within the project team and with suppliers—increases speed and flexibility. Fuji-Xerox shortened the development time from 38 months for an earlier model to 29 months for the FX-3500.

If sashimi defines the Fuji-Xerox approach, then rugby describes the overlapping at Honda. Like a rugby team, the core project members at Honda stay intact from beginning to end and are responsible for combining all of the phases.

In the relay-like PPP system, the crucial problems tend to occur at the points where one group passes the project to the next. The rugby approach smooths out this problem by maintaining continuity across phases.

The Auto Boy project proceeded with much overlapping across phases as well. Canon's design engineers stayed alert throughout the process to make sure their design was being converted into what they had in mind. The production people intruded onto the design engineers' turf to make sure that the design was in accord with production scale economies.

The overlapping approach has both merits and demerits. Greater speed and increased flexibility are the "hard" merits. But the approach also has a set of "soft" merits relating to human resource management. The overlap approach enhances shared responsibility and cooperation, stimulates involvement and commitment, sharpens a problem-solving focus, encourages initiative taking, develops diversified skills, and heightens sensitivity toward market conditions.

The more obvious demerits result from having to manage an inten-

Exhibit II.   *Fuji-Xerox's product development schedule*

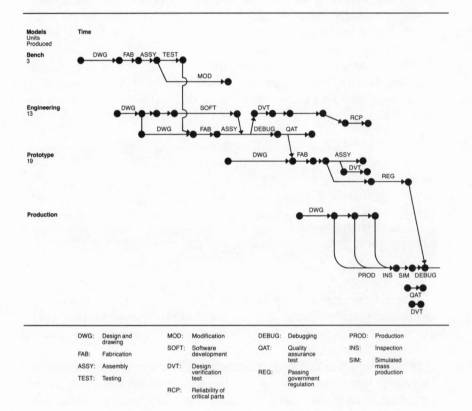

DWG:	Design and drawing	MOD:	Modification	DEBUG:	Debugging	PROD:	Production
FAB:	Fabrication	SOFT:	Software development	QAT:	Quality assurance test	INS:	Inspection
ASSY:	Assembly	DVT:	Design verification test			SIM:	Simulated mass production
TEST:	Testing			REG:	Passing government regulation		
		RCP:	Reliability of critical parts				

sive process. Problems include communicating with the entire project team, maintaining close contact with suppliers, preparing several contingency plans, and handling surprises. This approach also creates more tension and conflict in the group. As one project member aptly put it, "If someone from development thinks that 1 out of 100 is good, that's a clear sign for going ahead. But if someone from production thinks that if 1 out of 100 is not good, we've got to start all over. This gap in perception creates conflict."

The overlapping of phases also does away with traditional notions about division of labor. Division of labor works well in a type A system, where management clearly delineates tasks, expects all project members to know their responsibilities, and evaluates each on an individual basis. Under a type B or C system, the company accomplishes the tasks through what we call "shared division of labor," where each team member feels responsible for—and is able to work on—any aspect of the project.

MULTILEARNING

Because members of the project team stay in close touch with outside sources of information, they can respond quickly to changing market conditions. Team members engage in a continual process of trial and error to narrow down the number of alternatives that they must consider. They also acquire broad knowledge and diverse skills, which help them create a versatile team capable of solving an array of problems fast.

Such learning by doing manifests itself along two dimensions: across multiple levels (individual, group, and corporate) and across multiple functions. We refer to these two dimensions of learning as "multilearning."

MULTILEVEL LEARNING. Learning at the individual level takes place in a number of ways. 3M, for example, encourages engineers to devote 15% of their company time to pursuing their "dream." Canon utilizes peer pressure to foster individual learning. A design engineer for the PC-10 project explained, "My senior managers and some of my colleagues really study hard. There is no way I can compete with them in the number of books they read. So whenever I have time, I go to a department store and spend several hours in the toy department. I observe what's selling and check out the new gadgets being used in the toys. They may give me a hint or two later on."

Learning is pursued emphatically at the group level as well. Honda, for example, dispatched several members of the City project team to Europe for three weeks when the project reached a dead end at the concept development phase. They were told simply to "look around at what's happening in Europe." There they encountered the Mini-Cooper—a small car developed decades ago in the United Kingdom—which had a big impact on their design philosophy.

While it was developing the PC-10 copier, Canon team members left the project offices to hold a number of meetings in nearby hotels. In one of the early meetings, the entire project team broke up into subgroups, each with a representative from the design team and the production team. Each subgroup was told to calculate the cost of a key part and figure out ways of reducing that cost by one-third. "Since every subgroup faced the same mandate and the same deadline, we had no choice," recalled one project member. Learning took place in a hurry.

Learning at the corporate level is best achieved by establishing a company-wide movement or program. Fuji-Xerox, for example, used the total quality control (TQC) movement as a basis for changing the corporate mentality. TQC was designed to heighten the entire organization's sensitivity toward simultaneous quality and productivity improvement, market orientation, cost reduction, and work simplification. To achieve these goals, everyone in the organization had to learn the basics of techniques like statistical quality control and value engineering.

Hewlett-Packard embarked on a four-phased training program in marketing as part of the corporation's aim to become more market-oriented. The company now brings in top academics and business consultants to spread the marketing message. It also applies techniques borrowed from the consumer packaged goods industry, such as focus group interviews, quantitative market research, and test marketing. Further, the company has created a corporate marketing division to accelerate what one insider calls "the transition from a company run by engineers for engineers to one with a stronger marketing focus."

MULTIFUNCTIONAL LEARNING. Experts are encouraged to accumulate experience in areas other than their own. For instance:

> All the project members who developed Epson's first miniprinter were mechanical engineers who knew little about electronics at the start. So the leader of the project team, also a mechanical engineer, returned to his alma mater as a researcher and studied electrical engineering for two years. He did this while the project was under way. By the time they had completed the miniprinter project, all the engineers were knowledgeable about electronics. "I tell my people to be well-versed in two technological fields and in two functional areas, like design and marketing," the leader said. "Even in an engineering-oriented company like ours, you can't get ahead without the ability to foresee developments in the market."
>
> The team working on NEC's PC 8000 consisted of sales engineers from the Electronic Devices Division. They acquired much of the know-how

---

Corporate Rugby Scores

Some companies are already making headway in speeding up new product development:

A new copier—the 9900—took Xerox three years to develop, whereas the company spent more than five years developing a comparable earlier model.

A portable Brother printer—the EP-20—was developed in less than two years. It took the company more than four years to develop an earlier model.

One of John Sculley's top priorities, when appointed president of Apple in 1984, was to cut the company's product development time from 3.5 years down to one year.

Other organizations are beginning to add flexibility to product development:

Black & Decker recently unveiled 50 new power tool products at the National Hardware Show in Chicago to compete more effectively with Japanese power tool makers.

When Yamaha threatened its leadership position in the Japanese market in 1982, Honda unleashed some 30 new motorcycle models within a six-month period.

IBM broke from its tradition of designing everything internally and used a microprocessor designed by Intel Corporation and a basic operating system designed by Microsoft Corporation to develop its personal computer.

---

to develop the company's first personal computer by putting together TK 80, a computer kit, and introducing it on the market two years in advance of the PC 8000; and by stationing themselves for about a year, even on weekends, at BIT-IN, an NEC service center in the middle of Akihabara, talking with hobbyists and learning the user's viewpoint.

These examples show the important role that multilearning plays in the company's overall human resource management program. It fosters initiative and learning by doing on the part of the employees and helps keep them up to date with the latest developments. It also serves as a basis for creating a climate that can bring about organizational transition.

SUBTLE CONTROL

Although project teams are largely on their own, they are not uncontrolled. Management establishes enough checkpoints to prevent instability, ambiguity, and tension from turning into chaos. At the same time, management avoids the kind of rigid control that impairs creativity and spontaneity. Instead, the emphasis is on "self-control," "control through peer pressure," and "control by love," which collectively we call "subtle control."

Subtle control is exercised in the new product development process in seven ways:

1. Selecting the right people for the project team while monitoring shifts in group dynamics and adding or dropping members when necessary. "We would add an older and more conservative member to the team should the balance shift too much toward radicalism," said a Honda executive. "We carefully pick the project members after long deliberation. We analyze the different personalities to see if they would get along. Most people do get along, thanks to our common set of values."

2. Creating an open work environment, as in the case of Fuji-Xerox.

3. Encouraging engineers to go out into the field and listen to what customers and dealers have to say. "A design engineer may be tempted to take the easy way out at times, but may reflect on what the customer had to say and try to find some way of meeting that requirement," noted an engineer from Fuji-Xerox.

4. Establishing an evaluation and reward system based on group performance. Canon, for example, applied for patents for products from the PC-10 project on a group basis.

5. Managing the differences in rhythm throughout the development process. As mentioned earlier, the rhythm is most vigorous in the early phases and tapers off toward the end.

6. Tolerating and anticipating mistakes. Engineers at Honda are fond of saying that "a 1% success rate is supported by mistakes made 99% of the time." A Brother executive in charge of R&D said, "It's natural for young engineers to make a lot of mistakes. The key lies in finding the mistakes early and taking steps to correct them immediately. We've taken steps to expedite the trial production cycle for that reason." A 3M executive noted, "I believe we learn more from mistakes than from successes. That's not to say we should make mistakes easily. But if we do make mistakes, we ought to make them creatively."

7. Encouraging suppliers to become self-organizing. Involving them early during design is a step in the right direction. But the project team should refrain from telling suppliers what to do. As Xerox recently found out, suppliers produce better results when they have the problem explained to them and are allowed to decide how to furnish the parts.

TRANSFER OF LEARNING

The drive to accumulate knowledge across levels and functions is only one aspect of learning. We observed an equally strong drive on the part of the project members to transfer their learning to others outside the group.

Transfer of learning to subsequent new product development projects or to other divisions in the organization takes place regularly. In several of the companies we studied, the transfer took place through "osmosis"—by assigning key individuals to subsequent projects. A Honda executive explained, "If the factory is up and running and the early-period claims are resolved, we dismantle the project team, leaving only a few people to follow through. Since we have only a limited number of unusually able people, we turn them loose on another key project immediately."

Knowledge is also transmitted in the organization by converting project activities to standard practice. At Canon, for example, the Auto Boy project produced a format for conducting reviews that was used in later projects. One team member recalled, "We used to meet once a month or so to exchange notes on individual subprojects in progress and once in three months or so to discuss the project from a larger perspective. This pattern later became institutionalized into the monthly and quarterly progress reviews adopted from the PC-10 minicopier project."

Naturally, companies try to institutionalize the lessons derived from their successes. IBM is trying to emulate the personal computer development project—which was completed in 13 months with outside help—throughout the company.

At Hewlett-Packard, the personal computer group is reprogramming the way the entire company develops and sells new products. In the past, the company was famous for designing a machine for a particular customer and charging a premium price. But it recently engineered its

ThinkJet—a quiet inkjet printer—for low-cost mass production and priced it low. Within six months of its introduction, the printer captured 10% of the low-end market. Hewlett-Packard began to apply what it had learned from designing and pricing ThinkJet to its minicomputer line. Within months of putting ThinkJet on the market, the company introduced a minicomputer system for a broad corporate audience at a modest price.

But institutionalization, when carried too far, can create its own danger. Passing down words of wisdom from the past or establishing standard practices based on success stories works well when the external environment is stable. Changes in the environment, however, can quickly make such lessons impractical.

Several companies have tried to unlearn old lessons. Unlearning helps keep the development team in tune with the realities of the outside environment. It also acts as a springboard for making more incremental improvements.

Much of the unlearning is triggered by changes in the environment. But some companies consciously pursue unlearning. Consider these examples:

> Epson's target is to have the next-generation model in development stages as a new model is being introduced on the market. The company tells its project teams that the next-generation model must be at least 40% better than the existing one.
>
> When Honda was building the third-generation Civic model, its project team opted to scrap all the old parts and start anew. When the car made its debut before the public, all the new parts were displayed right next to the car at the request of the project members. The car won the 1984 Car of the Year Award in Japan.
>
> Fuji-Xerox has refined its sashimi approach, first adopted for the FX-3500. Compared with that effort, a new product today requires one-half of the original total manpower. Fuji-Xerox has also reduced the product development cycle from 4 years to 24 months.

Some Limitations

Some words of caution are in order. The holistic approach to product development may not work in all situations. It has some built-in limitations:

It requires extraordinary effort on the part of all project members throughout the span of the development process. Sometimes, team members record monthly overtime of 100 hours during the peak and 60 hours during the rest of the project.

It may not apply to breakthrough projects that require a revolutionary innovation. This limitation may be particularly true in biotechnology or chemistry.

It may not apply to mammoth projects like those in the aerospace business, where the sheer project scale limits extensive face-to-face discussions.

It may not apply to organizations where product development is masterminded by a genius who makes the invention and hands down a well-defined set of specifications for people below to follow.

Some limitations also stem from the scope of our research. Our sample size was limited to a handful of companies and our findings were drawn, for the most part, from observing how the development process was managed in Japan. General conclusions, therefore, must be made with some caution. But as new approaches to product development gain acceptance in the United States, the difference between the two countries may not be so much a difference of kind as a difference of degree.

Managerial Implications

Changes in the environment—intensified competition, a splintered mass market, shortened product life cycles, and advanced technology and automation—are forcing managements to reconsider the traditional ways of creating products. A product that arrives a few months late can easily lose several months of payback. A product designed by an engineer afflicted with the "next bench" syndrome—the habit of designing a product by asking the coworker on the next bench what kind of a product he or she would like—may not meet the flexible requirements of the marketplace.

To achieve speed and flexibility, companies must manage the product development process differently. Three kinds of change should be considered.

First, companies need to adopt a management style that can promote the process. Executives must recognize at the outset that product development seldom proceeds in a linear and static manner. It involves an iterative and dynamic process of trial and error. To manage such a process, companies must maintain a highly adaptive style.

Because projects do not proceed in a totally rational and consistent manner, adaptability is particularly important. Consider, for example, situations where:

> Top management encourages trial and error by purposely keeping goals broad and by tolerating ambiguity. But at the same time, it sets challenging goals and creates tension within the group and within the organization.

> The process by which variety is amplified (differentiation) and reduced (integration) takes place throughout the overlapping phases of the development cycle. Differentiation, however, tends to dominate the concept development phase of the cycle and integration begins to take over the subsequent phases.

> Operational decisions are made incrementally, but important strategic decisions are delayed as much as possible in order to allow a more flexible response to last-minute feedback from the marketplace.

Because management exercises subtle forms of control throughout the development process, these seemingly contradictory goals do not create total confusion. Subtle control is also consistent with the self-organizing character of the project teams.

Second, a different kind of learning is required. Under the traditional approach, a highly competent group of specialists undertakes new product development. An elite group of technical experts does most of the learning. Knowledge is accumulated on an individual basis, within a narrow area of focus—what we call learning in depth.

In contrast, under the new approach (in its extreme form) nonexperts undertake product development. They are encouraged to acquire the necessary knowledge and skills on the job. Unlike the experts, who cannot tolerate mistakes even 1% of the time, the nonexperts are willing to challenge the status quo. But to do so, they must accumulate knowledge from across all areas of management, across different levels of the organization, functional specializations, and even organizational boundaries. Such learning in breadth serves as the necessary condition for shared division of labor to function effectively.

Third, management should assign a different mission to new product development. Most companies have treated it primarily as a generator of future revenue streams. But in some companies, new product development also acts as a catalyst to bring about change in the organization. The personal computer project, for example, is said to have changed the way IBM thinks. Projects coming out of Hewlett-Packard's personal computer group, including ThinkJet, have changed its engineering-driven culture.

No company finds it easy to mobilize itself for change, especially in noncrisis situations. But the self-transcendent nature of the project teams and the hectic pace at which the team members work help to trigger a sense of crisis or urgency throughout the organization. A development project of strategic importance to the company, therefore, can create a wartime working environment even during times of peace.

Changes affecting the entire organization are also difficult to carry out within highly structured companies, especially seniority-based companies like the ones commonly found in Japan. But unconventional moves, which may be difficult to pull off during times of peace, can be legitimized during times of war. Thus management can uproot a competent manager or assign a very young engineer to the project without encountering much resistance.

Once the project team is formed, it begins to rise in stature because of its visibility ("we've been hand-picked"), its legitimate power ("we have unconditional support from the top to create something new"), and its sense of mission ("we're working to solve a crisis"). It serves as a motor for corporate change as project members from a variety of functional areas begin to take strategic initiatives that sometimes go beyond the company's conventional domain and as their knowledge gets transferred to subsequent projects.

The environment in which any multinational company—from the United States or Japan—operates has changed dramatically in recent years. The rules of the game for competing effectively in today's world market have changed accordingly. Multinationals must achieve speed and flexibility in developing products; to do so requires the use of a dynamic process involving much reliance on trial and error and learning by doing. What we need today is constant innovation in a world of constant change.

Notes

1. Booz Allen & Hamilton survey reported in Susan Fraker, "High-Speed Management for the High-Tech Age," *Fortune*, March 5, 1984, 38.

2. See, for example, Ilya Prigozine, *From Being to Becoming* (San Francisco, Calif.: Freeman, 1980); Eric Jantsch, "Unifying Principles of Evolution," in Eric Jantsch, ed., *The Evolutionary Vision* (Boulder, Colorado: Westview Press, 1981); and Devendra Sahal, "A Unified Theory of Self-Organization," *Journal of Cybernetics*, April–June, 1979, 127. See also Todao Kagono, Ikujiro Nonaka, Kiyonari Sakakibara, and Akihiro Okumura, *Strategic vs. Evolutionary Management: A U.S.-Japan Comparison of Strategy and Organization* (Amsterdam: North-Holland, 1985).

3
Fast-Cycle Capability for Competitive Power

Joseph L. Bower and Thomas M. Hout

All managers appreciate, at least intuitively, that time is money, and most will invest to save time—and the money it represents—if they see a clear opportunity. The travel agent computerizes to be able to confirm customers' reservations instantly. The apparel manufacturer develops a just-in-time production process to make what's wanted and avoid the inevitable discounts caused by overproduction.

But actions like these don't create much competitive advantage, because competitors will soon see the same opportunity and most will do the very same thing. Taking time out of a business gets interesting, however, when it represents a systematic change in the way a company accomplishes its work and serves its customers. Then saving time can provide sustainable competitive advantage.

Fast cycle time is not a new operating concept in business strategy. It has long been a key factor in the success of businesses ranging from Hong Kong's custom tailors to McDonald's. But today, executives in more and more large, complex businesses are achieving sustained competitive advantage by making radical changes in how they manage time within their companies. These companies make decisions faster, develop new products earlier, and convert customer orders into deliveries sooner than their competitors. As a result, they provide unique value in the markets they service, value that can translate into faster growth and higher profits.

In these top-performing companies, fast cycle time plays two important roles. First, it is an organizational capability, a level of performance that management shapes and builds into the company's operating systems and the attitudes of its employees. The basic idea is to design an organization that performs without the bottlenecks, delays, errors, and inventories most companies live with. The faster information, decisions, and materials can flow through a large organization, the faster it can respond to customer orders or adjust to changes in market demand and competitive conditions. Less time is spent fighting fires and coordinating. More time is available for planning, for initiating competitive activity.

Second, fast cycle time is a management paradigm, a way of thinking about how to organize and lead a company and how to gain real advantage over competitors. It is a powerful organizing message because its basic premise is so simple. It is also extremely effective since compressing time reinforces and supports what capable managers are already trying to do.

Analysis of competitive developments in a wide range of industries indicates that fast-cycle capability contributes to better performance across the board. Costs drop because production materials and information collect less overhead and do not accumulate as work-in-process inventory. Customer service improves because the lead time from receipt of order to shipment diminishes. Quality is higher because you cannot speed up the production cycle overall unless everything is done right the first time. Innovation becomes a characteristic behavior pattern because rapid new-product development cycles keep the company in close touch with customers and their needs.

Developing fast-cycle capability isn't easy nor can it be done overnight. It requires fundamental rethinking of how a company's goods or services are delivered to customers, and it means that various parts of the organization will have to work together in new and different ways. But these days, the penalty for standing still is far higher than the cost of change.

Every Company Is a System

People in fast-cycle companies think of themselves as part of an integrated system, a linked chain of operations and decision-making points that continuously delivers value to the company's customers. In such organizations, individuals understand how their own activities relate to the rest of the company. They know how work is supposed to flow, how time is supposed to be used.

In small companies, this way of thinking is usually second nature.

People find it easy to stay focused on creating value because almost everyone works directly on the product or with a customer. Policies, procedures, practices, or people that interfere with getting the product out the door are easy to see and can be dealt with quickly.

As companies grow, however, the systemlike nature of the organization often gets hidden. Distances increase as functions focus on their own needs, support activities multiply, specialists are hired, reports replace face-to-face conversations. Before long the clear visibility of the product and the essential elements of the delivery process are lost. Instead of operating as a smoothly linked system, the company becomes a tangle of conflicting constituencies whose own demands and disagreements frustrate the customer. "I don't care what your job is," the overwhelmed customer finally complains. "When can I get my order?"

Fast-cycle companies—especially the big ones—recognize this danger and work hard to avoid it by heightening everyone's awareness of how and where time is spent. They make the main flow of operations from start to finish visible and comprehensible to all employees, and they invest in this understanding with training. They highlight the main interfaces between functions and show how they affect the flow of work. They are aware of the way policies and procedures in one part of the company influence work in others. They compensate on the basis of group success. And, most important, they reinforce the systemic nature of the organization in their operations architecture.

To illustrate, let's look at Toyota, a classic fast-cycle company. Exhibit I presents a simplified diagram of the company's key operating activities. As the diagram shows, the heart of the auto business consists of four interrelated cycles: product development, ordering, plant scheduling, and production. Over the years, Toyota has designed its organization to speed information, decisions, and materials through each of these critical operating cycles, individually and as parts of the whole. The result is better organizational performance on the dimensions that matter to customers—cost, quality, responsiveness, innovation.

Self-organizing, multifunctional teams take charge of product development, focusing on a particular model series. In rapid response to demand patterns, they develop products and manufacturing processes simultaneously to collapse time and ensure better manufacturability. The teams are responsible for managing ongoing styling, performance, and cost decisions, and they control their own schedules and reviews. They also select and manage suppliers, who are brought into the

Exhibit I.

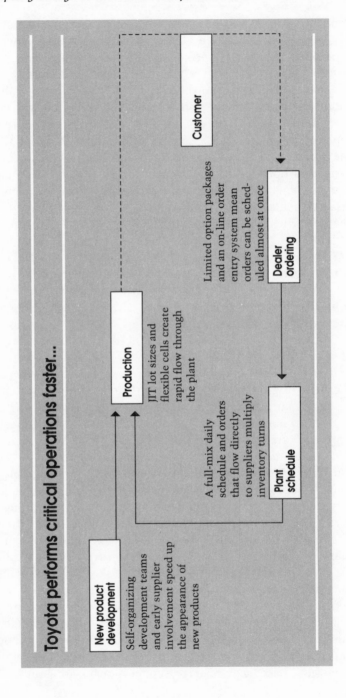

Toyota performs critical operations faster...

New product development

Self-organizing development teams and early supplier involvement speed up the appearance of new products

Production

JIT lot sizes and flexible cells create rapid flow through the plant

Plant schedule

A full-mix daily schedule and orders that flow directly to suppliers multiply inventory turns

Dealer ordering

Limited option packages and an on-line order entry system mean orders can be scheduled almost at once

Customer

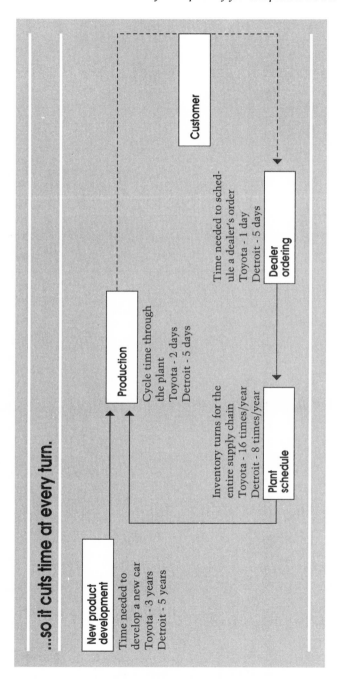

...so it cuts time at every turn.

New product development

Time needed to develop a new car
Toyota - 3 years
Detroit - 5 years

Production

Cycle time through the plant
Toyota - 2 days
Detroit - 5 days

Plant schedule

Inventory turns for the entire supply chain
Toyota - 16 times/year
Detroit - 8 times/year

Dealer ordering

Time needed to schedule a dealer's order
Toyota - 1 day
Detroit - 5 days

Customer

design process early on. The result is an ever-faster development cycle—three years, on average, as compared with four or five years in Detroit—frequent new product introductions, and a constant flow of major and minor innovations on existing models.

The production cycle begins as soon as a customer orders a car from a dealer. Dealers in Japan are connected on-line to the factory scheduling system, so that an order, complete with specifications and the customer's option package, can be entered and slotted into the factory schedule right away. Toyota schedules its plants to minimize sharp fluctuations in daily volume and to turn out a full mix of models every day. Customers get on-the-spot confirmation of their expected delivery date. Suppliers are automatically notified of the new order and given a stable production schedule so that they won't deliver the wrong components on the day of final assembly.

Actual production is executed in small lots by flexible manufacturing cells that can accommodate a mixed flow of units with little changeover time. Plants are managed to maintain high uptime (all the steps in the production sequence are functioning) and high yield (all the production processes are under control and turning out quality products). The result is a fast-paced production cycle, which squeezes out all the overhead except what's needed to get work done right the first time through, and a reliable, continuous manufacturing process.

Much of Toyota's competitive success is directly attributable to the fast-cycle capability it has built into its product development, ordering, scheduling, and production processes. By coming up with new products faster than competitors do, it puts other manufacturers on the marketing defensive. By translating a customer's order into a finished product delivered faster, it captures large numbers of time-sensitive buyers and puts cost and inventory pressure on other manufacturers. By continuously bringing out a variety of fresh products and observing what consumers buy or don't buy, it stays current with their changing needs and gives product development an edge market research cannot match. The faster Toyota can develop and deliver automobiles, the more it can control the competitive game.

In their ability to preempt new sources of value and force other companies to respond to their initiatives, Toyota and other fast-cycle companies resemble the World War II fighter pilots who consistently won dogfights, even when flying in technologically inferior planes. The U.S. Air Force found that the winning pilots completed the so-called OODA loop—Observation, Orientation, Decision, Action—faster than their opponents. Winning pilots sized up the dynamics in each new encounter, read its opportunities, decided what to do, and acted before their opponents could. As a result, they could take control of the dogfight, preempt the opposition's moves, and throw the enemy plane into a confused reactive spiral.

Companies in many industries are operating in much the same way today. Responding to a challenge from Yamaha, Honda nearly doubled its range of motorcycle models in less than two years—destroying Yamaha's short-lived edge. Liz Claiborne has introduced two additional apparel seasons to match consumer buying patterns more closely. Seiko has strengthened its hold on the watch market with a highly automated factory capable of producing new models each day. In semiconductors, the battle for global share is being fought largely on the basis of the speed with which new technology can be applied to larger chips.

Other manufacturing companies go beyond their own boundaries to include customers and suppliers in one integrated delivery system. Milliken, the large U.S. textile manufacturer, collaborates with General Motors on auto interiors, with Sears on upholstery fabrics, and with Wal-Mart on apparel. Because they see one another as partners in delivering a product, not separate operations, Milliken and its customers have been able to share upstream order input and scheduling information, coordinate production cycles to minimize imbalances, and eliminate duplicate inspections and buffer inventories. The results are dramatic. Costs have fallen. Inventory turns have typically doubled. Sales have risen. Stock shortages and markdowns occur less often. The time it takes the Milliken-customer system to fill an order has been cut in half.

Finally, competing through fast-cycle capability is as powerful a strategy in services as it is in manufacturing. By automating its analysis and trading functions, Batterymarch, the Boston-based equity fund manager, collapsed the time it takes to decide on a portfolio change for a customer and put it through. The customer gets into rising stocks and out of falling ones faster than before. Batterymarch has lower costs and higher profits: revenues per employee triple the industry average.

What Makes Fast-Cycle Companies Run

Fast-cycle companies differ from traditional organizations in how they structure work, how they measure performance, and how they view organizational learning. They favor teams over functions and departments. They use time as a critical performance measure. They insist that *everyone* learn about customers, competitors, and the company's own operations, not just top management.

Each of these characteristics is a logical outgrowth of the management mind-set Toyota exemplifies, the mind-set that sees a company as an integrated system for delivering value to customers. Conversely, practices and policies that compartmentalize the company—a strong functional organization, for example, or buffer inventories, or measurement and control systems that focus exclusively on the numbers—have to be modified or done away with. In a fast-cycle company they're counterproductive, however useful they've been in the past and however reassuring they are to employees.

Organize work in multifunctional teams. To compress time and gain the benefits, a company has to work in and manage through relatively small, self-managing teams made up of people from different parts of the organization. The teams must be small because large groups create communication problems of their own and almost always include members whose areas of responsibility are peripheral to the team's task. The teams must be self-managing and empowered to act because referring decisions back up the line wastes time and often leads to poorer decisions. The teams must be multifunctional because that's the best—if not the only—way to keep the actual product and its essential delivery system clearly visible and foremost in everyone's mind.

AT&T and Ford have used teams staffed with members from different disciplines to develop new telephones and new cars. By bringing people from product engineering, manufacturing, marketing, and purchasing together throughout the development process and giving them the authority to make the real business decisions, these companies have cut enormous time and expense out of their new product efforts. In the telephone business, for example, it takes laggards three to four times as long to bring their products and services to market.

Fast-cycle companies use multifunctional teams for everyday work at all levels, not just for special projects. One bank we're familiar with successfully reorganized its personal lending practices and collapsed the time it takes for a customer to get a decision from several days to 30 minutes. Formerly loan applications were handled by a series of supervisors, with clerks as intermediaries to do the processing work. Now an application comes to a single group made up of a credit analyst, an experienced collateral appraiser, and a bank procedures expert who can draw on their collective knowledge and experience to respond to the customer almost at once.

As this example suggests, putting together a successful team often means broadening the scope of individual jobs, organizing the team around market-oriented purposes rather than departmentally defined tasks, and placing business responsibility as far down in the organization as possible.

In effect, it redefines what is commonly meant by multifunctional work. In our experience, many large companies like to think that they work multifunctionally because they form special task forces that cross organizational lines or encourage managers to wander around informally and share their observations. And devices like these can make employees more aware of a company's working mechanisms and opportunities to improve them incrementally, to be sure. But they cannot create well-designed, day-in and day-out, cross-functional relationships down in the organization, where the work gets done and the opportunities to learn are greatest.

Similarly, skunk works that bypass the organization's regular review mechanisms won't develop fast-cycle capability or help managers root out quality and time problems in their operation. Fast-cycle managers know that routine work determines a company's effectiveness, not special projects. So rather than circumvent a slow-moving core by creating outlying units that are smaller, quicker, and more responsive, these executives work to build those qualities into the company as a whole—even if that means taking themselves out of some critical decision loops.

Senior managers typically have lots of good ideas to contribute. But their interventions also carry great weight and often come at awkward times in a project's life. Moreover, their calendars are so crowded that the more they get involved in a project, the harder it becomes to schedule important meetings and keep decisions on track. Senior executives in fast-cycle companies understand this problem and appreciate the way the bottlenecks they create can demotivate junior people. They concentrate on improving the system, therefore, and delegate routine operating decisions to others.

Because of all these differences, the organization charts of fast-cycle companies bear little resemblance to the traditional pyramid of hierarchical boxes. Neither responsibility nor authority is so neatly decentralized and isolated. Instead, the organization chart is more likely to be a set of interlocked circles or a systems flow chart with arrows and feedback loops indicating the actual path of decisions and work. The

Exhibit II.

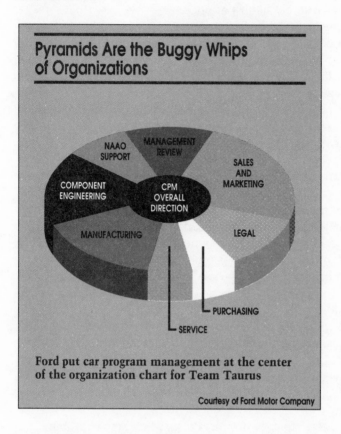

Pyramids Are the Buggy Whips of Organizations

Ford put car program management at the center of the organization chart for Team Taurus

Courtesy of Ford Motor Company

organization chart for the Taurus-Sable product development effort at Ford, for example, was a circle with the core project management team in the center and working groups branching out in all directions (see Exhibit II).

Track cycle times throughout the organization. To assure that information and materials will move through the entire organization with little or no delay, fast-cycle companies manage both the cycle time of individual activities and the cycle time of the whole delivery system—the number of days it takes to ship a customer's order, for instance, or develop a new product. Managers in these companies track each stage's output to see that it is flowing easily into the next and meeting that user's specifications. They make continuing efforts to reduce each activity's characteristic cycle time and therefore the time of the entire sequence. And they are alert to opportunities to compress time by eliminating stages, for example, combining once-separate data preparation and processing activities.

Most organizations manage the cycle time of the longest or most visible part of their operation, but neglect others that are less obvious like order processing or engineering tests. They also allow information in process and decisions to pile up between stages. In-company studies indicate that often less than 10% of the time between receipt of an order and shipment of the product is spent adding value. Material and information spend the rest of the time waiting to be acted on. In factories, for instance, processing in large batches slows down total plant throughput because each workstation has to wait for a large batch to accumulate before it can begin to work. And the same thing happens in white-collar work such as scheduling shipments and pricing orders. Often the only measures used to control these buildups are limits on working capital and overhead expense. Those costs are merely a crude approximation of the lost value to customers.

In contrast, Toyota appears to manage all the cycle times in its operation chain. As we have seen, for example, its management recognized that applying just-in-time principles to production would not greatly change the time a customer had to wait for a new car if retail orders spent weeks moving through the company's regional sales and scheduling departments. So Toyota's order-entry and scheduling procedures are designed to couple without intermediate steps or queues. Toyota's near-term goal is to produce and deliver a new car within a few days of the customer's order.

Benetton, the well-known Italian sportswear producer and retailer, is another company that owes much of its explosive growth and success to across-the-board cycle time reduction. Time compression starts in new product development, where a CAD system automatically explodes the new design into a full range of sizes, then transmits these patterns to computer numerically controlled fabric-cutting machines to await orders for the new product. Fabric is inventoried in neutral greige and then cut and dyed to order. This allows the company to minimize rolled-goods inventory and still respond quickly to the full range of customer demand. Orders are sent to a chain of pull-scheduled, just-in-time factories that allow Benetton to replenish its U.S. retail shelves in 15 days, a response time previously unimaginable in fashion retailing. That not only satisfies customers but lets the company avoid under- and over-production as well.

Finally, fast-cycle companies know just where in the system compressing time will add the most value for customers. Not surprisingly, those are the activities they attack first and upgrade regularly. For example, consider Freightliner, which has more than doubled its share of the U.S. heavy-duty, on-highway truck market over the last decade. Unlike many companies in this customized business, Freightliner didn't invest heavily in speeding up its in-plant production process. Instead, its management invested in pre-engineering hundreds of possible truck combinations, so that customers can order the drive trains, cabs, and other optional features they need from a pretested menu. The company avoids the on-line errors that plague some competitors and make hasty redesign and rework necessary. And it can deliver a truck weeks ahead of most of the industry at a lower price.

A key factor in achieving end-to-end, fast cycle time is a disciplined approach to schedules. Time-based competitors avoid the seemingly inevitable delays of organizational life by creating calendars for important events and insisting that *everyone* meet their commitments, so review and decision activities stay on track.

Build learning loops into the organization. Markets, products, and competitors move so quickly today that organizations with centralized intelligence functions simply cannot keep up. This is why fast-cycle managers want active sensors and interpreters of data at every level of the company. And why they emphasize on-line learning, which is the catalyst for continuous process innovation.

Designing rapid feedback loops into routine operations is a standard practice in fast-cycle companies. Benetton, for example, collects data daily at the retail level so it knows what is selling and what is not. Because what sells changes from month to month and from neighborhood to neighborhood, these data help the company decide what to produce currently, what new styles and colors to develop, and what merchandise to stock in particular outlets. Fast-cycle companies like Benetton don't waste time building inventory that won't be used immediately to satisfy customer needs.

Companies with fast-cycle capability also emphasize informal, ad hoc communication. Current information goes straight to where it can be most useful. It doesn't get lost in the chain of command. At Marks & Spencer, the great U.K. retailer, for example, managers at all levels are taught to bring important market information to senior management's attention at once. Thus the manager of a key store would be expected to call a vice chairman immediately if deliveries of basic products suggested the possibility of a systemwide shortage. From retail sales assistants, who are expected to reject defective merchandise and provide feedback on customer satisfaction, to a hands-on top management, everyone works to speed goods through the stores and information to the managers who can use it.

Companies with fast-cycle capability don't stay that way automatically. Their managers frequently renew and redesign the delivery system, continually gathering information about what makes it effective and what is getting in the way. They study competitors and superior performers in other industries for helpful ideas. They use new technologies like artificial intelligence to cut time out of routine activities. They encourage an unusual degree of mobility and initiative among their employees. At Du Pont, for example, production workers now visit customers just as salespeople and product engineers do to learn their needs firsthand.

Getting the Clock Started

Delivery dates, lead times, upcoming production dates—managers deal with time every day in an episodic manner. But they rarely stand back and consider time systematically or as a key to competitive position. Two facts of organizational life explain why time is so easily overlooked and undermanaged.

First, decision options are rarely presented to managers in terms of the effect they would have on time. A proposal for a new production process may highlight cost and labor savings but neglect to mention that the larger economic batch size will slow the whole organization down. Proponents of a new headquarters building will talk about more space and amenities but fail to point out that the floor plan separates marketing from engineering and thus will lengthen the new product development process. In short, it takes a special effort for executives to focus routinely on elapsed system time as something to be managed.

Second, and more problematic, most people in organizations like to have stability in their working procedures and social patterns. Serious efforts at cycle time reduction disrupt both. Multifunctional teams break up existing departments and routines. Compressing cycle time sweeps away long-standing crutches such as quality inspection and redundant data entry that existed only because work wasn't designed or done right the first time through. Some valued specialists are exposed as the cause of bottlenecks, while others become completely unnecessary. You don't need sophisticated short-term market forecasts if you can respond immediately to any change in the level of demand.

Strong as these internal forces are, however, today's executives have an even stronger incentive to manage their company's cycle time—the competitive world outside. Fast, smooth, skillful operations and an ability to learn in real time are potent sources of competitive advantage. Based on our observations in successful companies, here are some suggestions that can help management get started.

Examine cycle times and raise standards. First, calibrate your performance against that of your toughest competitors, not only on response time but also on cost, quality, and rate of innovation because all these are causally related. Then use these performance benchmarks as *minimum* targets in your strategic plan: improvements of 5% per year won't challenge the status quo. When Toyota set out to achieve a one-minute die change on a 50-ton press to make a cheap custom car possible, that wasn't incremental; it was inconceivable! But it is a foundation of Toyota's new level of competitiveness.

Map and model your company's decision making and operations flows so you can identify major interfaces, bottlenecks, and behavior patterns. Find out exactly where and how time is wasted and where quality problems arise, and share this intelligence with all of your employees. The organization has to learn how it actually works before it can usefully talk about changes.

Describe and highlight past successes in making changes, even modest ones, in how the company works. Build a belief that the company's circuitry is not fixed, that people can design and implement better ways to operate. Keep raising performance standards.

Set up unusual organization mechanisms to focus on cycle time. Form temporary teams to study what's slowing down a few key cross-functional activities in the company. Staff these teams with energetic, well-respected middle managers who must make the eventual solutions work. Ask them to articulate and evaluate a few options, especially radical ones. Crudely remap how the company would work under each proposal, then test it and determine what changes in policies and behavior would be needed to make it work. Keep discussing the best proposals until people begin to accept their feasibility.

Pursue conflict in meetings as a way to uncover and explore how the organization's working mechanisms slow down and where people's assumptions and beliefs diverge. After identifying the core of the conflict, develop a way to resolve it with data, not more opinion.

Treat bottlenecks, downtime problems, and other breakdowns as opportunities to learn. Don't just ascribe them to "life in a large organization" and assume they have to be lived with.

Keep asking "why" until you get to the root of a problem. Companies vary greatly in how they attack operating problems. Many fix today's problem: they adjust the machine that's turning out bad parts. Some go further and find the immediate cause of the problem: they adjust the machine and replace the worn tool that's throwing it off. Superior companies don't stop until they find the root cause—the poorly designed process or defective part that made the tool wear down in the first place.

Develop information systems to track value-adding activities. Distinguish the main operating sequence—the organization's central, value-adding activities—from time-consuming support and preparatory steps. Move the latter off-line. Give decision authority and responsibility for results to employees involved in the main sequence.

Organize working units around the flow of decisions, information, and material, not to accommodate departmental neuroses that have deformed the process over the years. Use training to give these groups the skills and support they need.

Connect stages in the operations chain as directly as possible. Design away gaps and queues. Develop target cycle times for specific stages, and schedule decisions and work flows so that people can meet them routinely.

Make time count in managing employees. Evaluate individuals on the basis of their contribution to the working team of which they are part. Be explicit about the group's cycle time and quality objectives and the individual's role in meeting them.

Avoid creating specialists unless they're absolutely essential. Specialists tend to be cut off from other perspectives and often have difficulty understanding new contexts. They also tend to push issues higher up in the organization where valuable management time gets taken up resolving them. Multifunctional teams can usually settle these issues at a working level.

Ask each individual to have at least an informal plan for the positive changes he or she intends to make. Get people accustomed to challenging and rethinking their activities continuously in the working-team context.

Position your people to accelerate their learning. Vary interactions among key managers, especially senior executives. Have them spend more time with peers on work substance and less time on policy problems. Imagine what would happen if you moved your senior managers' desks into a single room for three months, as Honda sometimes does, so that they could get to know the day-to-day business from their colleagues' point of view.

Devote meeting time to the effect of cycle time on the company's competitive position. Make sure everyone knows where the bottlenecks are, especially those they contribute to themselves.

Maximize key managers' exposure to operations downstream that depend on them. Sometimes an exchange of jobs between adjacent department heads is useful. With good people, a tour of duty that brings the vice president of marketing and sales to manufacturing—and vice versa—can be positive all around.

Ask each senior manager to prepare a flow chart that maps out how key reports make decisions and relate to one another operationally. Then compare the map with what the organization chart says. Explore the contrast and how it affects cycle time.

Implementation—a delicate balance. Managers who begin to move their organizations toward time compression face an inescapable dilemma: how to achieve faster cycles in the long term without being badly damaged by work interruptions in the short term. Most organizations cover their delays and errors with slack resources and loosely fitting interfaces. But when a company begins to compress its cycles, the delays and errors can rarely be fixed as quickly as the slack is taken away. Temporary breakdowns occur, and fast response to customers—the whole objective—is undermined.

Every management must find its own pace and mechanisms to walk this tightrope. A pilot project—walking before running—often helps. So does a simulation of new procedures before they are fully implemented. Temporary buffers of material or information may also help as long as they are deliberately reduced during the transition period. What's critical is that managers keep pushing the change process and don't suspend their efforts when the inevitable problems arise. As fast-cycle competitors everywhere remind us, operating crises are opportunities to learn and improve.

Many of these suggestions run counter to traditional ideas about good management. Efficiency was often thought to follow from fixed objectives, clear lines of organization, measures reduced to profit, and as few changes in basic arrangements as possible. But that was the logic of the mass-production machine. It has been superseded by the logic of innovation. And that logic, in turn, demands new organization and management practices.

PART

II

Managing the Creation of New Technologies

1
What Strategy Can Do for Technology

Kim B. Clark

There is a Japanese maker of high-precision dies that serves the burgeoning consumer electronics industry—the company's name will not ring a bell. Over the past five years, this small company has organized itself around an electronic network linking it to such giant electronics companies as Hitachi and to a highly specialized family of suppliers.

Designers at Hitachi sketch a new part and send it by fax to the diemaker. Die engineers review the sketch and, using computer-aided design (CAD) systems, generate the specifications for a new die in a matter of hours. The company then decides whether to make the die itself or subcontract it to one of the suppliers—all of whose skills, current capacity, and work-in-progress have been logged. As often as not, it chooses a supplier and sends the specifications by fax, along with supplementary information about materials and stresses. The supplier, using advanced numerical control tools, makes the die, also in a matter of hours. It is not uncommon for Hitachi to get the die for some parts back in one day: the sketch arrives in the morning, the die is finished in the afternoon.[1]

This diemaker comes to mind whenever I consider how science and technology pattern the world of business. We know that competition is intense, international, and unforgiving. But it is only when we come across a minor diemaker striving so hard to compete with technology that we know we are living in a new age. Five trends give shape to it:

- Worldwide dissemination of expanding scientific knowledge.
- The striking growth in the number of global competitors.

- Fragmented markets and shifting customer preferences.
- Diverse and transforming process technologies—leading to greater flexibility and responsiveness.
- A proliferation in the number of technologies relevant to any given product.

And notice the paradox. Technology has never been more important; yet building a competitive advantage by means of technology alone has never been more difficult. An expanding science base in communications, design, and manufacture puts enormous pressure on business, including such traditional crafts as diemaking. Markets are more fragmented and global precisely because competitors have the means to cater to increasingly particular customers and deliver products worldwide almost instantly; computers, materials science, and biology offer numerous, powerful, even astounding ways to improve products and the processes that make them.

But technology cannot be management's primary solution because it is every competitor's potential solution. A good offense can seem to be only defense. It is nearly impossible to build a lasting edge through a unique device developed by R&D or through an innovative, computer-driven process. There is no theoretical limit to getting good at making things, no permanent advantage to being first.

New technologies, whose sources are also worldwide, are critical to every company's struggle for existence. Even comparatively simple products like laundry detergent or breakfast cereal require enormously sophisticated process controls. We all assume that innovative engineers and scientists are at the core of high-technology industries like telecommunications or semiconductors, as well as biotechnology, artificial intelligence, or advanced materials. But creating and using new technology is no less essential to companies that compete in mature fabricated products like automobiles and appliances or to long-established processing industries like aluminum and chemicals.

Who wins? The advantage goes, as it always has gone, to superior strategy and execution. Take another look at the diemaker. It flourishes not because of any technological advantage per se but because it positioned itself at the center of a system of its own making—a system that exploits its own engineers' distinctive competence: rapid design of dies.

Any company that participates in the design of products today will use intelligent systems undreamed of a generation ago; advanced software and new forms of artificial intelligence equip designers with marvelously interactive tools for drawing, simulating, testing, and problem solving. That diemaker proves that unlocking the power of CAD systems requires creating not only new skills—individual engineers work away at CAD screens backed up by real-time databases, not drafting tables with dusty handbooks—but a new design process as well.

Within the Japanese automobile industry, the design system shifts the locus of critical pieces of knowledge; it presupposes greater communication among corporate functions—marketing with design, design with manufacturing. It even assumes new ways of characterizing customer requirements. An advanced design process, then, may lead to the elimination of whole departments and levels of management—it fundamentally changes the way design is accomplished in the organization.

Moreover, when factories provide the means to serve customers more individually, marketing discovers the means to probe markets more deeply. Mazda, surely, cannot be said only to have had more marketing savvy than Ford or GM when it came up with the Miata, a nostalgic little sports car with a convertible top. What it has is the highly scientific manufacturing capacity to make a profit with a run of no more than 40,000 cars—mixed-model assembly procedures, highly automated and flexible welding processes, sophisticated short-cycle stamping. By analogy, a nineteenth-century textile company could not have developed markets for mass-produced, inexpensive cloth if it had failed to exploit steam power or retained an organization derived from cottage, handloom weaving.

New design and manufacturing strategies are perhaps the most interesting ways of turning technology into advantage. The most conspicuous strategies are found in industries based on new science. Consider advances in molecular control, for example. Materials science and condensed matter physics are now creating many new commercial opportunities. Engineers at DuPont and Dow, for example, can control basic molecular structures, leading to new, high-performance materials with novel properties—for example, tough ceramics and high-strength polymer alloys.

Commercial production of such materials requires a manufacturing science that is equal to the science underlying the potential product. Scale and speed require the application of new sensor technology. They require new control algorithms based on mathematical models of the process and new equipment designs, with ultrahigh precision operation. They will also require, and this is imperative, an organization capable of managing an integrated, science-based process, one that develops and integrates customer knowledge into the development process—a further revolution in marketing.

It is no wonder, therefore, that managing the implications of scientific and technological advances has become an exciting, at times daunting, task. Senior managers particularly have a right to be perplexed. They commit to ambitious capital investments, many of which have dark corners. They are inundated with information from vendors of machines, software, and systems. They are justifiably eager to harness expertise.

Managers want to wed scientific and technical knowledge with existing strengths in engineering, marketing, human resource management, and manufacturing. They want to make better choices in targeting new technologies for development. And they especially want to shorten the lag between laboratory discovery and implementation—to link technical capabilities with customer requirements. In meeting these challenges, the best managers have uncovered some fascinating principles of action.

Know the technological core and link it to strategic intent. Technical questions cannot be the concern of only the technical community. General managers must know the value and advantage of the company's own processes and methods and know how to match their potential technical capabilities with opportunities to serve customer needs.

Managers need to link the world of technology with the world of business. People who are used to speaking of gross margins, focused differentiation, and convertible subordinated debentures need to share their language with people who are used to speaking of beta-blockers, biocompatibility, viral inactivation, and protein synthesis. Both groups need to acknowledge that new techology is futile unless it creates value.

Top managers must descend into the technological black box. They must help scientists and engineers ask searching questions about customers and competitors: How will needs change over the next five years? What are our competitors likely to do? Where do we need to be? What are the technical alternatives? What capabilities do we need to build? Where should we focus our resources?

Technology, in short, cannot be divorced from strategy. In implementing flexible manufacturing technology, general managers have to deal with the particular characteristics of software and hardware—not all of the details, perhaps, but the comprehensive benefits to the company. They have to understand the equipment and technologies of communication and control. Most important, they have to commit to a market strategy and a company organization that fits a flexible manufacturing system's advantages. Why buy an FMS just to increase volume?

Take a global view of technical competence. Even very large international companies cannot master through in-house research alone all the technical developments relevant to their industry. There are multiple centers of scientific and engineering expertise, as the competences of people from once-underdeveloped countries converge with those of Europe, Japan, and the United States. Managing technology flows among companies and labs often means using new organizational and administrative mechanisms—strategic partnerships and consortia.

Managers who once thought of competition as a straightforward test of one product against another, or simply rivalry among companies, must now contend with competitors backed by various alliances and confederations, including universities and governments. They have to consider leveraging technological development in their companies by forming alliances and strategic partnerships of their own.

Such forms of competition have been developing for a generation. Boeing and McDonnell Douglas compete against Airbus, a consortium of four companies from four European countries with the strong financial backing of four governments. On the horizon looms the prospect of a Japanese consortium, buttressed by joint ventures with jet engine manufacturers (like Rolls Royce) and seeded by Japanese government-sponsored research and defense production programs.

The merchant market in semiconductors is dominated by large, vertically integrated Japanese companies that have developed outstanding engineering and manufacturing capability. Japanese success has prompted collaborative efforts in Europe, spearheaded by Philips and Siemens. More recently, IBM and several other U.S. semiconductor and computer companies have agreed to form a new company called U.S. Memories, Inc. to produce advanced memory products for the commercial market.

But alliances are not to be thought of as one-shot collaborations. Rather, they are the basis for ongoing transfers of knowledge. Executives need to consider how technical knowledge really crosses borders and how it may be mustered from distant sources through strategic partnerships—Motorola and Toshiba, for example. They must be open to the possibility that a venture formed to access, say, outside manufacturing know-how may in fact lead to new approaches to product design, quality, and marketing and that new strategic concepts may be integral to the know-how that is transferred back to domestic operations.

In 1988, Quantum Corp., a manufacturer of high-performance disk drives, launched a new venture called Plus Development.[2] Its goal was to design, manufacture, and market a 10 MB hard disk mounted on an expansion board for IBM-compatible personal computers. Quantum and an experienced Japanese manufacturing company formed a partnership.

The Japanese engineers surprised Quantum with an enormous devotion to the product design to ensure that it would be manufacturable. Quantum product designers were skeptical at first—it seemed that Japanese fussing was going to delay product launch—but the American engineers eventually developed new skills in process technology. These lessons, in turn, led to a significant redesign of the product, creating greater robustness, which turned out to be an essential improvement for marketing the hard disk. Ultimately, Japanese manufacturing engineers stimulated the development of a more rigorous approach to quality throughout Quantum.

Time is of the essence. Today companies make history, or are consigned to it, quickly. In many industries, even six months can be packed with moves and countermoves. Products are born, sold, and phased out. Information moves very quickly. Customers will not wait; indeed, they will pay a premium for responsiveness.

That competition rewards quickness may seem somewhat removed from technological matters. It is not. Evidence is mounting that the effort to reduce cycle time can be critical to improving the technological self-consciousness of a company's whole organization. Companies that shorten product development time often prompt associated improvements in product quality and lower development costs. Their personnel become better at knowing what "better" is.

Japanese automobile companies develop stamping dies in half the time of their European competitors. This shortened lead time actually represents an improved understanding of the design process in the technology of die manufacturing; it presupposes more effective organizational approaches to technology as a whole—simultaneous engineering of product and process, for example.

Similarly, the speed with which a prototype is generated is often critical to commercializing a new technology. Yet finding out just what determines the speed of the prototyping cycle may have a profound influence on the technological competence of a company. It requires an understanding of the flows of materials and information and the nature of the production processes used. When you learn what you must do to make a prototype quickly, you expose the nerves of your core technology.

Discipline functions around the science of production. People who once worked in separable domains of technical knowledge or in research activities that could be conducted at arm's length—product engineering and manufacturing ramp-up, say, or materials development and assembly automation—must now be integrated. The focus of integration is a scientific understanding of the manufacturing process.

In steel, for example, advanced casting processes require the integration of machine design with sophisticated sensors to track temperature and speed, and the sensors require mathematical models of heat transfer to build control algorithms. If development work is to proceed rapidly and effectively, materials scientists must work closely with machine designers, software engineers, mathematicians, process specialists, and operating personnel.

Advanced plastics, used in structural elements of cars (like door frames), yield significant advantages, such as high strength at low weight. But mounting a door on a plastic frame requires extraordinary integration of product with process. One cannot twist, hit, or pull plastic. The door has to fit perfectly in the body. This imposes tight discipline on people responsible for door design, door processing, material design, door assembly, and hinge design and function. All engineers need greater insight into the sources of processing variation.

Integrate operations around the information system. Information technology fundamentally alters what knowledge is useful, where that knowledge is located, who has access to it, and how it gets increased and applied. One cannot exploit the virtues of information systems without aiming for structural changes compatible with them: the integration of product and process engineering, flattened hierarchies, distributed intelligence.

Competitive advantage often derives from undertaking projects that change the equipment, procedures, and software governing design, development, and assembly. Each of these elements is part of a system, ultimately linked through the computer; a change in one element requires complementary adaptation in the others.

This transformation toward greater integration will not be limited to the company's traditional boundaries. A broader structure—such as that diemaker's network—may arise, providing a new means for designing, producing, and servicing the product. Suppliers will be linked to designers, manufacturers to retailers, the R&D teams of international partners to each other.

Benetton, the Italian fashion company that pioneered such networks, has been widely celebrated in the business press, but one cannot help marvel at its continuing success.[3] It manufactures and markets its apparel on the strength of its information system, which links retail stores (most of them owned by franchisees) to warehouses, flexible factories, and suppliers. Information on hot-selling items and colors is available immediately and can be used to adjust production schedules to catch rapidly changing trends in the market. Without this network, Benetton would never be able to keep its prices moderate, the sine qua non of its marketing strategy.

Competing on science and technology means competing on the organization of information; inevitably, one thinks of a battle of computers. But the machine is not at the center of competition. If there is a hidden thread connecting these principles, it is that knowledge workers are the only corporate assets that last. They embrace machines and engender new systems, which they ultimately outgrow.

Executives who have thus been concerned primarily with capital investment and its return or who have put their faith in systems and procedures they thought would last almost forever now have to concentrate on creating a dynamic environment in which their most creative people can work hard in concert. Capitalizing on and expanding corporate knowledge requires relentless effort. Learning does not appear to be something that all organizations do naturally or well.

Another way of saying this is that senior managers, deliberately or by default, build the company's technical core. Senior managers hold the levers and mechanisms of change. They determine the rate and direction of learning in an organization. They organize the force of technology in the context of world competition. In the final analysis, they integrate human imagination.

Notes

1. This example is described more fully in Toshi Nishiguchi, "Competing Systems of Automotive Components Supply," paper prepared for the First Policy Forum, International Motor Vehicle Program (Cambridge: MIT, May 1987).

2. Steven C. Wheelwright and Nan S. Langowitz, "Plus Development Corporation (A)," 9-687-001, Boston: Harvard Business School, 1987.

3. James L. Heskett and S. Signorelli, "Benetton (A)," 9-685-014, Boston: Harvard Business School, 1985.

2

From the "Ladder of Science" to the Product Development Cycle

Ralph E. Gomory

U.S. business needs to understand how science and technology influence industrial competitiveness. Even in high-tech products, like computer memories, the U.S. trade surplus declined sharply early in the 1980s, and we were in deficit by 1986. How could this be happening to the greatest scientific power in the world—the home of the most Nobel laureates and innumerable scientific breakthroughs?

Too often the discussions about remedies center on the wrong questions: Which country invests the most of its GNP in basic research? Who has the most engineers and scientists? And then there are various statistics about how U.S. corporations are still outspending Japan, our biggest competitor, on research and development and the disquieting reports about the large number of foreign students picking up advanced degrees at our universities.

In fact, the United States is learning only now the hard lesson it taught the rest of the world earlier this century: Product leadership can be built without scientific leadership if companies excel at design and the management of production.

The United States was the leading industrial power well before it became the leading scientific power. When, during the 1920s, the capitals of science were the European universities, the United States excelled in worker productivity and per capita income and had the biggest trade surplus—it was preeminent by almost any industrial measure. Now U.S. universities are the capitals of science, and Japan has the trade surplus.

Given current Japanese superiority in manufacturing technology, this may seem a grim message to U.S. managers. It is not meant to be, but rather should be the basis for cautious optimism. If Japanese companies are by and large competing more successfully than U.S. companies right now, they aren't doing anything we cannot learn.

Again and again I read about the radical "macro" changes Americans must make if our major corporations are to regain their edge—a new, Zen-like attitude toward excellence, perhaps, rigorous new incentives for consumers to save money, a reformed system of basic education, a cultural merging of science with entrepreneurship. There are important insights and valid long-range directions implied by these rather sweeping demands, yet they miss the point. There is a great deal we can do now.

The *first* things high-technology companies should busy themselves with are doable "micro" changes in the way they manage the product development process. They should concentrate on comparatively small things—immediately doable things—like designing for manufacture, getting product into customers' hands more quickly, or pulling the right know-how into the development of products at just the right time. It is all fine and well to perfect the conditions that engender creativity. But technology-driven companies first have to organize to make the best fourth version of a product, not the best first. Often it hardly matters who made the first.

These urgent corporate tasks are very difficult, but they are not mysterious. If, on the whole, Japanese executives bring them off more successfully than we do nowadays, there is nothing inscrutable about their actions. Our fate certainly doesn't rest with business schools teaching about exotic new corporate culture. Once U.S. managers know what their companies are supposed to do, they too will work out the ways to manage their people. The point is to get clear what has to be done.

Two Concepts of Innovation

THE LADDER. The most common, reasonable perception of the relationship of innovation to production is the step-by-step reduction to practice of new scientific knowledge that then generates a radically new product. The Manhattan Project springs to mind, or DuPont's development of nylon. I think of the process as a kind of "ladder" because usable things come as the culmination of cumulative scientific research—as in nuclear physics or organic chemistry; the process then moves, step-by-step, toward increasing practicality. Science seems to yield what the Victorians called "progress."

While this ladder process goes on, those who understand the idea or technology best—most often scientists—play a leading role in shaping products. Their ideas dominate; the customers' needs are taken for granted.

When revolutionary commercial products emerge out of scientists' labs, they succeed by providing a great business opportunity. Windfall profit comes from doing what nobody else can. You are first, and you have what everybody wants or can be expected to want. You invent nylon, and you sell millions of stockings. If you could actually produce a cold-fusion reaction, you can expect to sell a great deal of electricity.

The first crude forms of the transistor, available by 1948, were the result of a buildup since the 1920s of fundamental knowledge about quantum mechanics and solid-state physics. Scientists descended the rungs to practical application. Crude transistors gave way to a series of increasingly usable devices, which started to appear in radios in the early 1950s. Finally, they found their way into computers. The transistor was essentially a new idea when scientists created the chip around it.

The great ladders of science are by no means all in the misty past. We see reductions to practice today in molecular biology and perhaps superconductivity. Any company that is first to exploit these new technologies in unexpected ways can count on winning millions of customers worldwide for revolutionary products. For a short while, that company will not have to bother about competitors cutting into profits.

THE PRODUCT CYCLE. There is another, wholly different, less dramatic, and rather grueling process of innovation, which is far more critical to commercializing technology profitably. I call it, naturally enough, the "cyclic development" process, governed as it is by the product cycle. Its hallmark is incremental improvement, not breakthrough. It requires turning products over again and again; getting the new model out, starting work on an even newer one. This may all sound dull, but the achievements are exhilarating.

Many products, after going through the ladder process, are absorbed into cyclic development. Quite apart from features ceremoniously introduced to win new customers, a product's stuff is quietly improved. Year after year, refrigerators are changed; plastic replaces steel, glass becomes more and more resistant to breaking, compressors become more energy efficient. In this way, the engine that powered the Model T gave way, by generations, to the Quad-4. The computer chip became denser and much more powerful—16 memory-bits 25 years ago, more than a million bits today.

There is no brand new product here, no revolutionary technology. Cyclic development is a competition among ordinary engineers in bringing established products to market. The contest is between my car and your car, not my car and your helicopter. Another way of saying this is that production is a relentless race, not a collegial puzzle. The company works assiduously to refine the product, customize it for more and more consumer segments, make it more reliable, or get it to market more cheaply.

To be sure, there are times when incremental improvements in one area of application suddenly become the solution for engineers stymied in a quite different area. Amorphous silicon had been developed and slowly improved in the production of solar cells. It was only after engineers had gone through several cycles of improvement in small liquid-crystal displays that they imported amorphous silicon into their work on very large displays. Amorphous silicon allowed them to deposit transistors inexpensively on the back of the display. Similarly, HDTV will merge more computer technology with established, many-times-refined ways of making televisions—a definite advantage for the Japanese.

I cannot stress enough that what ground U.S. consumer electronics and automobile producers have already lost *cannot* be attributed to failures of new science or to failures of innovation. We originated those industries and then fell behind in making refinements—behind the Japanese commitment to quality design and careful manufacturing, not behind in science and new ideas. If proponents of a U.S. industrial policy assume that Japanese competitiveness derives mainly from the Ministry of International Trade and Industry's targeting advanced technology for concentration and expansion, they are getting only part of the story right—and the smaller part at that.

MITI *has* orchestrated national research, such as the very large-scale integration project, and it has encouraged Japanese corporations to pursue Western technology actively. More recently, MITI has facilitated ladder-style innovation in such things as "fifth generation" supercomputing by funding and coordinating national research programs.

And yet I have trouble thinking of a single product Japanese companies have introduced first—one that sprung from their own basic research in new technology. Their strength is not science. Our weakness will not be cured by doing better science. We must reform the way we approach cyclic product improvement. In the key industries that are problems today, we have been good starters, the Japanese have been good finishers.

The Hard Facts of Cyclic Development

Most development work is done *just one step ahead of manufacturing.* While the company's plants are making the 256K chip, R&D is working on designing, refining, and processing the 1-megabit chip. When the 1-megabit chip is ready, manufacturing ramps up, increases volume—and the 256K chip is phased out. This triggers development work on the 4-megabit chip so that the process can start all over again. This pattern appears in all kinds of manufacturing—cars, consumer electronics, jet engines.

One cannot overestimate the importance of getting through each turn of the cycle more quickly than a competitor. It takes only a few turns for the company with the shortest cycle time to build up a commanding lead.

Even if a company starts out with an inferior product, it can overtake the industry leader if it has the capacity to turn out a new line 6 to 12 months more quickly. Our Japanese competitors believe that, in the shortest of long runs, quick development beats market research every time. I once made the mistake of asking a Japanese colleague, my counterpart in an electronics company, whether he had researched how customers were likely to respond to a particular kind of ink jet for printers. Why, he politely retorted, should he study whether customers are *likely* to respond positively to this or that jet if his company can get out a wholly redesigned printer in a year to 18 months? Why not adapt to actual buying patterns? (Why, he implied, should I be bothering with such questions?)

Moreover, people often observe that company engineers tend to be *impervious to ideas from outside sources.* R&D people often call this the not-invented-here syndrome—an inappropriately psychological phrase to describe an objective difficulty. By common prejudice, the resistance of designers to new ideas is ascribed to a certain mental inertia: we tend to think of the resistance of U.S. car designers to disc brakes, radial tires, and computer-governed, electronic fuel-injection systems; or of how long it took consumer electronics companies to replace metal parts and casings with molded plastics.

The facts are that design engineers cannot easily work with newness and keep to their timetables. Engineers need new ideas that snap into the skills they already have. They want to use the tools they've mastered. They want to finish in 18 months. Perhaps the hardest kind of knowledge for engineers to absorb is work done at research universities—work that is potentially useful but that appears to them at an early stage of development or that simply is packaged in a form alien to the product team.

Product development has a timetable that cannot be interrupted to accommodate some unexpected piece of technology. A better print head proposed for a printer one year into a two-year cycle is useless. New solutions, however sweet, *have to be available to designers at the beginning of the cycle*. Halfway through is too late.

Incidentally, even at the start of the cycle, new ideas are useful only if they've been pretty well fleshed out and tested so that the development team can incorporate them without breaking stride. R&D can rarely afford to see the schedule slip over the details of a component. Few incremental changes are significant enough to warrant being beaten to the market by competitors, which would mean losing business, revenue, customer loyalty. You don't risk losing a part of the base from which to compete next time around.

Tie Design to Manufacturing

Since design is one step ahead of manufacturing in the race to the end of the product cycle, one of the most important challenges for high-technology managers is to get manufacturing expertise contributing directly to product development early on. American companies have to give far more attention to design for manufacture.

In the United States, a kind of caste system has emerged in product development. Design engineers are focused on product features and performance, which have more prestige in the engineering world. Manufacturing people are mired in the grim and gritty details of production—in intermediate costs, in the ways components are actually put together. ("We've built one," says design to manufacturing, "now you build 10,000.")

Nothing could be further from Japanese practice, where design specialists and manufacturing people work side by side, often in product teams, so that the designers will be more cost-conscious and oriented toward manufacturing simplicity. Japanese design engineers typically start out their careers in manufacturing plants, so they're intuitively thinking about the control processes that are needed to maintain consistently high quality.

Without manufacturing's early participation in design, latent production problems are bound to remain obscure. Product engineers will ignore opportunities to improve quality and speed things up. Improvements can be as elementary as using a single screw size throughout the chassis of a processor—the IBM 9370 uses only one screw size. Alternatively, improvements may be very complex indeed.

When I was at IBM, one of the company's most notable turnarounds pivoted on the Proprinter, a dot-matrix printer to be used with the IBM PC. That the Proprinter came out of nowhere to gain a dominant share of the market is well known by now. What is less well understood is how much of its quick triumph resulted from IBM's attention to design for manufacture.

The company was hardly the industry leader in personal printers at the time. When it announced its original PC in 1983, the least expensive model IBM built cost some $5,500—more than twice the cost of the PC itself, and the company had little choice but to supply a Japanese-made printer along with the IBM computer. So the company mustered a small technical team—designers, manufacturing engineers, and automation specialists—in Charlotte, North Carolina, knowing full well that the luxury of a traditional multiyear cycle was out of the question.

IBM urged team members to work together, not sequentially. It gave them a mandate to simplify the product—and share the same coffee machine. One of the first things they discovered was that the typical PC-attachable printer contained about 150 parts. This was too many parts, and it was an invitation to wasted motion: the more parts you had, the more you had to design, purchase, account for, and store.

Team members determined to reduce that number to only 60 parts, some of these performing multiple functions. In one case, 20 parts were found to be replaceable by one molded-plastic frame. Manufacturing engineers discerned that they could substantially lower assembly costs by designing the product in layers so that robots could put components together from the bottom up. They saw that parts should be self-aligning so that jigs would be minimal. They eliminated all screws, springs, pulleys, and other items requiring human adjustment. Finally, they decided to use molded plastics wherever possible so they could design parts to clip together without fasteners.

Remarkably, the Proprinter came out essentially as planned. It was made from only 62 parts. It printed faster and had more features than the competition—and the team developed it in half the usual time. The product was so well designed for automated manufacture that it turned out to be extremely easy and inexpensive to assemble by hand—so easy, in fact, that IBM eventually shifted a good deal of Proprinter production from the automated plant in Charlotte to a manual plant in Lexington, Kentucky.

An additional benefit was that the Proprinter proved unusually reliable in the field. Fewer parts meant fewer assembly errors, fewer adjustments, and fewer opportunities for things to go wrong later. No screws will loosen in the customer's office if there are no screws in the product.

Five months after launch, the Proprinter became the best-selling PC printer in the industry. Now, just five years after launch, the future of dot-matrix printing is itself in doubt.

Keeping Engineers Up-to-Date

I noted how difficult it is, especially as product cycles shorten, for new ideas or new technology to enter the product cycle from the outside—and for good reasons, not just psychological ones. A lack of familiarity with a particular technology or exposure to it at the wrong time in the product cycle would strain resources and schedules. Only the engineers themselves can deal with these difficulties. They are the only ones who know in detail exactly when they can accept new ideas and what technologies require the tools they don't have.

Engineers need to go out and find what they *can* use and "pull" it into the company. This works far better than anyone trying to "push" ideas from the outside that really may not fit.

Management must encourage engineers to keep up-to-date and know what is going on in the outside world so that when the time is right engineers can pull new technology rather than oppose the unfamiliar being pushed at them. The prerequisite for keeping up-to-date is attending engineering conferences, reading the technical literature, and participating actively in the engineering community. Management must fund these activities rather than regard them as sops to engineers' professional ambitions and cut them at each budget crisis.

Many Japanese companies encourage their engineers not only to attend conferences but to present papers too. This may sound time-consuming; of course it is. But presentations force research scientists and engineers to stand up before their peers, to keep up with the relevant literature and anticipate questions and objections.

Companies can certainly facilitate communication among professionals in the research organization, regardless of distance. IBM's internal electronic network, VNET, allows company engineers and scientists to exchange message and data files, engage in computer conferencing, draw from among the many databases at the IBM Technical Information Retrieval Center, and search the catalog of IBM's technical libraries. In addition, VNET is a gateway to such academic research networks as BITNET and CSNET, which permit exchanges with university researchers.

Another way for companies to foster technical dialogue is through funding research programs with universities on problems of common interest. IBM has over $100 million in contractual agreements with universities around the world. Although some of the projects are substantial in scope, most are small, engaging only a few researchers. Where possible, IBM lends its own researchers to joint studies and experimental partnerships, and it often supplies extra funding or needed equipment. The mutual stimulation and professional relations fostered by such partnerships can outlast what is learned on a project.

The Sources of New Technology

Any company's relationship with universities, no matter how science-based, has limits. University presidents I've talked with agree that the proper work of universities (and national laboratories) is the ladder of science, not the product cycle—and they are right. They have a superb record in getting basic science done, and they cultivate the intellectual freedom that is far removed from the staggered starts and finishes of product development.

Even when they want to, university researchers can't be much help to companies struggling with their product cycles. How could university specialists in metallurgy know that IBM components engineers working in Fishkill, New York really need to learn more about how solder balls age? Impossible. University people shouldn't be expected to push their findings into the product cycle. It is the responsibility of the company to pull knowledge into the process when it is needed.

Japanese companies have learned to pull research effectively. They routinely send their best engineers and scientists to the graduate programs of our best universities and research institutes not only to study

Exhibit I.

Too Much Support for R&D from Corporate Sources...

Source of R&D Funds:	Corporate Labs and Technical Centers	Group, Sectorial, and Divisional Labs
Corporate	50.3%	23.1%
Business Units	41.1%	70.7%
Transfers from Other Labs	0.7%	0.8%
External to Company	7.2%	3.4%

...Too Little Support for Process R&D

Percent of Technical Effort Spent on:	
Basic Research	>1%
Applied Research	23%
Product Design, Development, and Engineering	34%
Process Design, Development, and Engineering	23%
Technical Service	20%

Charts supplied to HBR by Center for Innovation Management Studies at Lehigh University. Responses are drawn from questionnaires sent to R&D executives in the 210 U.S.-based companies comprising the membership of the Industrial Research Institute.

high science but also to get a clear idea of what academic research is being conducted by whom. They scout for science. U.S. companies should be doing the same, even if it means sparing leading design personnel for a year or more.

Compared to universities, an in-house industrial-research organization is naturally in a much better position to serve as an engine for cyclic development. A corporate research laboratory's greater technical depth, scientific knowledge, and ties with universities, however attenuated, can directly assist its business units. It is not enough, however, to put the lab up on a hill and hope that ideas will just trickle down to products.

To succeed, the corporate research organization must accept primary responsibility for technology transfer to its business units. And it may be time to start experimenting with new ways of funding corporate R&D. Some corporations—like Philips Industries, N.V. and General Electric—are experimenting with new strictures on their corporate labs that require them to gain a portion of their support directly from the various business units. The theory is that research and development people would more likely work on viable, commercial projects if their research depended on the people who would actually be applying it.

IBM has had considerable success since 1981 setting up joint programs between its research division and various product development laboratories. There are now 19 such programs in areas as diverse as advanced silicon technology to software technology and workstation systems. From the start, such programs were governed by agreements on technical road maps, division of labor, and migration of responsibility. The corporate research division has also worked directly with various manufacturing plants.

Technique and Common Sense

There are technique-oriented ways to shorten product cycles, among them wider use of computerized simulation, which allow manufacturers to avoid much of the cost and time needed to build actual hardware models and prototypes. IBM uses a highly parallel, special-purpose supercomputer called EVE (Engineering Verification Engine)—which simulates the performance of even very large-scale processors before they are built—to toy with different system configurations or spot and correct systems errors.

Of course, every manufacturing business cannot build an EVE. But businesses can do some very nice simulations on a PC. Today's enhanced PS/2 or Macintosh II is nearly as powerful as the Cray supercomputer of just ten years ago.

Yet high-tech simulations should not obscure how shortening product cycles is mostly a matter of managerial common sense. For exam-

Exhibit II.

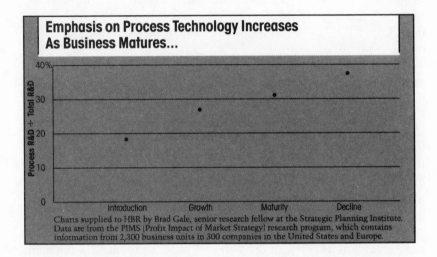

Emphasis on Process Technology Increases As Business Matures...

Charts supplied to HBR by Brad Gale, senior research fellow at the Strategic Planning Institute. Data are from the PIMS (Profit Impact of Market Strategy) research program, which contains information from 2,300 business units in 300 companies in the United States and Europe.

ple, management checks and hurdles should help the product development team make a clear business case, or clear up any ambiguities about what the product is trying to be—the market it is directed to, the options it would offer, and the technology that would produce it. Once the project is launched, however, there can be such a thing as too much review, with attendent changes and loss of time.

IBM used to have many hurdles at nearly every step of the process, which encumbered the product team with paperwork and unnecessary fussing. Now the company has only four or five, all at the beginning.

Finally, products should be developed around standard modules, such as keyboards, power supplies, monitors, and standard electronic components. By combining standard modules with more proprietary building blocks—usually sophisticated, specialized electronics and circuit boards—companies can develop the unique characteristics of each of their new models very quickly. One group at IBM, working on a new series of display terminals, trimmed five months off the previous development cycle for the same line of products—just by using standard components.

As citizens, we debate reforms in our schools, military, and budget—changes that will influence our competitiveness ten years down the line. But managers must make changes sooner than that. If our leading high-technology companies do not perform consistently well in

Exhibit III.

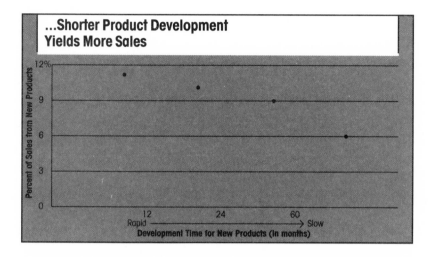

the short run, nothing the government eventually does will save the industry from decline. By itself, our population of brilliant, independent scientists will certainly not guarantee a relatively high standard of living. The leads those scientists generate are easily dissipated. Increasingly, our science is a storehouse of ideas that benefits the world nearly as much as it does us.

Yet there is no reason to lose heart. The course is clear enough. We can solve our problems, and cultural change is not a prerequisite. We need to execute elementary, practical reforms that are waiting to be instituted right outside our offices. Speed up the product cycle, encourage close ties between development and manufacturing people, keep engineers up-to-date—there is nothing here that U.S. industry cannot try today.

The United States has managed to be successful on the ladder of innovation. We simply must learn to be equally adept at managing the product cycle. Fix the product and fix the factory. *Then* think about fixing the country.

3
Technology Fusion and the New R&D

Fumio Kodama

From apparel to aerospace, steel to software, the pace of technological innovation is quickening. No longer can companies afford to miss a generation of technology and expect to remain competitive. Adding to the pressure, innovations are increasingly crossing industry boundaries: a new fiber developed by the textile industry has potential for building materials and medical equipment. Some companies are adept at using a diversity of technologies to create new products that transform markets. But many others are floundering because they rely on a technology strategy that no longer works in such a fast-changing environment. The difference between success and failure is not how much a company spends on research and development, but how it defines it.

There are two possible definitions. Either a company can invest in R&D that replaces an older generation of technology—the "breakthrough" approach—or it can focus on combining existing technologies into hybrid technologies—the "technology fusion" approach. The former is a linear, step-by-step strategy of technology substitution: the semiconductor replaced the vacuum tube, the CD replaced the record album. Technology fusion, on the other hand, is nonlinear, complementary, and cooperative. It blends incremental technical improvements from several previously separate fields of technology to create products that revolutionize markets. For example, marrying optics and electronics created optoelectronics, which gave birth to fiber-optics communications systems; fusing mechanical and electronics technologies produced the mechatronics revolution, which has transformed the machine-tool industry.

In a world where the old maxim "one technology–one industry" no longer applies, a singular breakthrough strategy is inadequate; companies need to include both the breakthrough and fusion approaches in their technology strategies. Relying on breakthroughs alone fails because it focuses the R&D effort too narrowly (say, within one electronics specialty), ignoring the possibilities of combining technologies (innovations in mechanics and electronics). Yet many Western companies still rely almost exclusively on the breakthrough approach. The reasons are complex: a distrust of outside innovations, a not-invented-here engineering arrogance, an aversion to sharing research results. Part of the breakthrough tradition in the United States stems from the defense-driven technology policy. The Department of Defense funds university research that it then transfers to a limited number of defense contractors for exploitation; the process is chronological, with very little technology transfer or cooperation.

It is among leading high-technology manufacturers in Japan that technology fusion has found its strongest proponents. Over the last two decades, companies such as Fanuc, Nissan, NEC, Sharp, and Toray have developed their own versions of technology fusion and incorporated them into their overall research and product development strategies. Consider the following examples:

> Starting in the late-1960s, a number of Japanese companies, including Nippon Telephone and Telegraph, NEC, Nippon Sheet Glass, and Sumitomo Electric Industries, fused glass, cable, and electronics technologies to produce Japan's first fiber optics. Today Japanese fiber-optics companies have established a significant share of the global fiber-optics equipment markets.

> A leader in mechatronics during the 1970s, Fanuc fused electronic, mechanical, and materials technologies to develop an affordable computerized numerical controller, a cabinet-sized system that controls the movements of industrial machine tools. Today Fanuc is the world market leader in computerized NCs and one of Japan's most profitable companies.

> In the early 1980s, Sharp developed the first commercially viable liquid crystal display for pocket calculators from the fusion of electronic, crystal, and optics technologies—another branch of optoelectronics. Today the company controls 38% of the worldwide LCD market, valued at over $2 billion; the market is expected to more than triple by 1995.

In each of these cases, the companies added one technology to another and came up with a solution greater than the sum of its parts—in technology fusion, one plus one equals three. Because it combines rather than replaces technologies, fusion requires a different mind-set and a new set of management practices. In the Japanese companies I have studied over the last decade, I have identified three basic principles essential to technology fusion.

First, the market drives the R&D agenda, not the other way around. If the customer wants a cheaper, smaller, and more reliable numerical controller for a machine tool, then that is the starting point for setting up R&D projects—not what the technologist has produced in the lab. Developing such a market-driven approach begins with *demand articulation*.

Second, companies need intelligence-gathering capabilities to keep tabs on technology developments both inside and outside the industry. Good surveillance goes beyond formal efforts, such as monitoring patent applications around the world. All employees, from senior managers to frontline workers, should be part of the collection and dissemination process as *active receivers*. In many Japanese companies, keeping ears and eyes open to usable innovations has become second nature, just another aspect of the job.

Third, technology fusion grows out of long-term R&D ties with a variety of companies across many different industries. Investment in research consortia, joint ventures, and partnerships goes beyond tokenism. It is both *reciprocal* and *substantial*—all participating companies are on more-or-less equal footing in terms of responsibility for and reward from the investment. Even though the risk of participation in many of these R&D ventures is high, the risk of nonparticipation is often much higher. Therefore, management must accept that it cannot evaluate each research investment on a short-term financial basis.

There is ample evidence of Japan's commitment to the three principles of technology fusion. Honda, NEC, Sharp, Sony, and others are zealots when it comes to involving the customer in the product conceptualization process; they have developed demand articulation to a fine art. And most Japanese companies have elaborate intelligence-gathering networks, both formal and informal, that can be traced back to post–World War II reconstruction. From the 1950s through the 1970s, Japan's R&D efforts were directed primarily at absorbing foreign technologies; the Japanese Ministry of International Trade and Industry (MITI) estimates that during the 1960s and 1970s, Japanese manufacturers devoted over one-quarter of all their R&D investments to "digesting" imported technologies.

Most important for fusion, however, is the ever-increasing emphasis

Japanese companies place on fusion research. Not only has R&D spending risen sharply in Japan over the last decade—among the top 50 industrial companies, R&D spending exceeded capital spending for the first time in 1986—but according to the Management and Coordination Agency of Japan, all major Japanese industries have been diversifying their R&D spending into noncore technologies. For instance, between 1980 and 1986, Japan's textile industry spent 70% of its total R&D outside its principal product area. Fabricated metals and the iron and steel industries both averaged about 50%, communications equipment, electronics, and precision machinery averaged around 35%.

Technology fusion is also reflected in changes in the types of joint research projects these companies undertake. An analysis of membership in Japanese research associations reveals that the average number of industries per project is increasing, while the number of participating companies per industry is decreasing. In other words, collective research in Japan is beginning to bring together companies from different industries rather than different companies within the same industry.

In 1988, for instance, there were 27 cases of collective research in which just 1 of the 5 rival computer makers—Toshiba, Hitachi, Fujitsu, Mitsubishi, and NEC—took part with other industries; many of these were technology fusion projects. Earlier in the decade, a typical joint research project would have included all 5 computer makers working together on an industry-specific problem. The same diversification trend is observable in other industries: in 1988, there were 27 research projects involving only 1 of the 5 major steel companies; 17 projects that included only 1 of 3 major shipbuilders; and 11 cases in which 1 of 3 textile companies took part.

Of course, any discussion of Japan's cooperative research must make mention of industrial policy and the country's industrial groups, or *keiretsu*. MITI, in particular, actively promotes technology fusion through legislation and government-funded research projects. Since 1961, MITI's industrial research associations have encouraged diffusion of technologies and the creation of intercompany engineering infrastructure through tax incentives and direct sponsorship. In all, there have been over 75 such associations formed in the past 3 decades.

Some observers argue that the mechatronics revolution was born out of MITI-sponsored industrial legislation enacted in Japan in 1971 and 1978 that encouraged joint research between the precision machinery and electronics industries. And, say these same observers, Japan's keiretsu provide a safe environment for cross-industry R&D.

The country's fiber-optics industry, for instance, owes a large part of its existence to collaborative R&D efforts within the Sumitomo Group.

I contend, however, that the roles of both the government and the keiretsu are, at most, secondary to a successful technology fusion strategy. In the evolution of mechatronics, neither the laws promoted by MITI nor MITI's direct guidance materially changed industrial behavior—the research and development would have taken place with or without the government's prompting. In the case of liquid crystal displays, for example, Sharp developed its products without the help of a powerful industrial group. Even in the fiber-optics market, the drive to create viable products was fueled by the market in the form of intense competition from companies in the United States and Europe—AT&T, Corning, Northern Telecom, Alcatel, Ericsson, Philips, and Siemens—not because of the existence of the Sumitomo Group.

By far the most important factor for a successful fusion strategy is how well senior management incorporates the three fusion principles—demand articulation, intelligence gathering, and collaborative R&D—into the company's existing technology strategy. It is a long-term process of change, but it is also a necessary one if companies expect to survive. Given this mandate, management's first task is to revisit the relationship between the customer and research and development.

Articulating Demand

Unlike a breakthrough strategy that starts in the laboratory, technology fusion starts with a new understanding of the market. Converting demand from a vague set of wants into well-defined products requires a sophisticated translation skill, demand articulation. Articulating demand is a two-step process: first, translate market data into a product concept; and second, decompose the concept into a set of development projects.

Consider the first step in Fanuc's development of the computerized numerical controller. Soon after its 1972 spinoff from Fujitsu, the company methodically analyzed the market to evaluate its opportunities. The then-current generation of numerical controller had changed little since it was invented in 1952 by researchers at Massachusetts Institute of Technology. With 2,000 mechanical valves, it was the size of a small room and still very expensive to buy and to operate. In its analysis, Fanuc identified a huge segment of midsized and small industrial customers that were going unserved because the NC was too costly and too large. Targeting this lucrative niche, Fanuc's management set a goal to develop a controller that was at once cheaper, simpler, and more compact than the current generation.

Fanuc then decomposed its product concept into a series of R&D projects. One of these projects looked at all the possibilities for substituting mechanical components with electronics. The rationale was simple: electronics were smaller, cheaper, and more reliable. Through its close connection with Fujitsu, which retained 35% ownership after the spinoff, Fanuc researched the necessary systems and developed the software and hardware for the new computer-based NC. One result was Fanuc's new electrohydraulic stepping motor, in which electrical pulses were converted directly into mechanical movements known as steps. The stepping motor removed many operational complexities and eliminated the need for much of the bulk of the MIT machine.

Sharp followed a similar demand approach when it translated the customer's desire for a more powerful and sleek electronic calculator into a set of specific R&D projects for a thinner, lower powered, easy-to-read display. These R&D projects included research in LCDs and in low-powered complementary metal oxide semiconductors (CMOS). Sharp was quick to identify the liquid crystal display as a promising technology, and the fact that the technology was still considered exotic was not a deterrent. Instead, Sharp saw LCDs as a way to solve specific technical problems and change the rules of competition in the marketplace.

Demand articulation flourishes when an industry is very competitive and technically sophisticated. Brisk competition, almost to the point of excess, motivates companies to keep their attention on the customer. And the more technically competent the industry is as a whole, the higher the absorption rate of technologies from other industries. In the case of Sharp, the competition included the likes of Hewlett-Packard and Texas Instruments, both pioneers in electronics. Such a competitive environment spurred Sharp to experiment with alternatives that it probably would not have explored had the competition been less intense.

Demand articulation also requires management to take a long-term view of the product development process. Instead of planning R&D investments out 1 or 2 years, companies should think out 10 or even 20 years, to how R&D efforts can satisfy today's latent demand even when the technology does not exist or is just emerging. Thinking long-term was critical in the evolution of the home-use video recorder market. The product concept can be traced back to 1955, when Toshiba's Noritake Sawazaki invented the helical scanning system for video recording and playback. Sawazaki's innovation enabled professional broadcasters to use narrower tape and smaller systems. But just as important, it set Toshiba and other equipment manufacturers thinking about the potential for home use. By shrinking the machine and developing ways to mass produce it, they could develop a viable home unit. Over time, with great effort and expense, they solved both problems, and by the mid-1970s, Sony launched the first home-use video recorder using a helical scanner, beating out Toshiba by a few months. Today Sony dominates the second-generation, eight-millimeter video market.

One of today's 20-year product development visions in the entertainment industry involves what Japanese engineers called "media design," a concept that involves the fusion of audio and video hardware and software with the creativity and artistry of the entertainment industry. One product concept being toyed with now is interactive cinema, where a moviegoer dons a lightweight headset fitted with a pair of goggles and slips on a pair of electronic gloves, becoming an "actor" in a virtual-reality movie. By shrinking the componentry and bundling it into an affordable home unit, the virtual-reality theater could become the twenty-first century equivalent of today's videocassette recorder.

While this idea sounds like pure science fiction, companies like Sony and Matsushita are taking it seriously. They are setting long-term research and business agendas that they expect will deliver a new generation of such innovative products within the next two decades. Both companies have already taken the first steps toward this vision: Sony acquired Columbia Pictures Entertainment in 1989, and Matsushita purchased MCA Inc. in 1990. As Michael Schulhof, vice chairman of Sony Corporation of America, said, "The acquisition of a major film studio extends Sony's long-term strategy of building a total entertainment business around the synergy of audio and video hardware and software." Both purchases open immediate opportunities for replacing analog production systems that use film as the medium with digital systems that use computer-generated images as the medium. Once the industry is all digital, then a whole new set of computer-based innovations such as high-definition television and digital audio-tape technology becomes feasible.

While imaginative demand articulation is an important starting point for companies like Sony and Matsushita, it is just that—a starting point. A well-defined R&D agenda is worthless without a sophisticated knowledge of the full range of technical alternatives to choose from. Broadening technical horizons begins with a system for monitoring technological innovations outside the organization and outside the industry.

Becoming Intelligent

When it comes to gathering intelligence on technological innovations, most companies do a poor job. They typically focus on the immediate competition and rely on a limited number of channels for collecting information. They lack the breadth of knowledge necessary for a technology fusion strategy. By analogy, a company might have a very sophisticated instrument for picking up and analyzing light waves, but if the instrument cannot read radio waves or microwaves, the company is at a distinct disadvantage. What most companies need is an instrument that collects information across the entire spectrum of both visible and invisible competitors.

The visible competitor is a known quantity. In the auto industry, Toyota has to watch developments at rivals Nissan, Honda, General Motors, and Ford; in the DRAM market, Toshiba has to keep tabs on Hitachi, Mitsubishi, NEC, Oki, Fujitsu, and Texas Instruments; and in disk drives, Seagate must monitor Conner Peripherals, IBM, Quantum, and others. In all cases, the "enemy" uses similar technologies and production systems; the difference is one of degree.

Invisible competitors, on the other hand, are unfamiliar and often unknown. They are companies from outside the industry that possess a technological capability that could be a threat if turned to new markets. For example, the makers of small, form-factor disk drives face a possible long-term threat from the vendors of storage devices that use flash memory semiconductors, solid-state components that offer comparable storage capacity but are much smaller and consume less power. Developed initially for the portable computer market by such companies as Intel, AT&T, Fujitsu, and Mitsubishi, industry watchers expect flash-based storage devices to migrate into other segments of the office equipment market—fax machines, cellular phones—over the next few years. In response, Conner Peripherals has teamed with Intel to develop a fusion version of a flash chip that marries disk-drive technology with semiconductor technology so the host computer thinks it's talking to a disk drive.

Of course, monitoring invisible competitors is not only a good defensive strategy but also a way for companies to spot innovations worthy of investment. But keeping tabs on an ever-growing diversity of technologies demands sophisticated intelligence gathering that includes both a formal and an informal capability. The formal capability includes such things as a network of offices around the world to monitor patent applications, a process for sifting through volumes of published information, and a system for finding innovative companies and technologists. Informal systems are based on a tacit understanding by employees, from senior managers to research assistants, that they have a responsibility to the company for gathering and disseminating technical information, wherever it may reside.

Management's biggest dilemma is deciding what technologies to focus on and where to look. To be effective in the search process, it must set realistic boundaries. To help do this, many Japanese companies use imaginative phrases and metaphors. NEC uses the image of a tree to represent the company: the branches are the five product modules (communications equipment and systems, electronic devices, home electronics, computers and industrial systems, and "new opportunities"); the roots are the set of core generic technologies (materials, devices, systems, and software); and the sun is the customer. NEC devotes considerable time and effort to understanding and choosing its set and subsets of core technologies. This is perfectly logical in the context of the tree metaphor: how the roots develop is vital to the health of the branches.

Choosing NEC's core technologies involves a well-planned, formalized program that was developed in 1975 by Michiyuki Uenohara, NEC's executive adviser. For 2 years every decade, a group of 50 middle and seniors managers from across the company—marketing, operations, and research and development—collectively analyze the company's overall technological needs for the coming 10 years. The corporate research laboratories work as catalysts and mediators to focus the discussion. In 1975, NEC defined 27 core technologies; by 1990 the number had increased to 34.

In the process of coming up with the set of technologies, the 50 participants sift through a broad assortment of market and technological information that, ordinarily, none of them would bother to look at. The job not only requires a considerable formal intelligence-gathering capability but also instills in management an appreciation for looking outside the company for new ideas, which is the basis of informal intelligence gathering. This informal method for gathering information requires all employees to become active receivers.

Mitsubishi Materials, a diversified company that produces everything from copper to cement to advanced materials, relies almost exclusively on its active receivers at all levels in the organization to drive its R&D process. Indeed, Mitsubishi has no formal technology "gatekeepers," according to Hiroshi Sakurai, former president of Mitsubishi Materials American Corporation. At every level, employees assume responsibility for keeping tabs on the marketplace and for bringing new innovations into the organization.

In one instance in 1981, one of Japan's national research institutes reported results for a new process for depositing a diamond coating on solid surfaces called chemical vapor deposition (CVD). Up until that point, Mitsubishi had been researching an alternative coating process on industrial cutting tools called physical vapor deposition (PVD). Simultaneously, but independently, Mitsubishi senior management, research management, and individual researchers found out about the CVD process and each began working to integrate it into the company's research pipeline. Senior management, including Takeshi Nagano, who is now the company chairman, realized the importance of the new CVD process on its mainline cutting tool business and instructed research management to reevaluate and replan the coating research program and explore investment and expense implications. On its own, research management applied for and got a research contract from the government and began negotiations for a technology license. Before formal approval, the researchers reduced activities on their PVD coating research and started work on the CVD process. Because of its speed, flexibility, and nearly ten years of substantial R&D effort, Mitsubishi was the first to market with a CVD diamond-coated cutting tool in 1990.

Informal integration of new innovations succeeds in Japan in part because there are few concrete job descriptions to begin with. If an electrical engineer is hired by the company, then he or she accepts to do whatever is necessary to excel as an engineer and improve the company's performance—including keeping tabs on all relevant technological developments going on outside the company. While it may not be appropriate or even possible for non-Japanese companies to develop an informal intelligence-gathering process quickly, senior management should make it clear to employees that they share the responsibility for the company's technological direction. To drive this home, it needs to communicate forcefully the importance of broad-based involvement in the technology search process.

Japanese High Technology and the Techno-Paradigm Shift

Technology fusion is embodied in the changes that have swept across industry in the last decade. With the emergence of high technology, changes are occurring in the whole framework of corporate strategy. From my past studies I derived the following four categories of this paradigm shift:

1. Manufacturing companies—from producing to *thinking* organization.
2. Business dynamics—from single to *multitechnologies* basis.
3. R&D activities—from visible to *invisible* ememies.
4. Technology development—from linear to *demand articulation* process.

First, a redefinition of the manufacturing company is taking place. The manufacturing company is traditionally a site for production, and the economist's formulation is a production function: capital plus labor equals output. But in many Japanese manufacturing companies, R&D investment surpassed capital investment quite recently in Japan, and the change occurred rapidly. So as R&D investment surpasses capital investment, the corporation shifts from being a place for production to being a place for thinking.

Second, there are changes in the business environment. In the past, one technology corresponds to a company. But now, especially in Japan, technological diversification has progressed so much that it is hard to distinguish a company's principal business from its secondary business. In many cases, the principal business of a company is now overtaken by its secondary business. Today's leading Japanese companies have entered the stage where they survive by adapting to the environment, relying on consistent, dependable R&D.

Third, major changes are observed in the field of research investment decision making in industry. Investment decisions are no longer based on rates of return. It is more like the principle of surfing: the waves of innovations come one after another and you have to invest; if you miss even one you are left behind. The pattern of competition is also changing. Competitors used to come solely from companies within the same industry, but that's no longer true. Thus high-tech companies have to monitor not only direct competitors in their own sector but also companies in other industries. In effect, this means that high-tech companies must engage in R&D competition with "invisible enemies."

Fourth, there are changes in the technology development process. In the high-tech era, the key issue of technology strategy has become not how to break through technological bottlenecks but how to put existing technology to the best possible use. Accordingly, a day of reckoning has come for technology strategy, which traditionally has emphasized the supply side of technology development. A need has now arisen for a technology strategy that works from the demand side. In developing new strategies to meet this need, the most important element is the process of demand articulation. Through this process, the need for a specific technology manifests itself and the R&D effort is targeted toward developing and perfecting it.

It is easy to synthesize these four categories of techno-paradigm shift around the concept of technology fusion. There is a strong relationship between technology fusion and manufacturing companies becoming thinking organizations. Technical terms are increasingly being used as catchphrases for corporate identity and for defining a corporate business domain. For example, C&C (computer and communication) is used by NEC, E&E (energy and electronics) by Toshiba, and IM&M (information movement and management) by AT&T in the United States. As those phrases imply, technology fusion is envisioned clearly, and such phrasing has helped shift these companies into growth markets.

Technological diversification is a necessary condition for technology fusion. In Japan, technology fusion is attained through diversification of R&D. Through the technological diversification efforts already made, Japanese companies have built the fundamental basis for technology fusion.

The techno-paradigm shift in R&D activities will facilitate the realization of technology fusion. Because of the competitive threat from companies in other industrial sectors solving critical technical problems first, some companies are forming alliances with outside companies. Alliances between companies in different industrial sectors work not only as a competitive hedge against major technological surprises that might be brought about by companies in different industrial sectors but also as a device that facilitates technology fusion.

Technology fusion is intrinsic to the process of demand articulation. Demand articulation is a process of converting the customer's vague wants into a set of research and development projects. Because R&D is demand driven, companies may very well not have the technological capabilities in-house to solve the technical challenges. To accumulate the necessary expertise requires a search and selection process outside the company. As companies develop their skill at articulating demand, they will also develop a skill at fusion. Indeed, demand articulation drives technology fusion.

The changing focus of manufacturing companies, the diversification of R&D, the changing pattern of R&D activities, and the increasing importance of demand articulation are all related. Taken together, the message to management is clear: technology fusion is becoming an increasingly important strategy for creating new products and new materials.

Cross-Industry R&D

Intelligence gathering increases the awareness of outside technologies, but to round out the fusion strategy, companies need to participate in cross-industry R&D projects. If they have done a good job articulating demand and gathering intelligence, then the choice of partners and projects should be relatively straightforward.

Leading high-tech companies in Japan are implementing an aggressive strategy of technological diversification. Japan's textile industry, for instance, spends considerable sums on R&D in other, unrelated fields. Asahi-Kasei, a leading textile producer, is now applying its fiber technology to produce building materials and to manufacture a filtration system for kidney dialysis machines.

Of course, not all diversification strategies involve technology fusion. To qualify as fusion, cross-industry R&D must be both substantial and reciprocal. Substantiality means management makes a commitment to the joint R&D project, from early exploratory research work through to advanced product development. Substantiality gives both the company's partners and its employees needed assurances that once senior management buys into the technology, the funds will be there to see the project through to completion.

While substantiality is important, reciprocity is the very essence of technology fusion. It means that all participants in the joint research project enter as equals (mutual respect) and each assumes a responsibility for contributing a certain expertise (mutual responsibility). Reciprocity also means that all companies share in the success of the development (mutual benefit). Ceramics is a case in point. Until a few years ago, companies such as Kyocera had invested heavily in research for new packaging materials for electrical and electronic equipment. But it was not until the electrical and electronic industries began investing jointly with ceramics companies that a new generation of industrial ceramics emerged as a technical field, benefiting both.

Typically, fusion is sparked when a new company or group of companies from a new industry enters the scene. This happened in the evolution of Japan's fiber-optics systems. The fiber-optic cable developed by Nippon Sheet Glass (NSG) in the 1970s lacked mechanical strength, and the quality of transmission over long distances was poor. So cable maker Sumitomo Electric Industries (SEI) developed a coating technology that strengthened the cable, solving the mechanical fragility problem. NTT and SEI together solved the transmission loss problem through a joint research effort using longer wavelengths.

Reciprocity and substantiality do not require that the cooperating companies be of equal size and stature. Fanuc played a pivotal role in the evolution of the computerized numerical controller in the 1970s, even though it was a small company. In one project, Fanuc teamed with Nippon Seiko (NSK), Japan's leading maker of bearings, to develop a new way to harness the controller's stepping motor to the machine tool's worktable. At the other extreme, Nissan took the lead in a fusion project with ceramics suppliers Nihon Tokushu Tohgyou Company (NGK Spark Plug Inc.) and Nihon Gaishi Company (NGK Industries) to develop a ceramic rotor for its turbocharger that was both lighter and stronger and allowed for faster acceleration than the traditional alloy rotor, giving Nissan a clear competitive advantage. Nissan introduced the new rotor in the 1985 Fairlady Z model sold in Japan, and today offers it in a number of models. Because of reciprocity, all Nissan's partner-suppliers benefited from the development effort.

Joint R&D is arguably the most important element of fusion. But as the scope of technologies widens every year, so does the expense of cooperative research. It is important for management to acknowledge that fusion-based R&D is essential for long-run success. To do so, it must discard traditional return-on-investment calculations for picking investments. Instead, it should trust in its ability to articulate demand and gather intelligence. These two capabilities, above all else, should shape the R&D investment strategy.

The Future of Fusion

Fusion will play an increasingly important role in product development efforts in the future as more and more companies integrate it into their overall technology strategies. And as the scope of fusion expands, it will open the floodgates for an even greater degree of cross-industry R&D. In the 1970s and 1980s, technology fusion was limited to fabrication industries—both the mechatronics and optoelectronics revolutions occurred *within* the manufacturing sector. In the future, however, fusion will occur more frequently *between* industrial sectors.

One immediate and compelling example of this trend is the fusion of the materials sector, drawing on both biology and chemistry, with manufacturing to create "fourth-generation" materials. First-generation materials are stones and woods, which are used primarily in their raw form. Second-generation materials are copper and iron, which become usable by extracting components from the naturally available materials. Third-generation materials are plastics, which are not available in nature but are synthesized artificially. The fourth generation will allow engineers to custom design new materials by manipulating atoms and electrons. Many leading technology fusion companies in Japan are already taking steps to harness the power of this new generation of materials. As NEC president Tadahiro Sekimoto has said, "The company that controls materials development will dominate in the electronics industry."

The main actors in the materials revolution will not be the materials industry, but manufacturers who use the materials technology to solve specific customer problems. Just as NTT "pulled" fiber-optics development to satisfy market demand, so will a new breed of manufacturing companies pull materials technology to the market in order to differentiate their products. Aeronautical engineers and semiconductor engineers, for example, will design materials for fuselages and computer chips based on their customers' needs for flexibility, strength, conductivity, environmental stress, and a host of other critical factors.

Consider how Toray, one of Japan's leading chemical companies and a pioneer in new materials, is letting its customers pull one fourth-generation material, carbon fiber, to the market. Toray's first carbon-fiber product was the shaft of a golf club. It designed the material in close cooperation with customer companies to meet the specific requirements of the golfer. Having cut its teeth on golf clubs, Toray next developed a carbon fiber for airframes with slightly different characteristics, again in close cooperation with customers. Today Toray's carbon fiber is the main advanced composite material used in 20% of the structural materials in Airbus's A320 model. Not only does the material have significantly greater strength than comparable alloys but it can also be manufactured in one piece, eliminating the need for complex and costly assembly. For instance, the number of parts in Airbus's tail wing has dropped from 600 to 335.

Toray is a textbook example of technology fusion. It articulated a need for new products in both sporting goods and airframes. It monitored the first development of carbon fiber by Union Carbide in 1959 and kept tabs on developments made by the Britain's Royal Aircraft Establishment during the 1960s, as well as developments at the Government Research Institute of Osaka in Japan. Finally, through extensive joint research projects with its customers, Toray came to market quickly with innovative products that outperformed the competition.

Carbon fiber is just an early indicator of the beginning of commercial fourth-generation materials. For fusion pioneers like Toray, the opportunities to define new products and new markets will be significant. But for companies that choose to rely on an inward-looking breakthrough strategy, the future is limited and, in some cases, nonexistent. The breakthrough companies must change the way they think about technology and begin moving toward a balance of breakthrough and fusion research. As they do, the basis on which they compete will begin to shift—instead of 1 plus 1 equaling 2, it will add up to 3 or 4 or 11.

4

Real-World R&D: Jumping the Product Generation Gap

Marco Iansiti

In most companies, the R&D process follows a well-trodden, familiar path. First comes basic research, in which the scientists in charge explore a new concept—say, a new polymer. Next, scientists with specific knowledge of the research area improve the concept until they identify an application for the polymer, such as a new insulating material. Finally, they hand off the job of actually developing a commercial product and its manufacturing process to engineers down the line.

I think of this traditional R&D approach as a series of successive refinements, one group of experts after another adding its contribution to the developing product. Such a linear approach tends to compartmentalize specific knowledge; a particular part of the R&D process may even be restricted to a single researcher.

Certainly the traditional R&D pipeline, based on the assumption that the greatest challenge to developing new products lies in making scientific discoveries, has led to significant innovations, such as the transistor and the color television. Yet I will argue that many of the best high-tech companies, particularly in the computer industry, have evolved a fundamentally different approach to new product development, one that is much more efficient and better suited to today's R&D complexities.

This new approach, which I call *system focus*, integrates the entire R&D process, rather than just shooting projects down a narrow pipeline. Based on a study of the R&D organizations of 12 mainframe computer companies—AT&T, Bull, DEC, Fujitsu, Hitachi, IBM, ICL, Mitsubishi Electric, NEC, Siemens, Toshiba, and Unisys—my research associates and I have determined that system-focused companies achieve the best product improvements in the shortest time and at the lowest cost. This is no small feat in the high-tech industry, where rolling out new, technically challenging products at the right time has been the key to success for more than a decade.

We compared the approaches these R&D organizations took during the 1980s in developing new technology for a particular product: the multichip module. Mainframe multichip modules house and connect the computer's most crucial integrated circuits, affecting the entire system's speed and reliability. They thus present an extremely complex and technically challenging development task, precisely the type of R&D hurdle most companies now face, whether they produce computers, cars, or pharmaceuticals.

The different approaches these companies took toward the multichip module demonstrate how a product, its manufacturing process, and the needs of its users constitute a system and should be developed as such. Any change in this product system—for example, the use of a more reliable material in the production of the module's substrate—will change the entire design and manufacturing process. In turn, these changes can lead to development dead ends, longer product rollouts, and many wasted hours if not accounted for from the very beginning. Therefore, the goal of new product development shifts from simply incorporating a powerful new element to optimizing the whole system.

High-tech companies are most affected by volatile markets and the rapid pace of technological change. But while industries that have traditionally been considered science-based, such as aerospace and semiconductors, may feel the most pressure to adapt their R&D approach, the challenge of incorporating new technical developments into commercial products is now a reality of competition in many other industries as well. From the application of laser-welding in the Lexus LS 400 automobile to the use of composite materials in the construction industry, new technical concepts have fueled innovations in a wide range of products. Improving the speed and efficiency of product development has, indeed, become a major competitive weapon.

The Integration Team

When it comes to R&D resources, principally the time and people involved, the most striking characteristic of a system-focused approach is the central role of *technology integration*. By this I mean the integration of the R&D process within a company, not the "fusion" of different technologies to create new products, although technology fusion often does result in complex components like the multichip module.

System-focused companies form a core group of managers, scientists, and engineers at the earliest stages of the R&D process. This *integration team* investigates the impact of various technical choices on the design of the product and the manufacturing system. The team's main objective is to balance new research from the lab with the manufacturing system's existing capabilities. A good integration team adapts new technologies to what a company already knows how to do. And more than that, it enhances the current system to take advantage of those new ideas.

In fact, all of the system-focused companies in our study established integration teams in the early stages to handle technology integration for the multichip module. Some of the companies went so far as to build pilot plants in order to experiment with new technologies, a sizable but worthwhile investment since it often provided unambiguous information on future production yields and manufacturing costs.

What follows is a typical profile for a successful integration team. In general, the members are the foundation of a system-focused approach to R&D. They possess a T-shaped combination of skills: they are not only experts in specific technical areas but also intimately acquainted with the potential systemic impact of their particular tasks. On the one hand, they have a deep knowledge of a discipline like ceramic materials engineering, represented by the vertical stroke of the T. On the other hand, these ceramic specialists also know how their discipline interacts with others, such as polymer processing—the T's horizontal top stroke.

Note that in the system-focused companies we studied, the fact that team members had this combination of skills was no accident. Team leaders considered their most important job to be assigning projects that would develop individuals by providing learning opportunities in other areas. According to one of the project managers we interviewed, "Each engineer is responsible for lots of different parts of the project. We choose the pieces to stretch their knowledge."

Successful integration teams specify and design both the product and the manufacturing process, leading the way in choosing new equipment. The team works with both system and component designers (for example, both mainframe designers and chip developers), facilitating a clearer understanding of how individual product components will interact. In fact, the integration team is usually in daily

Exhibit I.

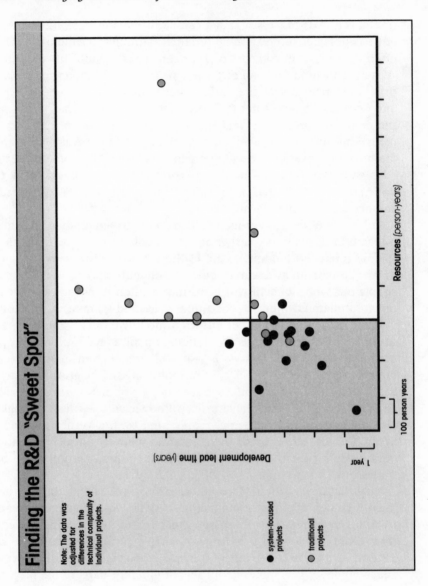

Finding the R&D "Sweet Spot"

Note: The data was adjusted for differences in the technical complexity of individual projects.

● system-focused projects

○ traditional projects

Resources (person-years)

Development lead time (years)

100 person years

1 year

contact with the manufacturing plant. Team members often deal with major production problems on ongoing product lines, which allows them to evaluate the impact of new technology on production. And as a development project progresses, the team physically moves to the site of major technical difficulties, such as the pilot or manufacturing facility.

Perhaps most important of all, the integration team works on a stream of related products, forming a cohesive unit of engineers who develop from project to project. Retained over multiple product generations, team members become the company's repository of technically integrated "system" knowledge. While various research groups continue to develop and present new options, it is the integration team that turns new ideas into useful work by conceptualizing new products and providing continuity.

Such continuity over product generations pays off. Even when it comes to individual research projects, system-focused companies can save many years of staff effort and development time (see Exhibit I). Even one less engineer working on a project saves roughly $100,000 a year; for projects like the multichip module, which extend over a decade and across product generations, the difference between traditional R&D and system focus can amount to hundreds of millions of dollars.

Of course, an emphasis on technology integration should not cut into the status of a company's research organization. I believe that for system focus to succeed, basic researchers must provide the integration team with a broad array of technical possibilities. Most integration teams will have a natural bias toward using older approaches to materials and manufacturing, because that's what team members are familiar with. However, research (whether conducted internally or by outside suppliers) must offset this potential inertia by championing a variety of alternatives. Though they frequently used suppliers to provide additional technical options, the most successful companies in our study had vibrant internal research organizations of their own.

Research: System Focus vs. the Traditional Pipeline

When the traditional research pipeline and system focus are examined side by side, their differences are clear. Let's start by comparing them during the research phase, when scientist-engineers investigate new technical possibilities for upcoming product generations. The following case histories of "Traditional Company A" and "System-Focused Company B," loosely based on companies in our study, illustrate the differences.

Note that the multichip module provides a good example of *development complexity* and its inherent research challenges (see "Development Complexity and System Focus"). For instance, the latest IBM multichip module, which makes up the core of its new ES9000 mainframe computer, contains more than 65 stacked layers of electrical circuits that total about one mile of wiring—all packed on a five-inch-square flat piece of ceramic.

Development Complexity and System Focus

When the entire R&D process becomes system-focused, companies are in a much better position to wrestle with the development complexity inherent in the creation of today's new products. Development complexity refers to the complications of the R&D process itself, not what the end product looks like or how difficult it is to manufacture.

For example, the development of drugs involves integrating many different research decisions based on knowledge of pharmacology, toxicology, physiology, relevant body systems, regulatory requirements in dozens of countries, and differences in medical practice and custom in those countries. But ironically enough, the pill that results from such a complicated set of R&D decisions is often so simple it can be manufactured in a home laboratory. This illustrates how bringing successful drugs quickly to market depends much more on integrating the knowledge of all R&D factors at every point in the process than on pure scientific prowess.

Of course, the development complexity that characterizes an industry can change over time, often in response to competitive pressures for products that deliver higher performance. Twenty years ago, automobiles were assembled from discrete and largely independent parts. But today's cars can be more accurately described as integrated systems rather than assembled parts. Consequently, a tight fit between individual design decisions is essential to satisfying customer expectations.

Now automobile manufacturers frequently "tune" the noise characteristics of a car to match the expectations of the market it is designed to serve. That means a high-revving sports car has a much different sound quality—as well as overall ride—than a luxury car. Such specific R&D challenges require a focus on the entire system, since decisions in basic engine design must be linked to the structural properties of the chassis, right down to the acoustical properties of the felt used in floor mats.

In such complex projects, the research phase involves more than coming up with a new material or production technique. It also includes technology integration in the form of a *technical concept*: a detailed specification of how the complete set of technical options will combine to provide the new product with good quality and low cost. While the research group controls technology integration in traditional companies, in a system-focused company the integration team takes charge.

TRADITIONAL COMPANY A. The research group at Company A explored a new ceramic material composition that could conduct a lot of heat. Using scaled-down equipment in the lab, these researchers fabricated small quantities of the material. They surveyed the literature, communicated intensively with scientists at universities, and performed many small-scale experiments aimed at characterizing the new material's properties, including its detailed microstructure. All of their research led them to believe that this new ceramic material could increase the speed and reliability of their company's multichip module.

Obviously, these researchers had much to gain if their ceramic was adopted, and they aggressively championed this material. They subsequently won: senior managers allowed them to develop their concept for the entire module system. Therefore, the same scientists who had launched the initial investigations were then responsible for integrating their new materials into a functional system.

Yet their sole criterion for success was feasibility: they had only to fabricate a small number of prototypes using lab equipment. The group eventually produced several partially functional modules, which showed that it ought to be possible to build a real module based on the new ceramic.

Once the technical concept had proved feasible, technology integration, driven by the research group, was complete. The basic technologies and the product design were set—which is fine, if both hold up in the real world of manufacturing. But in this case, the technical concept became a foregone conclusion without an active investigation of the challenge of future high-volume production. In fact, the activities of the research group ended at this point, and the module project was deemed ready for development.

Exhibit II.

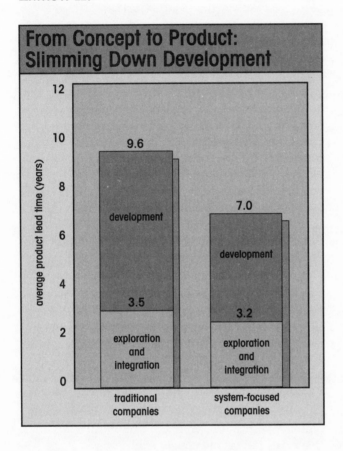

From Concept to Product:
Slimming Down Development

SYSTEM-FOCUSED COMPANY B. Here an integration team, formed at the very beginning of the R&D process, led the multichip module project. These 20 scientists and engineers monitored the basic investigations conducted by the research group as well as those contracted to several outside ceramic materials suppliers. As the results from initial research came in, the integration team began selecting the most promising of the various new techniques and worked on combining the elements into one technical concept. They investigated several possible technical concepts in parallel, based on different combinations of materials, such as aluminum and glass ceramic substrates.

This stage took much more time and involved more resources than the explorations of Company A (see Exhibit II). As the integration team learned more about the systemic effects of the various alternatives, some were dropped, others postponed for future generations, and others refined and kept for further study. Of course, this weeding of alternatives contrasted sharply with the process at Company A, where the initial research group championed their ceramic material and focused on demonstrating its feasibility.

In fact, Company B's integration team did not identify feasibility as an explicit requirement for their technical alternatives. They gradually selected the most promising concepts, using a steady, ongoing selection process designed to solve problems largely ignored by Company A's researchers: manufacturability, yield, and reliability.

And as the integration process steadily continued, other groups became more involved. Equipment suppliers, for example, worked directly with integration team members to specify the production tooling for the new system. Engineers from various development groups and the manufacturing facility discussed the details of the production process. It was only at this point that the integration team finally committed to a single new concept and froze the basic design of their company's multichip module.

COMPETING PHILOSOPHIES.   Clearly, Company A and Company B represent fundamentally different approaches to the exploration and selection of new technology. Under the traditional R&D philosophy of companies like A, researchers assume that discovering new scientific possibilities is the critical challenge and involves the identification and early exploration of new ideas. While the traditional R&D pipeline certainly allows for freedom in early investigations, its main aim is to select a concept that includes the technical possibilities with the maximum *theoretical* impact on future product characteristics, as proven "feasible" in the lab.

The critical weakness of the traditional method, however, is that it does not characterize the *actual* impact of the technical concept on the product and manufacturing process before selecting a winning concept. This is particularly a problem when a given research project is part of a much larger and complex "product system" like the multichip module. The research group first optimizes the technology chosen, and the development group is left with the problem of making the system work. As one frustrated development engineer put it, "By the time we got involved, the basic technologies were more than 90% established."

In contrast, the system-focused philosophy emphasizes discovering and capturing knowledge about the interactions between new research in the lab and the company's existing product and manufacturing systems. At Company B, the goal was joint optimization of system and technology, even though that initially consumed more time and resources. An integration team encouraged unbiased investigation of many alternatives, but its selection was greatly influenced by the details of the existing system. One engineer at a system-focused company in our study said, "The most essential part of choosing a new technology is to establish its impact on the production process. And we still never get it quite right."

That in no way means that system-focused companies like B settle for less aggressive results. In our study, we repeatedly observed that traditional companies like A often developed individual elements that were superior to B's—for example, ceramic materials with better electrical and thermal properties. Yet system-focused companies still achieved superior overall performance because technology integration from the start of the R&D project more than compensated for apparently inferior materials. In other words, the traditional R&D pipeline adds up to a whole that is less than the sum of its parts, while system focus produces a whole greater than the sum of its parts.

Development: How System-Focused Companies Get Results

Although comparing the research phases in Company A and Company B shows the importance of system focus, it's in the development of new products that the approaches yield dramatically different results. Exhibit III provides graphic evidence of why system-focused companies ultimately save on both time and money in rolling out new products and their subsequent generations.

COMPANY A. When it came time for Traditional Company A to implement the new ceramic material for the multichip module, the resources devoted to the project mushroomed. As you can see in the project map for Company A, a large development group was necessary because of the difficulty of increasing production yields and product reliability. Many of the details of the winning technical concept turned out to be extremely difficult for Company A to implement.

As the head of development for a traditional company in our study observed, "We completely underestimated what it would be like to ramp up." After extensively redesigning the product and manufacturing process, the development group transferred the new multichip

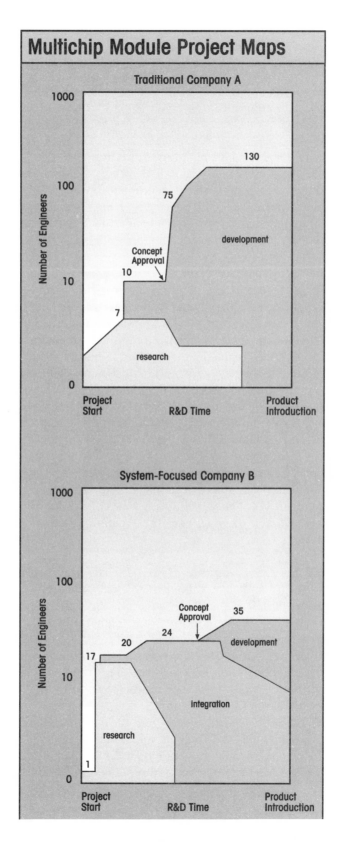

Exhibit III.

module system to the production facility. But pilot production also proved difficult, requiring additional design changes. After many false starts, targeted yields were finally achieved, volume production began, and the development group moved on to the next generation of module, taking over their end once more from the research group.

Due to promotions and individual career choices, many of these development engineers shifted to unrelated projects. In all, it took Company A over 6½ years of development time and about 800 person-years of engineering and scientific activity to complete the development phase.

COMPANY B. In contrast, System-Focused Company B completed the development phase in less than 4½ years and 300 person-years. Exhibit IV indicates the big difference in average resources used during development. In Company B, the integration team, which had been responsible for the basic conceptual design, remained in charge of the project during development. A few team members worked part-time on integration of the next generation. Most were deeply involved with development, working directly at the plant or with materials suppliers.

As development progressed, integration team members gradually shifted to work on the next generation; yet the team still led the process until the plant had achieved full production yields. Many members continued to be responsible for production yields even after the product had been introduced, and they were called into the plant when major problems occurred. In fact, the same people who were responsible for improving production yields of the current generation also often worked on specifying the technical concept for the next generation.

ORGANIZATIONAL LEARNING. System-focused companies like Company B capture knowledge about the different elements of the entire R&D process and feed that knowledge back in at the technology integration stage. At Company B, involving engineers in the integration of several product generations allowed them to transfer valuable knowledge all along the line. This *upstream* transfer of information provides not only continuity from generation to generation but also continual learning about the impact of new technology on the complex production capabilities of an organization.

And this transfer of knowledge goes beyond good communication. Organizational learning promotes individual learning, especially for integration team members. As one team leader noted, "At this point, one person is product engineer and production engineer at the same

Exhibit IV.

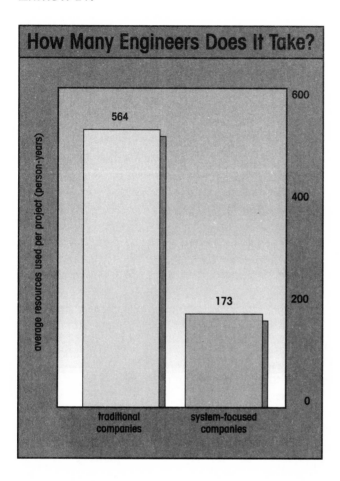

time. Basically, we no longer have the luxury of spending a lot of time communicating." "A System-Focused Résumé" illustrates how an engineer gains integration knowledge over several product generations.

A System-Focused Résumé

The hypothetical "Mr. Furube," a typical engineer at a system-focused main-frame computer company, is 30 years old. In less than a decade, he has worked on three generations of the same product.

Mr. Furube

1991–1992	Engineer
	Currently designing chip set for *gen 3* mainframe.
1989–1990	Massachusetts Institute of Technology: M.S. in electrical engineering
1987–1989	Worker and Trainer
	Developed *gen 2* module assembly process, working with suppliers. Designed, ordered, and set up production machines for microchip carrier.
1985–1986	Worker
	Improved production process for *gen 1.5* module. Conducted feasibility study for new *gen 2* module concept. Worked on basic conceptual design of *gen 2* module; applied for patent.
1983–1984	Trainee
	Developed production process for LSI modules for *gen 1* mainframe; set up specialized machines and trained workers on pilot production line. Designed production process for *gen 1.5* module.
1979–1983	Tokyo University: degree in mechanical engineering

Traditional companies like Company A devote substantial attention to the transfer of knowledge but only *downstream*—through the narrow pipeline of research to development to manufacturing. Under this approach, there is no mechanism for transferring knowledge back upstream so that it can improve the next round of technology selection and integration. Moreover, the compartmentalized knowledge typical of traditional R&D pipelines often disappears as scientists, engineers, and product developers shift from one project to another or take other jobs.

Given this distinction in organizational learning, it's not surprising that the system-focused companies in our study were faster and more productive on individual projects *and* that the performance gap between traditional companies and system-focused ones actually increased over time. We found a substantial difference between resources used in subsequent product generations for traditional and system-focused companies. The resources used by the system-focused companies each decreased dramatically as integration teams learned more and more about the product and its manufacturing system. When it comes to jumping the product generation gap, efficiently transferring knowledge is essential.

In contrast, companies that relied on the traditional R&D pipeline decreased in productivity over successive product generations. Competitive pressures to keep up with increasing technological innovations led them to increase the resources they sunk into technology development. Yet without fundamental changes to the whole R&D process—namely, the use of integration teams to facilitate organizational learning—their R&D became even less efficient than before.

Integrated Problem Solving

The companies I've been calling system-focused depart from the traditional R&D pipeline both in philosophy and organizational design. They also differ significantly in their approach to solving problems. Our study included 61 different problem-solving attempts. While the traditional companies took a relatively narrow approach to solving problems, the system-focused companies were remarkable for the breadth of theirs. Consider the following example.

PROBLEM. The core of this multichip module contains more than 40 ceramic layers, each one carrying a complex circuit. The layers first are patterned, then stacked, and finally fired together at a high temperature. However, as the ceramic bakes, it shrinks. Therefore, the challenge is to achieve uniform shrinkage without buckling so that the module retains its shape and has a smooth surface for connecting integrated circuits.

SOLUTION A. Scientists at Company A identified the buckling problem early on in the research phase. At this point, they worked with a simplified model of the multichip module core, using scaled-down equipment in the lab. After making a number of adjustments to the ceramic composition and the firing process, they succeeded in eliminating the buckling.

Later, during the development phase, a more representative model of the multichip module was used on a new pilot production line, which closely—though not exactly—represented the manufacturing conditions of volume production. The buckling problem reoccurred. Development engineers spent much time and energy adjusting the ceramic material and the production process in order to fix the problem again.

At the end of the development phase, the new product was moved to the actual manufacturing plant. Once again, the buckling reoccurred, causing additional delays in the production schedule. After a great deal of effort, the third and final round of reengineering succeeded in eliminating the problem for good.

SOLUTION B. For scientists at Company B, the problem wasn't narrowly defined as "how to eliminate all buckling" but instead as "how to get the entire system to function effectively." The integration team focused earlier on a prototype of the product and the manufacturing process, using a pilot production line with equipment representative of actual conditions but flexible enough to allow experimentation.

Developing a module prototype that was representative of high-volume production conditions allowed the team at Company B to characterize precisely the extent of the buckling. And by asking a broader question at the start and drawing on a broader knowledge base, the integration team found a faster and cheaper solution: controlling the buckling and coating the ceramic substrate with a polymer to smooth the surface. When the project moved from research into development, the buckling problem did not reoccur.

In fact, the system-focused companies in our study were only slightly better at identifying problems early on; they identified 74% of the significant problems in multichip module development, but the more traditional companies found 61% of their own early problems. The most striking difference came in achieving real rather than apparent solutions. Only 40% of the early fixes made by traditional companies stood up to the requirements of later project phases. Yet 77% of the early solutions discovered by system-focused companies actually worked in the long run.

A New R&D Philosophy

System focus is a philosophy rather than a specific technique, one that underpins and reinforces the importance of technology integration: the mutual adaptation of new technology, product design, manufacturing process, and user needs. An engineer from a system-focused company said, "We get together with the semiconductor and systems group people to discuss future possibilities. Everyone talks about this, and negotiations occur throughout. There's lots of give-and-take."

Compare this remark with that of an R&D manager from a traditional company: "The strategy is always to take a piece of the technology and set up a group to own it. If coordination problems exist, we set up a task force." These two remarks reveal fundamentally different assumptions about what R&D is all about.

Most companies that live by a system-focused philosophy emphasize the work of an integration team during all phases of a project. Yet the substantial advantages of technology integration don't come without investment and the commitment of senior managers as well. It takes time to develop the skills of integration teams. The new approach may appear slow and cumbersome at first. And even after good results start to roll in, team leaders and senior managers still may need periodically to redirect the work of individual team members, helping them to fight inertia.

Still, the most effective companies in our study demonstrated the value of system focus in an environment that is both complex and changeable. Their experience shows that an integration team can build a solid and powerful base of knowledge about the interactions between the most critical decisions in the design of a new product. Of course, while similar in purpose and character, integration teams of various organizations will develop different focuses depending on the nature of the technical environment. In high-performance computer processor design, the link between material choice and manufacturability presents the toughest challenge. Therefore, successful integration teams, like those responsible for the multichip module projects in our study, will emphasize retaining detailed knowledge of the impact past materials choices have had on manufacturing.

In contrast, the pharmaceutical industry provides a very different set of R&D challenges. Integration teams there would find that the most complex interactions are between the chemical formulation of a new drug and its safety and efficacy, as perceived by both users and regulatory agencies. In this case, these would replace manufacturing difficulties and history as the foundation of a rich R&D knowledge base.

But regardless of the industry, the traditional R&D pipeline is not up to managing technology integration in any environment that is characterized by development complexity. A company marketing cosmetics, for example, had to postpone rolling out a new product because its novel chemical formulation proved incompatible with the planned packaging. A forest products company barely avoided the complete failure of a new venture in engineered wood products; it discovered in the nick of time that there were subtle inconsistencies between the preset production process (which had been optimized for northern pine) and the properties of southern pine.

And a pharmaceutical company failed to obtain approval for a new cancer drug due to poor integration of regulatory requirements and the development process. A competitor with a more system-focused approach integrated its regulatory activities and drug formulation accordingly and was able to roll out the new drug, gaining sole access to a very large market.

With sophisticated customers who demand greater performance and new, aggressive, and often subtle product characteristics, developing successful products requires managing an increasing number of complex design decisions. Compared with old-line industries, which carefully nurtured deep knowledge of narrow specifics, today's shifting markets call for a flexible breadth of experience, backed by the organizational and technical ability to integrate.

For system focus to work, then, the company must have a consistent technology strategy and view the whole R&D process as a continuous stream of competence-building projects, not as a series of isolated efforts. Successful companies will target core technical areas and gradually build technology integration in those areas. Such a consistent approach, driven by the long-term commitment of senior managers, will allow integration teams to acquire the knowledge, tools, and procedures necessary for the efficient integration of new technology, ultimately producing the innovative products that customers want.

5

Managing Innovation in the Information Age

Rebecca Henderson

The continued vitality of the most successful U.S. and European pharmaceutical companies, in the face of accelerating scientific and technological change, holds valuable lessons for managers in all industries trying to respond to turbulent times. The pharmaceutical industry faces some serious challenges in the future, most notably the proposed reform of the U.S. health care system. Yet its success to date in the crucial area of research can serve as a benchmark for companies seeking to become more innovative in the overloaded environment of the information age.

New competitors skillfully exploiting a wave of technological change have displaced or seriously challenged the companies that once dominated such industries as machine tools, steel, xerography, automobiles, semiconductors, and computers. In contrast, companies founded in

Author's note: This study was funded by the Sloan Foundation and four pharmaceutical companies, drawing on the internal records of ten major European and U.S. pharmaceutical companies and a variety of public data. The companies account for approximately 28% of U.S. research-and-development and sales. Professor Iain Cockburn and I believe that they are representative of the industry in terms of size and technical and commercial performance.

Our statistical results rely on a database that contains information about the inputs and outputs of more than 120 programs over a period of up to 30 years. Our primary input measure is research spending on discovery; our output measures include important patents, numbers of investigational new drug applications, new drug applications, new drug approvals, sales, and market share. These data were supplemented by interviews with 84 people at the sample companies, a number of industry experts, and a variety of measures of scientific opportunity and pharmaceutical demand derived from public sources.

the 1940s and 1950s continue to dominate the pharmaceutical industry. These companies have demonstrated an ability to learn and grow that confounds conventional wisdom. Despite their age, size, and success, the best of these companies have found ways to retain the flexibility and responsiveness of companies one-tenth their size and age. And they have already solved some of the competitive challenges in the research arena that companies in other industries are just starting to grapple with.

New research that I conducted with Iain Cockburn, professor of strategic management at the University of British Columbia, suggests that the longevity of pharmaceutical companies attests to a unique managerial competency: the ability to foster a high level of specialized knowledge within an organization, while preventing that information from becoming embedded in such a way that it permanently fixes the organization in the past, unable to respond to an ever-changing competitive environment.

GM, IBM, and DEC are not in trouble today because they are run by incompetents. Rather, their difficulties are the natural result of their success. They have become prisoners of the deeply ingrained assumptions, information filters, and problem-solving strategies that make up their world views, turning the solutions that once made them great into new problems to be resolved. The best pharmaceutical companies have not fallen into this trap. Instead, they have managed to remake themselves even as the science on which they rely has changed dramatically. Studying these successful companies provides an opportunity to learn how to innovate continuously in the face of rapidly changing scientific and technological information.

Management Matters

To outside observers, the drug-discovery process can seem a random procedure in which inspired scientists, working around the clock, come upon major breakthroughs in the middle of the night. Drug discovery is risky, but the process is much less random than it appears. While 20 years ago, organic chemists might have had little more than hunches to guide them in the synthesis and elaboration of new compounds, today's chemists have much more information and far more sophisticated tools to guide them in their work. The random screening of compounds remains important, but leading-edge drug discovery is most often the result of a guided search. And effective management can greatly increase the efficiency of the discovery process.

In a three-year study of ten pharmaceutical companies, Professor Cockburn and I found that the research efforts of the most successful pharmaceutical companies can be as much as 40% more productive than their rivals. Interpreted with some care, this result is substantial enough to suggest that it takes more than hiring the best possible people and giving them funds to be successful. Indeed, management plays a crucial role in the innovation process. The best managers do not merely administer a static system. Instead, they constantly challenge the company's conventional wisdom and stimulate the dynamic exchange of ideas.

Modern-day drug discovery requires the integration of knowledge from a broad array of disciplines. A major drug house, for example, today employs large numbers of molecular biologists, physiologists, and biochemists, as well as specialists in the traditional disciplines of synthetic chemistry and pharmacology, and more esoteric specialists like molecular kineticists. All of these disciplines are advancing at an extraordinarily rapid rate. For instance, there were over 80,000 articles published in the cardiovascular field alone in just the last half of 1992. Good drug discovery, therefore, requires tight ties to the larger intellectual community. But a unique competence in just one scientific specialty—say, in synthetic chemistry—is not enough to sustain a prolonged competitive advantage. Successful companies must keep abreast of the changes within particular scientific disciplines and successfully integrate this knowledge within and across company boundaries, often in new and unexpected ways (see Exhibit I).

As a result, successful pharmaceutical companies have been forced to acquire the key competitive advantage of the 1990s: the ability to innovate in an information-intensive environment. Over a period of 30 years, the most successful companies in our study obtained more than twice the number of patents per research dollar, advanced to clinical trials more often, and, most important, were more than twice as likely to bring new drugs to market than their less successful competitors. As a result, these companies had sales and profits far above the industry average.

In addition, the managers of these companies did all the things that business pundits recommend: they used sophisticated resource-allocation procedures, hired the best people, and encouraged cross-functional and cross-disciplinary communication. More important, they didn't view these innovations as quick fixes to a static system. Instead, they focused on continuously refurbishing the innovative capabilities of the organization. They actively managed their companies' knowledge and resources.

Exhibit I.

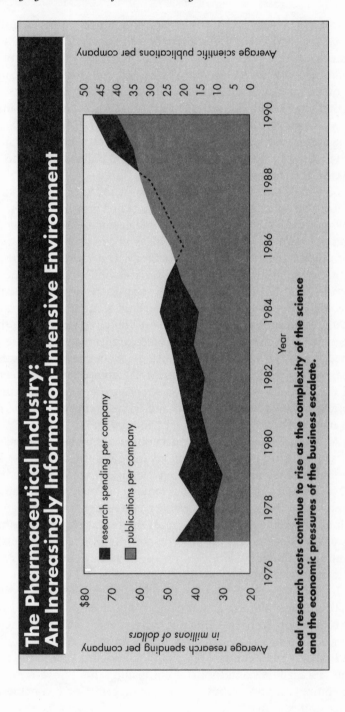

The Pharmaceutical Industry:
An Increasingly Information-Intensive Environment

Real research costs continue to rise as the complexity of the science and the economic pressures of the business escalate.

Our study revealed three characteristics shared by the most successful pharmaceutical companies: first, they kept abreast of the changes in their field by making and maintaining close connections with the scientific community at large; second, they allocated resources across a wide range of therapeutic areas, ending up with the most advantageous mix of projects; and, finally, they actively confronted the tension between organizing by function and organizing by product group.

Keeping Connected

The scientific and medical knowledge needed to make significant advances in drug discovery is changing too fast for any one company to hope to master it all. The most successful companies in our study therefore ensured that they were efficiently connected to the scientific community and to their peers.

All companies in our sample had scientific advisory boards, for example, but the boards had been in existence for many years in the most successful companies. All companies permitted their employees to publish in scientific journals and to attend conferences, but, in the most successful companies, eminence in the scientific community was an important criterion for promotion. At one of the less successful companies, for example, the director of research commented, "Of course people are free to publish if they want, but in general I haven't encouraged it. After all, the effort that goes into writing a paper could be employed to search for new drugs." In sharp contrast, the research director at one of the most successful companies was proud to have recently sponsored a major scientific conference in the field.

Of course, a company that focuses on scientific excellence alone runs the risk of creating an organization staffed by world-class scientists who produce excellent papers but no useful drugs. The successful companies balanced the ability to reach out beyond the company for new scientific knowledge with the ability to link that knowledge to therapeutically useful goals.

Allocating Scarce Resources

Budgeting is a contentious process. Yet in the pharmaceutical industry, it is made more difficult because large amounts of money must be invested years before any return can be expected.

Successful resource allocation is not simply a matter of picking winners or diversifying financial risk. Our study suggests that the most productive companies are those whose project portfolios are not only diverse enough to enable them to leverage their specialized scientific expertise but also related sufficiently to allow them to benefit from the cross-fertilization of ideas (see Exhibit II). Well managed resource-allocation processes also have important implications for the effective management of knowledge within a company. Effective resource-allocation processes encourage lively debate and in turn stimulate the rapid transfer of information across the company, while ensuring that the opportunities this information flow presents are reflected in the set of projects chosen.

In companies with relatively little communication across boundaries, resource allocation was more likely to be managed with a "last year plus 5%" or a "don't bother me, and I won't bother you" tactic. Strong individuals carved out personal fiefdoms, and resources rarely shifted dramatically from year to year across disciplines or therapeutic classes. Any individual area might conduct world-class science or make the occasional breakthrough. However, the static nature of the resource-allocation process encouraged a certain narrowness of vision.

In contrast, in the successful companies, resource allocation was a much more contentious process. Two models seemed to work particularly well. In the first model, a single, highly respected and knowledgeable individual took primary responsibility. He or she was widely read in the field and actively questioned the leading scientists on every project, pushing for more detail and suggesting new connections, questions, and perspectives. This method of decision making is risky because its effectiveness is solely dependent on the ability of the key decision maker. Some of the worst performing companies, for instance, were commanded by resource-allocation dictators who made the wrong calls or alienated key personnel with their arrogance. Still, when this method works well, it works very well, because the cross-boundary connections are made in the mind of a single individual who can encourage those around him or her to think in boundary-breaking terms.

The second successful resource-allocation model was the relatively high-conflict committee. Key decisions were made at annual or biannual meetings. There, each group presented its project and budget requirements, and decisions were arrived at through constructive confrontations across the group. While at its worst this type of decision making tends toward "last year plus 5%," at its best it encourages

Exhibit II.

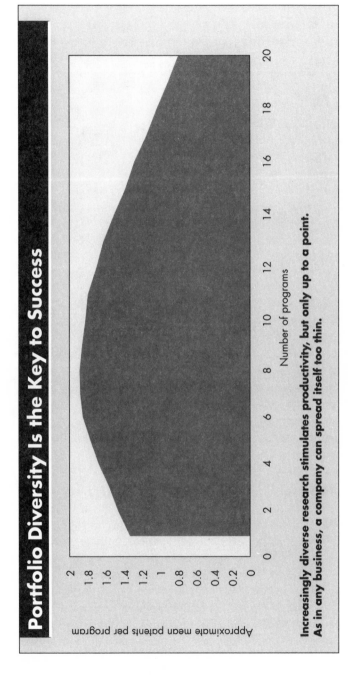

Portfolio Diversity Is the Key to Success

Approximate mean patents per program

Number of programs

Increasingly diverse research stimulates productivity, but only up to a point. As in any business, a company can spread itself too thin.

Exhibit III.

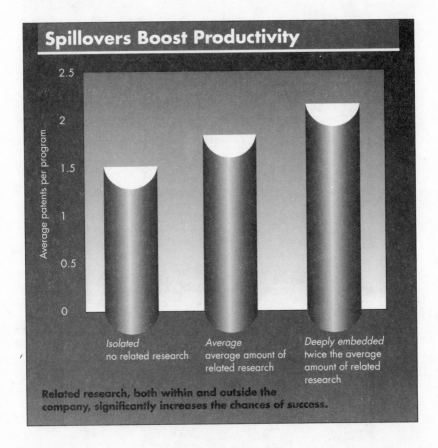

Spillovers Boost Productivity

Average patents per program

Isolated	no related research
Average	average amount of related research
Deeply embedded	twice the average amount of related research

Related research, both within and outside the company, significantly increases the chances of success.

senior scientists to be aware of the nature and status of research being conducted in other areas of the company, encouraging the fluid flow of information and ideas throughout the organization.

Our results suggest that the companies that take advantage of knowledge generated from all areas of the organization are significantly more productive than their rivals (see Exhibit III). All other things being equal, for example, our results suggest that moving a program from one of the least diversified companies in the sample to one running twice the number of programs would increase its productivity by more than 20%. The best resource-allocation processes not only encourage the flow of information across the company, they also reflect an awareness that choosing the right set of projects is more than a financial decision. If projects are interrelated, failure in one program can be redeemed by the ability to use the knowledge it generated in other areas of the company. And if projects are diverse, then the company can remain open to unexpected possibilities and unanticipated connections.

Managing Tension in Organizational Design

Every organization must choose between organizing by function and organizing by product. Organization by function ensures that the in-depth, specialized knowledge fundamental to long-term innovation is preserved and enhanced. However, it opens the company to developing the "functional silos" that have bedeviled so much of U.S. industry. Organization by product, on the other hand, focuses the energies of the organization on the customer and encourages rich communication across functions. But it often does so at the cost of a steadily eroding base of functional knowledge. After a while, the functional specialists have spent so much time thinking about the whole product that they lose the functional expertise that was their core strength.

Our study suggests that either approach to organizational design can be, at best, only a temporary solution. A senior research manager at one of the most successful companies reflected, "We've tried organizing by therapeutic class. We've tried organizing by scientific discipline. We've tried using project teams. Nothing works as well as being continually aware of the need to be both at the leading edge of the science and in total command of the important developments in other areas."

Success is not a function of a particular organizational choice or a particular form of boundary-spanning mechanism. Indeed, the most successful companies in our study were those that were never satisfied with any single answer. They continually expended organizational energy to ensure that neither the disciplinary nor the therapeutic perspective took the upper hand for too long. In some companies, this meant refocusing from disciplinary to therapeutic area and vice versa on a regular basis. In others, it meant continuous experimentation with boundary-spanning devices such as tiger teams or "heavyweight" team leaders. In still others, it meant the active cultivation of a culture in which every individual was continually reminded to wear "two hats": a functional, or disciplinary, hat and a product-oriented, or therapeutic, hat. A senior scientist at one of the most successful companies said of his company's tactic, "They have given me all the resources that I could have asked for, and we've been able to do some world-class science. But I'm very much aware that if we don't come up with some promising new compounds soon, my role here will be called into question. And that's OK. I want to see the science used to make some major therapeutic breakthroughs."

The problem of innovation is never solved. Cross-functional teams, organizing by product, or organizing by function may increase cross-disciplinary communication, but they may do so at the expense of disciplinary excellence. Companies succeed by attending to this tension, devoting organizational energy to ensuring that neither end of the continuum dominates the process. Their experience underlines the need to revisit and rebalance the organization's flow of knowledge continuously.

Success Is Dangerous

Health care reform presents the pharmaceutical industry with a new set of challenges. Can the industry respond with the flexibility that it has shown in adapting its research efforts to the biomedical revolution? For example, in their development functions (the processes of testing drugs on humans), some companies in our study displayed the kinds of deeply ingrained assumptions and rigid behavior patterns that have crippled established companies in other industries.

If it is to avoid the fate of so much of U.S. industry, the pharmaceutical industry will have to be just as sophisticated in developing and selling its products as it has been in generating them.

PART

III

Creating a Development Strategy

1
Managing Technological Change: A Box of Cigars for Brad

Frederick W. Gluck and Richard N. Foster

Brad Youngman, brash young vice president for corporate development at Diversified Manufacturing Corporation, handed his boss, Miles Atkinson, a lengthy memo just as the CEO was about to board a jet for a welcome vacation in Jamaica. The memo from the troubleshooter essentially asked, "Who the hell is running this business?" Youngman's analysis of what constitutes the strategic direction of a technology-based company leads to a reexamination by Atkinson and his top management group of their roles in the operation of the company. The lesson that Atkinson learns is a valuable one for any high executive.

I don't think I've ever been so glad to get on an airplane in my life, thought Miles. *Another 15 minutes with Brad and I probably would have fired him.*

Miles Atkinson settled into his seat on the 747 flight to Jamaica. He was on his way to join his wife, Moira, at their villa in Montego Bay for their first real vacation since he had become president and chief executive of Diversified Manufacturing Corporation five years before. It had been a tremendous but demanding five years for the manufacturer of construction, medical, and (now) oil-drilling equipment: sales up 120%, profits up 80%, some successes, and some failures. Moira had really been after him lately. She said he had begun to stew about his problems and needed a rest.

She's probably right, he thought. *Look at how frustrated I am with Brad. But goddamn it, I know he's a good man.*

The immediate cause of his frustration was the lunch he'd just had with Bradford Youngman, his vice president for corporate development. Brad was a real tiger. DMC had picked him up three years before when it acquired Dynamic Controls, a small, high-technology company that Brad and two partners had built from scratch. Six months ago Miles had persuaded Brad to leave the subsidiary, which was clearly too small to test him rigorously, and give him a hand with strategy at corporate headquarters.

Miles admitted to himself that he didn't have quite the same handle on the business that he'd had five years before when he'd stepped up from executive VP of manufacturing to the presidency. So he wanted Brad to develop a corporate planning system that would pull things together and help him set a clear strategic direction for Diversified. It had been quite a struggle persuading Brad that the move made sense for him.

Now, ironically, the question was whether it had made sense for the company—Brad was turning out to be bad news. Instead of working on a planning system, he was minding everybody else's business. In particular, he was constantly second-guessing the technical people on technical decisions. Cutler Sims, VP for finance, and Jim Pasinaro, VP for R&D, were livid over Brad's nit-picking at one of the most sophisticated R&D project evaluation systems in the industry. And two hours ago at lunch Brad had implied none too subtly that top management— that is, Miles himself—wasn't providing the leadership that DMC needed. To top it off, Brad had dropped another of his memos on Miles and insisted that he take it along on his vacation.

Could the guy possibly have his eye on my job? thought Miles. *If he does, he's sure telegraphing his punches. Well, the hell with him and his memo. I'll look at it later.*

Two weeks later, on the flight back to New York, Miles reflected that Moira had been right again. *I really needed that vacation; I was getting paranoid. Imagine seeing a threat in Brad's criticism. Why, the guy was only—oh, Lord, that memo of his. I'd better look at it or he'll be all over me.*

Shaking Up the CEO

MEMORANDUM

TO: Miles Atkinson, President, Diversified Manufacturing Corporation
FROM: Bradford Youngman, Vice President, Corporate Development

It's been six months since you sweet-talked me into this boondoggle at headquarters, and I'll bet you're sitting there at 35,000 feet wondering whether it was the right thing to do. I know I've been a royal pain you know where, and some people think I've been sticking my nose in places where it doesn't belong. Well, if these six months have been difficult for you, they haven't been exactly comfortable for me. But I think all the snooping I've done may turn out to be worthwhile.

To get at the substance of our problems, as you asked me to do, I had to dig into the business. Since we're a technology-based company, that meant digging into the technology, and specifically into our key product and process design decisions. If I learned one thing at Dynamic, it's that a superior product line and superior cost structure are one hell of a leg up on the marketplace. And in technology-based businesses like Dynamic and Diversified, the only way to get those advantages in the long run is by effectively managing technological advances in the product lines—a very different thing from calculating possible returns from R&D. In fact, the more I dug and the more I thought about it, the more I realized that the way we manage technological development is the heart of our whole strategic planning. You could call it the "strategic control of technology."

Nice phrase, thought Miles. *So what else is new?*

Once I'd gotten that far, things really began to fall into place. It was obvious that the leverage to influence the outcome of a product design is way up front—not months before you go into production, but even before you start the design. We're damned effective at manufacturing cost reduction, but if we're cost-reducing a design that's inherently more expensive than a competitor's, we're playing catch-up ball. And I don't have to tell you that if the design misses the market or challenges the regulations, we're really in the soup.

Exhibit I.   Miles Atkinson's activity profile

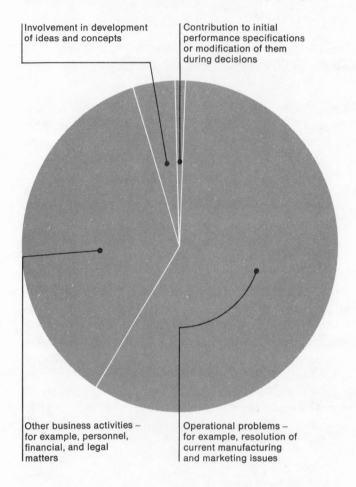

Involvement in development
of ideas and concepts

Contribution to initial
performance specifications
or modification of them
during decisions

Other business activities –
for example, personnel,
financial, and legal
matters

Operational problems –
for example, resolution of
current manufacturing
and marketing issues

Touché. We spent a small fortune on dust-proofing those ore conveyors after we put them on the market.

By the way, Miles, do you recall the last time you had a hand in deciding the performance characteristics of a new design, or really understood why we needed it? I went through your appointment books for last year—the ones you asked me to look at to become familiar with your modus operandi. Take a look at the first chart that I prepared (see Exhibit I). You spend, at most, 5% of your time on the substance of the major product and process decisions that not only establish our technological strategy but also largely define our business strategy. Fire fighting and other operating problems take up 60% of your time, and you devote 35% to legal, financial, personnel, and other matters.

In the second chart that I made (see Exhibit II), I've applied your time profile to a diagram showing how our flexibility to set the strategic direction of DMC decreases as an idea moves through concept and design and into the marketplace. It looks like you're apportioning your time in roughly inverse relation to the strategic importance of each phase. This suggests a rather basic question: Who the hell is running the business?

Brad, old buddy, thought Miles grimly, *if you don't know, rest easy. You'll find out.*

As I mentioned before, we're intervening in the wrong spots. At the top level of the company we're primarily exercising operational, not strategic, control because we've become so far removed from the substance of technological decisions. Sure, that's the nuts and bolts, in a sense; but in a company like ours the nuts and bolts *are* strategy. The technological options are so diverse and the market needs are so much in flux that the strategic performance parameters of every product and line—the features that make us or break us—are constantly shifting. And I don't believe that you or anyone else at the decision-making level is systematically analyzing these shifts and modifying our technical strategies to reflect them. Most of the time we're content to rubber-stamp the technical guys' decisions quite a while after design gets under way and when the strategic direction has long since been cast in concrete.

Rubber-stamp, hell. I go over those things with a fine-toothed comb. Sure, maybe the R&D reviews could be advanced a bit, but it wouldn't change the outcome much. Our evaluation system weeds out the losers long before they reach me. Or is that what he's driving at?

Five years ago, when you were made CEO, I'll bet you could have told me the important design parameters of every one of our major products and exactly why they were the way they were. But can you tell me now why we still have electromechanical controls on our

Exhibit II.   Miles's time allocation, showing his ability to influence strategy

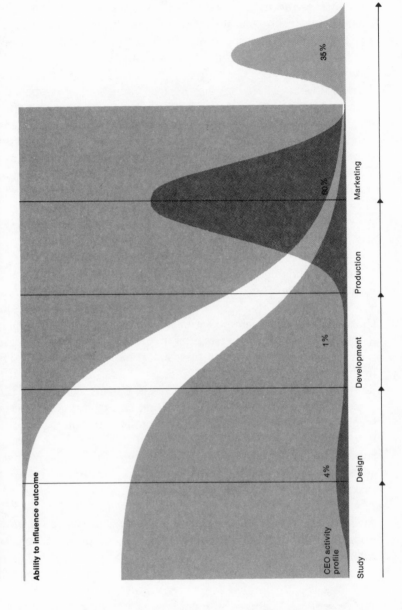

heavy earthmovers? That's not an idle question, Miles. Five years ago our controls for this equipment were the best and most reliable on the market, and everyone knew it. That gave us a clean competitive edge. On top of that, over the years we'd cost-reduced them to the point where we could price them very competitively and still throw off loads of cash. But over the past five years, as you know, our edge has been eroding as our competitors put solid-state devices into their controls.

And next fall, of course, Focused Industries is introducing integrated circuits on all its heavy equipment control systems. Meanwhile, our study team is still trying to decide which supplier to work with. Pasinaro says our electromechanical systems have done the trick for seven years and the new ones still have some bugs in them. I've looked into it and I'm not persuaded. Meanwhile, Sid Rogers and half of his sales guys are saying that the market for electromechanical controls will dry up so fast it won't be funny once FI's new line comes out. Personally, I don't think Sid is just preparing an alibi; I think there's a very good chance he's right. Remember what happened to Mechanical Cash Register?

I remember, all right. They stuck to their last and kept producing better and better mechanical machines while their competitors went electronic—and mopped up the floor with MCR. But hell, calculators aren't earthmovers.

For somebody in your position, there's a natural but extremely dangerous temptation to focus on financial and mathematical abstractions instead of coming to grips with the realities of our business economics and competitive product-line position. The literature is full of sophisticated analytical and mathematical procedures for R&D management: DCF analysis, project-ranking procedures, experience curves, nonlinear programming for project selection under uncertainty, multidimensional scaling techniques for determining desirable product characteristics, industrial dynamics simulations of entire companies, and so on, ad infinitum.

We've invested a good deal of money in systems and procedures based on these techniques, which gives us a comfortable feeling that we've reduced our problems to hard, reliable figures. So we don't worry nearly as much as we should about all those subtle, elusive, qualitative factors that the figures don't reflect. We forget that our job as top managers is to manage product lines, not financial abstractions. Sure, we need to reduce a lot of data to sophisticated digests, but to do the job we're paid for we also need plenty of unabstracted information, with all the fuzziness of reality in it.

There's no substitute for fact-founded judgment on technological issues. And while these techniques and the financial analyses are useful and have their place, they simply don't tell the whole story. That's the nature of the beast.

Agreed, Brad, agreed—you can't have too much information. But where am I supposed to get the time to dig down to that level of detail? Who's going to mind the store?

I think we've lost strategic control of the company because we've let a group of guys about three levels below Pasinaro make our basic technical and business decisions. And they don't have the perspective needed to handle them. We hardly ever tell *them* what to do; they tell *us* what they're doing. At the most, we judge whether what they've got in the works will fly in the marketplace. We've become overdependent on management by exception, but I doubt we're even very effective at that. When was the last time, Miles, that you shut off a project as a result of an R&D review?

Maybe four years ago. Well, not shut off exactly; I didn't approve the A-300 until they'd redesigned it to a higher level of maintainability.

Look at the way we've been depending on the R&D people and the marketing people to set priorities for our technology. Most of the time we haven't even defined the missions to be accomplished, except in financial terms. Sometimes, when it comes to reviewing our alternatives, we pass the buck to a committee or task force. Nine times out of ten they follow some variation of the Chinese menu approach. You get three options—Option A boils down to doing nothing, Option B is radical and terrifyingly risky, and Option C is a nice, safe, well-balanced compromise with something for everybody, backed up with lots of reassuring analysis. And you get to sprinkle holy water.

Meanwhile, up in the corporate stratosphere, we've allowed ourselves to become insulated from the technological realities—when to shift from electromechanical to solid-state, say, or from discrete components to integrated circuits. And we've even become insulated from some of the market realities—when to try to segment a market by creating unique performance specs, as you did with the Model A-300. We even fumble over developing control systems that will meet new

EPA and OSHA regulations. We let the lawyers and the R&D staff worry about the problem.

In general, we're allowing big technological decisions to be made by some very bright people who are at such a low level in the organization that they can't see the trees for the undergrowth, let alone the forest for the trees. Subtle but critical trade-offs involving manufacturing cost, product features, reliability, and date of introduction are made almost daily at the design level. We could be missing a major market opportunity or crippling our economics just because a single designer or his boss would rather walk over his grandmother than exceed his budget.

That may have been MCR's problem—maybe it could be traced to the company's brittle financial control, everyone frightened of spending a dollar, no one rocking the boat. How many millions has MCR written off now?

Well, Miles, this memo has gone on longer than I intended, and I'm going to cut it off. Before doing so, however, I want to say two more things.

First, I don't believe our situation is all that bleak yet. I've talked to people in a lot of other companies about these problems, and most of them, outside of the really top performers, seem to be muddling along pretty much the way we are. And we *have* made quite a few good decisions. But we owe half of them to luck or dumb decisions by our competitors, which I guess is much the same thing. We can thank our stars that the quality of our people has partly compensated for our failure to manage technological change. On the other hand, we've always been the industry leader, and we don't want to let that slip away from us.

Second, I want to ask you to take the attached list of questions to the annual R&D budget review meeting the Tuesday after you get back from Montego Bay. If you see fit, ask a few of the questions then. I'm going to be uncharacteristically quiet.

Well, Miles, I hope I haven't given you indigestion. See you on Tuesday.

Probing Questions

Thoroughly aroused by Brad's comments, Miles pored over the list. He added a couple of questions to it, rearranged the order of the questions, and wrote out a final list, as follows:

Finance (Cutler Sims)

1. How many R&D projects have been proposed to top management in the past five years? How many has it turned down or substantially modified?
2. Of the projects we have approved, what was the distribution of projected rates of return?

R&D and Sales (Jim Pasinaro, Sid Rogers)

1. How do our present electromechanical control systems stack up against Focused Industries' line in terms of technology, reliability, maintenance, and cost structure?
2. How will Focused's new integrated-circuit line affect us? What do we plan to do in response?
3. What do our customers regard as the three most important performance parameters of our control systems in earthmoving equipment? In medical equipment? In oil-drilling equipment?
4. How do we stack up against Focused in each of these markets in terms of these parameters?
5. Are there any anticipated changes in external developments—e.g., legislative or regulatory action or shifts in raw material availability—that could change the strategic performance parameters of our products in these markets?
6. How do our R&D programs reflect these considerations? How much technological risk are we taking in introducing the new drilling-equipment line? How much marketing risk?

Back at his desk at 9 A.M. Monday, Miles dictated three brief memoranda, one to each of the three VPs, listing the relevant questions and requesting each man to bring the answers with him to the review the next day. Then he shut himself up for the rest of the day and dealt with two weeks' accumulation of paper.

Confrontation on Tuesday

Reviews of the budget, of the ratios of R&D expense to sales, and of the other customary financial gauges of the R&D effort took up the first part of the meeting. Pasinaro had just finished with the chart summarizing new-project ROIs and was about to start the project-by-project ROI reviews when Miles asked the finance VP his first question: "Cutler, your finance guys track our project selection system pretty closely. What percent of the projects that are proposed to us have been turned down since we started this process?"

"Well, Miles," said Cutler, "I'd never really looked at that before, but I followed it up for you. It looks as if we'd never actually turned a project down. Once they get to us, it's pretty automatic because the losers have already been screened out. I'd say that's as it should be."

Score one for Brad, thought Miles. *He said that's what they'd say.* "I see," he said. "And what about the distribution of projected rates of return?"

"I have that one too," said Cutler. "Of course, given that we've never turned a project down, no projection has fallen below the 20% hurdle rate. But I was a little surprised to find that 95% of the projections over the past three years, since we got the system on line, have come in between 20% and 25%. It's possible that some of the boys down the line have been plugging numbers. You know how hard it is to project sales from new products."

"Yes, I know." *"Possible," my foot; it's a dead certainty, and he knows it.* "Jim," said Miles, turning to Pasinaro, "I know we have high hopes for those new drilling-equipment controls. If that line succeeds, it will have a major impact on next year's earnings. How much technical risk are we taking in that project?"

"Miles, I'm happy to report that there's nothing to worry about there. The system is a classic design, and there isn't a component in it that hasn't been proved out over time in our electromechanical devices. The whole project is solid as a rock, technically. Being conservative," Pasinaro concluded, "I'll say it's 99% risk free."

That's great, Miles thought wryly. *You'll guarantee the product will work if anyone happens to buy it.*

"Jim," he continued, "what features of our control systems are most important to potential customers in this market, and how will the program help our market position relative to, say, Focused Industries?"

"I'm not sure I follow you, Miles. We've never looked at it in quite that way. Our customers want four main things—low cost, high performance, low maintenance, and high reliability. We're tops in every single one of these counts, and we aim to stay that way."

"Staying tops in market share is what I had in mind," Miles said dryly. "Thanks anyway, Jim. Sid, how would you estimate the marketing risk in this introduction?"

"Well, you know how hard it is to estimate sales of new products," Rogers said. "I hate to commit myself, but we've got a solid cadre of loyal customers in that market segment, and we're going to hold them and add to them with this new line. Cutler, you've got the charts. What are we projecting that market as?"

Miles interrupted him. "No, Sid, I know we've got the projections. I want to know about the risk. What's the chance that the projections won't materialize?"

"I hope I don't seem to be ducking the question, Miles, but we haven't really looked at it that way. How the hell could we calculate that risk? To be honest, a number of my salesmen are getting kind of nervous about Focused Industries' all solid-state approach. You know salesmen—always crying wolf. Anyway, our headquarters guys have ironed this all out with Jim's people."

"They sure have, Sid." Pasinaro chimed in. "Your guys have extrapolated the market based on some very sophisticated smoothing techniques, and my guys have nailed down the cost and reliability to a gnat's eyeball. I don't see how we can miss."

This is unreal, thought Miles.

But before he could speak, Seymour Crawford, the general counsel, interrupted. Miles was rather surprised; Seymour had never been known to say a word at an R&D budget meeting. Usually he had to be coaxed into attending.

"Jim, Sidney," Crawford said, "pardon me for butting in. I just wanted to make sure you're aware of the possibility of some new OSHA legislation prohibiting the use of electromechanical relay contacts on drilling equipment. It's not a certainty this year by any means, but I think the handwriting's on the wall. My assistant, Hal Masterson, took it up with one of your engineers a few weeks ago and got roughly nowhere. Your guy's position, as I heard it, was that our electromechanical devices had the best safety record in the business and that anyway we had no alternative, since we don't make semiconductors. Hal thought that was rather beside the point, but your guy's back was up so he didn't pursue it at the time. I thought you ought to know the story. Mind you, I'm not pushing the panic button."

Horace Bender, the manufacturing VP, spoke up for the first time: "Let's not forget all that electromechanical capacity we just put in, Jim."

"That's right," said Pasinaro. "We're already committed, and, anyway, I think OSHA's a paper tiger."

"I don't know, Jim," Crawford said. "They've been taking some tough stands lately, and the courts have been backing them up. Still, we're probably OK for a while."

They could swat us like a gnat, eyeballs and all, Miles thought.

"Come to think of it," said Rogers, "one of my guys was going on about OSHA last week too. Maybe we should check our contacts in Washington."

They'll have to treat me for depression when this is over. Glancing around the table, Miles saw Cutler, so cool and confident a moment ago, now looking decidedly ill at ease; Sid was pensive; and Seymour was rather above it all. Only Jim and Horace seemed relaxed. Brad was quietly watchful.

As Miles was about to put his next question, Jim Pasinaro took the floor again. "Miles, we're falling way behind schedule with this speculation. I know our guys have studied all these things, and they're satisfied. Now, if you want to finish reviewing the numbers, we'd better get back on track."

"OK, Jim. But before we go on, I'd like to ask you to elaborate a bit on my point about performance parameters. What do you think are the most important features to our customers in the drilling segment, and how will the project under consideration help our competitive position in those areas?"

"Miles, as I said before: cost, reliability, maintainability, performance. That's what all our customers want. Now, if you want details on what our competitors' equipment is like, we've got the complete literature and specs on every one of them in our files. One of our guys can dig them out and answer any questions you might have by the end of the week. But it seems to me that here and now we ought to be concerned with approving our own projects instead of sitting around speculating about a competitor's product line.

"As far as the solid-state issue is concerned, you'll recall that we had a task force look at it two years ago. They concluded that solid-state controls wouldn't take over the market for six to ten years, so we could afford to relax. Or, if we wanted to push it, we could retread half of our engineering staff, hire a bunch of high-priced, solid-state hotshots, and scoop the industry. Nobody was very keen on that one, you remember. What did make sense was to go ahead with our proven electromechanical technology, watch the trends in semiconductors, and review the bidding in two years' time. That's next spring, I reckon."

Now Sims spoke up. "It seems to me, Jim, that we may have let our decision making in these areas get a little too routine. Your down-the-line engineers seem to be making an awful lot of key decisions."

"I don't see anything wrong with that," Pasinaro retorted. "That's exactly what—" whereupon Sid interrupted angrily, and others joined in the hubbub. But in a few minutes Miles had restored order, and the group completed the agenda as planned.

Then Miles took the floor. "Gentlemen," he said, "it's now past one o'clock. Although personally I seem to have lost my appetite, I suggest we move over to the dining room for lunch. There's no sense in coming back here afterwards, however. It seems clear to me, based on this morning's rather depressing performance, that we're superbly prepared to discuss things of little importance and totally at sea when it comes to assessing the strategic significance of our R&D programs. Obviously, we've all got some hard thinking to do about our approach to managing technological change.

"Since we've never turned down an R&D project before, let's consider this year's R&D budget approved as proposed for the moment and spend the afternoon reflecting on why we seem to be so distant from the realities of our businesses. You'll all be getting a memo on the subject from me early next week."

Shape of a Solution

MEMORANDUM

TO: R&D Planning Committee
FROM: Miles Atkinson, President

I've had a few days to reflect on our meeting last Tuesday and discuss its implications with each of you, so now I want to share my thoughts with you. We agree that we have a serious problem with our approach to managing technological change. We can deal with that problem if we avoid defensiveness, figure out precisely what needs to be done, and do it.

Fortunately, our company is still the leader in its industry, our financial position is sound, and our basic functional skills and technical capabilities are adequate—apart from a few weak spots. So we have the time to analyze and deliberate; but we must also be decisive.

Let me give you some insight into the nature and extent of the problem. Brad, Jim, and Sid have collaborated on a quick-and-dirty analysis that puts it into perspective. In 1970, our competitive position looked roughly like this:

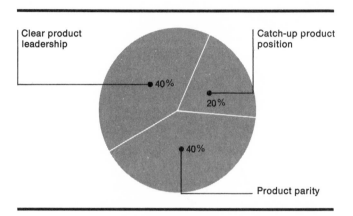

These are the percentages for particular product items in our line, weighted by sales. Today we estimate our competitive position to be as follows:

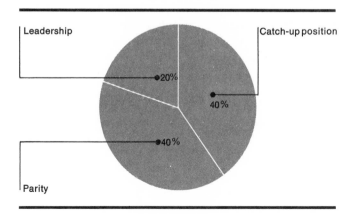

When Focused introduces its new line, it could go to this extreme:

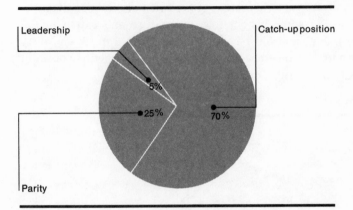

Brad, Sid, and Jim feel that this analysis needs further refining, but that the trend is disturbingly clear. We are steadily losing our competitive position. We haven't felt it too badly yet because we are so well established in our markets, with an extremely loyal customer base. Nevertheless, the trend helps to explain why our sales have gone up half again as fast as our profits over the past five years. And it strongly suggests to me that we've lost our ability to manage technological change effectively.

By now all of you have read and discussed with me Brad's original memo on the subject. We agree that it's an incisive analysis of this insidious loss of strategic control. We've been working so hard to capitalize on our traditional strengths that we've forgotten to look at the strategic performance parameters of our product lines and markets. We've become the captives of tradition and the slaves of procedures. In particular, I have noted the following.

Item: Instead of monitoring the constant changes in technology and in our markets, and modifying our strategy to maintain our leadership, we have followed the incremental approach that has worked so well in the past—giving our customers more and better of our established products.

Item: We have never tried to balance technological risks and marketing risks. As a result, it appears that our overconservative approach to technological risk is exposing us to a dangerous level of marketing risk.

In short, we simply haven't learned to adapt to change. Let me assure you, I take the largest share of responsibility for the state of affairs that I've just described. But let me also assure you that all of us will have to change our ways radically, starting now. Here are the two main changes we will make:

1   A NEW KIND OF REVIEW

As top managers, we will participate much earlier in the R&D project selection process; when we do, we will be prepared to make substantive contributions. To this end we will institute monthly, full-day competitive product position reviews, starting one month from today. At these sessions, Sid's marketing people will take the lead in providing an in-depth analysis of one of our major product lines and/or market segments. These analyses will be circulated to each of us in hard copy a week before the meeting so that we can prepare to deal with the questions they raise. Their contents will consider, at a minimum:

- The strategic performance parameters of our products in each product/market segment, how they have shifted over the past five years, and how we can expect them to shift in the next five.
- Our position in each paramenter compared with that of our principal competitors.
- The improvements that our customers would value most in each such parameter.
- The changes in each paramenter that could lead to either further market segmentation or reaggregation of the market at a level giving us a competitive advantage.
- Potential moves of competitors that might undermine our company's advantages in each parameter.
- Potential changes in the environment (government action, activity of consumer groups, availability of raw materials) that could weaken our position in, or require changes in, each parameter.
- Any other internal or external factor that might make such an impact.

At these sessions we will also evaluate every effort under way to improve each strategic performance parameter, and we will assess these efforts against those of competitors and potential competitors.

Jim will report to us on the status of each project and, if possible, of competitive efforts. Supporting the description of each paramenter will be a qualitative and, where possible, quantitative estimate of its susceptibility to further modifications through technology. In addition, we will try to pinpoint opportunities for further segmentation or for aggregation of the markets where this strategic factor is relevant.

Note that these reviews will necessarily include some financial analyses. But their focus will be to provide the judgmental raw material required by our top management group to deal effectively with strategic technological issues.

When we start these reviews, we will naturally have some growing pains. Our first sessions may be uneven. But they should rapidly improve, particularly if we discipline ourselves to record the strategic issues that emerge in these sessions and follow them up to see that they are resolved. I've asked Brad to take responsibility for that follow-up.

These monthly sessions will continue until we have reviewed our entire product line and have identified and understood all the major strategic issues in each of our businesses. At that time we will reassess this new approach and modify it as necessary. Our goal is to develop an exact understanding of what we are doing in R&D, and why.

2   A NEW BOLDNESS IN INTERVENTION

We will adopt a much more disciplined approach to monitoring the progress of R&D projects. Brad and Jim are still researching the details, but we have already come to a decision on some major requirements.

Henceforth, our new-product introduction process will be divided into discrete phases, as shown in the attached chart (see Exhibit III). Of course, we do this now to a certain extent, but God knows we lack discipline. From now on, before any major project can move from one phase to the next, our top-management group will sign it off. At each sign-off point, we will agree on whether to continue the project and, if we decide to continue it, whether and how the project plan should be modified in the light of new conditions.

I fully expect that this procedure will result in some cancelled projects and substantial redirections of projects as they develop, as we gain better information on technological possibilities and difficulties and, increasingly, as we attune ourselves to developments and changes

Exhibit III. Top management's monitoring of project

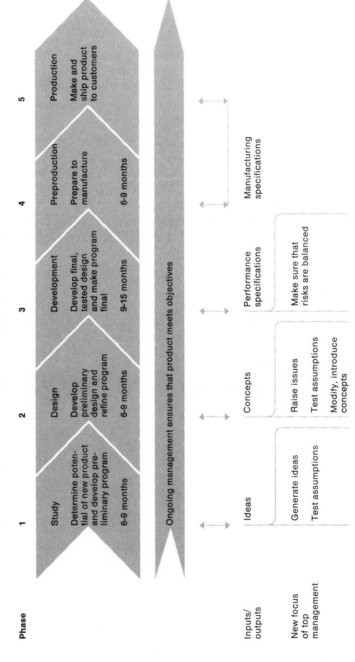

in the marketplace. This, of course, will differ sharply from our past practice of leaving product development in the hands of R&D once a project had been initially approved and subjecting it to only the most cursory review at our annual budget meetings.

Further, before each sign-off, we will review the competitive position of the product to make sure that the technological and marketing risks remain in balance. We will be less concerned with minimizing schedule delays and cost overruns than with capturing every significant opportunity to strengthen our competitive position through improvements in product performance.

In contrast to our future role, let me note a fact that Cutler has unearthed: with one minor exception, every development project we have undertaken over at least the past five years has been completed with essentially no revision to the original performance specifications, even though substantial shifts in market, competitive, and governmental conditions have taken place. This must never be allowed to happen again. It won't happen if we apply the informed judgment in these matters for which our stockholders are paying us.

Beyond these immediate steps, I am contemplating further moves to streamline our decision making and pinpoint responsibilities for individual businesses and product lines. Since these moves are not yet formed in my mind, I would appreciate suggestions about them from each of you. In the meantime, I know you will cooperate in the fullest with me and also with Brad, as we move to seize strategic control of our technology.

Decisions at the Top

Miles breathed a sigh of relief as he shut off his dictating machine. *I deserve one of those Macanudos I brought back from Jamaica,* he thought. *Sara's gone for the day, and she'll never notice that I've been smoking if I remember to clean out the ashtray. I think we're on the way to solving this problem.*

He was feeling pleased with himself. But as the first puffs of his cigar created a gray halo of smoke over his head, he reflected that he was still troubled about the tone of the corporation and the attitudes that underlay the problems he was now moving to solve. If the tone and attitudes were wrong, it was up to him as CEO to change them. He was not yet sure how, but he was beginning to get a handle on the problem.

He had begun with a simple question: What types of technological decisions should his top management team make? The more he thought about it, the more convinced he became that three decisions were key to managing technological change. And as long as DMC was organized as a single profit center, ensuring the soundness of those decisions was his responsibility.

The first was the decision on what to do—that is, what problems or opportunities to deploy technological resources against. Most of the raw material for this decision would have to come from his top functional people during the review sessions. But he would have to immerse himself sufficiently in the issues to be able to ask the right questions and test the assumptions underlying the answers he got. And ultimately he would have to provide direction with respect to the product parameters that would have to be changed to gain a competitive edge.

The second decision concerned how to do it and, particularly, how much risk to take in each instance. This was a tricky decision, balancing (at the least) technological and marketing risks. It was also a critical decision because it determined timing. As he and Brad had agreed the other day, the widespread availability of technology and the proliferation of multiple approaches to meet market needs had put a premium on the appropriate timing. And it was becoming increasingly difficult to sit on a technological lead.

The final decision concerned when to stop and when to redirect projects. The work and preparation necessary to make the first two decisions properly would, of course, really help them all to review each project's progress from the standpoint of its continued strategic significance. Nevertheless, decisions to cut off projects were notoriously tough to make—and making them stick sometimes even tougher. He knew how difficult it was to factor in the opportunity costs of continuing to commit scarce technological resources to projects that had lost their relevance or chance for success. Too often, he knew, investments in ego turned out to be the controlling factor in letting projects continue.

The steps he had already taken were, of course, aimed at forcing these decisions on top management, but he knew he was asking a great deal of some of his executives and he was unsure whether all of them were able to change. There would be a powerful tendency, reinforced by the sheer magnitude of the task, to slip back into the habit of pushing numbers instead of coming to grips with technological and competitive realities.

Has Diversified become too diversified to manage as a single profit center? he wondered. *If so, I'll have to bring more top management focus on particu-*

lar products or markets. Or maybe the company should slow down its diver-sification until the executives learn how to manage it better. That was one reason Miles had alluded in his memo to some possible further moves.

But Miles was most concerned about the company's attitude toward change, as reflected by its top management. *If the signals coming from the top pointed so clearly to an ultraconservative technological strategy, what else could I expect from the down-the-line people? There are bound to be a few innovative souls out there, not all of them in Jim Pasinaro's department.* But the evidence of the past two weeks had shaken him.

I suppose that to an independent observer DMC has been as much a hotbed of innovation as the Catholic Church or the railroads. Well, that's my *problem. Even if it means knocking some heads together, I've got to create a positive attitude toward change. And I will.*

He had finished his cigar. He made a note to himself to send a box of Macanudos to Brad first thing in the morning.

2
The New Product Development Map

Steven C. Wheelwright and W. Earl Sasser, Jr.

No business activity is more heralded for its promise and approached with more justified optimism than the development and manufacture of new products. Whether in mature businesses like automobiles and electrical appliances, or more dynamic ones like computers, managers correctly view new products as a chance to get a jump on the competition.

Ideally, a successful new product can set industry standards—standards that become another company's barrier to entry—or open up crucial new markets. Think of the Sony Walkman. New products are good for the organization. They tend to exploit as yet untapped R&D discoveries and revitalize the engineering corps. New product campaigns offer top managers opportunities to reorganize and to get more out of a sales force, factory, or field service network, for example. New products capitalize on old investments.

Perhaps the most exciting benefit, though, is the most intangible: corporate renewal and redirection. The excitement, imagination, and growth associated with the introduction of a new product invigorate the company's best people and enhance the company's ability to recruit new forces. New products build confidence and momentum.

Unfortunately, these great promises of new product development are seldom fully realized. Products half make it; people burn out. To understand why, let's look at some of the more obvious pitfalls.

1. *The moving target.* Too often the basic product concept misses a shifting market. Or companies may make assumptions about channels of distri-

bution that just don't hold up. Sometimes the project gets into trouble because of inconsistencies in focus; you start building a stripped-down version and wind up with a load of options. The project time lengthens, and longer projects invariably drift more and more from their initial target. Classic market misses include the Ford Edsel in the mid-1950s and Texas Instruments' home computer in the late 1970s. Even very successful products like Apple's Macintosh line of personal computers can have a rocky beginning.

2. *Lack of product distinctiveness.* This risk is high when designers fail to consider a full range of alternatives to meet customer needs. If the organization gets locked into a concept too quickly, it may not bring differing perspectives to the analysis. The market may dry up, or the critical technologies may be sufficiently widespread that imitators appear out of nowhere. Plus Development introduced Hardcard®, a hard disc that fits into a PC expansion slot, after a year and a half of development work. The company thought it had a unique product with at least a nine-month lead on competitors. But by the fifth day of the industry show where Hardcard® was introduced, a competitor was showing a prototype of a competing version. And within three months, the competitor was shipping its new product.

3. *Unexpected technical problems.* Delays and cost overruns can often be traced to overestimates of the company's technical capabilities or simply to its lack of depth and resources. Projects can suffer delays and stall mid-course if essential inventions are not completed and drawn into the designers' repertoire before the product development project starts. An industrial controls company we know encountered both problems: it changed a part from metal to plastic only to discover that its manufacturing processes could not hold the required tolerances and also that its supplier could not provide raw material of consistent quality.

4. *Mismatches between functions.* Often one part of the organization will have unrealistic or even impossible expectations of another. Engineering may design a product that the company's factories cannot produce, for example, or at least not consistently at low cost and with high quality. Similarly, engineering may design features into products that marketing's established distribution channels or selling approach cannot exploit. In planning its requirements, manufacturing may assume an unchanging mix of new products, while marketing mistakenly assumes that manufacturing can alter its mix dramatically on short notice. One of the most startling mismatches we've encountered was created by an aerospace company whose manufacturing group built an assembly plant too small to accommodate the wingspan of the plane it ultimately had to produce.

Thus new products often fail because companies misunderstand the most promising markets and channels of distribution and because they misapprehend their own technological strengths or the product's technological challenges. Nothing can eliminate all the risks, but clearly the most important thing to do early on when developing a new product is to get all contributors to the process communicating: marketing with manufacturing, R&D with both. Products fail from a lack of planning; planning fails from a lack of information.

Developing a new generation of products is a lot like taking a journey into the wilderness. Who would dream of setting off without a map? Of course, you would try to clarify the purpose of the journey and make sure that needed equipment is available and in order. But once committed to the trip, you need a map of the terrain, something everybody can study—the focus for discussion, the basis for planning alternative courses. Knowing where you've come from and where you are is essential to knowing how to get where you want to go.

Mapping Existing Products

We have often used this analogy of a map with corporate managers involved in product development, and gradually it became clear to us that an actual map is needed, not just an analogy. Managers need a way to see the evolution of a company's product lines—the "where we are"—in order to expose the markets and technologies that have been driving the evolution—the "where we've come from." Such a map presents the evolution of current product lines in a summary yet strikingly clear way so that all functional areas in the organization can respond to a common vision. The map provides a basis for sharing information. And by enabling managers to compare the assumptions underlying current product lines with the ideal assumptions of new research, it points to new market opportunities and technological challenges. Why, for example, should an organization build for department stores when specialty discount outlets are the emerging channels of distribution? Why bend metals when you can mold ceramics?

Exhibit I illustrates a generic map that indicates how the product offerings in one generation may be related to each other. These relations are the building blocks that allow us to track the evolution of product families from one generation to another.

The map categorizes product offerings (and the development efforts they entail) as "core" and "leveraged" products, and divides leveraged

Exhibit I.

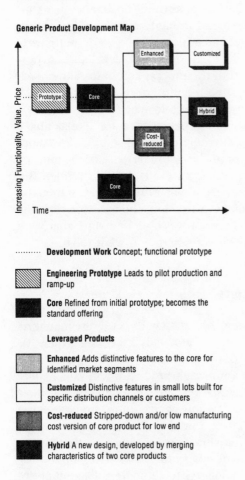

Generic Product Development Map

.... **Development Work** Concept; functional prototype

Engineering Prototype Leads to pilot production and ramp-up

Core Refined from initial prototype; becomes the standard offering

Leveraged Products

Enhanced Adds distinctive features to the core for identified market segments

Customized Distinctive features in small lots built for specific distribution channels or customers

Cost-reduced Stripped-down and/or low manufacturing cost version of core product for low end

Hybrid A new design, developed by merging characteristics of two core products

products into "enhanced," "customized," "cost reduced," and "hybrid" products. (These designations seem to cover most cases, but managers should feel free to add whatever other categories they need.) A core product, first an engineering prototype, is the engineering platform, providing the basis for further enhancements. The core product is the initial, standard product introduced. It changes little from year to year and is often the benchmark against which consumers compare the rest of the product line.

Enhanced products are developed from the core design; distinctive features are added for various, more discriminating markets. Enhanced products are the first products leveraged from the capabilities put in place to produce the core and the first aimed at new or extended market opportunities. Often companies even identify them as enhanced versions, for example, IBM's DisplayWrite 3.1 is an enhanced version of DisplayWrite 3. But a leveraged product isn't necessarily more costly: the idea is simply to get more out of a fixed process—more "bang for the buck." As companies leverage high-end products, they may customize them in smaller lots for specific channels or to give consumers more choice. The cost-reduced model starts with essentially the same technology and design as the core product but is a stripped-down version, often with less expensive materials and lower factory costs, aimed at a price-sensitive market. (Think of the old Chevrolet Biscayne, which was many times the vehicle of choice for taxicabs and business fleets.)

Finally, there is the hybrid product, developed out of two cores. The initial two-stage thermostat products—accommodating a daytime and nighttime temperature setting—were hybrids of a traditional thermostat product and high-end, programmable thermostat lines.

On the generic map, from left to right is calendar time, and from bottom to top designates lower to higher added value or functionality, which usually also means a shift from cheaper to more expensive products.

These distinctions—core, hybrid, and the others—are immediately useful because they give managers a way of thinking about their products more rigorously and less anecdotally. But the various turns on the product map—the various "leverage points"—also serve as crucial indicators of previous management assumptions about the corporate strengths and market forces shaping product evolutions.

A map that shows a proliferation of enhanced products toward the high end, for example, says something important about the market opportunities managers identified after they had introduced the core. A map's configuration raises necessary questions about dominant channels of distribution—then and now. That products could have been leveraged in particular ways, moreover, says something important about in-house technological and manufacturing capabilities—capabilities that may still exist or may need changing. The map generates the right discussions. When managers know how and why they have leveraged products in the past, they know better how to leverage the company in the present.

Exhibit II.

The First Generation of Coolidge Vaccuum Cleaner (1952–1968)

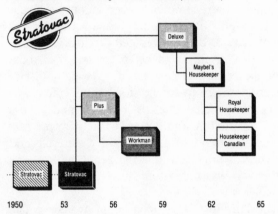

The First Generation

How can managers plan, develop, and position a set of products—that is, how do they build a dynamic map? With the generic map in mind, let us track offerings from generation to generation, as shown in Exhibit II. Imagine a very simple line of vacuum cleaners, Coolidge Corporation's "Stratovac," introduced, say, in 1952. The core product, the Stratovac, was a canister-type appliance with a 2.5 horsepower motor. Constructed mainly from cut and stamped metals, it was distributed through department stores and hardware chains.

The following year, reaching for the somewhat more affluent suburban household, Coolidge brought out the "Stratovac Plus," an enhanced Stratovac delivered in a choice of three colors, with a 4 horsepower motor and a recoiling cord. In 1959, the company introduced the "Stratovac Deluxe"—a Stratovac Plus with a vacuum resistance sensor (which cut off the power when the bag was full) and a power head with a rotating brush for deep pile or shag carpeting. By 1959, the basic Stratovac cost $89, the Stratovac Plus, $109, and the Stratovac Deluxe, $159.

To reach the industrial market at $79, Coolidge had decided to offer the "Stratovac Workman," a stripped-down Plus model—one color, no recoiling cord. That was introduced in 1956. And when Deluxe sales rocketed, Coolidge offered Maybel's department store chain a customized version of it, the Stratovac "Maybel's Housekeeper." This came out in 1960, in Maybel's blue gray, with the power head. The price was "only" $129. (Coolidge eventually customized the "Housekeeper Canadian" for the Simpton's chain in Canada, and the "Royal House-keeper" for the Mid-Lakes chain in England.)

Again, this is a simple product line, but even so, the map raises interesting questions, especially for younger managers who came after this era. Why the Stratovac Plus? Why a proliferation of products toward the high end?

In fact, during the 1950s, most companies marketed home appliances through department stores with product families visibly shaped by the distribution channels. Products stood side by side in the stores, to be demonstrated by a salesperson. The markup was similar for each product on the floor.

What differentiated products in product families at the time was an appliance manufacturer's reach to satisfy more or less obvious customer segments—customers differentiated by factors like income and marital status. (In the 1950s, most vacuum cleaner purchasers were women, with more or less money, time, and patience.)

How Coolidge leveraged its products also points to certain fixed—and not especially unique—manufacturing capabilities. During the 1950s, company engineers designed appliances for manual assembly and traditional notions of economies of scale. By the end of the 1950s, Coolidge acquired new vacuum sensor innovations from the auto industry. It also learned certain flexible manufacturing techniques, making different colors and options possible.

By 1958, Coolidge had solved most of the technical problems of the Stratovac line and had recruited a number of ambitious design engineers to integrate vacuum sensor and power heads into the line. The life cycle of the product—including development time, which stretched back to 1949—was typical for core products of that time: 10 to 15 years. Demand for the Stratovac remained strong throughout the 1950s, and Coolidge sold to department stores in roughly the same proportion as its competition, except for companies organized around the door-to-door trade.

The company's increased (and not fully utilized) technical competence and the steadiness of its key distribution channels are crucial pieces of information to add to the map (see Exhibit III). The map summarizes technical competence in the box beneath the product lines, and Coolidge's gross sales by distribution channel in the box

Exhibit III.

The First Generation of Coolidge Vaccuum Cleaner (1952–1968)

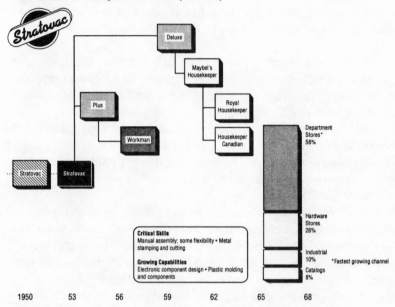

graph. The fastest growing distribution channel in the industry—in this case, department stores—is shaded for emphasis.

The Second Generation

With so much technical talent in-house, and a society growing increasingly affluent, Coolidge could not be expected to rest on the Stratovac's success indefinitely. Sales were steady, but by the mid-1960s customers assumed there would be some innovations. The age of plastics was dawning; the vanguard of the baby boom was taking apartments; it was the "new and improved" era.

Moreover, marketing people at Coolidge began to detect a new potential market at the low end. People who had relied on their Stratovacs for a decade were looking around for a second, lighter weight appliance for quick cleanups or for the workroom or garage. Lighter weight and cheaper naturally meant more reliance on plastic components.

In the early 1960s, Coolidge managers decided on two product families, each with its own core product (see Exhibit IV). The design team that had brought out the old core Stratovac would handle the "Stratovac II," and company new hires would design a second line, the all-plastic, mass-produced "Handivac" ("any color, so long as it's beige").

The Stratovac II, introduced in 1968, was heavier and had a 4.3 horsepower motor, resulting in a slightly noisier operation, "jet noise," which the marketing people reasoned would actually increase respect for its power. Half of the case was now plastic for a "streamlined" appearance. The core Stratovac II boasted a new dust-bag system, which virtually eliminated the need for handling dust. A retractable cord was also standard.

The Stratovac II "Sentry," an enhanced version of the core, included electronic controls for variable speed and came in many colors. The Stratovac II "Imperial," like the old Deluxe model, came with the power head. The Stratovac II Workman continued to sell steadily to the light industrial market, as did the Stratovac II Housekeeper line to the department store chains that still sold the vast majority of units.

Most notable about the Stratovac II was how little changed it was, certainly on the manufacturing end. Assembly was still chiefly manual, along the lines of the 1950s—no priority given to modularity, design for manufacturability, or any of the considerations that would drive designers later on. There was some outsourcing of components to Mexico and Taiwan but no real attention to automation. The only significant change in the Stratovac II came in 1973, when inflationary pressures pushed management to develop a fully plastic casing and critical plastic components—in effect, a hybrid developed by merging technologies of the high-end vacuum cleaner with the low-end Handivac.

Handivac, the second core product, introduced in 1969, was something of a disappointment—mostly because of the inexperience of the team managing its development. Reliability was a problem, given Handivac's almost complete dependence on plastic components, components subjected to higher than expected temperatures from an old, slightly updated 2.5 horsepower motor. Weight was also a problem: it was not as light as promised. Mass-production lines, which were partially automated, were considered a success when they were finally debugged.

Perhaps the greatest problem with the Handivac, however, was the fact that, like the Stratovac II, it was sold mainly through department stores and hardware chains, where markups were too large to permit it a significant price advantage over the more expensive core product.

Exhibit IV.

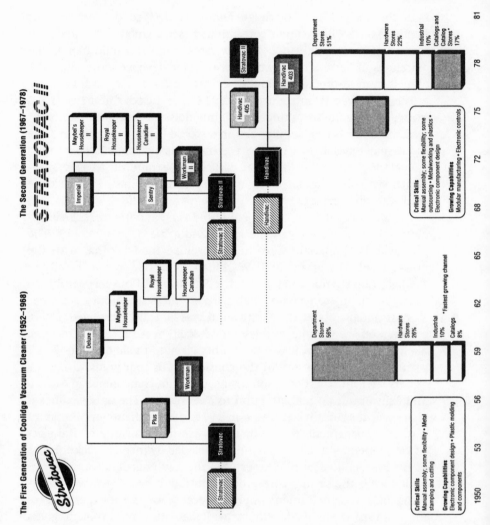

The First Generation of Coolidge Vaccuum Cleaner (1952–1968)

The Second Generation (1967–1978)

Handivac sold for $79, while the Stratovac II sold for $99. Handivac managers tried to cut costs by going to an overseas supplier for a lighter weight, somewhat less powerful motor—over the vehement objections of Stratovac II designers, who had depended on Handivac's participation in their motor plant to keep their own costs in line.

Eventually, Handivac introduced a cost-reduced "Handivac 403," which sold for $69, importing a 3.0 horsepower motor and cord sub-assembly from Japan. The enhanced "405" sold for $83. Handivac engineers began at this time to interact with Japanese manufacturing managers. But there were still no distribution channels where Handivac could enjoy the "price busting" opportunity it needed. The most promising channel, though hardly dominant, was the growing chains of catalog stores, which sold the Handivac 403 for $63, a 10% reduction in the department store price.

The Third Generation

During 1976 and 1977, a number of external and internal pressures led to a redesign of the entire product line. Department stores were still the major source of revenue, but competitors were proliferating and the Stratovac II group felt the need to offer an increasing number of more enhanced and more customized products to maintain demand at the profitable high end. Consumers would pay a premium, marketing people believed, only if the company could produce so many versions that all customers felt they were getting the right color with the right options. Moreover, Coolidge had canvassed Stratovac II customers, who hadn't appreciated the "jet sound," as designers had assumed. Bulk was also a problem, as was the vacuum's unattractive look.

Inside the company, Coolidge's two design teams had become more cooperative, particularly as the advantages of molded plastic became obvious to everyone. The hybrid Stratovac II, which had been redesigned in plastic wherever possible, was something of a victory for the young Handivac designers over the more traditional group. Flexibility and cost were the keys to satisfying many markets, and plastics answered both needs. Eventually the more traditional designers also came to see the advantage of going to Japan for a smaller, lighter, more reliable motor—and for a number of subassemblies critical to the company's goal of offering arrays of options.

Concurrently in the mid-1970s, the Handivac designers were pressing for a complete merging of the design engineering teams and for studying Japanese manufacturing techniques. They argued that if flexibility, cost, and quality were going to be crucial, the manufacturing people would have to become more involved in product design. The young guard also believed that Coolidge could produce motors domestically—at required levels of quality—if it adopted certain innovations in machine tool and winding automation and instituted statistical process control at its existing motor plant.

Where the younger design group still lacked credibility, however, was on the bottom line. Top management was reluctant to give up on a two-track approach when the Handivac group had failed to deliver an appliance that made even as much as the Housekeeper line. The number of catalog stores was growing, and newer discount appliance chains were springing up in big cities, but the Handivac faced intense competition. Could the younger designers hope to come in with enough products, offering enough features, and at low enough costs to meet this competition?

In the end, Coolidge management decided to develop two core product families in its third generation (see Exhibit V). The Stratovac II team redesigned the high-end vacuum cleaner in six models, the "Challenger 6000" series. All appliances in this series came with a power head and a new bag system. By steps—6001, 6002, and upward—consumers could buy increasingly sophisticated electronic controls. And they could order the 6004 and 6005 in an array of colors.

The 6000 series was constructed almost entirely of molded plastic. Manufacturing came up with an automated way of applying hot sealant to critical seams, and the Challenger's motor was quieter. Top management agreed with the younger engineers that a more advanced motor factory could be constructed in the United States. The design teams didn't merge, but they found themselves working more closely together and increasingly with manufacturing.

The traditional design group simultaneously came out with the "Pioneer 4000" series. This was a middle-range product, somewhat smaller than the Challenger 6000, and not offering a power head. The marketing people felt that department stores would want a cost-reduced model to compete with the proliferating "economy" products that discount chains were now offering. (The 4001, 4002, and 4003 were distinguished, again, by electronic controls.) The Pioneer 4000 series was leveraged largely from the Challenger 6000 as a cost-reduced version.

Since both series offered stripped-down models, Coolidge did not introduce a specific industrial product and eliminated the Workman.

Exhibit V.

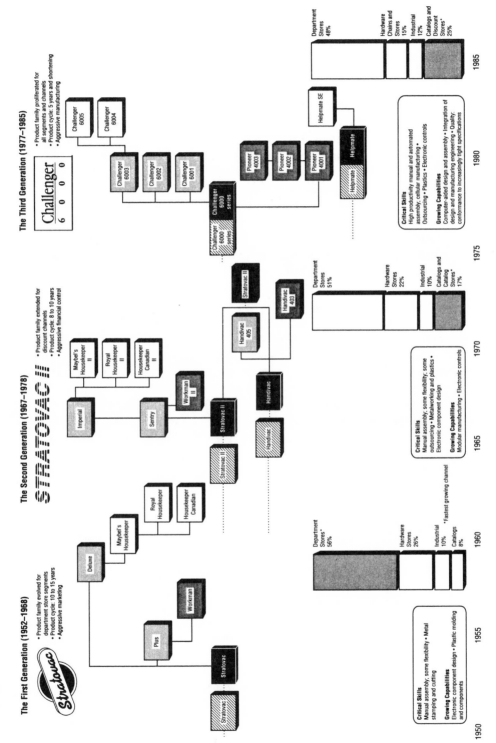

The First Generation (1952–1968)
- Product family evolved for department store segments
- Product cycle: 10 to 15 years
- Aggressive marketing

Critical Skills
Manual assembly; some flexibility • Metal stamping and cutting
Growing Capabilities
Electronic component design • Plastic molding and components

The Second Generation (1967–1978)
- Product family extended for discount channels
- Product cycle: 8 to 10 years
- Aggressive financial control

Critical Skills
Manual assembly; some flexibility; some outsourcing • Metalworking and plastics • Electronic component design
Growing Capabilities
Modular manufacturing • Electronic controls

The Third Generation (1977–1985)
- Product family proliferated for all segments and channels
- Product cycle: 5 years and shortening
- Aggressive manufacturing

Critical Skills
High productivity manual and automated assembly; cellular manufacturing • Outsourcing • Plastics • Electronic controls
Growing Capabilities
Computer-aided design and assembly • Integration of design and manufacturing engineering • Quality: conformance to increasingly tight specifications

Coolidge executives also believed that it was no longer worthwhile to customize models for particular department stores where margins were shrinking, so they eliminated the Housekeeper line.

A year after they introduced the Challenger 6000, the Handivac team brought out its new series of products, the "Helpmate." With minor modifications, Helpmate was customized as "Helpmate SE," targeted at different low-end market segments—college students, apartment dwellers, do-it-your-selfers, and the industrial market. The cleaner was lightweight. Attachments varied, as did graphic design: the company expected a Spartan gray color and a longer hose to appeal to commercial customers and bright pastels and different size brushes to appeal to women college students.

The key to the Helpmate line, however, was its manufacturing. The motor was no longer outsourced, and designers worked with manufacturing engineers on modular components and subassemblies. Top management agreed to set aside manufacturing space in the assembly plants for cellular construction of the Helpmate so that the company could respond quickly to demand for particular models. And Helpmate came in at two-thirds the price of the Pioneer 4000.

There was still some debate among Helpmate's product development team members about most likely channels. Some saw it designed only for discount chains and catalog stores, which by 1978 had pretty much eclipsed hardware stores. Others saw the Helpmate as a low-end product for department stores too. In the end, Helpmate was a smash in the discount stores and all but disappeared from department stores.

The Next Generation?

Imagine that Coolidge managers are gathered in 1985 to consider the company's future. Their three-generation map has simplified a great deal of information—information the managers might intuitively understand but could not have looked at so clearly before. Where can they go from here?

Looking at their map, it's clear that Coolidge's product offerings are not appropriately matched to the new environment. They have aimed most of their products at department stores, and now discount chains are growing at a tremendous rate. They had devoted too much attention to figuring out how to leverage products at the high end, when the big battle was shaping up at the low end. Now Coolidge's managers wonder how long it will be before power options and accessories show up on cheaper, sturdier import lines distributed to high-volume outlets.

More growth in the company's manufacturing capabilities is obviously very important now. The map indicates the growing reciprocity between design and manufacturing engineers, owing largely to the initiatives of the younger design group. It would not be hard to imagine a merging of all engineering groups and the use of temporary dedicated development teams at this point. Product life cycles have obviously been shrinking; designers have to think fast now and cooperate across functional lines. To bring out a new line of inexpensive products that are both reliable and varied in options, Coolidge will need automated, flexible manufacturing systems. This development means bringing all parts of the company together—designers with marketing, manufacturing with both. It means, interestingly enough, a need for even clearer, more complete new product development maps.

The finished product development map presented here may appear elementary, but managers who have mapped their products' evolution have experienced substantial payoff in several areas. First, the map can be extremely useful to product development efforts. It helps focus development projects and limit their scope, making them more manageable. The map helps set specifications and targets for individual projects, provides a context for relating concurrent projects to one another, and indicates how the sequence of projects capitalizes on the company's previous investments. These benefits do much to minimize the likelihood of encountering two of the pitfalls we identified at the outset of this article, the moving target and the lack of product distinctiveness.

A second important benefit is the motivation the map provides the various functional groups—all with a stake in effective product development—to develop their own complementary strategies. As illustrated in the Coolidge Corporation example, the product development map raises a number of issues regarding distribution channels, product technology, and manufacturing approaches that must be answered in all parts of the company if the map is to represent the organization's agreed-on direction.

This point brings up the need for "submaps" in each functional area. In the Coolidge case, the first couple of product generations may not have shown the need for a more careful distribution channel map, but by the third the need is painfully clear. Capturing other strategic marketing variables in, say, a price map, a competitive product positioning map, and a customer map would enable the marketing function to identify and present important trends in the marketplace, define targets for future product offerings, and provide guidance for developing and committing sales and marketing resources.

Equally apparent by the third generation is the need for supporting maps in design engineering. A set of design engineering submaps can produce a clearer sense of the mix of engineering talent the company requires, how it should be organized and focused, and the rate at which the company should bring new technologies into future product generations. These maps would not only help managers integrate design resources with product development efforts but would also ensure that they hire and train new employees in a timely and effective manner and that they focus new project tools (such as computer-aided engineering) on pressing product development needs. The key is achieving technical agreement in advance of product development.

Toward the end of the third generation at Coolidge, the map reveals the need for more detailed manufacturing functional maps to bring out issues raised in the "critical skills" box. Such maps would focus on strategic issues relating to manufacturing facilities, vendor relationships, and automation technology.

Again, the development of such functional submaps not only benefits manufacturing but also helps the company maximize the return on new product development resources. The most interesting and useful benefits will come out of debates about what to put in the submaps.

Submaps capture the essence of the functional strategies, and when integrated with the new product development map, serve to tie those functional strategies together and provide both a foundation and a process for achieving a company's business strategy. The whole process facilitates the cross-functional discussion and resolution of strategic issues. How often have well-intentioned functional managers met to discuss their various substrategies only to have those from other functions tune out within the first two minutes, as the discussion becomes too technical, too detailed, or simply too parochial to comprehend?

Mapping provides a process for planning that avoids too much detail (like budgeting) and too much parochialism (like traditional functional strategy sessions). Managers will inevitably develop linkages across the organization by going through the steps of selecting the resources or factors to develop into a map, identifying the key dimensions to capture in the map, reviewing historical data to understand the relationships of those dimensions, and examining what is likely to drive future versions of the map. Functions can share their maps to communicate, refine, and agree on important product strategy choices. It is the sharing of functional capabilities—capabilities applied in a systematic, repetitive fashion to product development opportunities—that will become the company's competitive advantage.

3
Pitfalls in Evaluating Risky Projects

James E. Hodder and Henry E. Riggs

In recent years, the leaders of American companies have been barraged with attacks on their investment policies. Critics accuse American executives of shortsightedness and point out that managers in Japan and Europe often fix their vision on more distant horizons. Here, it is claimed, managers pay too much attention to quarterly earnings reports and not enough to such basic elements of industrial strength as research and development. Some analysts see the root of this problem in the tendency of American companies to rely on discounted cash flow techniques in weighing long-term investments.[1] These critics argue that DCF techniques have inherent weaknesses that make them inappropriate for evaluating projects whose payoffs will come years down the road.

We disagree with the contention that DCF techniques are inappropriate for evaluating long-term or strategic investment proposals. We do believe, however, that companies often misapply or misinterpret DCF techniques. Misuse is particularly serious in evaluating long-term capital investments, such as ambitious R&D projects, that appear to involve high risk.

Misapplication of DCF techniques can certainly contribute to an unwarranted aversion to making long-term investments. However, the problem lies not in the technique but in its misuse. Money has a time value in every economy, and cash is the lifeblood of every business. To evaluate cash flows (costs or revenues) generated in different periods requires a procedure for making comparisons. For evaluating and ranking investment proposals, whether they have short or long lives, and involve capital equipment, R&D, or marketing expenditures, we need techniques that recognize that cash flows occur at different times. Discounting provides a rational and conceptually sound procedure for making such evaluations.

Unfortunately DCF techniques, like computers, can yield impressive-looking but misleading outputs when the inputs are flawed. Managers with biased assumptions may end up with biased conclusions. The fault, however, lies not with the technique but with the analyst. The path to improved capital budgeting requires education in the proper use of rational techniques rather than their rejection out of hand.

In our view, DCF techniques provide valuable information to *assist* management in making sound investment decisions. We emphasize the word assist because it is people, rather than analytical tools, who make decisions. Managers may have many objectives and face many constraints in their decision making. Nevertheless, they need information on the relative financial merits of different options. Properly employed, DCF techniques provide such information. The alternative is to ignore the time value of money and implicitly assume that, for example, a dollar earned ten years from now will have the same value as a dollar today.

DCF procedures, as commonly applied, are subject to three serious pitfalls:

Improper treatment of inflation effects, particularly in long-lived projects.

Excessive risk adjustments, particularly when risk declines in later phases of a project.

Failure to acknowledge how management can reduce project risk by diversification and other responses to future events.

Awareness of these pitfalls should help managers avoid uncritical use of DCF techniques that may lead to poor decisions.

An R&D Project, for Example

Although the comments here apply to a variety of investment proposals, we shall illustrate these three major pitfalls with the analysis of an R&D project. (Exhibit I lists examples of other investment projects that are frequently misevaluated for the reasons described in this article.) Because of their risk characteristics, R&D projects present

Exhibit I.   Long-term risky investments frequently misevaluated

1	A consumer goods company considers test marketing the first of a proposed new family of products.
2	A paper company studies investment in a new processing technique that could revolutionize paper making.
3	A drug company looks at increasing its investment in biomedical research and the pilot plant that will be required if the research is successful.
4	A real estate developer analyzes the first-stage investment in improvements at a greenfield site for industrial-commercial facilities.
5	A financial services firm considers investment in a telecommunications facility that could radically alter the future distribution of its services.
6	A natural resources company evaluates a mineral-rights lease of a site that will require extensive development.

some especially thorny problems. The pronounced uncertainties in these projects affect the analysis of risk in many ways. As a result, R&D projects with acceptable—even exciting—risk/return profiles may fail to meet the payoff criteria that management has established.

Let's look at a typical (hypothetical) project that would be rejected on the basis of the incomplete DCF analysis common in industry today. Then we'll show how a more complete and careful analysis reveals the project to be not only acceptable but highly desirable.

Our project has three distinct phases, as shown in Exhibit II. If the research (Phase 1) is successful, the project moves to market development (Phase 2), after which the resulting product may enjoy a long and profitable period of production and sales. The research and market development phases are periods of investment; returns are forthcoming only during the third period (Phase 3) when the product is sold.

It is important to differentiate between these phases, since each has decidedly different risk characteristics. Market development (Phase 2) will not be undertaken unless the research (Phase 1) is successful; thus, considerable uncertainty disappears before Phase 2 proceeds. Similarly, the sales period (Phase 3) follows only after successful results from research and market development. The information from Phase 2 will refine market projections, and Phase 3 cash flows are relatively low risk. In sum, uncertainty about the project diminishes progressively as we acquire more information.

Exhibit II.   Project description

Phase 1	**Research or product development**
	$ 18 million annual research cost for 2 years
	60 % probability of success
Phase 2	**Market development**
	Undertaken only if product development succeeds
	$ 10 million annual expenditure for 2 years on the development of marketing and the establishment of marketing and distribution channels (net of any revenues earned in test marketing)
Phase 3	**Sales**
	Proceeds only if Phase 1 and Phase 2 verify opportunity
	Production is subcontracted
	The results of Phase 2 (available at the end of year 4) identify the product's market potential as shown below:

Product demand	Product life	Annual net cash inflow	Probability
High	20 years	$ 24 million	.3
Medium	10 years	$ 12 million	.5
Low	Abandon project	None	.2

Note:
For simplicity, we assume that production is subcontracted in Phase 3 and that all cash flows are after tax and occur at year end. This assumption permits us to ignore some potentially complex tax issues involving depreciation and financing strategies. While a radical departure from reality, this assumption allows us to focus on issues of cash flow timing and risk that appear to be less widely understood.

According to the probabilities shown in Exhibit II, the project viewed as a whole (rather than by phases) has the expected-value cash flows shown in Exhibit III and an expected internal rate of return (IRR) slightly over 10%. This appears distinctly unattractive, even ridiculous, when compared with customary rates of return (hurdle rates) of 20% or more for high-risk projects. Given this analysis and results, most managers would almost certainly reject the project unless other strategic reasons dictated the investment.

Many (if not most) U.S. companies, unfortunately, would probably analyze the project in this way, concluding that it is indeed risky and has an expected IRR below normal hurdle rates. The interpretation of these "facts" is far from obvious, however, and requires a deeper

Exhibit III.   Expected cash flows for the project in $ millions

Years	Expected value calculations	
1		−18
2		−18
3	.6 (−10)	= −6
4	.6 (−10)	= −6
5-14	.6 (.3 x 24 + .5 x 12)	=7.92
15-24	.6 (.3 x 24)	=4.32
Expected IRR = 10.1 %		

understanding of DCF calculation procedures. The issue is not which buttons to push on a calculator, but rather the appropriate interpretation of the inputs and consequent output since the DCF procedure is no more than a processing technique. The analysis appears sophisticated with its use of probabilities and discounting, but it is incomplete and seriously misleading.

Adjusting for Inflation

The most obvious shortcoming of the analysis is that it ignores how inflation will affect the various cash flows. At one extreme, they may not be affected at all. On the other hand, the cash flows may adjust directly and completely with inflation, that is, an 8% inflation rate next year will raise cash flows in that and following years by 8%. Most likely, inflation will affect different components of the cash flows in different ways and, when aggregated, the cash flows will adjust partially with inflation. Meaningful interpretation of the calculated IRR requires knowledge of this inflation adjustment pattern.

If complete adjustment were anticipated, the calculated IRR would represent an expected real return. However, comparing such real returns with nominal hurdle rates—including inflation—or nominal investment yields (for example, from government bonds) is not appropriate.[2] Historically, real yields on low-risk investments have averaged less than 5%, and the real yield on short-term U.S. Treasury securities has equalled close to zero. For higher risk investments, a frequent standard of comparison is the return (including dividends) on the

Standard & Poor's "500" stock index. Over a 53-year period (1926–1978) the real rate of return on the S&P "500" averaged 8.5%. While we cannot be certain that history will repeat itself, long-run averages do provide one standard for comparison. Since listed securities represent an alternative investment, projects of comparable risk reasonably should have expected returns at least as great.

Returning to our hypothetical project, if cash flows adjust fully with inflation, the project offers a real return greater than the historic 8.5% of the S&P "500."

Many types of cash flows, of course, do not adjust fully with inflation, and some do not adjust at all. For example, depreciation tax shields, many lease payments, fixed-rate borrowing (like debentures), and multiyear fixed-price purchase or sales contracts do not change with the inflation rate. Consequently, a proper analysis requires an understanding of the inflation adjustment patterns for different cash flow segments.

While American managers' awareness of the impact of inflation on project evaluation has risen in the last decade, even today many of them have at best a cursory understanding of it. Failure to incorporate inflation assumptions in DCF analyses can be particularly troublesome in decentralized companies. Corporate financial officers commonly specify companywide or divisional hurdle rates based on a current (nominal) cost of capital. Furthermore, analysts at the plant or division level often estimate future cash flows (particularly cost savings) based on current experience. Unless those analysts consciously include anticipated inflation, they will underestimate future cash flows and, unfortunately, many good projects may be rejected.

Parenthetically, the converse is unlikely to occur: it is hard to conceive of an analyst using inflated cash flows with real discount or hurdle rates. Also, projects that go forward usually undergo several reviews that are likely to result in some tempering, or lowering, of overly optimistic cash flow assumptions. By contrast, rejected projects are seldom given subsequent reviews that might reveal unrealistically low inflation assumptions.

The mismatch of inflation assumptions regarding cash flows and hurdle rates is generally most pronounced for projects with payoffs years down the road. So long as the inflation rate is positive (even if declining), the gap between projected real cash flows and their nominal equivalents grows with time. For example, suppose that inflation rates for the next three years are expected to be 8, 6, and 4% respectively. Consider an item that sells for $1 now. If its price will increase at the rate of inflation, its nominal price should be $1.08 next year, $1(1.08)(1.06) = $1.14 in two years, and $1(1.08)(1.06)(1.04) = $1.19 in three years. These inflated prices, rather than the current $1 price, should be incorporated into the DCF analysis if discounting is to occur at nominal rather than real interest rates.

The error that arises from the failure to include inflation in cash flow estimates compounds with time as long as inflation is positive. Under these circumstances, distant cash flows, such as those characteristic of research and development investments, have present values that are more seriously understated. It is difficult to know how widespread such errors have been during recent years, but almost surely they explain in part the shift toward shorter lived projects and myopic investment decisions in many businesses.

Avoiding Excessive Risk Adjustments

A second flaw in the original DCF calculations for our hypothetical R&D project is the use of a single discount rate (IRR) for a project in which risk declines dramatically over time. As a result, the project appears less attractive than it really is. If we make appropriate adjustments for the differing risks in different stages of the project, the investment becomes much more attractive.

A typical discount rate (k) used in DCF analyses may be viewed as composed of three parts: a risk-free time value of money (RF), a premium for expected inflation $(E\pi)$, and a risk premium (Δ) that increases with project risk. This relationship can be represented as:

$$1 + k = (1 + RF)(1 + E\pi)(1 + \Delta)$$

For example, a risk-free rate of 3% with 10% expected inflation and a 6% risk premium would imply $1 + k = (1.03)(1.10)(1.06) = 1.20$, or a nominal discount rate of approximately 20%.

Since inflation, as well as project risk and even the risk-free rate (RF), can vary over time, we should permit k to have different values at different times. The subscript t indicates the relevant time period; thus k_t is a function of the RF_t, $E\pi_t$, and Δ_t values for that period. To focus on situations where project risk is expected to change significantly through time, we will use real (deflated) cash flows and real discount rates with RF constant. It is, of course, very important to adjust for expected inflation properly. Without losing sight of that point, let's shift the focus of discussion to risk adjustments by assuming that the inflation adjustments have been executed properly.

Denoting the real (risky) discount rate for period t as r_t, we have:

$$1 + r_t = (1 + RF)(1 + \Delta_t)$$

This differs from k_t simply by the removal of the inflation factor $(1 + E\pi_t)$. Then by definition, the *NPV* of a project with expected real cash flows (CF_t) occurring in two periods is:

$$NPV = \frac{CF_1}{1 + r_1} + \frac{CF_2}{(1 + r_1)(1 + r_2)}$$

$$= \frac{CF_1}{(1 + RF)(1 + \Delta_1)}$$

$$+ \frac{CF_2}{(1 + RF)^2 (1 + \Delta_1)(1 + \Delta_2)}$$

This brings us to a key point. If $\Delta_1 = \Delta_2 = \Delta$, this formula collapses into the familiar form with a single discount rate:

$$NPV = \frac{CF_1}{(1 + RF)(1 + \Delta)} + \frac{CF_2}{(1 + RF)^2 (1 + \Delta)^2}$$

$$= \frac{CF_1}{1 + r} + \frac{CF_2}{(1 + r)^2}$$

In practice, virtually all DCF calculations are performed using a constant discount rate such as r. Indeed, financial calculators are programmed that way. Under what conditions, however, can we assume that $\Delta_1 = \Delta_2$ (even approximately)?

This assumption is reasonable if we anticipate that errors in predicting real cash flows result from a random walk process—that is, predictions one period into the future always entail the same uncertainty. Thus if we were at time 1, each dollar of real cash flow in period 2 would look just as risky as each dollar of CF_1 looks now. However, predicting two periods into the future is more risky; thus CF_2 viewed from the present deserves a larger risk adjustment. Consequently, CF_2 is multiplied by $1/(1 + \Delta)^2$ as opposed to simply $1/(1 + \Delta)$ for CF_1. In more general terms, the risk adjustment factor for a cash flow t period in the future is $1/(1 + \Delta)^t$. The risk adjustment grows geometrically with time.

Using a single risk-adjusted discount rate, therefore, implies an important and somewhat special assumption about the risks associated with future cash flow estimates: such risks increase geometrically with chronological distance from the present. On the infrequent occasions when this assumption is mentioned, it is usually justified on the grounds that the accuracy of our foresight decreases with time. While that argument has merit, consider what can happen when an investment proposal does not fit this pattern.

Recall our R&D project. If the cash flows of Exhibit II are in real terms, the project has an expected real IRR of 10%; but there is a 40% chance of investing $36 million (real, after tax, but undiscounted) during the first two years and receiving nothing. Many decision makers would demand a much higher return than 10% (real or otherwise) to undertake such an investment. If the project proceeds to Phase 3, the cash flows in that phase are considered relatively low risk. The large risk adjustments that were appropriate for early phases are no longer appropriate once we reach Phase 3.

To highlight this point, let's suppose that Phase 3 could be sold if the project successfully proceeds through the first two phases. Given its low risk, potential investors might evaluate Phase 3 with a low discount rate such as 5% (real). Suppose market research reveals a high demand for the product during Phase 3: 20-year life with annual net cash inflows of $24 million. Discounting these flows at 5%, we reach a value at the beginning of Phase 3 (end of year 4) of $299 million. Thus if strong demand develops for the product, it's possible the rights to produce and market it could be sold for a considerable sum. This value depends, however, on the marketing results from Phase 2. Thus we need to check what happens if less favorable demand conditions are revealed in Phase 2. Performing similar calculations for the other possible market conditions, we obtain the values in Exhibit IV.

Even though there is a 20% chance of low demand, the overall expected value of selling Phase 3 is $136 million. Suppose we now recalculate the project's expected IRR assuming such an outright sale of Phase 3 for its expected value: $136 million. Using the 60% probability of Phase 1 success, we calculate the expected cash flows to be those in Exhibit V. Those net expected cash flows are equivalent to an expected IRR of approximately 28%. In other words, the prospect that Phase 3 could be sold as just discussed leads us to revise the overall expected IRR for investing in the project from 10 up to 28%. Since these calculations are in real terms, the project now appears quite attractive.

Pushing this analysis one step further, let's assume the project could also be sold at the end of Phase 1 if the research is successful. That is, the new owner after purchasing the project would pay an estimated

Exhibit IV.   Anticipated Phase 3 values if sold
in $ millions

Demand	Probability	Value of Phase 3 year 4
High	.3	299
Medium	.5	93
Low	.2	0
Expected value =		136

Exhibit V.   Expected cash flows with Phase 3 sale
in $ millions

Year	Outflow	Inflow	Net
1	−18		− 18
2	−18		− 18
3	−10 x .6		− 6
4	−10 x .6	136 x .6	75.6

Exhibit VI.   Expected cash flows for purchaser of
Phase 2   in $ millions

Year	Outflow	Inflow	Net
3	−10		− 10
4	−10	136	126

$10 million per year of Phase 2 costs and receive the Phase 3 value (depending on marketing research results) as shown in Exhibit IV. The purchaser would now encounter the expected cash flows indicated in Exhibit VI.

Clearly this proposition is riskier than just buying Phase 3, since the marketing research results of Phase 2 are not yet known. Suppose a potential purchaser evaluated the cash flows in Exhibit VI using a 20% discount rate (well over twice the historic real return on the S&P "500"). The implied purchase price (present value at the beginning of Phase 2) is slightly over $79 million. But what is the implied return to the first owner—the initial developer of the product who undertakes the risky proposition of investing $18 million for each of two years in research—if a successful project could be sold at the end of two years for $79 million? The expected real return (including the 40% chance of Phase 1 failure) is over 63%—a far cry from our initial estimate.

This analysis illustrates a pitfall in evaluating projects with risk patterns that differ significantly from the simple random walk assumption. In our example, uncertainty is greatest during the first two years. But it is unreasonable to penalize more than 20 years of subsequent cash flows for that risk. To dramatize this point, we have assumed that the project can be sold in its latter phases. Indeed, the project acquires a dramatically high value if Phase 1 succeeds—a point missed by the initial IRR calculation, which implicitly discounted all cash flows at the same rate.

The difficulty with using a single risk-adjusted discount rate (or IRR) is that the analysis blends time discount and risk adjustment factors. Unless project risk follows a simple random walk pattern, this blending is inappropriate. Although this problem is discussed in the academic literature,[3] it is generally ignored in practice. For projects with dramatically different risk phases, the result can be a serious misestimation of project value.

A more appropriate procedure for evaluating such projects is to separate timing and risk adjustments using the concept of certainty equivalent value (CEV). The CEV of a cash flow in a given year is simply its risk-adjusted value in that year. If we converted all future cash flows to CEVs, we could then discount the CEVs to the present using a single risk-free discount rate. With the timing and risk adjustments thus separated, we avoid the possibility of compounding risk adjustments unintentionally.

As a practical matter, attempting to convert each year's cash flow into a CEV can be cumbersome since the CEV for period t may depend on probabilities for cash flows in the previous period $(t-1)$, which in turn depend on probabilities from $t-2$, and so on. In our example, the cash flows in Phase 3 depend on results from Phases 1 and 2. Indeed, we have assumed that management would abandon the project altogether if the research is unsuccessful or market tests indicate low demand.

Although it is important to consider interactions among cash flows in different periods, the analysis of all possible management responses or other contingencies would be extraordinarily complex and unwieldy. Thus we need reasonable approximations. Managers and analysts must exercise judgment regarding which risks and possible actions should be included in the analysis. We recommend that high-risk projects be evaluated as a sequence of distinct risk phases (of perhaps several years each).

In our example, we did not attempt to calculate CEVs for each year in Phase 3. Rather, we estimated a value for the whole phase conditional on the demand level. Similarly, our calculated $79 million value for the project if Phase 1 succeeded is a CEV (at the beginning of year three) for Phases 2 and 3 combined. In both cases, these CEVs are estimates of the project's potential selling price—its market value at the end of years two and four respectively. While the project might be worth more to the company if it retained all phases, the market CEVs represent opportunity costs for retaining Phases 2 and 3 that are useful (and conservative) yardsticks for evaluating the entire project.

Estimating market values for different phases is obviously an imprecise process. Using a single risk-adjusted rate for an entire phase (rather than separate rates or CEVs for each cash flow) produces only an approximation, unless risks within that phase have a random walk pattern. The approximation is reasonable, however, if the discount rate is low and/or the phase covers a fairly short period of time (as in Phases 1 and 2 above). If a phase is both long and risky, analysts should divide it into subphases.

To restate our argument, we recommend segmenting projects into risk phases, then valuing sequentially each phase, working backward from the last. This procedure can be used to determine either an expected IRR on the initial phase (as already illustrated) or an NPV for the project. In general, we prefer calculating NPVs since this avoids technical problems with IRR, including scale ambiguities. Although slightly more complex than a standard expected NPV or IRR calculation, our approach is not difficult per se. It simply entails a short sequence of expected NPV calculations using different interest rates to value different risk phases. When a project's risk pattern differs sub-

Calculating Inflation's Effects

To correctly allow for inflation in a DFC analysis, some analysts include it in the cash flows and use nominal discount rates. If inflation rates are expected to vary, different discount rates can be used for different years in a net present value (NPV) calculation. Such a procedure, however, entails cumbersome calculations. Furthermore, consistency on a companywide basis requires specifying the annual series of discount and inflation rates to be used by analysts. The simple approach is to use a single "average" inflation rate with a single nominal discount rate, but this is not ideal. Although in many cases the distortion associated with this approximation is not serious, the pattern of cash flows and projected inflation affects the size of the distortion.

A preferable procedure is to use deflated cash flows with real discount rates. In this approach, analysts estimate the cash flow in each period, including the increase from inflation applicable to each of its segments (for example, zero for depreciation tax shields). Analysts then deflate the cash flow to present (for example, 1985) dollars using the projected inflation between now and that period. If the cash flow is expected to adjust fully with inflation, the deflation adjustment will exactly cancel the included inflation. If not, the real value of that future cash flow will be altered by the extent to which it does fully adjust with inflation. The series of deflated (real) cash flows can then be discounted using real discount rates. Since the real time value of money appears to be considerably more stable than its nominal counterpart, this second procedure is superior to using a single nominal discount rate.

stantially from the simple random walk assumption, such differences should be recognized and the evaluation procedure modified accordingly. As we have shown, evaluation based on inappropriate analysis can be very misleading.

Considering the Eye of the Beholder

A third major problem in project evaluations is correctly assessing project risk and how managers can influence its nature and level. Here it is important to consider the perspective of the analyst. Risk that seems excessive to an R&D or project manager may appear reasonable to a corporate executive or a shareholder who can diversify the risk by spreading it across other investments. Also, managers can influence the level of risk by future actions that affect the ultimate payoff of a project investment.

Frequently, the major uncertainty in R&D investments is whether the research phase will produce a viable product. From the perspective of financial market theories such as the Capital Asset Pricing Model (CAPM), risks associated with the research phase are apt to be largely diversifiable. Consequently, a public shareholder with a well-diversified securities portfolio will probably voice little or no concern about these risks. Success or failure in the lab is probably correlated weakly (if at all) with broad economic forces or other systematic nondiversifiable factors that affect returns in the stock market as a whole.

The CAPM and related theories stress that a project's total risk normally contains both diversifiable and nondiversifiable components. To the extent shareholders can easily diversify their holdings in the financial markets, they can reduce *their* portion of the project's diversifiable risk to a very small level. Under these circumstances, the shareholders need worry only about the systematic portion of project risk. Thus a financial market approach suggests that the typical R&D project is much less risky from the perspective of a well-diversified public shareholder than it may appear to the individual performing the DCF analysis.

In contrast, managers, creditors, and even suppliers may focus on total risk (including both diversifiable and systematic components) at the company level. These groups have interests that are not easily diversified in the sense that the CAPM assumes. Thus they are concerned about total cash flow variability but at the company (not project) level. Even at the company level, however, the R&D budget may be spread across many projects. A multi-industry company of even moderate size is probably sufficiently diversified to allow large reductions in cash flow variability per dollar of R&D investment. Once again, the risk of a particular project appears lower from a portfolio perspective than from the perspective of an analyst looking only at the project itself.

Most managers are aware of portfolio effects and the arguments regarding shareholder welfare based on financial market models such as the CAPM. Nevertheless, it is understandable that they view a project with over a 50% chance of no payoff (as in our example) as highly risky. Under such circumstances, it is easy to ignore portfolio

Exhibit VII.   Expected cash flows if the project can be abandoned during Phase 1 in $ millions

Year	Expected outflow	Expected inflow	Expected net cash flow
1	−18		−18
2	−18 x .8	79 x .6	33

effects and worry too much about the risk of that particular investment opportunity. This excessive risk aversion is frequently mani-
fested in a too-high discount or hurdle rate, thus compounding the
pitfalls already discussed.

Analysts may also use conservative estimates: overestimates of development time or costs and underestimates of both the magnitude
and duration of subsequent payoffs. Although the tendency toward
excessive conservatism is both inevitable and difficult to overcome,
management needs to be aware of its existence and sensitive to its
consequences. As we said earlier, projects that have been rejected are
seldom reevaluated. It is all too easy for a good project to be lost.

While excessive risk adjustments are certainly not unique to R&D
proposals, the problem may be more severe here because R&D projects
involve large and obvious uncertainties. The key is that these risks are
likely to be highly diversifiable. Failure to recognize this fact represents
a systematic bias against R&D projects.

Managers can also affect the level of risk by influencing the distribution of project payoffs. In our example, there is a 30% chance that
Phase 3 will be worth $299 million. There is not a symmetric chance
of losing $299 million—because the company will abandon the project
if faced with low product demand. The result is an *expected* value for
Phase 3 ($136 million) which is $43 million above the *most likely*
estimate of $93 million. Unfortunately, many project evaluations con-
sider only the most likely cash flow estimates and ignore the asymme-
try or skewness of the payoffs. This practice understates the project's
true value in situations in which future management actions can
improve profits or limit losses.

This problem is more significant for R&D projects than for other
investments because the company has greater flexibility to expand
production for highly successful products and to abandon apparently

unprofitable efforts. Such managerial actions can result in greater returns than estimated originally (larger revenues over a longer period) as well as reduced downside risk.

In our example, suppose progress can be monitored throughout Phase 1, and management has the option to abandon the project at the end of the first year if certain goals are not met. If the probability of research failure is equally divided between years one and two (20% each), the expected IRR from an initial investment in Period 1 research increases from 63% to 83%, with no change in our other assumptions (Exhibit VII shows the relevant cash flows). Clearly management's ability to skew a payoff distribution in the company's favor can have an important influence on a project's desirability.

DCF Analysis in Perspective

How much the misuse of DCF techniques has contributed to the competitive troubles of American companies is a matter of conjecture. It is clear, though, that incomplete analysis can severely penalize investments whose payoffs are both uncertain and far in the future. Given these perils, one might argue that DCF procedures should be avoided or should be accorded little weight in long-term investment decisions. We strongly disagree. It is foolish to ignore or to indict useful analytical tools simply because they might be used incorrectly or incompletely. Rather, analysts and decision makers should recognize potential problems and be careful to ensure that evaluations are performed correctly. Managers cannot treat a DCF evaluation like a black box, looking only at the output. They need to break open the box, examine the assumptions inside, and determine how those assumptions affect the analysis of a project's long-term profitability.

DCF procedures can help evaluate the implications of altered price, cost, or timing assumptions, but managers must first specify the correct assumptions. These procedures can also be used to examine the effects of different capacity expansion or R&D strategies under many scenarios. However, again managers must specify the strategies or scenarios to be examined. In short, discounting is only one step in evaluating alternative investment opportunities. This fact has frequently been lost in the arguments (pro and con) about the use of discounting procedures.

Blaming DCF procedures for short-sightedness, biased perceptions, excessive risk aversion, or other alleged management weaknesses does not address the underlying problems of American industry. However, understanding the pitfalls in the casual use of DCF techniques can both improve the analysis of capital investment projects and place these techniques in a more appropriate perspective.

It is important to remember that managers make decisions. DCF techniques can assist in that process, but they are only tools. Correctly used, these techniques provide a logical and consistent framework for comparing cash flows occurring at different times—an important aspect of virtually every investment project.

Notes

1. See, for example, Robert H. Hayes and David A. Garvin, "Managing as if Tomorrow Mattered," *Harvard Business Review*, May–June 1982, 71.

2. James C. Van Horne, "A Note on Biases in Capital Budgeting Introduced by Inflation," *Journal of Financial and Quantitative Analysis*, January 1971, 653.

3. See, for example, Alexander A. Robichek and Stewart C. Myers, "Conceptual Problems in the Use of Risk-Adjusted Discount Rates," *Journal of Finance*, December 1966, 727.

4
Creating Project Plans to Focus Product Development

Steven C. Wheelwright and Kim B. Clark

The long-term competitiveness of any manufacturing company depends ultimately on the success of its product development capabilities. New product development holds hope for improving market position and financial performance, creating new industry standards and new niche markets, and even renewing the organization. Yet few development projects fully deliver on their early promises. The fact is, much can and does go wrong during development. In some instances, poor leadership or the absence of essential skills is to blame. But often problems arise from the way companies approach the development process. They lack what we call an "aggregate project plan."

Consider the case of a large scientific instruments company we will call PreQuip. In mid-1989, senior management became alarmed about a rash of late product development projects. For some months, the development budget had been rising even as the number of completed projects declined. And many of the projects in the development pipeline no longer seemed to reflect the needs of the market. Management was especially troubled because it had believed its annual business plan provided the guidance that the marketing and engineering departments needed to generate and schedule projects.

To get to the root of the problem, the chief executive first asked senior managers to compile a list of all the current development projects. They discovered that 30 projects were under way—far more than anticipated, and, they suspected, far more than the organization could support. Further analysis revealed that the company had two to three times more development work than it was capable of completing over its three-year development planning horizon (see Exhibit I).

Exhibit I.

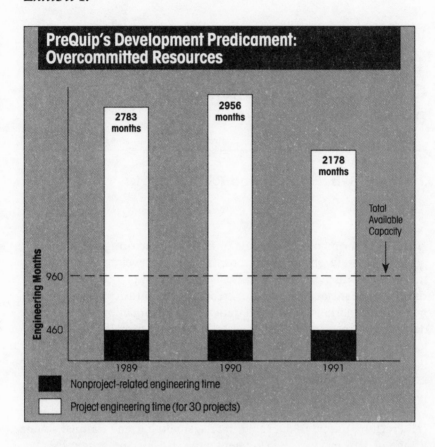

PreQuip's Development Predicament: Overcommitted Resources

With such a strain on resources, delays were inevitable. When a project ran into trouble, engineers from other projects were reassigned or, more commonly, asked to add the crisis project to their already long list of active projects. The more projects they added, the more their productivity dropped. The reshuffling caused delays in other projects, and the effects cascaded. Furthermore, as deadlines slipped and development costs rose, project managers faced pressure to cut corners and compromise quality just to keep their projects moving forward.

The senior management team also discovered that the majority of PreQuip's development resources—primarily engineers and support staff—was not focused on the projects most critical to the business. When questioned, project leaders admitted that the strategic objectives outlined in the annual business plan had little bearing on project selection. Instead, they chose projects because engineers found the technical problems challenging or because customers or the marketing department requested them. PreQuip had no formal process for choosing among development projects. As long as there was money in the budget or the person making the request had sufficient clout, the head of the development department had no option but to accept additional project requests.

Many engineers were not only working on noncritical projects but also spending as much as 50% of their time on nonproject-related work. They responded to requests from manufacturing for help with problems on previous products, from field sales for help with customer problems, from quality assurance for help with reliability problems, and from purchasing for help with qualifying vendors. In addition to spending considerable time fixing problems on previously introduced products, engineers spent many hours in "information" and "update" meetings. In short, they spent too little time developing the right new products, experimenting with new technologies, or addressing new markets.

PreQuip's story is hardly unique. Most organizations we are familiar with spend their time putting out fires and pursuing projects aimed at catching up to their competitors. They have far too many projects going at once and all too often seriously overcommit their development resources. They spend too much time dealing with short-term pressures and not enough time on the strategic mission of product development.

Indeed, in most organizations, management directs all its attention to individual projects—it micromanages project development. But no single project defines a company's future or its market growth over time; the "set" of projects does. Companies need to devote more attention to managing the set and mix of projects. In particular, they should focus on how resources are allocated between projects. Management must plan how the project set evolves over time, which new projects get added when, and what role each project should play in the overall development effort.

The aggregate project plan addresses all of these issues. To create a plan, management categorizes projects based on the amount of resources they consume and on how they will contribute to the company's product line. Then, by mapping the project types, management can see where gaps exist in the development strategy and make more informed decisions about what types of projects to add and when to add them. Sequencing projects carefully, in turn, gives management greater control of resource allocation and utilization. The project map also reveals where development capabilities need to be strong. Over time, companies can focus on adding critical resources and on developing the skills of individual contributors, project leaders, and teams.

Finally, an aggregate plan will enable management to improve the way it manages the development function. Simply adding projects to the active list—a common practice at many companies—endangers the long-term health of the development process. Management needs to create a set of projects that is consistent with the company's development strategies rather than selecting individual projects from a long list of ad hoc proposals. And management must become involved in the development process *before* projects get started, even before they are fully defined. It is not appropriate to give one department—say, engineering or marketing—sole responsibility for initiating all projects because it is usually not in a position to determine every project's strategic worth.

Indeed, most companies—including PreQuip—should start the reformation process by eliminating or postponing the lion's share of their existing projects, eventually supplanting them with a new set of projects that fits the business strategy and the capacity constraints. The aggregate project plan provides a framework for addressing this difficult task.

How to Map Projects

The first step in creating an aggregate project plan is to define and map the different types of development projects; defining projects by type provides useful information about how resources should be allocated. The two dimensions we have found most useful for classifying are the degree of change in the product and the degree of change in the manufacturing process. The greater the change along either dimension, the more resources are needed.

Using this construct, we have divided projects into five types. The first three—derivative, breakthrough, and platform—are commercial development projects. The remaining two categories are research and development, which is the precursor to commercial development, and alliances and partnerships, which can be either commercial or basic research (see Exhibit II).

Each of the five project types requires a unique combination of

Exhibit II.

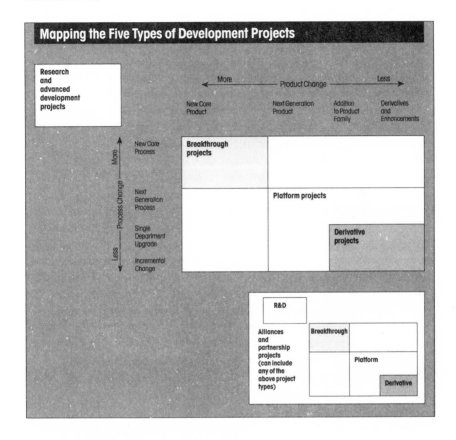

Mapping the Five Types of Development Projects

development resources and management styles. Understanding how the categories differ helps managers predict the distribution of resources accurately and allows for better planning and sequencing of projects over time. Here is a brief description of each category:

Derivative projects range from cost-reduced versions of existing products to add-ons or enhancements for an existing production process. For example, Kodak's wide-angle, single-use 35mm camera, the Stretch, was derived from the no-frills Fun Saver introduced in 1990. Designing the Stretch was primarily a matter of changing the lens.

Development work on derivative projects typically falls into three categories: incremental product changes, say, new packaging or a new feature, with little or no manufacturing process change; incremental process changes, like a lower cost manufacturing process, improved reliability, or a minor change in materials used, with little or no product change; and incremental changes on both dimensions. Because design changes are usually minor, incremental projects typically are more clearly bounded and require substantially fewer development resources than the other categories. And because derivative projects are completed in a few months, ongoing management involvement is minimal.

Breakthrough projects are at the other end of the development spectrum because they involve significant changes to existing products and processes. Successful breakthrough projects establish core products and processes that differ fundamentally from previous generations. Like compact disks and fiber-optics cable, they create a whole new product category that can define a new market.

Because breakthrough products often incorporate revolutionary new technologies or materials, they usually require revolutionary manufacturing processes. Management should give development teams considerable latitude in designing new processes, rather than force them to work with existing plant and equipment, operating techniques, or supplier networks.

Platform projects are in the middle of the development spectrum and are thus harder to define. They entail more product and/or process changes than derivatives do, but they don't introduce the untried new technologies or materials that breakthrough products do. Honda's 1990 Accord line is an example of a new platform in the auto industry: Honda introduced a number of manufacturing process and product changes but no fundamentally new technologies. In the computer market, IBM's PS/2 is a personal computer platform; in consumer products, Procter & Gamble's Liquid Tide is the platform for a whole line of Tide brand products.

Well-planned and well-executed platform products typically offer fundamental improvements in cost, quality, and performance over preceding generations. They introduce improvements across a range of performance dimensions—speed, functionality, size, weight. (Derivatives, on the other hand, usually introduce changes along only one or two dimensions.) Platforms also represent a significantly better system solution for the customer. Because of the extent of changes involved, successful platforms require considerable up-front planning and the involvement of not only engineering but also marketing, manufacturing, and senior management.

Companies target new platforms to meet the needs of a core group of customers but design them for easy modification into derivatives through the addition, substitution, or removal of features. Well-designed platforms also provide a smooth migration path between generations so neither the customer nor the distribution channel is disrupted.

Consider Intel's 80486 microprocessor, the fourth in a series. The 486 introduced a number of performance improvements; it targeted a core customer group—the high-end PC/workstation user—but variations addressed the needs of other users; and with software compatibility between the 386 and the 486, the 486 provided an easy migration path for existing customers. Over the life of the 486 platform, Intel will introduce a host of derivative products, each offering some variation in speed, cost, and performance and each able to leverage the process and product innovations of the original platform.

Platforms offer considerable competitive leverage and the potential to increase market penetration, yet many companies systematically underinvest in them. The reasons vary, but the most common is that management lacks an awareness of the strategic value of platforms and fails to create well-thought-out platform projects. To address the problem, companies should recognize explicitly the need for platforms and develop guidelines for making them a central part of the aggregate project plan.

Research and development is the creation of the know-how and know-why of new materials and technologies that eventually translate into commercial development. Even though R&D lies outside the boundaries of commercial development, we include it here for two reasons: it is the precursor to product and process development; and, in terms of future resource allocation, employees move between basic research and commercial development. Thus R&D projects compete with commercial development projects for resources. Because R&D is a creative, high-risk process, companies have different expectations about results and different strategies for funding and managing it than they do for commercial development. These differences can indeed be great, but a close relationship between R&D and commercial development is essential to ensure an appropriate balance and a smooth conversion of ideas into products.

Alliances and partnerships, which also lie outside the boundaries of the development map, can be formed to pursue any type of project—R&D, breakthrough, platform, or derivative. As such, the amount and type of development resources and management attention needed for projects in this category can vary widely.

Even though partnerships are an integral part of the project development process, many companies fail to include them in their project planning. They often separate the management of partnerships from the rest of the development organization and fail to provide them with enough development resources. Even when the partner company takes full responsibility for a project, the acquiring company must devote in-house resources to monitor the project, capture the new knowledge being created, and prepare for the manufacturing and sales of the new product.

All five development categories are vital for creating a development organization that is responsive to the market. Each type of project plays a different role; each requires different levels and mixes of resources; and each generates very different results. Relying on only one or two categories for the bulk of the development work invariably leads to suboptimal use of resources, an unbalanced product offering, and eventually, a less than competitive market position.

PreQuip's Project Map

Using these five project types, PreQuip set about changing its project mix as the first step toward reforming the product development process. It started by matching its existing project list to the five categories. PreQuip's product line consisted of four kinds of analytic instruments— mass spectrometers, gas and liquid chromatographs, and data handling and processing equipment—that identified and isolated chemical compounds, gases, and liquids. Its customers included scientific laboratories, chemical companies, and oil refineries—users that needed to measure and test accurately the purity of raw materials, intermediate by-products, and finished products.

PreQuip's management asked some very basic questions in its attempt to delineate the categories. What exactly was a breakthrough product? Would a three-dimensional graphics display constitute a breakthrough? How was a platform defined? Was a full-featured mass spectrometer considered a platform? How about a derivative? Was a mass spectrometer with additional software a derivative?

None of these questions was easy to answer. But after much analysis and debate, the management team agreed on the major characteristics for each project type and assigned most of PreQuip's 30 projects to one of the five categories. The map revealed just how uneven the distribution of projects had become—for instance, less than 20% of the company's projects were classified as platforms (see Exhibit III).

Exhibit III.

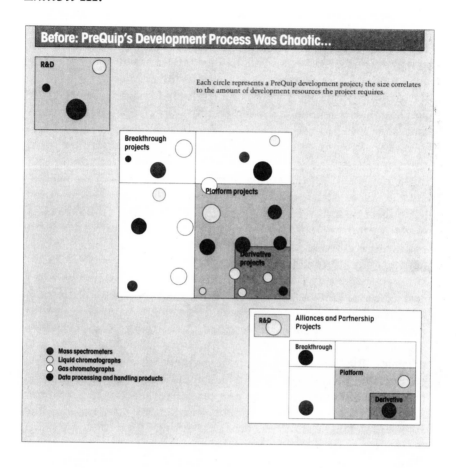

Before: PreQuip's Development Process Was Chaotic...

Each circle represents a PreQuip development project; the size correlates to the amount of development resources the project requires.

Management then turned its attention to those development projects that did not fit into any category. Some projects required substantial resources but did not represent breakthroughs. Others were more complicated than derivative projects but did not fall into PreQuip's definition of platforms. While frustrating, these dilemmas opened managers' eyes to the fact that some projects made little strategic sense. Why spend huge amounts of money developing products that at best would produce only incremental sales? The realization triggered a reexamination of PreQuip's customer needs in *all* product categories.

Consider mass spectrometers, instruments that identify the chemical composition of a compound. PreQuip was a top-of-the-line producer of mass spectrometers, offering a whole series of high-performance equipment with all the latest features but at a significant price premium. While this strategy had worked in the past, it no longer made sense in a maturing market; the evolution of mass spectrometer technology was predictable and well defined, and many competitors were able to offer the same capabilities, often at lower prices.

Increasingly, customers were putting greater emphasis on price in the purchasing decision. Some customers also wanted mass spectrometers that were easier to use and modular so they could be integrated into their own systems. Others demanded units with casings that could withstand harsh industrial environments. Still others required faster operating speeds, additional data storage, or self-diagnostic capabilities.

Taking all these customer requirements into account, PreQuip used the project map to rethink its mass spectrometer line. It envisaged a single platform complemented with a series of derivative products, each with a different set of options and each serving a different customer niche. By combining some new product design ideas—modularity and simplicity—with some features that were currently under development, PreQuip created the concept of the C-101 platform, a low-priced, general-purpose mass spectrometer. In part because of its modularity, the product was designed to be simpler and cheaper to manufacture, which also helped to improve its overall quality and reliability. By adding software and a few new features, PreQuip could easily create derivatives, all of which could be assembled and tested on a single production line. In one case, a variant of the C-101 was planned for the high-end laboratory market. By strengthening the casing and eliminating some features, PreQuip also created a product for the industrial market.

Mapping out the new mass spectrometer line and the three other product lines was not painless. It took a number of months and involved a reconceptualization of the product lines, close management, and considerable customer involvement. To provide additional focus, PreQuip separated the engineering resources into three categories: basic R&D projects; existing products and customers, now a part of the manufacturing organization; and commercial product development.

To determine the number of breakthrough, platform, derivative, and partnered projects that could be sustained at any time, the company first estimated the average number of engineering months for each type of project based on past experience. It then allocated available engineering resources according to its desired mix of projects; about

Exhibit IV.

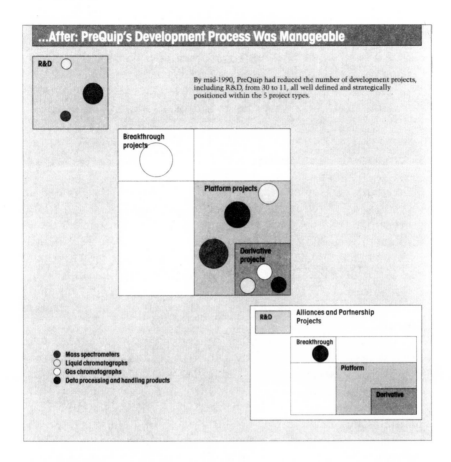

...After: PreQuip's Development Process Was Manageable

R&D

By mid-1990, PreQuip had reduced the number of development projects, including R&D, from 30 to 11, all well defined and strategically positioned within the 5 project types.

Breakthrough projects

Platform projects

Derivative projects

R&D — Alliances and Partnership Projects

Breakthrough

Platform

Derivative

● Mass spectrometers
○ Liquid chromatographs
○ Gas chromatographs
● Data processing and handling products

50% to platform projects, 20% to derivative projects, and 10% each to breakthrough projects and partnerships. PreQuip then selected specific projects, confident that it would not overallocate its resources.

In the end, PreQuip canceled more than two-thirds of its development projects, including some high-profile pet projects of senior managers. When the dust had settled in mid-1990, PreQuip had just eleven projects: three platforms, one breakthrough, three derivatives, one partnership, and three projects in basic R&D (see Exhibit IV).

The changes led to some impressive gains: between 1989 and 1991, PreQuip's commercial development productivity improved by a factor of three. Fewer projects meant more actual work got done, and more work meant more products. To avoid overcommitting resources and to improve productivity further, the company built a "capacity cushion" into its plan. It assigned only 75 full-time-equivalent engineers out of a possible 80 to the 8 commercial development projects. By leaving a small percent of development capacity uncommitted, PreQuip was better prepared to take advantage of unexpected opportunities and to deal with crises when they arose.

Focus on the Platform

PreQuip's development map served as a basis for reallocating resources and for rethinking the mix of projects. Just as important, however, PreQuip no longer thought about projects in isolation; breakthrough projects shaped the new platforms, which defined the derivatives. In all four product lines, platforms played a particularly important role in the development strategy. This was not surprising considering the maturity of PreQuip's industry. For many companies, the more mature the industry, the more important it is to focus on platform projects.

Consider the typical industry life cycle. In the early stages of growth, innovative, dynamic companies gain market position with products that have dramatically superior performance along one or two dimensions. Whether they know it or not, these companies employ a breakthrough-platform strategy. But as the industry develops and the opportunity for breakthrough products decreases—often because the technology is shared more broadly—competitors try to satisfy increasingly sophisticated customers by rapidly making incremental improvements to existing products. Consciously or not, they adopt a strategy based on derivative projects. As happened with PreQuip, this approach ultimately leads to a proliferation of product lines and overcommitment of development resources. The solution lies in developing a few well-designed platform products, on each of which a generation of products can be built.

In the hospital bed industry, for example, companies that design, manufacture, sell, and service electric beds have faced a mature market for years. They are constantly under pressure to help their customers constrain capital expenditures and operating costs. Technologies are stable and many design changes are minor. Each generation of product typically lasts 8 to 12 years, and companies spend most of their time and energy developing derivative products. As a result, companies find themselves with large and unwieldy product lines.

In the 1980s, Hill-Rom, a leading electric-bed manufacturer, sought a new product strategy to help contain costs and maintain market share. Like other bed makers, its product development process was reactive and mired in too many low-payoff derivative projects. The company would design whatever the customer—a single hospital or nursing home—wanted, even if it meant significant commitments of development resources.

The new strategy involved a dramatic shift toward leveraging development and manufacturing resources. Hill-Rom decided to focus on hospitals and largely withdraw from the nursing home segment, as well as limit the product line by developing two new platform products—the Centra and the Century. The Centra was a high-priced product with built-in electronic controls, including communications capabilities. The Century was a simpler, less complex design with fewer features. The products built off each platform shared common parts and manufacturing processes and provided the customer with a number of add-on options. By focusing development efforts on two platforms, Hill-Rom was able to introduce new technologies and new product features into the market faster and more systematically, directly affecting patient recovery and hospital staff productivity. This strategy led to a less chaotic development cycle as well as lower unit cost, higher product quality, and more satisfied customers.

For companies that must react to constant changes in fashion and consumer tastes, a different relationship between platform and derivative projects makes sense. For example, Sony has pioneered its "hyper-variety" strategy in developing the Walkman: it directs the bulk of its Walkman development efforts at creating derivatives, enhancements, hybrids, and line extensions that offer something tailored to every niche, distribution channel, and competitor's product. As a result, in 1990, Sony dominated the personal audio system market with over 200 models based on just three platforms.

Platforms are critical to any product development effort, but there is no one ideal mix of projects that fits all companies. Every company must pursue the projects that match its opportunities, business strategy, and available resources. Of course, the mix evolves over time as projects move out of development into production, as business strategies change, as new markets emerge, and as resources are enhanced.

Management needs to revisit the project mix on a regular basis—in some cases every six months, in others, every year or so.

Steady Stream Sequencing: PreQuip Plans Future Development

Periodically evaluating the product mix keeps development activities on the right track. Companies must decide how to sequence projects over time, how the set of projects should evolve with the business strategy, and how to build development capabilities through such projects. The decisions about changing the mix are neither easy nor straightforward. Without an aggregate project plan, most companies cannot even begin to formulate a strategy for making those decisions.

PreQuip was no different. Before adopting an aggregate project plan, the company had no concept of project mix and no understanding of sequencing. Whenever someone with authority had an idea worth pursuing, the development department added the project to its active list. With the evolution of a project plan, PreQuip developed an initial mix and elevated the sequencing decision to a strategic responsibility of senior management. Management scheduled projects at evenly spaced intervals to ensure a "steady stream" of development projects (see Exhibit V).

A representative example of PreQuip's new strategy for sequencing projects is its new mass spectrometer, or C series. Introduced into the development cycle in late-1989, the C-101 was the first platform conceived as a system built around the new modular design. Aimed at the middle to upper end of the market, it was a versatile, modular unit for the laboratory that incorporated many of the existing electromechanical features into the new software. The C-101 was scheduled to enter manufacturing prototyping in the third quarter of 1990.

PreQuip positioned the C-1/X, the first derivative of the C-101, for the industrial market. It had a rugged casing designed for extreme environments and fewer software features than the C-101. It entered the development process about the time the C-101 moved into manufacturing prototyping and was staffed initially with two designers whose activities on the C-101 were drawing to a close.

Very similar to the C-1/X was the C-1/Z, a unit designed for the European market; the C-1/X team was expanded to work on both the

Exhibit V.

PreQuip's Project Sequence

Project Type	Development Resources Committed at Mid-1990 (% of Total Engineering Time)	Project Description	Project Number	Sequencing 1990 — 1991
R&D	(Separate)	Advanced pump Electronic sensors Software	RD-1 RD-2 RD-3	
Breakthrough	12.5%	Fully automated self-diagnostic system for gas chromatograph	BX-3	
Platform	52.5	Liquid chromatograph Gas chromatograph Mass spectrometer Data processing and handling equipment	A series B series C series D series	A-502, B-502 C-101, C-201 DX-52, DX-82
Derivative	18.75	Liquid chromatograph Gas chromatograph Mass spectrometer Data processing and handling equipment	A series B series C series D series	A-311, A-22, A-321, B-22, B-32, A-502X C-1/X, C-1/Z, C-101X D-333, D-433
Partnership	10.0	Medical/chemical diagnostic system	VMH	

C-1/X and the C-1/Z. The C-1/Z had some unique software and a different display and packaging but the same modular design. Pre-Quip's marketing department scheduled the C-101 to be introduced about 6 months before the C-1/X and the C-1/Z, thus permitting the company to reach a number of markets quickly with new products.

To leverage accumulated knowledge and experience, senior management assigned the team that worked on the C-1/X and the C-1/Z to the C-201 project, the next-generation spectrometer scheduled to replace the C-101. It too was of a modular design but with more computer power and greater software functionality. The C-201 also incorporated a number of manufacturing process improvements gleaned from manufacturing the C-101.

To provide a smooth market transition from the C-101 to the C-201, management assigned the remainder of the C-101 team to develop the C-101X, a follow-on derivative project. The C-101X was positioned as an improvement over the C-101 to attract customers who were in the market for a low-end mass spectrometer but were unwilling to settle for the aging technology of the C-101. Just as important, the project was an ideal way to gather market data that could be used to develop the C-201.

PreQuip applied this same strategy across the other three product categories. Every other year it planned a new platform, followed by two or three derivatives spaced at appropriate intervals. Typically, when a team finished work on a platform, management assigned part of the team to derivative projects and part to other projects. A year or so later, a new team would form to work on the next platform, with some members having worked on the preceding generation and others not. This steady stream sequencing strategy worked to improve the company's overall market position while encouraging knowledge transfer and more rapid, systematic resource development.

An Alternative: Secondary Wave Planning

While the steady stream approach served PreQuip well, companies in different industries might consider alternative strategies. For instance, a "secondary wave" strategy may be more appropriate for companies that, like Hill-Rom, have multiple product lines, each with their own base platforms but with more time between succeeding generations of a particular platform.

The strategy works like this. A development team begins work on a next-generation platform. Once the company completes that project, the key people from the team start work on another platform for a different product family. Management leaves the recently introduced platform on the market for a couple of years with few derivatives introduced. As that platform begins to age and competitors' newer platforms challenge it, the company refocuses development resources on a set of derivatives in order to strengthen and extend the viability of the product line's existing platform. The wave of derivative projects extends the platform life and upgrades product offerings, but it also provides experience and feedback to the people working on the product line and prepares them for the next-generation platform development. They receive feedback from the market on the previous platform, information on competitors' platform offerings, and information on emerging market needs. Key people then bring that information together to define the next platform and the cycle begins again, built around a team, many of whose members have just completed the wave of derivative products.

A variation on the secondary wave strategy, one used with considerable success by Kodak, involves compressing the time between market introduction of major platforms. Rather than going off to work on another product family's platform following one platform's introduction, the majority of the development team goes to work immediately on a set of derivative products. This requires a more compressed and careful assessment of the market's response to the just-introduced platform and much shorter feedback loops regarding competitors' products. If done right, however, companies can build momentum and capture significant incremental market share. Once the flurry of derivative products has passed, the team goes to work on the next-generation platform project for the same product family.

Before 1987, Kodak conducted a series of advanced development projects to explore alternative single-use 35mm cameras—a roll of film packaged in an inexpensive camera. Once used, the film is processed and the camera discarded or recycled. During 1987, a group of Kodak development engineers worked on the first platform project which resulted in the market introduction and volume production of the Fling 35mm camera in January 1988. (The product was later renamed the Fun Saver.) As the platform neared completion, management reassigned the front-end development staff to two derivative projects: the Stretch, a panoramic, double-wide image version of the Fling, and the Weekend, a waterproof version.

By the end of 1988, Kodak had introduced both derivative cameras and was shipping them in volume. True to the definition of a derivative, both the Stretch and the Weekend took far fewer development resources and far less time than the Fling. They also required less new tooling and process engineering since they leveraged the existing automation and manufacturing process. The development team then went to work on the next-generation platform product—a Fun Saver with a built-in flash.

No matter which strategy a company uses to plan its platform-derivative mix—steady stream or secondary wave—it must have well-defined platforms. The most advanced companies further improve their competitive position by speeding up the rate at which they introduce new platforms. Indeed, in a number of industries we've studied, the companies that introduced new platforms at the fastest rate were usually able to capture the greatest market share over time.

In the auto industry, for example, different companies follow quite different sequencing schedules, with markedly different results. According to data collected in the late 1980s, European car companies changed the platform for a given product, on average, every 12 years, U.S. companies every 8 years, and Japanese companies every 4 years. A number of factors explain the differences in platform development cycles—historical and cultural differences, longer development lead times, and differences in development productivity.[1]

In both Europe and the United States, the engineering hours and tooling costs of new products were much higher than in Japan. This translated into lower development costs for Japanese car makers, which allowed faster payback and shorter economic lives for all models. As a consequence, the Japanese could profitably conduct more projects and make more frequent and more extensive changes than both their European and U.S. competitors and thus were better positioned to satisfy customers' needs and capture market share.

The Long-Term Goal: Building Critical Capabilities

Possibly the greatest value of an aggregate project plan over the long-term is its ability to shape and build development capabilities, both individual and organizational. It provides a vehicle for training development engineers, marketers, and manufacturing people in the different skill sets needed by the company. For instance, some less experienced engineers initially may be better suited to work on derivative projects, while others might have technical skills more suited for breakthrough projects. The aggregate project plan lets companies play to employees' strengths and broaden their careers and abilities over time.

Thinking about skill development in terms of the aggregate project plan is most important for developing competent team leaders. Take, for instance, an engineer with five years of experience moving to become a project leader. Management might assign her to lead a derivative project first. It is an ideal training ground because derivative projects are the best defined, the least complex, and usually the shortest in duration of all project types. After the project is completed successfully, she might get promoted to lead a larger derivative project and then a platform project. And if she distinguishes herself there and has the other required skills, she might be given the opportunity to work on a breakthrough project.

In addition to creating a formal career path within the sphere of development activities, companies should also focus on moving key engineers and other development participants between advanced research and commercial development. This is necessary to keep the transfer of technology fresh and creative and to reward engineers who keep their R&D efforts focused on commercial developments.

Honda is one company that delineates clearly between advanced research and product development—the two kinds of projects are managed and organized differently and are approached with very different expectations. Development engineers tend to have broader skills, while researchers' are usually more specialized. However, Honda encourages its engineers to move from one type of project to another if they demonstrate an idea that management believes may result in a commercially viable innovation. For example, Honda's new lean-burning engine, introduced in the 1992 Civic, began as an advanced research project headed by Hideyo Miyano. As the project moved from research to commercial development, Miyano moved too, playing the role of project champion throughout the entire development process.

Besides improving people's skills, the aggregate project plan can be used to identify weaknesses in capabilities, improve development processes, and incorporate new tools and techniques into the development environment. The project plan helps identify where companies need to make changes and how those changes are connected to product and process development.

As PreQuip developed an aggregate project plan, for example, it identified a number of gaps in its capabilities. In the case of the mass spectrometer, the demand for more software functionality meant Pre-

---

Eight Steps of an Aggregate Project Plan

1. Define project types as either breakthrough, platform, derivative, R&D, or partnered projects.
2. Identify existing projects and classify by project type.
3. Estimate the average time and resources needed for each project type based on past experience.
4. Identify existing resource capacity.
5. Determine the desired mix of projects.
6. Estimate the number of projects that existing resources can support.
7. Decide which specific projects to pursue.
8. Work to improve development capabilities.

Quip had to develop an expertise in software development. And with an emphasis on cost, modularity, and reliability, PreQuip also had to focus on improving its industrial design skills.

As part of its strategy to improve design skills, the company introduced a new computer-aided design system into its engineering department, using the aggregate project plan as its guide. Management knew that one of the platform project teams was particularly adept with computer applications, so it chose that project as the pilot for the new CAD system. Over the life of the project, the team's proficiency with the new system grew. When the project ended, management dispersed team members to other projects so they could train other engineers in using the new CAD system.

As PreQuip discovered, developing an aggregate project plan involves a relatively simple and straightforward procedure. But carrying it out—moving from a poorly managed collection of ad hoc projects to a robust set that matches and reinforces the business strategy—requires hard choices and discipline.

At all the companies we have studied, the difficulty of those choices makes imperative strong leadership and early involvement from senior management. Without management's active participation and direction, organizations find it next to impossible to kill or postpone projects and to resist the short-term pressures that drive them to spend most of their time and resources fighting fires.

Getting to an aggregate project plan is not easy, but working through the process is a crucial part of creating a sustainable development strategy. Indeed, while the specific plan is extremely important, the planning process itself is even more so. The plan will change as events unfold and managers make adjustments. But choosing the mix, determining the number of projects the resources can support, defining the sequence, and picking the right projects raise crucial questions about how product and process development ought to be linked to the company's competitive opportunities. Creating an aggregate project plan gives direction and clarity to the overall development effort and helps lay the foundation for outstanding performance.

Note

1. Based on research by Kim B. Clark and Takahiro Fujimoto. See their article, "The Power of Product Integrity," *Harvard Business Review*, November–December 1990, 107.

PART
IV

Building
High-Performance Teams

1
The Discipline of Teams

Jon R. Katzenbach and Douglas K. Smith

Early in the 1980s, Bill Greenwood and a small band of rebel rail-roaders took on most of the top management of Burlington Northern and created a multibillion-dollar business in "piggybacking" rail services despite widespread resistance, even resentment, within the company. The Medical Products Group at Hewlett-Packard owes most of its leading performance to the remarkable efforts of Dean Morton, Lew Platt, Ben Holmes, Dick Alberting, and a handful of their colleagues who revitalized a health care business that most others had written off. At Knight-Ridder, Jim Batten's "customer obsession" vision took root at the *Tallahassee Democrat* when 14 frontline enthusiasts turned a charter to eliminate errors into a mission of major change and took the entire paper along with them.

Such are the stories and the work of teams—real teams that perform, not amorphous groups that we call teams because we think that the label is motivating and energizing. The difference between teams that perform and other groups that don't is a subject to which most of us pay far too little attention. Part of the problem is that *team* is a word and concept so familiar to everyone.

Or at least that's what we thought when we set out to do research for our book *The Wisdom of Teams*. We wanted to discover what differentiates various levels of team performance, where and how teams work best, and what top management can do to enhance their effectiveness. We talked with hundreds of people on more than 50 different teams in 30 companies and beyond, from Motorola and Hewlett-Packard to Operation Desert Storm and the Girl Scouts.

We found that there is a basic discipline that makes teams work. We

---

Not All Groups Are Teams: How to Tell the Difference

Working Group

- Strong, clearly focused leader
- Individual accountability
- The group's purpose is the same as the broader organizational mission
- Individual work-products
- Runs efficient meetings
- Measures its effectiveness indirectly by its influence on others (e.g., financial performance of the business)
- Discusses, decides, and delegates

Team

- Shared leadership roles
- Individual and mutual accountability
- Specific team purpose that the team itself delivers
- Collective work-products
- Encourages open-ended discussion and active problem-solving meetings
- Measures performance directly by assessing collective work-products
- Discusses, decides, and does real work together

---

also found that teams and good performance are inseparable; you cannot have one without the other. But people use the word *team* so loosely that it gets in the way of learning and applying the discipline that leads to good performance. For managers to make better decisions about whether, when, or how to encourage and use teams, it is important to be more precise about what a team is and what it isn't.

Most executives advocate teamwork. And they should. Teamwork represents a set of values that encourage listening and responding constructively to views expressed by others, giving others the benefit of the doubt, providing support, and recognizing the interests and achievements of others. Such values help teams perform, and they also promote individual performance as well as the performance of an entire organization. But teamwork values by themselves are not exclusive to teams, nor are they enough to ensure team performance.

Nor is a team just any group working together. Committees, councils, and task forces are not necessarily teams. Groups do not become teams simply because that is what someone calls them. The entire work force of any large and complex organization is *never* a team, but think about how often that platitude is offered up.

To understand how teams deliver extra performance, we must distinguish between teams and other forms of working groups. That distinction turns on performance results. A working group's performance is a function of what its members do as individuals. A team's performance includes both individual results and what we call "collective work-products." A collective work-product is what two or more members must work on together, such as interviews, surveys, or experiments. Whatever it is, a collective work-product reflects the joint, real contribution of team members.

Working groups are both prevalent and effective in large organizations where individual accountability is most important. The best working groups come together to share information, perspectives, and insights; to make decisions that help each person do his or her job better; and to reinforce individual performance standards. But the focus is always on individual goals and accountabilities. Working-group members don't take responsibility for results other than their own. Nor do they try to develop incremental performance contributions requiring the combined work of two or more members.

Teams differ fundamentally from working groups because they require both individual and mutual accountability. Teams rely on more than group discussion, debate, and decision; on more than sharing information and best practice performance standards. Teams produce discrete work-products through the joint contributions of their members. This is what makes possible performance levels greater than the sum of all the individual bests of team members. Simply stated, a team is more than the sum of its parts.

The first step in developing a disciplined approach to team management is to think about teams as discrete units of performance and not just as positive sets of values. Having observed and worked with scores of teams in action, both successes and failures, we offer the following. Think of it as a working definition or, better still, an essential discipline that real teams share.

A team is a small number of people with complementary skills who are committed to a common purpose, set of performance goals, and approach for which they hold themselves mutually accountable.

The essence of a team is common commitment. Without it, groups perform as individuals; with it, they become a powerful unit of collective performance. This kind of commitment requires a purpose in which team members can believe. Whether the purpose is to "transform the contributions of suppliers into the satisfaction of customers," to "make our company one we can be proud of again," or to "prove that all children can learn," credible team purposes have an element related to winning, being first, revolutionizing, or being on the cutting edge.

Teams develop direction, momentum, and commitment by working to shape a meaningful purpose. Building ownership and commitment to team purpose, however, is not incompatible with taking initial direction from outside the team. The often-asserted assumption that a team cannot "own" its purpose unless management leaves it alone actually confuses more potential teams than it helps. In fact, it is the exceptional case—for example, entrepreneurial situations—when a team creates a purpose entirely on its own.

Most successful teams shape their purposes in response to a demand or opportunity put in their path, usually by higher management. This helps teams get started by broadly framing the company's performance expectation. Management is responsible for clarifying the charter, rationale, and performance challenge for the team, but management must also leave enough flexibility for the team to develop commitment around its own spin on that purpose, set of specific goals, timing, and approach.

The best teams invest a tremendous amount of time and effort exploring, shaping, and agreeing on a purpose that belongs to them both collectively and individually. This "purposing" activity continues throughout the life of the team. In contrast, failed teams rarely develop a common purpose. For whatever reason—an insufficient focus on performance, lack of effort, poor leadership—they do not coalesce around a challenging aspiration.

The best teams also translate their common purpose into specific performance goals, such as reducing the reject rate from suppliers by 50% or increasing the math scores of graduates from 40% to 95%. Indeed, if a team fails to establish specific performance goals or if those goals do not relate directly to the team's overall purpose, team members become confused, pull apart, and revert to mediocre performance. By contrast, when purposes and goals build on one another and are combined with team commitment, they become a powerful engine of performance.

Transforming broad directives into specific and measurable performance goals is the surest first step for a team trying to shape a purpose meaningful to its members. Specific goals, such as getting a new product to market in less than half the normal time, responding to all customers within 24 hours, or achieving a zero-defect rate while simultaneously cutting costs by 40%, all provide firm footholds for teams. There are several reasons:

Specific team performance goals help to define a set of work-products that are different both from an organizationwide mission and from individual job objectives. As a result, such work-products require the collective effort of team members to make something specific happen that, in and of itself, adds real value to results. By contrast, simply gathering from time to time to make decisions will not sustain team performance.

The specificity of performance objectives facilitates clear communication and constructive conflict within the team. When a plant-level team, for example, sets a goal of reducing average machine changeover time to two hours, the clarity of the goal forces the team to concentrate on what it would take either to achieve or to reconsider the goal. When such goals are clear, discussions can focus on how to pursue them or whether to change them; when goals are ambiguous or nonexistent, such discussions are much less productive.

The attainability of specific goals helps teams maintain their focus on getting results. A product-development team at Eli Lilly's Peripheral Systems Division set definite yardsticks for the market introduction of an ultrasonic probe to help doctors locate deep veins and arteries. The probe had to have an audible signal through a specified depth of tissue, be capable of being manufactured at a rate of 100 per day, and have a unit cost less than a preestablished amount. Because the team could measure its progress against each of these specific objectives, the team knew throughout the development process where it stood. Either it had achieved its goals or not.

As Outward Bound and other team-building programs illustrate, specific objectives have a leveling effect conducive to team behavior. When a small group of people challenge themselves to get over a wall or to reduce cycle time by 50%, their respective titles, perks, and other stripes fade into the background. The teams that succeed evaluate what and how each individual can best contribute to the team's goal and, more important, do so in terms of the performance objective itself rather than a person's status or personality.

Specific goals allow a team to achieve small wins as it pursues its broader purpose. These small wins are invaluable to building commitment and overcoming the inevitable obstacles that get in the way of a long-term purpose. For example, the Knight-Ridder team mentioned at the outset turned a narrow goal to eliminate errors into a compelling customer-service purpose.

Performance goals are compelling. They are symbols of accomplishment that motivate and energize. They challenge the people on a team to commit themselves, as a team, to make a difference. Drama, urgency, and a healthy fear of failure combine to drive teams who have their collective eye on an attainable, but challenging, goal. Nobody but the team can make it happen. It is their challenge.

The combination of purpose and specific goals is essential to performance. Each depends on the other to remain relevant and vital. Clear performance goals help a team keep track of progress and hold itself accountable; the broader, even nobler, aspirations in a team's purpose supply both meaning and emotional energy.

Virtually all effective teams we have met, read or heard about, or been members of have ranged between 2 and 25 people. For example, the Burlington Northern "piggybacking" team had 7 members, the Knight-Ridder newspaper team, 14. The majority of them have numbered less than 10. Small size is admittedly more of a pragmatic guide than an absolute necessity for success. A large number of people, say 50 or more, can theoretically become a team. But groups of such size are more likely to break into subteams rather than function as a single unit.

Why? Large numbers of people have trouble interacting constructively as a group, much less doing real work together. Ten people are far more likely than fifty are to work through their individual, functional, and hierarchical differences toward a common plan and to hold themselves jointly accountable for the results.

Large groups also face logistical issues, such as finding enough physical space and time to meet. And they confront more complex constraints, like crowd or herd behaviors, which prevent the intense sharing of viewpoints needed to build a team. As a result, when they try to develop a common purpose, they usually produce only superficial "missions" and well-meaning intentions that cannot be translated into concrete objectives. They tend fairly quickly to reach a point when meetings become a chore, a clear sign that most of the people in the group are uncertain why they have gathered, beyond some notion of getting along better. Anyone who has been through one of these exercises knows how frustrating it can be. This kind of failure tends to foster cynicism,which gets in the way of future team efforts.

In addition to finding the right size, teams must develop the right mix of skills, that is, each of the complementary skills necessary to do the team's job. As obvious as it sounds, it is a common failing in potential teams. Skill requirements fall into three fairly self-evident categories:

Technical or functional expertise. It would make little sense for a group of doctors to litigate an employment discrimination case in a court of law. Yet teams of doctors and lawyers often try medical malpractice or personal injury cases. Similarly, product-development groups that include only marketers or engineers are less likely to succeed than those with the complementary skills of both.

Problem-solving and decision-making skills. Teams must be able to identify the problems and opportunities they face, evaluate the options they have for moving forward, and then make necessary trade-offs and decisions about how to proceed. Most teams need some members with these skills to begin with, although many will develop them best on the job.

Interpersonal skills. Common understanding and purpose cannot arise without effective communication and constructive conflict, which in turn depend on interpersonal skills. These include risk taking, helpful criticism, objectivity, active listening, giving the benefit of the doubt, and recognizing the interests and achievements of others.

Obviously, a team cannot get started without some minimum complement of skills, especially technical and functional ones. Still, think about how often you've been part of a team whose members were chosen primarily on the basis of personal compatibility or formal position in the organization, and in which the skill mix of its members wasn't given much thought.

It is equally common to overemphasize skills in team selection. Yet in all the successful teams we've encountered, not one had all the needed skills at the outset. The Burlington Northern team, for example, initially had no members who were skilled marketers despite the fact that their performance challenge was a marketing one. In fact, we discovered that teams are powerful vehicles for developing the skills needed to meet the team's performance challenge. Accordingly, team member selection ought to ride as much on skill potential as on skills already proven.

Effective teams develop strong commitment to a common approach, that is, to how they will work together to accomplish their purpose. Team members must agree on who will do particular jobs, how schedules will be set and adhered to, what skills need to be developed, how continuing membership in the team is to be earned, and how the group will make and modify decisions. This element of commitment is as important to team performance as is the team's commitment to its purpose and goals.

Building Team Performance

Although there is no guaranteed how-to recipe for building team performance, we observed a number of approaches shared by many successful teams.

Establish urgency, demanding performance standards, and direction. All team members need to believe the team has urgent and worthwhile purposes, and they want to know what the expectations are. Indeed, the more urgent and meaningful the rationale, the more likely it is that the team will live up to its performance potential, as was the case for a customer-service team that was told that further growth for the entire company would be impossible without major improvements in that area. Teams work best in a compelling context. That is why companies with strong performance ethics usually form teams readily.

Select members for skill and skill potential, not personality. No team succeeds without all the skills needed to meet its purpose and performance goals. Yet most teams figure out the skills they will need after they are formed. The wise manager will choose people both for their existing skills and their potential to improve existing skills and learn new ones.

Pay particular attention to first meetings and actions. Initial impressions always mean a great deal. When potential teams first gather, everyone monitors the signals given by others to confirm, suspend, or dispel assumptions and concerns. They pay particular attention to those in authority: the team leader and any executives who set up, oversee, or otherwise influence the team. And, as always, what such leaders do is more important than what they say. If a senior executive leaves the team kickoff to take a phone call ten minutes after the session has begun and he never returns, people get the message.

Set some clear rules of behavior. All effective teams develop rules of conduct at the outset to help them achieve their purpose and performance goals. The most critical initial rules pertain to attendance (for example, "no interruptions to take phone calls"), discussion ("no sacred cows"), confidentiality ("the only things to leave this room are what we agree on"), analytic approach ("facts are friendly"), end-product orientation ("everyone gets assignments and does them"), constructive confrontation ("no finger pointing"), and, often the most important, contributions ("everyone does real work").

Set and seize upon a few immediate performance-oriented tasks and goals. Most effective teams trace their advancement to key performance-oriented events. Such events can be set in motion by immediately establishing a few challenging goals that can be reached early on. There is no such thing as a real team without performance results, so the sooner such results occur, the sooner the team congeals.

Challenge the group regularly with fresh facts and information. New information causes a team to redefine and enrich its understanding of the performance challenge, thereby helping the team shape a common purpose, set clearer goals, and improve its common approach. A plant quality improvement team knew the cost of poor quality was high, but it wasn't until they researched the different types of defects and put a price tag on each one that they knew where to go next. Conversely, teams err when they assume that all the information needed exists in the collective experience and knowledge of their members.

Spend lots of time together. Common sense tells us that team members must spend a lot of time together, scheduled and unscheduled, especially in the beginning. Indeed, creative insights as well as personal bonding require impromptu and casual interactions just as much as analyzing spreadsheets and interviewing customers. Busy executives and managers too often intentionally minimize the time they spend together. The successful teams we've observed all gave themselves the time to learn to be a team. This time need not always be spent together physically; electronic, fax, and phone time can also count as time spent together.

Exploit the power of positive feedback, recognition, and reward. Positive reinforcement works as well in a team context as elsewhere. "Giving out gold stars" helps to shape new behaviors critical to team performance. If people in the group, for example, are alert to a shy person's initial efforts to speak up and contribute, they can give the honest positive reinforcement that encourages continued contributions. There are many ways to recognize and reward team performance beyond direct compensation, from having a senior executive speak directly to the team about the urgency of its mission to using awards to recognize contributions. Ultimately, however, the satisfaction shared by a team in its own performance becomes the most cherished reward.

Agreeing on the specifics of work and how they fit together to integrate individual skills and advance team performance lies at the heart of shaping a common approach. It is perhaps self-evident that an approach that delegates all the real work to a few members (or staff outsiders), and thus relies on reviews and meetings for its only "work together" aspects, cannot sustain a real team. Every member of a successful team does equivalent amounts of real work; all members, including the team leader, contribute in concrete ways to the team's work-product. This is a very important element of the emotional logic that drives team performance.

When individuals approach a team situation, especially in a business setting, each has preexisting job assignments as well as strengths and weaknesses reflecting a variety of backgrounds, talents, personalities, and prejudices. Only through the mutual discovery and understanding of how to apply all its human resources to a common purpose can a team develop and agree on the best approach to achieve its goals. At the heart of such long and, at times, difficult interactions lies a commitment-building process in which the team candidly explores who is best suited to each task as well as how individual roles will come together. In effect, the team establishes a social contract among members that relates to their purpose and guides and obligates how they must work together.

No group ever becomes a team until it can hold itself accountable as a team. Like common purpose and approach, mutual accountability is a stiff test. Think, for example, about the subtle but critical difference between "the boss holds me accountable" and "we hold ourselves accountable." The first case can lead to the second; but without the second, there can be no team.

Companies like Hewlett-Packard and Motorola have an ingrained performance ethic that enables teams to form "organically" whenever there is a clear performance challenge requiring collective rather than individual effort. In these companies, the factor of mutual accountability is commonplace. "Being in the boat together" is how their performance game is played.

At its core, team accountability is about the sincere promises we make to ourselves and others, promises that underpin two critical aspects of effective teams: commitment and trust. Most of us enter a potential team situation cautiously because ingrained individualism and experience discourage us from putting our fates in the hands of others or accepting responsibility for others. Teams do not succeed by ignoring or wishing away such behavior.

Mutual accountability cannot be coerced any more than people can be made to trust one another. But when a team shares a common purpose, goals, and approach, mutual accountability grows as a natural counterpart. Accountability arises from and reinforces the time, energy, and action invested in figuring out what the team is trying to accomplish and how best to get it done.

When people work together toward a common objective, trust and commitment follow. Consequently, teams enjoying a strong common purpose and approach inevitably hold themselves responsible, both as individuals and as a team, for the team's performance. This sense of mutual accountability also produces the rich rewards of mutual achievement in which all members share. What we heard over and over from members of effective teams is that they found the experience energizing and motivating in ways that their "normal" jobs never could match.

On the other hand, groups established primarily for the sake of becoming a team or for job enhancement, communication, organizational effectiveness, or excellence rarely become effective teams, as demonstrated by the bad feelings left in many companies after experimenting with quality circles that never translated "quality" into specific goals. Only when appropriate performance goals are set does the process of discussing the goals and the approaches to them give team members a clearer and clearer choice: they can disagree with a goal and the path that the team selects and, in effect, opt out, or they can pitch in and become accountable with and to their teammates.

The discipline of teams we've outlined is critical to the success of all teams. Yet it is also useful to go one step further. Most teams can be classified in one of three ways: teams that recommend things, teams that make or do things, and teams that run things. In our experience, each type faces a characteristic set of challenges.

TEAMS THAT RECOMMEND THINGS. These teams include task forces, project groups, and audit, quality, or safety groups asked to study and solve particular problems. Teams that recommend things almost always have predetermined completion dates. Two critical issues are unique to such teams: getting off to a fast and constructive start and dealing with the ultimate handoff required to get recommendations implemented.

The key to the first issue lies in the clarity of the team's charter and the composition of its membership. In addition to wanting to know why and how their efforts are important, task forces need a clear definition of whom management expects to participate and the time commitment required. Management can help by ensuring that the team includes people with the skills and influence necessary for crafting practical recommendations that will carry weight throughout the organization. Moreover, management can help the team get the necessary cooperation by opening doors and dealing with political obstacles.

Missing the handoff is almost always the problem that stymies teams that recommend things. To avoid this, the transfer of responsibility for recommendations to those who must implement them demands top management's time and attention. The more top managers assume that recommendations will "just happen," the less likely it is that they will. The more involvement task force members have in implementing their recommendations, the more likely they are to get implemented.

To the extent that people outside the task force will have to carry the ball, it is critical to involve them in the process early and often, certainly well before recommendations are finalized. Such involvement may take many forms, including participating in interviews, helping with analyses, contributing and critiquing ideas, and conducting experiments and trials. At a minimum, anyone responsible for implementation should receive a briefing on the task force's purpose, approach, and objectives at the beginning of the effort as well as regular reviews of progress.

TEAMS THAT MAKE OR DO THINGS. These teams include people at or near the front lines who are responsible for doing the basic manufacturing, development, operations, marketing, sales, service, and other value-adding activities of a business. With some exceptions, like new-product development or process design teams, teams that make or do things tend to have no set completion dates because their activities are ongoing.

In deciding where team performance might have the greatest impact, top management should concentrate on what we call the company's "critical delivery points," that is, places in the organization where the cost and value of the company's products and services are most directly determined. Such critical delivery points might include where accounts get managed, customer service performed, products designed, and productivity determined. If performance at critical delivery points depends on combining multiple skills, perspectives, and judgments in real time, then the team option is the smartest one.

When an organization does require a significant number of teams at these points, the sheer challenge of maximizing the performance of so many groups will demand a carefully constructed and performance-focused set of management processes. The issue here for top management is how to build the necessary systems and process supports without falling into the trap of appearing to promote teams for their own sake.

The imperative here, returning to our earlier discussion of the basic discipline of teams, is a relentless focus on performance. If management fails to pay persistent attention to the link between teams and performance, the organization becomes convinced that "this year we are doing 'teams.'" Top management can help by instituting processes like pay schemes and training for teams responsive to their real time needs, but more than anything else, top management must make clear and compelling demands on the teams themselves and then pay constant attention to their progress with respect to both team basics and performance results. This means focusing on specific teams and specific performance challenges. Otherwise "performance," like "team," will become a cliché.

TEAMS THAT RUN THINGS. Despite the fact that many leaders refer to the group reporting to them as a team, few groups really are. And groups that become real teams seldom think of themselves as a team because they are so focused on performance results. Yet the opportunity for such teams includes groups from the top of the enterprise down through the divisional or functional level. Whether it is in charge of thousands of people or a handful, as long as the group oversees some business, ongoing program, or significant functional activity, it is a team that runs things.

The main issue these teams face is determining whether a real team approach is the right one. Many groups that run things can be more effective as working groups than as teams. The key judgment is whether the sum of individual bests will suffice for the performance challenge at hand or whether the group must deliver substantial incremental performance requiring real, joint work-products. Although the team option promises greater performance, it also brings more risk, and managers must be brutally honest in assessing the trade-offs.

Members may have to overcome a natural reluctance to trust their fate to others. The price of faking the team approach is high: at best, members get diverted from their individual goals, costs outweigh benefits, and people resent the imposition on their time and priorities; at worst, serious animosities develop that undercut even the potential personal bests of the working-group approach.

Working groups present fewer risks. Effective working groups need little time to shape their purpose since the leader usually establishes it. Meetings are run against well-prioritized agendas. And decisions are implemented through specific individual assignments and account-abilities. Most of the time, therefore, if performance aspirations can be met through individuals doing their respective jobs well, the working-group approach is more comfortable, less risky, and less disruptive than trying for more elusive team performance levels. Indeed, if there is no performance need for the team approach, efforts spent to improve the effectiveness of the working group make much more sense than floundering around trying to become a team.

Having said that, we believe the extra level of performance teams can achieve is becoming critical for a growing number of companies, especially as they move through major changes during which company performance depends on broad-based behavioral change. When top management uses teams to run things, it should make sure the team succeeds in identifying specific purposes and goals.

This is a second major issue for teams that run things. Too often, such teams confuse the broad mission of the total organization with the specific purpose of their small group at the top. The discipline of teams tells us that for a real team to form there must be a *team* purpose that is distinctive and specific to the small group and that requires its members to roll up their sleeves and accomplish something beyond individual end-products. If a group of managers looks only at the economic performance of the part of the organization it runs to assess overall effectiveness, the group will not have any team performance goals of its own.

While the basic discipline of teams does not differ for them, teams at the top are certainly the most difficult. The complexities of long-term challenges, heavy demands on executive time, and the deep-seated individualism of senior people conspire against teams at the top. At the same time, teams at the top are the most powerful. At first we thought such teams were nearly impossible. That is because we were looking at the teams as defined by the formal organizational structure, that is, the leader and all his or her direct reports equals the team. Then we discovered that real teams at the top were often smaller and less formalized—Whitehead and Weinberg at Goldman, Sachs; Hewlett and Packard at HP; Krasnoff, Pall, and Hardy at Pall Corp; Kendall, Pearson, and Calloway at Pepsi; Haas and Haas at Levi Strauss; Batten and Ridder at Knight-Ridder. They were mostly twos and threes, with an occasional fourth.

Nonetheless, real teams at the top of large, complex organizations are still few and far between. Far too many groups at the top of large corporations needlessly constrain themselves from achieving real team levels of performance because they assume that all direct reports must be on the team; that team goals must be identical to corporate goals; that the team members' positions rather than skills determine their respective roles; that a team must be a team all the time; and that the team leader is above doing real work.

As understandable as these assumptions may be, most of them are unwarranted. They do not apply to the teams at the top we have observed, and when replaced with more realistic and flexible assumptions that permit the team discipline to be applied, real team performance at the top can and does occur. Moreover, as more and more companies are confronted with the need to manage major change across their organizations, we will see more real teams at the top.

We believe that teams will become the primary unit of performance in high-performance organizations. But that does not mean that teams will crowd out individual opportunity or formal hierarchy and process. Rather, teams will enhance existing structures without replacing them. A team opportunity exists anywhere hierarchy or organizational boundaries inhibit the skills and perspectives needed for optimal results. Thus, new-product innovation requires preserving functional excellence through structure while eradicating functional bias through teams. And frontline productivity requires preserving direction and guidance through hierarchy while drawing on energy and flexibility through self-managing teams.

We are convinced that every company faces specific performance challenges for which teams are the most practical and powerful vehicle at top management's disposal. The critical role for senior managers, therefore, is to worry about company performance and the kinds of teams that can deliver it. This means that top management must recognize a team's unique potential to deliver results, deploy teams strategically when they are the best tool for the job, and foster the basic discipline of teams that will make them effective. By doing so, top management creates the kind of environment that enables team as well as individual and organizational performance.

2

How to Integrate Work *and* Deepen Expertise

Dorothy Leonard-Barton, H. Kent Bowen, Kim B. Clark, Charles A. Holloway, and Steven C. Wheelwright

To be a leader in global manufacturing in the 1990s, a company must excel in two seemingly contradictory ways. First, it must constantly build and refresh its individual areas of expertise so it has the critical capabilities needed to stay ahead of the pack. And second, it must get its ever-changing mix of disciplines to work together in the ever-changing way needed to prevail in the ever-changing competitive environment. In other words, a company must find the way that best enables it at a given point in time both to come up with a product that meets customer needs better than the competition's *and* to create that product faster and more efficiently than competitors.

Most manufacturers, especially those companies that have reorganized themselves by cross-functional processes, have already discovered how difficult it is to integrate various disciplines and still maintain functional excellence. "Is it even possible to achieve both things?" executive after executive laments. There is a solution. It lies in the creative use of development projects.

As the critical juncture where functional groups meet, development projects are the true test of an organization's integrative abilities. More important, development projects can be used as a tool for strengthening the relationship among functions, while still giving them the room they need to advance their own expertise. To attain this leverage, though, executives must approach development projects with those goals in mind and must take into account how their company's strengths and weaknesses will help or hinder the project in trying to attain those goals.

Eastman Kodak learned this lesson when it developed its FunSaver camera in the late 1980s. Although the project was not all smooth sailing, it had a happy ending and, overall, superbly illustrates how a company can get functions to work together effectively, enhance functional expertise, and create a winning product to boot.

Looking to expand the company's product line, Kodak's technical-development group in the mid-1980s proposed an intriguing new product: a disposable camera. Film would be packaged in a simple, inexpensive, sealed plastic camera. Once the pictures had been taken, the consumer would hand the camera to a photofinisher, who would extract the film and discard the camera. (Later on, the company developed a system to recycle the used cameras.) Marketing would target this "single-use" camera at people who suddenly found themselves without their camera or who needed a camera for outdoor activities like boating or a beach outing, where they might be nervous about bringing an expensive camera. The disposable camera would be sold at convenience outlets and at major tourist attractions such as Disney World.

Initially, senior managers placed the project under the direction of the film division because they envisioned the FunSaver more as a premium film product than as a camera, but that proved to be a mistake. The project languished for months because the film division thought the camera would be a low-margin business that would cannibalize sales of film, a very high-margin business.

In the meantime, the camera division lobbied Kodak executives to take over the project, pointing out that Fuji intended to market a single-use camera in the United States that it had already introduced in Japan. The camera division also promised to structure the camera's costs and pricing so that its per-unit profit margin would match or exceed the company's current margin on a roll of film. Management gave the nod.

The project then took off. In a bid to streamline decision making, design the camera rapidly and efficiently, and ensure that its design would make it easy to manufacture, the camera division's development team decided to take several steps. It placed design and manufacturing, which traditionally were separate functional groups at Kodak, under one project leader. And it created a small, dedicated team of engineering, manufacturing, and marketing people, who shared the same work space. While this approach was new for Kodak, the team members believed it was essential to complete the project rapidly.

The project leader also strongly believed that computer-aided design and computer-aided manufacturing (CAD/CAM) could make a huge difference in designing the camera and optimizing its manufacturability. Kodak had used CAD/CAM systems in other projects, but they had been technical engineering systems used by specialists. The project leader wanted a CAD/CAM system that could do more—one that could help integrate the work of the entire team—and persuaded senior managers to buy into his vision of using the project to create this new capability. So, at the outset of the project, the team had three explicit goals: to produce the camera quickly; to create new methods for integration; and to develop new CAD/CAM technology that would enable Kodak to develop high-quality, easy-to-manufacture products faster and more efficiently.

Team members customized the new CAD/CAM system to make it easy for them to share information and get immediate feedback from one another. Each designer of a component, system, mold, or manufacturing subsystem would work on his or her part, then insert an updated drawing into the master schematic for the whole camera and/or the manufacturing process. Then each morning, a new composite design would be downloaded so that all engineers could see the effects of their combined efforts. Although only the original designer could alter the drawing of his or her part, anyone could critique any drawing and request changes. In addition, manufacturing engineers used the system to generate simulations of prototypes of the manufacturing process, which enabled them to work out kinks that would have shown up in the actual manufacturing system. As a result, they were able to reach full production much faster when actual manufacturing began.

Kodak introduced the FunSaver in 1988, just as Fuji's camera was hitting the U.S. market. But, aided by aggressive advertising, the Fun-Saver immediately grabbed the lead, and it has held on to it. Kodak quickly introduced two follow-on products, the Weekend, a waterproof camera, and the Panoramic, a camera with a wide-angle lens. These products contributed greatly to the overall success of the Fun-Saver: more than 100 million have been sold. Kodak was able to develop the Weekend and the Panoramic in record time by using not only the same basic product design and manufacturing process but also the same people, the same project-management procedures, and the same CAD/CAM system.

Besides creating a successful product, the FunSaver project proved to the company that integrating functions was possible and highly advantageous. In this case, the CAD/CAM technology fostered a significant degree of interaction among the design, tooling, and manufacturing engineers within engineering as well as between engineering and marketing. In addition, the CAD/CAM system provided discipline and a common set of principles for achieving the desired integration. Subsequent development teams at Kodak organized their work in a similar manner, and leaders of the FunSaver project implemented the new principles for achieving integration elsewhere, when they moved on to other projects.

The FunSaver project also gave Kodak a new technical capability: CAD/CAM. Rather than try to introduce this emerging technology on a companywide or divisional scale, Kodak—thanks to the inspiration of the project manager—gave it a test run on a manageable scale. Afterward, the company went on to widen its use of the CAD/CAM system, again by means of development projects, charging each team with customizing the system to best serve its needs.

The project also provided Kodak with a path leading away from a tradition that had become a major problem for the company: the autonomy of each functional group. Before the FunSaver, development projects had proceeded in sequential fashion, with one functional department completing its work and passing the results to the next in the chain. While this approach resulted in high performance and quality, it slowed decision making and meant that an extensive amount of rework typically had to be conducted during the development process in order to get all the components and subsystems of a product or process to mesh. In the new time-sensitive competitive environment, Kodak's design-engineering process, once a core capability, had become a rigidity.

Finally, the shaky beginning of the project provided a valuable lesson about development teams. It demonstrated that a project must fit the objectives of the organization that is responsible for carrying it out. The film division did not fully support the project. The camera division, however, got right behind it and refined its definition so that it would meet Kodak's profitability goals, advance companywide learning, and develop new capabilities.

Prototypes: Tools for Learning and Integrating

Effective development teams build prototypes often and early to learn rapidly, minimize mistakes, and successfully integrate the work of the many functions and support groups involved in the project. Prototypes can provide a common language and a focal point for people from a wide variety of disciplines. They help each group understand how its work affects the work of other groups and enable the team to spot problems that require cross-functional solutions. By doing so, prototypes not only enable products to be developed and launched more quickly but also result in products that are both higher-quality and more effective in fulfilling their intended purpose in the marketplace.

By prototypes, we do not mean merely the physical embodiments of the nearly final products made by craftspeople before production begins. We mean a series of representations, including early mock-ups, computer simulations, subsystem models, and models featuring system-level engineering, as well as production prototypes. The most successful teams studied by the Manufacturing Vision Group frequently and regularly built a variety of prototypes; started creating prototypes of the entire system very early in the development process; and made each successive model more closely approach the desired final product in terms of form, content, and the customer experience it provoked. This process provided each team with an invaluable progress report on its success in dealing with unresolved issues and in meeting its schedule. The most successful teams also built multiple copies of each prototype so that everyone involved in the development and eventual production, sale, use, and servicing of the product (including suppliers, prospective customers, and dealers) could rapidly evaluate it and offer feedback. Indeed, the best use of prototypes enabled companies to test regularly during the development process:

- the degree to which the decisions made about factors like design, specifications, and materials were executing faithfully the intent of the design;
- the cost and ease with which the manufacturing system—including production processes, purchasing, and test routines—could deliver the product;
- the extent to which the critical aspects of the unfolding product—including the functionality of individual subsystems and the way the subsystems work together—were satisfying the targeted customers' stated desires and latent needs (qualities or features they seem to want but have trouble articulating).

But the projects that exploited prototypes in this manner were the exception. Indeed, most of the projects studied by the Manufacturing Vision Group failed to create enough prototypes. And often the prototypes they did build (1) were not created early enough to solve problems that took more time and resources to solve later; (2) focused on only one or two components and not on the entire system; (3) were not used to test the manufacturing processes that would produce the final product;

and (4) were not widely tested in the field, meaning that an opportunity to glean potentially invaluable reactions from customers was missed.

Building prototypes early is critical for companies because decisions affecting about 85% of the ultimate total cost of the product (including its manufacture, use, maintenance, and disposal) are typically made during the first 15% of a development project. Changes that are made late in the project invariably upset the sought-after balance among product features, cost, and quality, and therefore cause subsequent delays and suboptimal solutions. Conversely, if needed changes in, say, one subsystem can be spotted early or proposed changes for improving performance can be tested and acted on early, the ripple effect—the impact on and changes that need to be made in other subsystems—can be minimized.

For example, when Ford was developing its 1991 Crown Victoria/ Grand Marquis in the late 1980s, it had its plant in St. Thomas, Ontario, build full-scale prototypes of the car on the same line producing the current model. As a result, line workers could suggest numerous ways to improve the manufacturability of the car relatively early in the project. This not only enabled the development team to alter designs without greatly disrupting the project but also gave plant employees in-depth information about the product that enabled them to move to full production relatively quickly when actual manufacturing began.

A process of building prototypes, testing and evaluating them internally and in the field, and then incorporating what is learned into the next prototype is a powerful mechanism for focusing a development team's efforts. These cycles also provide milestones, when management can review progress, assess what remains to be done, and consider whether alternative paths should be taken to complete the effort.

Companies can and should use prototypes in this way for the development of processes as well as products. At Chaparral Steel, for example, a team developing a new process will typically make small batches of steel using a prototype of the process, then refine the process, make more batches, refine the process more, and so on, gradually increasing the scale until the process reaches full-production levels. Chaparral also typically puts prototypes on the shop floor from the outset of a project. That approach has enabled the company to push a given new process's performance level 15% to 20% beyond what would have been possible had it taken the traditional approach of conducting most of the development work off-site.

All in all, the extensive use of prototypes provides a structure, discipline, and approach that significantly enhance the rate of learning and integration in development projects. It gives both the project team and senior managers a powerful tool for effectively monitoring, guiding, and improving the development effort.

Leveraging Capabilities, Breaking Rigidities

Core capabilities are not just technologies and workforce skills. They are a capacity for action. They are the essence of what makes an organization unique in its ability to provide value to customers over a long period of time. But this is hardly a revelation.

What many managers do not yet understand about capabilities, however, is that each consists of four elements whose interaction determines how effectively the organization can exploit it. Those elements are: *knowledge and skills*—technical know-how and personal "know-who," including ties to important groups such as government regulatory bodies or the scientific community; *managerial systems*—tailored incentive systems, in-house educational programs, or methodologies that embody procedural knowledge; *physical systems*—plant, equipment, tooling, and engineering work systems that have been developed over the years, and production lines and information systems that constitute compilations of knowledge; and *values*—the attitudes, behaviors, and norms that dominate in a corporation.

An interesting example of a core capability that encompasses several of these elements is networking at Digital Equipment. Workstations or terminals are on virtually everyone's desk and are connected with sophisticated software so that any employee around the world can reach any other. The physical system supports a very horizontal, networked style of management. Because individual freedom and responsibility are the values that DEC employees prize the most, any requests for action are more likely to be met, and met more quickly, if they are sent through the horizontal chain of the informal network than if they are passed through the vertical chain of command. This networking approach permeates the company's routines and culture and fosters a task-force approach to most issues.

Take DEC's CDA software project to develop a computer architecture for linking desktop-publishing products. During this project, which started in late 1986, DEC employees were asked to field-test prototype software sent to them over the network. Some 150 reviewers provided their feedback in an electronic notes file. The on-line file provided "living specs" that enabled the team to perfect the software code continually. Later, the team members estimated that 90% of the bugs in the software were found by this method. DEC's networking capability clearly enhanced the project's success.

DEC's networking system is also a reason why project ideas often originate in the ranks. Development teams are authorized to initiate projects off-line, which give rise to multiple, ongoing experiments, some of which became full-fledged projects. Corporate strategy evolves as much from these projects as from top-management direction. Such empowerment of employees engenders a tremendous sense of project ownership and spurs team members to make remarkable achievements, often in the face of great odds. Development teams charge ahead with little supervision, believing they will be able to alter the direction of their group significantly and turn the course of their mammoth corporation a critical degree or two.

The downside of a core capability, as we have pointed out, is that it can become a rigidity. A strength can become a weakness. The very reason for a company's traditional success can become an obstacle to developing new capabilities or maintaining the right balance of capabilities. This was most obvious in the technology-intensive companies that the Manufacturing Vision Group studied.

Consider the DECstation 3100 effort, which was undertaken in 1988 to develop DEC's first workstation based on reduced-instruction-set computing (RISC) technology. In this project, the internal field-testing capability that had served DEC so well in the past proved to be a liability. The project team recruited an internal "wrecking crew" of DEC volunteers to evaluate the prototype product and rewarded employees who found the most bugs with prototype workstations.

But both the DEC engineers designing the workstation and the volunteers who tested it focused almost exclusively on the machine's performance—on building a "hot box" of excellent hardware—rather than on the amount of applications software that could run on it. In hindsight, that is not surprising. DEC had become a giant in the computer industry as a result of its machines that shared DEC's proprietary VAX architecture and VMS operating system. A plethora of applications software was available for these machines. As a result, DEC engineers designing new machines typically did not worry about software availability. But the DECstation 3100 was aimed at giving DEC a foothold in the market dominated by RISC-based machines with UNIX operating systems.

Though the workstation was a technical gem and benefited from the wrecking crew's suggestions, it had difficulty penetrating the market because only 20 application programs had been developed by the time

DEC introduced the product. Potential customers chose competing workstations, even though they were less advanced, because they had many more application programs (more than 500 in some cases). The team members naïvely believed that the DEC volunteers provided a good test market, that a hot box would sell simply on its performance, and that users would develop their own applications. DEC's engineers might have been happy to do so, but potential customers clearly were not.

THE DARK SIDE OF VALUES

Of the four elements that determine the effectiveness of a core capability, the one most overlooked and most misunderstood—and most difficult to change—is also the one that is the most powerful when aligned with the other three. This element is values.

A project undertaken in the early 1980s at Hewlett-Packard to develop the company's first personal computer illustrates how values can trip up a project. In this case, HP consciously pitted the project against one of its core values, the fierce autonomy of its divisions, but underestimated how hard it would be to change that core value. Each HP division traditionally focused on specific product lines and had its own marketing, manufacturing, engineering, finance, and personnel functions. Division managers were expected to make a profit, and if one division developed a component for another, it would "sell" it at full price. This approach made a lot of sense when the challenge was attacking several distinctly separate, fast-growing markets at the same time and the key to success was to be able to respond quickly to the demands of disparate customers. HP's phenomenal growth was proof of that. But in the PC project, it certainly was not a plus.

HP senior managers decided to attack the fledgling PC market by coordinating the efforts of four divisions. While integrating the technologies of several divisions seemed logical, the company had virtually no mechanism for getting them to work closely together. HP senior managers also did not make integration an explicit project goal; they, like the division leaders, assumed that the traditional practice of divisions selling components to one another would suffice.

HP assigned the main responsibility for the PC to a team that had just started work on a new terminal for the HP 3000 minicomputer at HP's minicomputer division in Cupertino, California. Corporate executives reasoned that the team could squeeze enough computing power into the terminal, known as the HP 150, to enable it to perform as a PC.

The job of developing the keyboard was originally given to the desktop computers division in Fort Collins, Colorado. The HP 150 team required that the keyboard cost only $25. The existing Fort Collins keyboard, designed for big computers, cost $100, and the general manager of the division did not believe that the team's request for a $25 keyboard was a high priority. Keyboard design rapidly became a bottleneck. Finally, the work was brought back to the team in Cupertino for a "crash" effort that ended up taking six months.

The responsibility for the HP 150's disk drive fell to the disk-drive division in Greeley, Colorado. Rather than developing a new cost-effective drive, it simply modified an existing one. And following HP custom, the division's leaders priced the drive so that they could make a profit on the "contract." This made it harder for the team to achieve the targeted margins. In retrospect, the team would have been much better off had it turned to outside suppliers to develop the keyboard and disk drive.

As a terminal, the HP 150 did well. Customers liked it, and the division made a profit on the sales. As a personal computer, however, the HP 150 never became profitable and was unable to gain significant market share.

One value that often affects development projects is the status that companies accord different disciplines. The dominance of a given discipline can create powerful capabilities, but it can also result in dangerous rigidities. That was particularly evident at DEC and at Hewlett-Packard, where the belief that design engineering was the most critical function caused design engineers to become the elite. This status enabled both companies to grow very strong in design, which became a strategic core capability and led to the creation of a stream of sophisticated products. But it also led to an arrogance in that group that eventually turned this capability into a rigidity. The attitude at HP and at DEC was that marketing and manufacturing were less valuable than design. As a result, designers began to assume that they knew better than customers what product features and attributes were best.

The pervasive perception that manufacturing people and their concerns were relatively less important eventually became a significant problem at both companies. As a result, manufacturing problems were tackled only late in projects, causing delays, rework, and higher expenses. And because of manufacturing's perceived lower status, fewer skilled people were attracted to the function. That left manufacturing less able to solve difficult problems, which further convinced everyone that the lower status was deserved. In the United States, this problem persists in many industries, which helps explain this country's persistent weakness in manufacturing engineering and process-equipment development.

This problem was a big one in HP's Hornet project, which developed an inexpensive spectrum-analyzer instrument for testing and analyzing radio-frequency and microwave signals, that HP introduced in the mid-1980s. The manufacturing engineers on the project were assigned to it only part-time and were not added to the team until the testing phase had already begun. As a result, there was almost no thought given to manufacturability in designing the product, and the ramp-up to full production was long, complicated, and stressful for the people working in the plant.

OVERCOMING RIGIDITIES

HP's DeskJet project for developing a low-cost computer printer shows how a company can use a development project to overcome a rigidity. HP executives purposely designed the project to break the negative cycle that had sapped its strength in manufacturing and to get the company to start looking to other functions besides design engineering for creative solutions. Manufacturing was strongly represented from the beginning because the project involved—for HP— novel products, markets, and customers and, as a result, novel manufacturing cost and volume requirements. Once the project team was established, managers moved the manufacturing engineers to the R&D site and insisted that the R&D engineers consult with them continually regarding the design. Eventually, the manufacturing engineers became such valuable team members that the designers even lobbied for more of them.

Sure, the chief motive for initiating this new approach was to benefit the DeskJet project. But HP executives also wanted it to signal to the rest of the company that their view of the traditional status of design and manufacturing was changing. The project was a model for teamwork, and subsequent projects were organized along similar lines. Moreover, as the status of manufacturing engineers rose, the company began to attract stronger, broader, and more senior people to manufacturing.

Managing Development to Build Capabilities

In the wide range of products it studied, the Manufacturing Vision Group discovered several essential principles that can help companies correct conflicts and imbalances and build core capabilities. They are: an incremental approach to improving and expanding capabilities; a focus on process as well as product; innovative ways to challenge conventional thinking; and coherent vision, leadership, and organization.

INCREMENTAL ADVANCES

Companies must strive to "push the envelope" steadily and avoid reliance on great leaps. And to avoid overwhelming their development teams, they also must be careful not to push on too many fronts at the same time. As we described in the first article in this package, the Kodak team that sought to develop the "factory of the future" failed in part because it tried to push the envelope on too many fronts.

Chaparral Steel's failure to develop an electric-arc saw for cutting steel in 1985 to 1987 shows that even the best can succumb to the temptation to try to make a leap that is just too far. Chaparral wanted to find a faster and more efficient way to cut the steel it produced and discovered that the aerospace industry was using an intensely hot electric arc to cut stainless steel. But the aerospace industry had tried neither to cut sections thicker than eight inches nor to cut through high volumes of material with this process, which is what Chaparral wanted it to do. But Chaparral employees, who time and again had figured out how to get equipment to perform in ways never intended, were undeterred. They discovered, however, that they lacked the knowledge of physics and electromagnetics necessary for the project to succeed. Even with the help of an outside consultant versed in the required physics, the project was beyond Chaparral's ken.

FOCUS ON MANUFACTURING PROCESS

U.S. companies have tended to push new products but not manufacturing processes. The conventional wisdom is that efforts to develop superior product features, functionality, and ease of use, and to lower costs will create demand for new processes. But in this paradigm, process will always lag product, which can severely handicap a company because the lead time needed to develop a new process typically exceeds that for a new product.

As a company in a process industry, Chaparral naturally focuses on production processes. But the internal capability that it has developed, which enables it to obtain feedback on processes from customers, suppliers, and competitors, and to revise processes continually in almost real time is nonetheless extraordinary. Furthermore, Chaparral does this frequently *in advance of* specific product requirements, thereby creating additional new-product opportunities. With the exception of Kodak and Chaparral, the other companies that the Manufacturing Vision Group studied rarely made processes the primary target of a development project. And in those handful of instances when they did, it was virtually always in response to a desire to create specific new products.

DEC's RA90 project to develop a high-density disk drive in the 1980s, which is described in "Development Projects: The Engine of Renewal," is a good example. While the project did not achieve many of the original product goals, DEC viewed it as a success because it achieved a major strategic goal set at the beginning: to lay a strong foundation for future high-density storage products. DEC executives were willing to invest heavily—to the tune of $1 billion, including a new manufacturing plant—in the development of skills, market position, and critical manufacturing processes. Team members were inspired to redefine the state of the art, which would put DEC in a strong competitive position in the long run.

This view may constitute a bit of Monday-morning quarterbacking on the part of DEC managers. But, as we discussed, it is important to realize that a development project can result in a less-than-successful product and still create a strategically crucial new process.

Something similar happened with Chaparral's Microtuff 10 steel project to develop new high-quality forging steels. Although sales of the end product were limited, hardly yielding enough revenues to justify the investment, the Microtuff 10 extended the company's product line. And the fact that Chaparral, a minimill, could even produce the kind of high-quality product that only large, integrated steel companies previously could make, burnished Chaparral's reputation as a high-tech company and gave it a big advantage over other minimills.

Of course, the best projects to improve processes are those that also result in product successes, which was the case with Kodak's efforts to improve its antistatic coating process. For years, Kodak had been a leading manufacturer of micrographic films, which include the film used in microfiche machines in libraries. Studies showed that some users—the main customers are banks and insurance companies—thought that the images on Kodak films were less sharp than those on competitors' films. Kodak determined that the problem wasn't clarity; it was darkness. The images on its films appeared a bit darker because of a coating placed on the film to reduce the buildup of static electricity, which attracts dust.

The project team charged with developing a clearer antistatic coating spotted a recent process invention made by a Kodak unit in France and used it to develop quickly a new manufacturing process. New films reached the streets within a year—a feat that enabled Kodak not merely to maintain its market share but also to increase it.

"OUT-OF-THE-BOX" THINKING

A third ingredient for building capabilities and breaking rigidities is an ability to challenge conventional thinking. The Manufacturing Vision Group found several effective ways to create the out-of-the-box thinking needed to do this.

One method is the clever use of benchmarking. Most companies benchmark products or processes to find out what competitors are doing so that they can match the best or go them one better. But there are creative ways a company can use benchmarking to attain a sustainable leadership position. Chaparral demonstrated such creative thinking when it looked at practices outside its industry to develop the horizontal caster.

Another way to challenge conventional thinking—and stay ahead of competitors—is to be more resourceful and industrious in tapping the best minds in the field. When Chaparral began the Microtuff 10 project, it approached the Colorado School of Mines about cosponsoring a technical conference on forging steel, and the school agreed. The conference attracted technical papers and brought together experts who otherwise would not have convened. Chaparral employees learned enough to create new formulas for forging steel as well as related production processes.

Breaking the conventional flow of information is yet another way to challenge conventional thinking. Often, this can help a company alter its basic values so they help rather than hinder it in adapting to changes in its competitive environment. During HP's DeskJet printer project, marketing people conducted studies in shopping malls and brought back 24 suggestions for changes that they believed would ensure market acceptance. But design engineers heeded only 5, discounting the others largely as a "marketing wish list." The people from marketing and the project leaders were so convinced of the important nature of the information, however, that they insisted that the design engineers go to the malls to hear for themselves what test customers were saying. Grudgingly, the engineers went, listened, and then did an about-face and made 17 more changes.

In DEC's LAN Bridge 200 project to develop a communications product for linking computer networks, the marketing people discovered early on several important features that users wanted. However, they lacked the stature and self-confidence to persuade the design engineers to include the features. Not until two senior DEC technologists gathered the same information from customers was it actually used. By the time the new information had been incorporated into the design, however, the project schedule had slipped four months.

In subsequent projects at both HP and DEC, development teams made greater efforts to ensure that designers heard what customers were demanding and heeded it. In other words, the companies had learned.

VISION, LEADERSHIP, AND ORGANIZATION

While constantly striving to make incremental advances, focusing on process, and generating creative thinking are important, three things are even more crucial. More than anything, a project's success—and the success of a company's range of projects—in enhancing competitiveness and generating knowledge depends on a coherent vision, strong leadership, and organization. A clear vision enables projects to take off from the start. Then, when a project faces seemingly impossible odds or hits a point where failure seems inevitable, the right kind of leadership can pull it through.

There is no one right way to organize and lead a project. Companies that master the art of picking the best for each project will end up with more than a system for managing development projects effectively. They will end up with a system that cultivates leaders who excel in getting functions to work together and advance their knowledge. Such managers will enable manufacturers not merely to attain the lead but to keep it.

3

The Return Map: Tracking Product Teams

Charles H. House and Raymond L. Price

Once time was money. Now it is more valuable than money. A McKinsey study reports that, on average, companies lose 33% of after-tax profit when they ship products six months late, as compared with losses of 3.5% when they overspend 50% on product development. More and more, advanced manufacturers are learning that the time required to develop a new product has more influence on its success than its costs.

Little wonder, then, that senior managers are working hard to reduce their new product development cycles. At Hewlett-Packard, well over 50% of sales come from products introduced during the past three years, and more than 500 product development projects are going on at any given time. Even enterprises that develop just a few new products over several years, like Boeing Commercial Airplane Group, are focusing on reducing the time required to develop them.

It is a common belief in management practice today that one of the most effective ways to shorten development cycles is through the collaborative work of cross-functional development teams. But if anything is easier said than done, it is that marketing people, development engineers, and manufacturing engineers should collaborate rather than "throw product specifications over the wall" to one another.

Collaboration among people from different functions is difficult, uncertain, and suffers from too little mutual understanding. New product development teams are typically composed of people who do not have the experience or qualifications to criticize each other's judgments or performance—certainly not while the project is evolving. They do not, and cannot, know all that their colleagues from other functions know.

And uncertainty comes in many forms. What features do customers want? How do features translate into sales? Is the technology available to develop the features? Will the product be manufacturable at the desired price? Much of the challenge of new product development is centered on people from different functions finding answers to, and getting agreement on, just such questions.

Obviously, the more team members understand the work of other functions and the interrelationships among all functions, the more likely they are to make intelligent decisions that will enhance the success of the product. But what constitutes understanding? Bill Hewlett, a founder of Hewlett-Packard, used to say, "You cannot manage what you cannot measure," and his corollary was "What gets measured gets done." By inference, the real challenge for teams is to develop measures that will help individuals assess how well they are doing what they agree must be done. Advanced manufacturers must create new products that will make the most profit in the least time, but what metric can managers of interfunctional teams use to direct their employees' efforts toward this outcome?

Ideally, such a metric would encourage the ongoing monitoring of a new product development project. It would allow people from different disciplines to assess the impact of their decisions and their colleagues' decisions on the entire project. The metric would encourage collaboration among different functions: engender challenge and criticism without encouraging presumptuousness. It would serve as a prompt for learning and improvement. It would be easy to read and interpret, something to sketch on the back of an envelope while in a coffeepot discussion. And it would provide a way of visualizing progress holistically.

In fact, Hewlett-Packard has been using just such a metric since 1987—we named it the "Return Map"—and it is so simple and elegant that it has become a staple of the company's product development cycle. The Return Map graphically represents the contributions of all team members to product success in terms of time and money. First and foremost, it includes the critical elements of product development— the investment in product development and the return or profits from that investment. But the Return Map also shows the elapsed time to develop the product, introduce it, and achieve the returns.

Not surprisingly, the Return Map's crucial coordinate is the point at which product sales generate sufficient profit to pay back the initial development investment, that is, when the project breaks even. But the map's greatest virtue is not in what it says so much as in what it does. It provides a superordinate goal and measure for all the functions and thus shifts the team's focus from "who is responsible" to "what needs to get done." Even more important, the map forces members of the team to estimate and reestimate the time and money it will take to complete their tasks and the impact of their actions on overall project success. In giving a comprehensive picture of the common task, it helps to create the only discipline that works, namely, self-discipline.

The Basic Elements

The Return Map is intended to be used by all of the functional managers on the business team. Basically, it is a two dimensional graph displaying time and money on the x and y axes respectively. The x axis is usually drawn on a linear scale, while the y axis is drawn most effectively on a logarithmic scale because for successful products the difference between sales and investment costs will be greater than 100:1. It is important to remember when looking at the exhibit curves that the dollar amounts are rising cumulatively. The x axis is divided into three segments, showing partitioned tasks and responsibilities—Investigation, Development, and Manufacturing and Sales (see Exhibit I).

The purpose of Investigation is to determine the desired product features, the product's cost and price, the feasibility of the proposed technologies, and the plan for product development and introduction. At this point, all numbers are estimates. Investigation is usually the responsibility of a small team and requires a relatively modest investment. Obviously, Marketing and R&D should collaborate to determine what features customers want and how they could be provided. At the end of Investigation, the company commits to develop a product with specific features using agreed-upon technologies.

The Development phase is usually the primary domain of R&D in consultation with manufacturing; its purpose is to determine how to produce the product at the desired price. Challenges during this phase include changing product features, concurrent design of the product and the manufacturing processes, and, often, the problems associated with doing something that has not been done before.

The formal end of the Development phase is Manufacturing Release (MR)—that is, when the company commits to manufacture and sell the product. When the product is ready to be manufactured and shipped to customers, sales become a reality and manufacturing, mar-

Exhibit I.

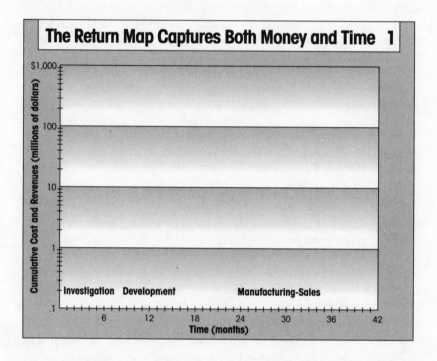

keting, sales costs, and profits are finally more than estimates. The transitions between these phases or the project checkpoints are key times for the Return Map.

Perhaps the best way to grasp how the Return Map evolves from these early stages is to examine a map for a completed project, where all the variables are known—in this case, the map for a recent Hewlett-Packard pocket calculator (see Exhibit II).

Investigation took 4 months and cost about $400,000; Development required 12 months and $4.5 million, with many new manufacturing process designs for higher quality and higher production volumes. Hence, the total product development effort from beginning to manufacturing and sales release took 16 months and cost $4.9 million (see the investment line on Exhibit II). Once the product was released, sales increased consistently for 5 months and then increased at a slightly faster pace during the next 9 months. Sales volume for the first year was $56 million and for the second year was $145 million (see the sales line on Exhibit II—and remember, the differences are greater

Exhibit II.

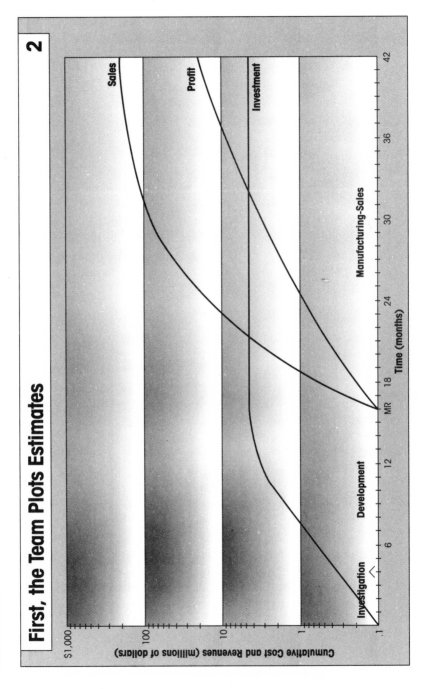

First, the Team Plots Estimates

than they appear owing to the log scale). Cumulative sales volume gives a sense of how quickly and effectively the product was introduced and sold.

In the first year, net profits of $2.2 million were less than expected due to the sales volume lag and the resulting increase in cost per unit. But profits (see the profit line in Exhibit II) increased significantly in the second year and passed through the investment line about 16 months after Manufacturing Release. For the second year, net profits reached $13 million. Profits are the best indicator of the contribution the product made to the customers since they reflect both the total volume of sales and the price the product can command in the marketplace.

So the critical lines that are systematically plotted on the Return Map include new product investment dollars, sales dollars, and profit dollars. Each of these is plotted as both time and money, with money in total cumulative dollars. Now that we have the basic elements of the map, we can focus on some novel metrics.

New Metrics

The map tracks—in dollars and months—R&D and manufacturing investment, sales, and profit. At the same time, it provides the context for new metrics: Break-Even-Time, Time-to-Market, Break-Even-After-Release, and the Return Factor. These four metrics (see Exhibit III, plotted for the pocket calculator) become the focus of management reviews, functional performance discussions, learning, and most important, they are the basis for judging overall product success.

Break-Even-Time, or *BET*, is the key metric. It is defined as the time from the start of investigation until product profits equal the investment in development. In its simplest form, BET is a measure of the total time until the break-even point on the original investment; for the pocket calculator, BET is 32 months. BET is the one best measure for the success of the whole product development effort because it conveys a sense of urgency about time; it shows the race to generate sufficient profit to justify the product in the first place.

Time-to-Market, or *TM*, is the total development time from the start of the Development phase to Manufacturing Release. For the calculator project, TM was 12 months. This time and its associated costs are determined primarily by R&D efficiency and productivity. TM makes

Exhibit III.

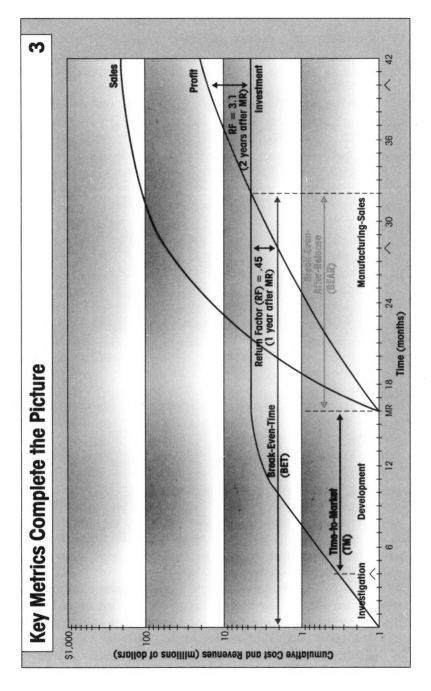

Key Metrics Complete the Picture

visible the major checkpoints of Investigation and Development. It is obviously the most important R&D measure.

Break-Even-After-Release, or *BEAR*, is the time from Manufacturing Release until the project investment costs are recovered in product profit. BEAR for the calculator was 16 months. This measure focuses on how efficiently the product was transferred to marketing and manufacturing and how effectively it was introduced to the marketplace. Just as TM is considered the most important R&D metric, BEAR is the most important measure for marketing and manufacturing.

Finally, the *Return Factor*, or *RF*, is a calculation of profit dollars divided by investment dollars at a specific point in time after a product has moved into manufacturing and sales. In the case of the pocket calculator, RF after one year was .45 (that is, cumulative profit of $2.2 million divided by total investment of $4.9 million) and was 3.1 (a profit of $15.2 million divided by $4.9 million) after two years. The RF gives an indication of the total return on the investment without taking into account how long it took to achieve that return.

The effectiveness of the Return Map hinges on the involvement of all three major functional areas in the development and introduction of new products. The map captures the link between the development team and the rest of the company and the customer. If the product does not sell and make money, for whatever reasons, the product development efforts were wasted. The team is accountable for designing and building products that the customers want, doing it in a timely manner, and effectively transferring the products to the rest of the company.

Making the Most of the Return Map

We have argued that an interfunctional team uses the Return Map most appropriately during the Investigation phase by generating estimates for a final map, including investment, sales, and profit. These initial estimates or forecasts are a "stake in the ground" for the team and will be used for comparison and learning throughout the project. By focusing on the accuracy of the forecasts, marketing, R&D, and manufacturing are forced to examine problems as a team; all three functions are thus sharing the burden of precision.

Too often, the whole burden during the initial phase of a project is placed on the R&D team—to generate schedules, functionality, and cost goals. But the Return Map requires accurate sales forecasts, which forces market researchers to get better and better at competitive analysis, customer understanding, and market development. Similarly, manufacturing involvement is essential for forecasting cost and schedule goals; manufacturing engineers should never be left to develop the manufacturing process after the design is set.

We cannot emphasize enough that missed forecasts generated for the Return Map in the Investigation phase should be viewed as valuable information, comparable with defect rates in manufacturing—deviations from increasingly knowable standards, proof that either the process is out of whack or the means for setting the standard are. The Return Map can be used to provide a visual perspective on sales forecasts and expected profits given any number of hypothetical scenarios. What if the forecasts varied by 20%, over or under? What are the implications of reaching mature sales six months earlier than expected? The Return Map allows for a kind of graphic sensitivity analysis of product development and introduction decisions; it sets the stage for further, indeed, continual investigation.

By no means should the Return Map be used by management to punish people whose forecasts prove inaccurate. Estimates are a team responsibility or at least a functional one—no individual should be held responsible for generating the information on which they are based. Moreover, if functions are penalized for being late, they will simply learn to estimate conservatively, building slack into a discipline whose very purpose is the elimination of slack.

Consider the estimated Return Map for a proposed ultrasound machine (see Exhibit IV). The Investigation phase is planned to last 5 months and cost $500,000, TM is estimated to be 9 months and cost $2.3 million, while anticipated BET is 18 months. Mature sales volume is expected to be 300 units a month, or $16 million, and mature profits are expected to be $2 million per month. These estimates were made by a project team that had developed two other ultrasound products and were quite knowledgeable about the medical instrument business. They wanted to take more time in the Investigation phase to completely understand the desired product features in order to move more quickly during the Development phase.

During the Development phase, that is, once product features and the customer requirements are understood, TM becomes vital and other concerns fade. The Return Map implicitly stresses execution now. The faster a product is introduced into a competitive marketplace, the longer potential life it will have—hence the greater its return. TM emphasizes the need to respond to market windows and competitive pressures.

Exhibit IV.

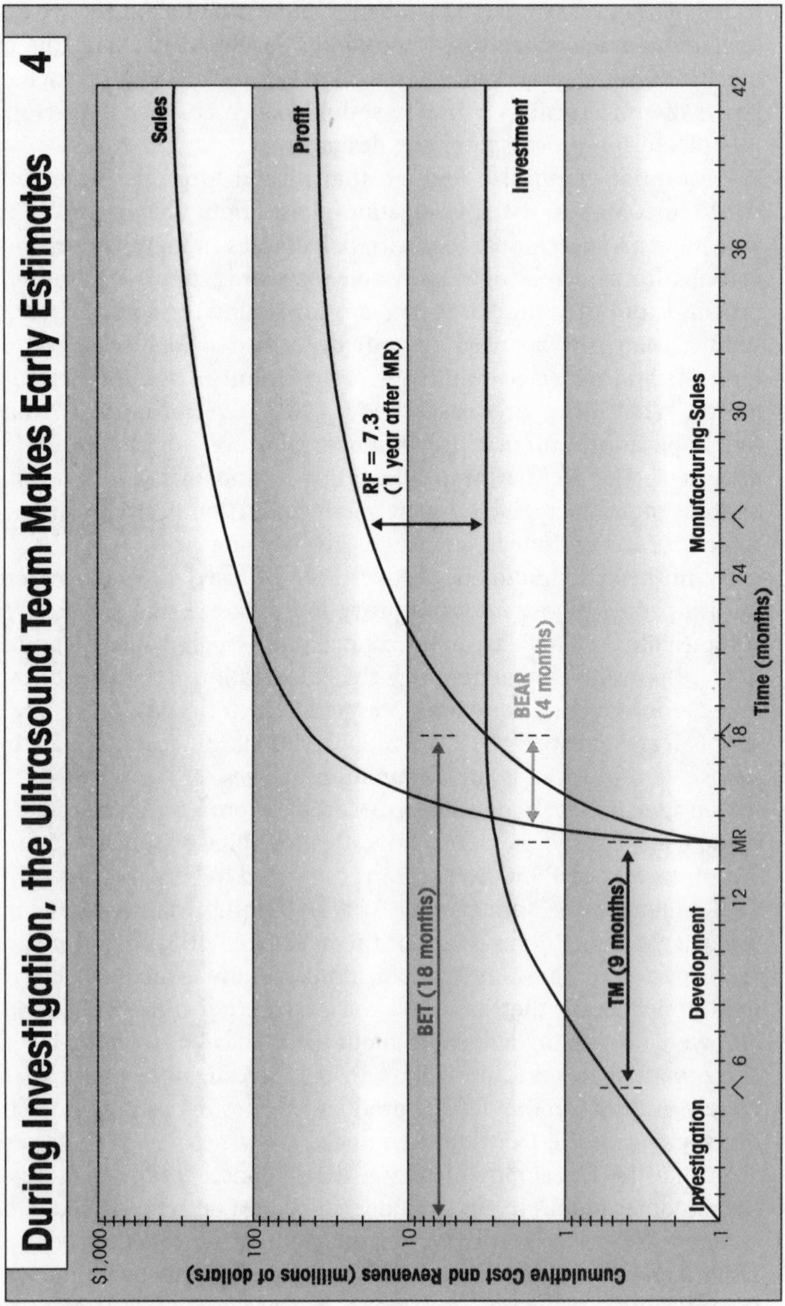

During Investigation, the Ultrasound Team Makes Early Estimates
4
Cumulative Cost and Revenues (millions of dollars)
$1,000
100
10
1
.1
Sales
Profit
Investment
RF = 7.3
(1 year after MR)
BET (18 months)
BEAR
(4 months)
TM (9 months)
Investigation
Development
Manufacturing-Sales
6
12
MR
18
24
30
36
42
Time (months)

It is difficult to keep project goals focused during development. Creeping features, management redirection, and "new" marketing data all push the project to change things in midstream, much to the detriment of engineering productivity and TM. The Return Map can help put this new information into perspective and help team members analyze the impact of changes on the entire project. For example, how much will new features increase sales and profits? If adding the features delays the introduction of the product, how will that affect sales and profit?

For example, two months into the Development phase of the ultrasound machine, Hewlett-Packard labs had a breakthrough in ultrasound technology that would enable the machine to offer clearer images. Should the project incorporate this new technology or proceed as planned? The project team determined that customers would value the features and they would result in more sales, though the new technology would be more expensive to produce. But would the changes be worth the extra expense?

The original Return Map was updated with a new set of assumptions (see Exhibit V). Development costs would increase by 40% to $3.2 million, the TM would be extended by at least 4 months, but the sales could increase by 50% and net profits could increase by 30%. The Return Map demonstrated that the BET for the project would extend to 22 months, the BEAR would remain the same, but the RF would be reduced slightly.

What on the surface seemed like a great idea proved not to increase significantly the economic return. In the end, the team decided to incorporate the new technology anyway, but in order to capture a greater market share, not to make more money. The team went into the changes with its eyes open; it made a strategic decision, not one driven by optimistic numbers.

Once the team gets beyond Investigation, the Development phase, represented by TM, can itself be segmented into subphases and submetrics that provide greater understanding and accuracy and more effective management. Teams that compare projects over time become more and more sophisticated about the development processes underlying TM forecasts. Within Hewlett-Packard, for instance, the time required for printed circuit board turnaround emerged as something of a bottleneck for many projects. So the company developed streamlined processes for printed circuit board development and eventually simulation tools that reduced the need for board prototypes.

Another HP study showed that company managers were much more

Exhibit V.

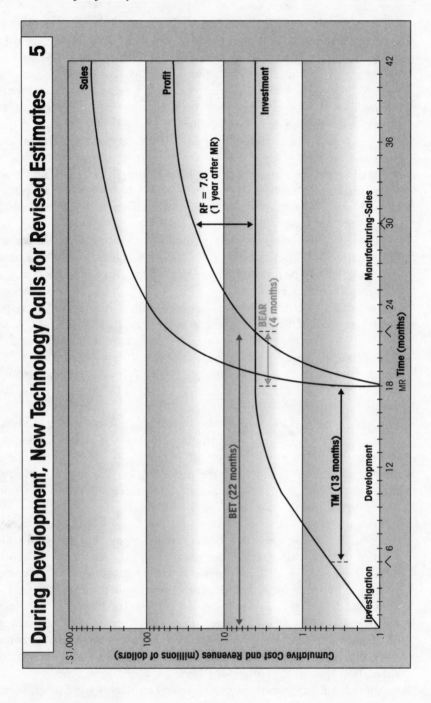

During Development, New Technology Calls for Revised Estimates   5

effective at predicting total engineering months than total calendar months (that is, effort rather than time). The big mistake here seemed to be a tendency on the company's part to try to do too many projects with the available engineers—resulting in understaffed projects. Once management focused on staffing projects adequately, the company experienced a significant reduction in this kind of forecast error.

Beyond Manufacturing Release

The Manufacturing Release, or MR, meeting is perhaps the single most important built-in checkpoint in the system. It is structured to allow the management team to focus on the original goals of the entire development effort and to compare the goals at the project's inception with the new estimates based on the realities of the Development phase. The team can now analyze the adjustments required by the marketing and manufacturing estimates, in consequence of any elapsed time, schedule slippages, or the changed competitive and economic scene.

Consider the updated Return Map for the ultrasound project showing the estimates that were made during the Development phase and the real development cost and TM (see Exhibit VI). The project took two extra months to complete and cost $700,000 more than estimated. At this time, the estimates for sales and profits are lower than Development phase estimates. The important point for team members to understand, obviously, is the effect of a slide in TM on the other measures, and they should take corrective action in the future to avoid delays. A series of MR meetings, supported by documentation, will sharpen any team's estimating and development skills.

During the Manufacturing and Sales phase, the emphasis shifts from estimates to real data for sales and profits. This is the moment of truth for the development team. As sales and profits vary from the forecast, everyone has the right—and responsibility—to ask why. One HP study tracked sales forecasts for 16 products over a two-year period. The targets were set rather broadly—a 20% deviation either way would be acceptable—on the assumption that manufacturing and sales could adjust successfully to either surging or weakening demand within that range. Nevertheless, only 12% of the forecasts fell into the acceptable range.

From our experience, this is the time when the project team gets the most constructive criticism, insight, and enthusiasm to do things right, now and the next time. At the MR stage, analysis, thoughtfulness,

Exhibit VI.

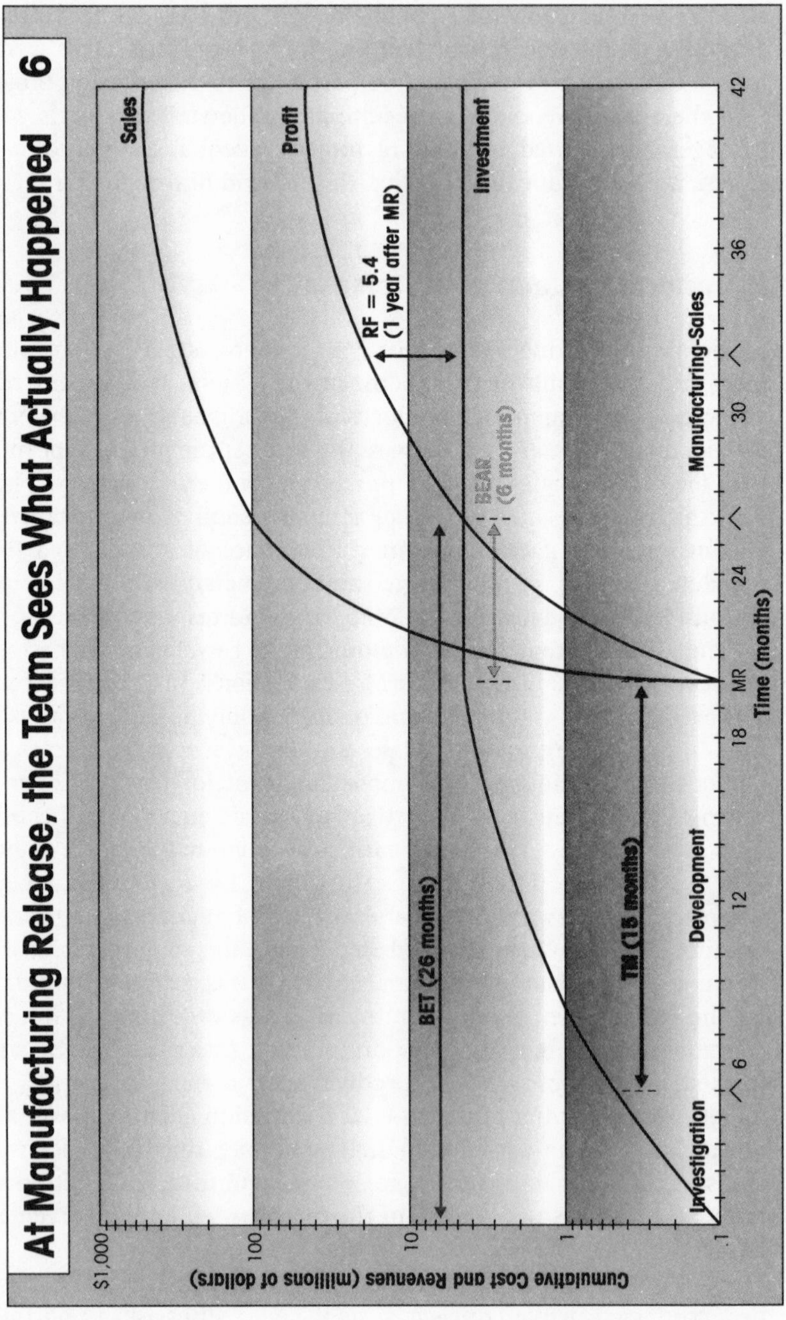
At Manufacturing Release, the Team Sees What Actually Happened
6
Cumulative Cost and Revenues (millions of dollars)
$1,000
100
10
1
.1
Sales
Profit
Investment
RF = 5.4
(1 year after MR)
BEAR
(6 months)
BET (26 months)
TM (15 months)
Investigation
Development
Manufacturing-Sales
6
12
18
MR
24
30
36
42
Time (months)

and responsiveness are vital. We have seen products falter because of such varied problems as unreliable performance, an unprepared sales force, or an inability to manufacture the product in appropriate volumes—all problems that should be correctable, even at this late date. Problems such as inappropriate features, high costs, and poor designs, however, will have to wait for the next generation.

Incidentally, one important lesson we have learned is the need to keep a nucleus of the project team together for at least six months after introduction. Team members should be available to help smooth the transition to full production and sales, and the company's next generation of products will benefit greatly from the team's collective learning.

In addition to helping manage and analyze individual products, the Return Map can be used for families of products, programs, and major systems. As companies establish a market presence with a product, it must be buttressed with corresponding products based on customer requirements and the next appropriate technologies. A complete program strategy for an important market usually embraces products from three overlapping generations, which we call a "strategic cycle."

A family of products can lead to overall success, even if some of the products do not reach standard return goals and are not seen as successful. The success of major new programs may not be obvious until the second generation is produced: it may take many years before success or failure is completely determined.

Table I illustrates the cumulative data for an entire product family, divided into three generations, with the second generation divided into five major products (A,B,C,D,E).

A quick scan of the second generation of products suggests that productivity could have been improved by doing only those products that end up with a low BET, low BEAR, and a high RF. Unfortunately, this requires more luck than foresight. One product in the series (product D) made much of the economic difference, but it is not possible to establish a full program with only one product. In fact, the success of product D was almost entirely dependent on the investment made in the technology for product C (note the long Time-to-Market) and the market understanding gained from product B.

To have a winning and sustained market presence usually requires at least three generations of products. Frequently, one of those generations will develop a new and significant technology, while the next generation will exploit that technology by means of rapid product development cycles—products tailored to specific markets.

Table I.

Product	R&D Investment (millions of dollars)	Investigation Time (months)	Time-to-Market (months)	Break-Even-After-Release (months)	Break-Even-Time (months)	Return Factor (months after MR)
Family	$19.0				68	3.1 at 60 months
First Generation	3.0	16	19	27	62	5.0 at 36 months
Second Generation	4.5	10	36	17	63	7.4 at 48 months
A	0.65	10	24	6	40	4.8 at 24 months
B	0.8	0	24	23	47	0.8 at 8 months
C	1.7	12	42	9	63	2.8 at 20 months
D	0.7	12	24	4	40	7.0 at 12 months
E	0.7	12	31	6	49	1.5 at 8 months
Third Generation	11.5	8	36	22	66	4.0 at 72 months

Easier Said Than Done

The Return Map, along with its BET, TM, BEAR, and RF measures, provides a useful indicator of the effectiveness of new product development and introduction. It provides a general management tool to track the development process and to take corrective action in real time. But while the map is simple, the difficulties of using it well are great, time-consuming, and require significant commitment. The first challenge is to get the forecast data out and to track the actual costs, sales, and profits against those forecasts. Unfortunately, most development teams will have to pull this data manually from the period expense reports, since most companies track costs, sales, and profits on a period rather than a project basis. If development teams can prove project data useful, though, accounting departments may start tracking numbers for major projects and not only aggregate numbers month by month. (HP is now overhauling its cost accounting systems to provide project as well as period data.)

Another challenge is to get functional managers to work together toward common goals and to share openly the subset measures that govern their function's contribution to BET, TM, and BEAR. The map exposes each function's weaknesses insofar as each function's performance is clearly measurable against its own predictions—predictions upon which important project decisions were based. Again, if there is going to be open sharing of data, the Return Map should not be used to penalize people for their forecasts. The race to market is a concerted effort that requires enthusiasm, not fear and apprehension. The judgments of the marketplace are generally all the correction a talented team requires.

The Return Map provides a visible superordinate goal for all the functions of the team and, in graphically representing the common task, helps them collaborate. No graph can substitute for judgment and experience—yet there is no substitute either for basing judgment on an accurate picture of experience.

4
How the Right Measures Help Teams Excel

Christopher Meyer

Many executives have realized that process-focused, multifunctional teams can dramatically improve the way their companies deliver products and services to customers. Most executives have not yet realized, however, that such teams need new performance-measurement systems to fulfill their promise.

The design of any performance-measurement system should reflect the basic operating assumptions of the organization it supports. If the organization changes and the measurement system doesn't, the latter will be at best ineffective or, more likely, counterproductive. At many companies that have moved from control-oriented, functional hierarchies to a faster and flatter team-based approach, traditional performance-measurement systems not only fail to support the new teams but also undermine them. Indeed, traditional systems often heighten the conflicts between multifunctional teams and functions that are vexing many organizations today.

Ideally, a measurement system designed to support a team-based organization should help teams overcome two major obstacles to their effectiveness: getting functions to provide expertise to teams when they need it and getting people from different functions on a team to speak a common language. Traditional measurement systems don't solve those problems.

The primary role of traditional measurement systems, which are still used in most companies, is to pull "good information" up so that

Author's note: The author would like to thank Steven C. Wheelwright, who provided valuable guidance for this article.

senior managers can make "good decisions" that flow down. To that end, each relatively independent function has its own set of measures, whose main purpose is to inform top managers about its activities. Marketing tracks market share, operations watches inventory, finance monitors costs, and so on.

Such *results measures* tell an organization where it stands in its effort to achieve goals but not how it got there or, even more important, what it should do differently. Most results measures track what goes on within a function, not what happens across functions. The few cross-functional results measures in organizations are typically financial, like revenues, gross margins, costs of goods sold, capital assets, and debt, and they exist only to help top managers. In contrast, *process measures* monitor the tasks and activities throughout an organization that produce a given result. Such measures are essential for cross-functional teams that are responsible for processes that deliver an entire service or product to customers, like order fulfillment or new-product development. Unlike a traditional, functional organization, a team-based organization not only makes it possible to use process measures but also requires them.

How should performance-measurement systems be overhauled to maximize the effectiveness of teams? Here are four guiding principles:

1. **The overarching purpose of a measurement system should be to help a team, rather than top managers, gauge its progress.** A team's measurement system should primarily be a tool for telling the team when it must take corrective action. The measurement system must also provide top managers with a means to intervene if the team runs into problems it cannot solve by itself. But even if a team has good measures, they will be of little use if senior managers use them to control the team. A measurement system is not only the measures but also the way they are used.

2. **A truly empowered team must play the lead role in designing its own measurement system.** A team will know best what sort of measurement system it needs, but the team should not design this system in isolation. Senior managers must ensure that the resulting measurement system is consistent with the company's strategy.

3. **Because a team is responsible for a value-delivery process that cuts across several functions (like product development, order fulfillment, or customer service), it must create measures to track that process.** In a traditional functional organization, no single function is responsible for a total value-delivery process; thus there are no good ways to measure those processes. In contrast, the purpose of

the multifunctional team approach is to create a structure—the team—that is responsible for a complete value-delivery process. Teams must create measures that support their mission, or they will not fully exploit their ability to perform the process faster and in a way that is more responsive to customer demands.

A process measure that a product-development team might use is one that tracks staffing levels to make sure that the necessary people are on a given team at the right time. Another measure is the number or percentage of new or unique parts to be used in a product. While such parts may offer a performance advantage, the more a product contains, the greater the likelihood that there will be difficult design, integration, inventory, manufacturing, and assembly issues.

Having sung the praises of process measures, let me throw in a qualification: while such measures are extremely important, teams still need to use some traditional measures, like one that tracks receivables, to ensure that functional and team results are achieved. Functional excellence is a prerequisite for team excellence.

4. **A team should adopt only a handful of measures.** The long-held view that "what gets measured gets done" has spurred managers to react to intensifying competition by piling more and more measures on their operations in a bid to encourage employees to work harder. As a result, team members end up spending too much time collecting data and monitoring their activities and not enough time managing the project. I have seen dozens of teams spend too much time at meetings discussing the mechanics of the measurement system instead of discussing what to *do*. As a general rule, if a team has more than 15 measures, it should take a fresh look at the importance of each one.

Trying to run a team without a good, simple guidance system is like trying to drive a car without a dashboard. We might do it in a pinch but not as a matter of practice, because we'd lack the necessary information—the speed, the amount of fuel, the engine temperature—to ensure that we reach our destination. Companies may find it helpful to create a computerized "dashboard," which inexpensive graphics software has made easy to do. (See "The Team Dashboard.")

The Team Dashboard

Spreadsheets are the most common format companies use to display their performance measures. But if a measurement system should function like a car's dashboard by providing a multifunctional team with the information it needs to complete its journey, why not actually construct a dashboard? The dashboard format, complete with colorful graphic indicators and other easy-to-read gauges, makes it much easier for a team to monitor its progress and know when it must change direction. A multifunctional team called Lethal, which designed and built a 2.5-inch disk drive for the Quantum Corporation in Milpitas, California, used the displayed dashboard.

Quantum had begun using multifunctional development teams only nine months before it established the Lethal team late in 1989. Lethal's core group included representatives from marketing, manufacturing, engineering, quality assurance, finance, and human resources. While Quantum was a strong player in the 3.5-inch drive segment, it had never made 2.5-inch drives. On top of this technical challenge, managers wanted Lethal to deliver the drive in 14 months—10 months less than similar projects had taken.

Larry, the team's principal leader, who came from engineering, was very skeptical about whether or not Quantum's past development practices would enable Lethal to reach its 14-month goal. When he asked leaders from previous teams what they would do differently, all said they would try to find a better way to detect problems early. The teams would gather all the right players, but too many problems still ended up being resolved in the functions. Larry recognized one reason for that situation: the teams had used measurement systems designed for hierarchical, functional organizations. He thought Lethal could do better.

When the team began trying to establish a schedule, its members quickly discovered that development engineering was the only function that had provided a complete schedule for performing its tasks. The others had only sketched out major milestones. In addition, individual team members were often unsure what the others' schedules meant, and none of the schedules had been integrated. Marketing had even gone ahead and set a date for the product launch without consulting development engineering!

After this revelation, the team members decided to spell out the details of all the functional schedules in terms that everyone could understand. They then integrated those schedules into one master product-development schedule, which product-development programs often lack.

In addition to this schedule monitor and a milestone gauge, the dashboard contains a variety of other results measures, which development teams typically use to track their progress in achieving the key strategic goals that will determine whether or not top managers consider the project a success. Lethal's goals included creating a product that could be

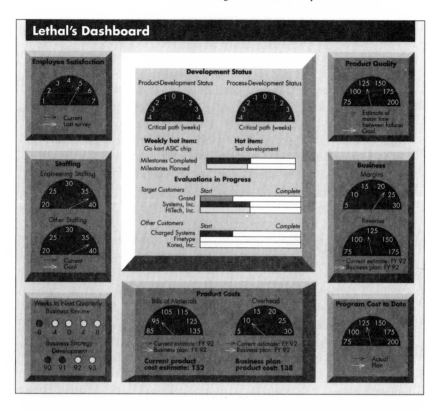

manufactured at a targeted cost (tracked by the "Overhead" and "Bills of Materials" gauges) and had a competitive quality level (tracked by the "Product Quality" gauge). The dashboard also has results measures for tracking the product's success in achieving profit margin and revenue targets once it is on the market. But such results measures tell a team only where it stands, not why it stands there. To do the latter, Lethal adopted the first process measures used by multifunctional teams in the company.

Previous teams at Quantum had focused on developing the product and treated as secondary such tasks as developing the methods and equipment for testing. Only after teams discovered that early prototypes couldn't be adequately tested did those issues receive attention. To avoid such a bottleneck, Lethal adopted a separate process-development gauge for all the tasks involved in manufacturing, including testing.

A similar discussion resulted in a decision to include staffing gauges on the dashboard. People for areas like testing, manufacturing, and marketing had to be hired early enough so that they would be on board when the team needed them. If the team waited until the development of testing methods and equipment were supposed to start before hiring test engineers, the schedule could slip by at least six weeks.

Larry's motive for suggesting the employee-satisfaction gauge was simple: unhappy team members won't keep to an ambitious schedule. The position of the "Current" needle reflects the team leaders' opinion of the team's morale. The position of the "Last survey" needle reflects the most recent survey of all team members. By forcing themselves to monitor morale, the leaders discovered that people were concerned about such things as the shortage of lab space and access to the workstations and were able to do something about those issues before they hurt morale.

The indicator lights in the lower left-hand corner of the dashboard were designed to ensure that the team allocated enough time to planning. While weekly team meetings were adequate for dealing with many issues, some, like product-launch planning, required more preparation. Because of the program's intensity, team members worried that issues that couldn't be solved quickly would eventually cause a bottleneck. Scheduling a half- or full-day meeting that everyone could attend would often take at least four weeks. John from marketing suggested that the team use the indicator lights as a reminder to schedule time for planning sessions.

The team quickly realized which gauges were not useful. John from finance argued that determining Lethal's expenses for the "Program Cost to Date" gauge was nearly impossible since the company did not have a project-based accounting system. Moreover, top managers rarely asked about an individual program's costs because they hardly varied from project to project. Since nobody on the team changed his or her behavior if the program-cost gauge dropped or increased, the team decided to eliminate it.

The team succeeded in getting potential customers for the 2.5-inch disk drive to approve the company as a qualified supplier in 16 months—2 months over the original target date but still 33% faster than previous teams. However, the drive took longer to move through the actual qualification phase than previous drives. The "Evaluations in Progress" gauges helped Lethal track its progress with potential customers but did not help the team discover a key problem until relatively late: Lethal's test procedures were more rigorous than those used by potential customers, which made it look as if the drives' failure rate was relatively high. On the basis of these data, potential customers would not qualify the company as a supplier.

> Could a dashboard with different gauges have detected the problem early enough to solve it? Probably not. Like any performance-measurement tool, the dashboard is not a replacement for the decision maker.

The lack of an effective measurement system, or dashboard, can even prevent teams from making it much past the starting line. After companies first adopt the team approach, teams must typically prove to skeptical senior and middle managers that the power these managers have wielded can be handed to the teams without the business spinning out of control. A team can offer no such proof if it lacks the tools to track its performance.

What operations executive, for example, would be willing to let a new-product development team manage the transition from an existing product to a new one if the team did not have a measure that tracked old product inventory from the factory throughout the distribution channel? Without such information, the company might end up stuck with lots of an unsellable old product. And what development executive would be willing to hand over responsibility for a project if he or she did not see that the product-development team was able to track cost, quality, and schedule?

Many managers fail to realize that results measures like profits, market share, and cost, which may help them keep score on the performance of their businesses, do not help a multifunctional team, or any organization, monitor the activities or capabilities that enable it to perform a given process. Nor do such measures tell team members what they must do to improve their performance.

An 8% drop in quarterly profits accompanied by a 10% rise in service costs, for example, does not tell a customer-service team what its service technicians should do differently on their next call. Process measures, however, examine the actions and capabilities that contributed to the situation. Knowing that the average time spent per service call rose 15% last month and that, as a result, the number of late calls rose 10% would explain to the technicians why service costs had gone up and customer satisfaction and profits had gone down.

The most commonly used results measures in product development are schedule and cost. But the fact that a program is six months late and $2 million over budget doesn't tell anyone what went wrong or what to do differently. In contrast, tracking staffing levels during the course of a project—a process measure that might include not only the number of bodies but also the years of experience in major job categories—can radically affect a team's performance. Many product-development teams, for example, do a poor job planning exactly when they will need people with a certain functional expertise. Not having all the necessary people at a particular stage often leads to expensive and time-consuming efforts to fix problems that the right people would have detected earlier.

This is exactly what I saw happen at a company that had given a multifunctional team seven months to develop a consumer product for testing blood-sugar levels. The team began work on July 1 and had a February 1 target date for launching the product. Although the company had named the people from the critical functions who would serve on the team well before the effort got under way, Mary, the manufacturing representative, did not join the team until mid-August. By then, people from marketing and development engineering had already made some best-guess decisions about significant packaging and manufacturing issues. After one week on the team, Mary raised serious questions about many of those decisions, and the team decided to adopt her suggestions and retrace its steps. Not only was Mary's arrival on the team very awkward, but also the program slipped by three weeks within the first two months.

A team's reliance on traditional measures can also cause its members to forget the team's goal and revert to their old functional way of working—or fighting—with one another. Consider the case of Ford Motor Company during the development of a luxury model in 1991. The project was one of Ford's first attempts to use multifunctional teams for product development. By and large, the team's measurement system was a collection of the individual measures that each function on the team (styling, body engineering, powertrain, purchasing, finance, etc.) had used for years.

Shortly before team members were to sign off on the car's design and begin engineering the body, a controversy developed over the door handle, which was different from the ones Ford had been using. One reason for the controversy was that each function made different assumptions about the relative importance of the factors contributing to the product's costs and competitiveness.

Members from the purchasing and finance departments feared that the handle would be too expensive. Their gauges were the cost of manufacturing the handle and its warranty costs. The people from design and body engineering responded that the handle's design was no more complex than that of existing handles. And because there was no basis for assuming that its warranty costs would be higher, they argued, the cost of manufacturing the handle should be the main issue in the cost debate. They submitted a bid from a vendor on Ford's approved vendor list as proof that the handle would be no more expensive to make. In addition, they argued, purchasing and finance were not giving enough weight to the importance of the handle's design in the overall design of the car.

The purchasing representative was still not satisfied about the warranty costs. He said that handles made by other approved vendors had had lower warranty costs than handles made by the vendor whose bid had been submitted. After a short shouting match, the design and engineering people gave up.

During the debate, no one asked the critical question: Would the new handle increase the car's ability to compete in the marketplace? Since the model's distinctive styling was a critical competitive element, the new handle might have helped the vehicle capture enough additional customers to more than compensate for higher warranty costs. Adopting the old handle was not necessarily the best decision, and this last-minute design change, which in turn required other changes, added at least one week to the development process. The members of this product-development team were still thinking as they did in their functions, where nobody had an overview of what would make the product succeed in the marketplace.

What kind of measures could have helped the team avoid its win-lose battle over cost versus style? One possibility would have been a measure that incorporated several product attributes, such as product cost, features, service, and packaging, to enable the team to assess trade-offs. This may have helped the team realize that an undetermined factor—the proposed handle's warranty costs—should not have influenced the decision so heavily.

When cross-functional teams are being established, many companies do not institute a measurement system that supports the company's strategy, ensures senior managers that there won't be unpleasant surprises, and, last but not least, truly empowers the teams. Let me offer a generic process that most companies can implement. I'll start with the role of top managers.

In two articles on the *balanced scorecard* ("The Balanced Scorecard—Measures That Drive Performance," *Harvard Business Review*, January–

February 1992, and "Putting the Balanced Scorecard to Work," *Harvard Business Review*, September–October 1993), Robert S. Kaplan and David P. Norton provide managers with a valuable framework for integrating a company's strategic objectives and competitive demands into its performance-measurement system. They urge managers to augment their traditional financial measures with measures of customer satisfaction, internal processes, and innovation and improvement activities.

What Kaplan and Norton do not explain is how such an approach can be applied to team-based organizations. I believe that it can, with one caveat: senior managers should create the strategic context for the teams but not the measures. Senior managers should dictate strategic goals, ensure that each team understands how its job fits into the strategy, and provide training so that the team can devise its own measures. But to ensure that ownership of and accountability for performance remains with the teams, managers must require the teams to decide which measures will best help them perform their jobs.

For example, the managers of a multinational computer company established an ambitious strategic goal for all of the company's product-development teams to reduce their cycle times by more than 50% within three years. But rather than dictating how the teams measure cycle time, managers asked each team to select its own measures. To help the teams in this effort, managers provided training in cycle-time reduction and a very broad selection of measures from which the teams could choose.

Top managers and a team should jointly establish rules about when or under what circumstances managers will review the team's performance and its measurement system. A team should know at the outset that it will have to review the measures it has selected with top managers to ensure that they are consistent with corporate strategy and that it may have to adjust its measures. The team should also promise to renegotiate with managers any major changes in the measures made during the course of the project. As I will discuss later, measures should not be carved in stone.

The team and senior managers should also set boundaries, which, if crossed, will signal that the team has run into trouble serious enough to trigger an "out-of-bounds" management review. Such an approach keeps managers informed without disenfranchising the team.

During an out-of-bounds review, teams and managers must define the problem and decide what corrective action to take. The team must retain responsibility for calling and running the review and executing any decisions. It must be clear that the purpose of the reviews is for senior managers to help the teams solve problems, not to find fault.

Some product-development teams actually negotiate written contracts with senior managers at the start of a project. The contracts define the product, including features and quality targets; the targeted cost to the customer; the program cost; financial information like revenues, gross margins, and cost of goods sold; and the schedule. During the contract negotiations, management ensures that the overall program, including the measures, supports the company's strategy.

The contract also establishes rules for management reviews. For example, one company requires only two planned reviews. The first comes at the end of the design phase so that management can confirm that the product still meets the market need before the company invests in expensive tooling. The second review is after production is under way so that management can learn about and pass on to other teams any advances that the team has made, like designing a particular component to be manufactured easily, and can solve unforeseen production problems early on. During the entire design phase, the team is free to proceed without any contact with management unless it has broken or knows it will break its commitments on product features, performance, product and development costs, or schedule.

The main problem at most companies that now use multifunctional teams is that top managers use a team's measurement system to monitor and control projects or processes. Even if unintentional, such behavior will inevitably undermine the effectiveness of any team.

This is what happened when a Ford manufacturing plant turned to multifunctional teams to improve product quality but didn't change management's command-and-control mind-set.

The company grouped line workers from various functional areas into teams and trained them to collect and analyze data so that they could resolve quality problems on their own. But then came the mistake: the division managers asked quality engineers, who supposedly had been sent to assist the teams, to send a monthly report on the plant's quality and plans for improving it. In turn, the quality engineers asked the teams for their data.

Over time, the teams began to depend on the quality engineers to analyze the data and waited for the engineers' directions before taking action. The engineers recognized what was happening but felt caught in a bind because the division managers wanted them, rather than the teams, to provide the reports. Problems that the teams had been able to resolve on their own in a day or two began to require the involvement of the quality engineers and twice the time. And the quality engineers asked for more engineers to help them support the teams.

The division managers became very frustrated. Given all their verbal support for empowering teams, they couldn't understand why the teams didn't act empowered.

When a group of people builds a measurement system, it also builds a team. One benefit of having a team create its own measurement system is that members who hail from different functions end up creating a common language, which they need in order to work as an effective team. Until a group creates a common language, it can't reach a common definition of goals or problems. Instead of acting like a team, the group will act like a collection of functions.

As a first step, the team should develop a work plan that can serve as a process map of the critical tasks and capabilities required to complete the project. The second step is to make sure that everyone understands the team's goals in the same way. Team members frequently start out believing that they share an understanding of their goals only to discover when they begin developing performance measures how wrong they were.

After the goals have been confirmed, the appropriate team members should develop individual measures for gauging the team's progress in achieving a given goal and identifying the conditions that would trigger an out-of-bounds review. In addition, each member should come to the next meeting with two or three gauges that he or she considers most effective for monitoring his or her functional area. In an attempt to push team members to focus on overall goals and the total value-delivery process as they develop measures, they should be encouraged to include process measures. (See "Creating Process Measures.")

Creating Process Measures

There are four basic steps to creating process measures: defining what kinds of factors, such as time, cost, quality, and product performance, are critical to satisfying customers; mapping the cross-functional process used to deliver results; identifying the critical tasks and capabilities required to complete the process successfully; and, finally, designing measures that track those tasks and capabilities. The most effective process measures are often those that express relative terms. For example, a measure that tracks the percentage of new or unique parts is usually more valuable than one that tracks the absolute number.

Here's how the parts and service operation of a Europe-based car company created process measures.

The warehousing function had traditionally measured its performance by tracking how often parts ordered by dealers could be filled immediately from the warehouse shelf. If a stock picker found a gasket on the warehouse shelf—meaning that it did not have to be ordered—that counted as a "first fill."

When the organization began using teams, it put the warehousing and the dealer-service groups on a multifunctional team charged with improving the total service process, from product breakdown through repair. The team reexamined the current performance measures and concluded that, from the dealer's perspective, the first-fill measure was meaningless. Dealers—and the final customers—didn't care where the part came from; they just wanted to know when they'd receive it. And just because a part was on the warehouse shelf did not ensure that it would get to a dealer quickly; the sloppy handling of orders and shipping problems could also cause delays.

Because the new team was responsible for the entire process, it mapped all the steps in the service cycle, from the moment the warehouse received a dealer's order to the moment the dealer received the part, and the time each step took. The team then identified its critical tasks and capabilities, which included the order-entry operation, the management-information system for tracking orders and inventories, warehouse operations, and shipping. The team created cycle-time measures for six to eight subprocesses, which helped the team see how much time was being spent on each step of the process relative to the value of that process. With this information, the team could begin figuring out how to reduce cycle time without sacrificing quality. The resulting changes included reducing the copies made of each order and the number of signatures required to authorize filling it. Within six months, the team was able to reduce the service cycle considerably. Not coincidentally, dealer complaints fell by a comparable amount.

At the next meeting, each member should explain what his or her proposed measures track and why they are important. Everyone should make an effort to define any terms or concepts that are unfamiliar to others. One important rule is that no question is a "dumb question."

So-called dumb questions are often the most valuable because they test the potential value of each measure in the most obvious terms.

Some measures will be either eliminated or agreed on very quickly. The hard work will be assessing those that fall in between. No final decisions should be made until all the gauges accepted or still in contention are tested as a unit against the following criteria:

- Are critical team objectives (like filling an order within 24 hours) tracked?
- Are all out-of-bounds conditions monitored?
- Are the critical variables required to reach the goal (like having enough skilled personnel to run an order-entry system) tracked?
- Would management approve the system as is or seek changes?
- Is there any gauge that wouldn't cause the team to change its behavior if the needle swung from one side to another? If so, eliminate it.
- Are there too many gauges? As I mentioned earlier, if a team has more than 15 measures, it should take a second look at each one.

After a team's measures have passed this test, the system is ready for the management review.

A team can preserve the value of its performance-measurement system by diligently adding and eliminating gauges, as required, during the project or task.

Measures that were relevant during the early stages in the development of a new product will undoubtedly become irrelevant as the product nears production. In most cases, teams realize that and plan for changes during the development of their measurement systems. But priorities often change during a project, which means that measures should be changed too. And sometimes measures prove not to be so useful after all and should be dropped. A team should also regularly audit the data being fed into its measurement system to make sure they are accurate and timely.

Managers are still in the early stages of learning how to maximize the effectiveness of multifunctional teams that are incorporated into their functional organizations. The same applies to the measurement systems used to guide both. As companies gain experience, they will discover that some specific measures can be used over and over again by different teams undertaking similar tasks or projects. But managers should be on their guard lest they do with performance-measurement systems what they have done with so many management tools: assume that one size fits all. Managers can systematize the process that teams use to create their measurement systems. They can also catalog the measures that appear to have been most effective in particular applications. But managers must never make the mistake of thinking that they know what is best for the team. If they do, they will have crossed the line and returned to the command-and-control ways of yore. And they will have rendered their empowered teams powerless.

5
The Power of Product Integrity

Kim B. Clark and Takahiro Fujimoto

Some companies consistently develop products that succeed with customers. Other companies often fall short. What differentiates them is integrity. Every product reflects the organization and the development process that created it. Companies that consistently develop successful products—products with integrity—are themselves coherent and integrated. Moreover, this coherence is distinguishable not just at the level of structure and strategy but also, and more important, at the level of day-to-day work and individual understanding. Companies with organizational integrity possess a source of competitive advantage that rivals cannot easily match.

The primacy of integrity, in products and organizations alike, begins with the role new products play in industrial competition and with the difficulty of competing on performance or price alone. New products have always fascinated and excited customers, of course. Henry Ford's Model A made front-page news after near-riots erupted outside dealers' showrooms. But today, in industries ranging from cars and computers to jet engines and industrial controls, new products are the focal point of competition. Developing high-quality products faster, more efficiently, and more effectively tops the competitive agenda for senior managers around the world.

Three familiar forces explain why product development has become so important. In the last two decades, intense international competition, rapid technological advances, and sophisticated, demanding cus-

Authors' note: We gratefully acknowledge the help of Nobuhiko Kawamoto, CEO of Honda Motor Company, and Tateomi Miyoshi, large product leader for the Honda Accord.

tomers have made "good enough" unsatisfactory in more and more consumer and industrial markets. Yet the very same forces are also making product integrity harder and harder to achieve.

Consider what happened when Mazda and Honda each introduced four-wheel steering to the Japanese auto market in 1987. Although the two steering systems used different technologies—Mazda's was based on electronic control, while Honda's was mechanical—they were equally sophisticated, economical, and reliable. Ten years earlier, both versions probably would have met with success. No longer. A majority of Honda's customers chose to install fourwheel steering in their new cars; Mazda's system sold poorly and was widely regarded as a failure.

Why did consumers respond so differently? Product integrity. Honda put its four-wheel steering system into the Prelude, a two-door coupe with a sporty, progressive image that matched consumers' ideas about the technology. The product's concept and the new component fit together seamlessly; the car sent a coherent message to its potential purchasers. In contrast, Mazda introduced its four-wheel steering system in the 626, a five-door hatchback that consumers associated with safety and dependability. The result was a mismatch between the car's conservative, family image and its racy steering system. Too sophisticated to be swayed by technology alone (as might have been the case a decade before), Mazda's potential customers saw no reason to buy a car that did not satisfy their expectations in every respect, including "feel." (Mazda's new advertising slogan, "It just feels right," suggests the company's managers took this lesson to heart.)

Product integrity is much broader than basic functionality or technical performance. Customers who have accumulated experience with a product expect new models to balance basic functions and economy with more subtle characteristics. Consumers expect new products to harmonize with their values and lifestyles. Industrial customers expect them to mesh with existing components in a work system or a production process. The extent to which a new product achieves this balance is a measure of its integrity. (One of integrity's primary metrics is market share, which reflects how well a product attracts and satisfies customers over time.)

Product integrity has both an internal and an external dimension. Internal integrity refers to the consistency between a product's function and its structure: the parts fit smoothly, the components match and work well together, the layout maximizes the available space. Organizationally, internal integrity is achieved mainly through cross-functional coordination within the company and with suppliers. Efforts to enhance internal integrity through this kind of coordination have become standard practice among product developers in recent years.

External integrity refers to the consistency between a product's performance and customers' expectations. In turbulent markets like those in which Honda and Mazda were competing, external integrity is critical to a new product's competitiveness. Yet for the most part, external integrity is an underexploited opportunity. Companies assign responsibility for anticipating what customers will want to one or more functional groups (the product planners in marketing, for example, or the testers in product engineering). But they give little or no attention to integrating a clear sense of customer expectations into the work of the product development organization as a whole.

Of course, there are exceptions. In a six-year study of new product development (see "Focus on Development"), we found a handful of companies that consistently created products with integrity. What set these companies apart was their seamless pattern of organization and management. The way people did their jobs, the way decisions were made, the way suppliers were integrated into the company's own efforts—everything cohered and supported company strategy. If keeping the product line fresh and varied was a goal, speed and flexibility were apparent at every step in the development process, as were the habits and assumptions that accustom people and organizations to being flexible and to solving problems quickly. For example, product plans relied on large numbers of parts from suppliers who focused on meeting tight schedules and high quality standards even when designs changed late in the day. Product and process engineers jointly developed body panels and the dies to make them through informal, intense interactions that cut out unnecessary mistakes and solved problems on the spot. Production people built high-quality prototypes that tested the design against the realities of commercial production early in the game and so eliminated expensive delays and rework later on.

Focus on Development

What are the sources of superior performance in product development? What accounts for the wide differences in performance among companies in the same industry? To answer those questions, we studied 29 major development projects in 20 automobile companies around the world. (Three companies are headquartered in the United States, eight in Japan, and nine in Europe.) The projects ranged from micro-mini cars and small vans to large luxury sedans, with suggested retail prices from $4,300 to more than $40,000. Our research methods included structured and unstructured interviews, questionnaires, and statistical analysis. Throughout the study, we strove to develop a consistent set of data (including both measures of performance and patterns of organization and management) so that we could identify the constants among projects that differed greatly in scope and complexity.

We chose to concentrate on the automobile industry because it is a microcosm of the new industrial competition. In 1970, a handful of auto companies competed on a global scale with products for every market segment; today more than 20 do. Customers have grown more discerning, sophisticated, and demanding. The number of models has multiplied, even as growth has slowed, and technology is ever-more complex and diverse. In 1970, for example, the traditional V-8 engine with 3-speed automatic transmission and rear-wheel drive was the technology of choice for 80% of the cars produced in the United States. By the early 1980s, consumers could choose among 34 alternative configurations. In this environment, fast, efficient, effective product development has become the focal point of competition and managerial action.

The examples we draw on in this article all come from the auto industry. We chose to look at a single industry worldwide so that we could identify the factors that separate outstanding performers from competitors making similar products for similar markets around the globe. But our basic findings apply to businesses as diverse as semi-conductors, soup, and commercial construction. Wherever managers face a turbulent, intensely competitive market, product integrity—and the capacity to create it—can provide a sustainable competitive advantage.

The Power of a Product Concept

Products are tangible objects—things you can see, touch, and use. Yet the process of developing new products depends as much on the flow of information as it does on the flow of materials. Consider how a new product starts and ends.

Before a customer unpacks a new laptop computer or sets up a high-speed packaging machine, and long before a new car rolls off the showroom floor, the product (or some early version of it) begins as an idea. Next, that idea is embodied in progressively more detailed and concrete forms: ideas turn into designs, designs into drawings, drawings into blueprints, blueprints into prototypes, and so on until a finished product emerges from the factory. When it is finally in customers' hands, the product is converted into information once again.

If this last statement sounds odd, think about what actually happens when a potential buyer test-drives a new car. Seated behind the wheel, the customer receives a barrage of messages about the vehicle's performance. Some of these messages are delivered directly by the car: the feel of the acceleration, the responsiveness of the steering system, the noise of the engine, the heft of a door. Others come indirectly: the look on people's faces as the car goes by, comments from passengers, the driver's recollection of the car's advertising campaign. All these messages influence the customer's evaluation, which will largely depend on how he or she interprets them. In essence, the customer is consuming the product *experience*, not the physical product itself.

Developing this experience—and the car that will embody it—begins with the creation of a product concept. A powerful product concept specifies how the new car's basic functions, structures, and messages will attract and satisfy its target customers. In sum, it defines the character of the product from a customer's perspective.

The phrase "pocket rocket," for example, captures the basic concept for a sporty version of a subcompact car. Small, light, and fast, a pocket rocket should also have quick, responsive handling and an aggressive design. While the car should sell at a premium compared with the base model, it should still be affordable. And the driving experience should be fun: quick at the getaway, nimble in the turns, and very fast on the straightaways. Many other design and engineering details would need definition, of course, for the car to achieve its objectives. But the basic concept of an affordable and fun-to-drive pocket rocket would be critical in guiding and focusing creative ideas and decisions.

By definition, product concepts are elusive and equivocal. So it is not surprising that when key project participants are asked to relate the concept for a new vehicle, four divergent notions of value emerge. Those for whom the product concept means *what the product does* will couch their description in terms of performance and technical functions. Others, for whom the concept means *what the product is*, will describe the car's packaging, configuration, and main component technologies. Others, for whom product concept is synonymous with *whom the product serves*, will describe target customers. Still others, reflecting their interpretation of the concept as *what the product means to customers*, will respond thematically, describing the car's character, personality, image, and feel.

The most powerful product concepts include all these dimensions. They are often presented as images or metaphors (like pocket rocket) that can evoke many different aspects of the new product's message without compromising its essential meaning. Honda Motor is one of the few auto companies that make the generation of a strong product concept the first step in their development process.

When Honda's engineers began to design the third-generation (or 1986) Accord in the early 1980s, they did not start with a sketch of a car. The engineers started with a concept—"man maximum, machine minimum"—that captured in a short, evocative phrase the way they wanted customers to feel about the car. The concept and the car have been remarkably successful: since 1982, the Accord has been one of the best-selling cars in the United States; in 1989, it was the top-selling car. Yet when it was time to design the 1990 Accord, Honda listened to the market, not to its own success. Market trends were indicating a shift away from sporty sedans toward family models. To satisfy future customers' expectations—and to reposition the Accord, moving it up-market just a bit—the 1990 model would have to send a new set of product messages.

As the first step in developing an integrated product concept, the Accord's project manager (the term Honda uses is "large product leader") led a series of small group discussions involving close to 100 people in all. These early brainstorming sessions involved people from many parts of the organization, including body engineering, chassis engineering, interior design, and exterior design. In line with Honda tradition, the groups developed two competing concepts in parallel. The subject of the discussions was abstract: what would be expected of a family sedan in the 1990s. Participants talked frequently about "adult taste" and "fashionability" and eventually came to a consensus on the message the new model would deliver to customers—"an adult sense of reliability." The ideal family car would allow the driver to transport family and friends with confidence, whatever the weather or road conditions; passengers would always feel safe and secure.

This message was still too abstract to guide the product and process engineers who would later be making concrete choices about the new Accord's specifications, parts, and manufacturing processes. So the next step was finding an image that would personify the car's message to consumers. The image the product leader and his team emerged with was "a rugby player in a business suit." It evoked rugged, physical contact, sportsmanship, and gentlemanly behavior—disparate qualities the new car would have to convey. The image was also concrete enough to translate clearly into design details. The decision to replace the old Accord's retractable headlamps with headlights made with a pioneering technology developed by Honda's supplier, Stanley, is a good example. To the designers and engineers, the new lights' totally transparent cover glass symbolized the will of a rugby player looking into the future calmly, with clear eyes.

The next and last step in creating the Accord's product concept was to break down the rugby player image into specific attributes the new car would have to possess. Five sets of key words captured what the product leader envisioned: "open-minded," "friendly communication," "tough spirit," "stress-free," and "love forever." Individually and as a whole, these key words reinforced the car's message to consumers. "Tough spirit" in a car, for example, meant maneuverability, power, and sure handling in extreme driving conditions, while "love forever" translated into long-term reliability and customer satisfaction. Throughout the course of the project, these phrases provided a kind of shorthand to help people make coherent design and hardware choices in the face of competing demands. Moreover, they were a powerful spur to innovation.

Consider this small slice of the process. To approximate the rugby player's reliability and composure ("stress-free"), the engineers had to eliminate all unnecessary stress from the car. In technical terms, this meant improving the car's NVH, or noise, vibration, and harshness characteristics. That, in turn, depended on reducing the "three gangs of noise," engine noise, wind noise, and road noise.

To reduce engine noise, the product engineers chose a newly developed balance shaft that rotated twice as fast as the engine and offset its vibration. The shaft made the Accord's compact 4-cylinder engine as quiet as a V-6 and conserved space in the process. But since the shaft was effective only when the engine was turning over reasonably quickly, the product engineers also had to design a new electrically controlled engine mount to minimize vibration when the engine was idling.

Moreover, once the engine was quieter, other sources of noise became apparent. The engineers learned that the floor was amplifying noise from the engine, as was the roof, which resonated with the engine's vibration and created unpleasant, low-frequency booming sounds. To solve these problems, the engineers inserted paper honeycomb structures 12 to 13 millimeters thick in the roof lining—a solution that also improved the roof's structural rigidity and contributed to the car's tough spirit. They also redesigned the body floor, creating a new sandwich structure of asphalt and sheet steel, which similarly strengthened the body shell.

Multiply this example hundreds of times over and it is clear why a strong product concept is so important. At its core, the development process is a complex system for solving problems and making decisions. Product concepts like those developed at Honda give people a clear framework for finding solutions and making decisions that complement one another and ultimately contribute to product integrity.

Organizing for Integrity

When cars were designed and developed by a handful of engineers working under the direction of a Henry Ford, a Gottlieb Daimler, or a Kiichiro Toyoda, organization was not an issue. What mattered were the engineers' skills, the group's chemistry, and the master's guidance. These are still vital to product integrity; but the organizational challenge has become immeasurably more complex. Developing a new car involves hundreds (if not thousands) of people working on specialized pieces of the project in many different locations for months or even years at a time. Whether their efforts have integrity—whether the car performs superbly and delights customers—will depend on how the company organizes development and the nature of the leadership it creates.

Efforts to organize development effectively are rooted in the search for solutions to two basic problems. One is designing, building, and testing the product's parts and subsystems so that every element achieves a high level of performance. In a car, this means that the brakes hold on wet or icy roads, the suspension gives a smooth ride on rough roads, the car corners well on sharp turns, and so on. Because performance at this level is driven by expertise and deep understanding, some specialization, both for individuals and for the organization, is essential. Yet specialization is a double-edged sword. By complicating communication and coordination across the organization, it complicates the second problem that development organizations face: achieving product integrity.

When markets were relatively stable, product life cycles long, and customers concerned most with technical performance, companies could achieve product integrity through strong functional organizations. Managers could commit whatever resources and time it took to make products that worked well, and external integrity (matching the product to customer expectations) was simply a by-product of those efforts. But as competition intensified and customers' needs and wants grew harder to predict, integration became an explicit goal for most product developers. By the late 1980s, even the most resolutely functional development organizations had established formal mechanisms such as coordination committees, engineering liaisons, project managers, matrix structures, and cross-functional teams to improve product development.

Structural mechanisms like these are only a small part of achieving product integrity, however. At best—when they are reinforced and supported by the behaviors, attitudes, and skills of people in every part of the development organization—they speed problem solving and improve the quality of the solutions. But by design, they are focused inward; they do not address integrity's external dimension. So unless the company makes a deliberate effort to integrate customers into the development process, it is likely to create products that are fresh, technologically advanced, and provide good value but that often fall short with sophisticated consumers.

For this reason, external integration is the single most important task for new product development. It represents a conscious organizational effort to enhance the external integrity of the development process by matching the philosophy and details of product design to the expectations of target customers. Generating a distinctive product concept that anticipates future customers' needs and wants is the first step in external integration. Infusing this concept into drawings, plans, detailed designs, and, ultimately, the product itself is the substance of its ongoing work.

To get some sense of how thorough (and hard) this infusion process actually is, consider a few of the conflicts Honda faced during the planning stage for the third-generation Accord.

The vehicle's product concept (man maximum, machine minimum) included maximum space and visibility for the occupants, minimum space for the car's mechanisms, a wide, low body for aesthetics, superb handling and stability, and superior economy in operation. To convey a feeling of spaciousness, the design called for a low engine hood and a larger-than-usual front window. Both features increased the driver's visibility and sense of interaction with the outside world. But the window size also meant that the cabin would get uncomfortably hot on sunny days unless the car had a big air conditioner—as well as a powerful engine to run it.

A large engine—the obvious solution—was precluded by the deci-

286 Building High-Performance Teams

sion to keep the hood low, since the only suspension system that would work was an expensive, double-wishbone construction that narrowed the engine chamber. And in any case, the engineers wanted the engine to be light so that the car would handle sharply.

The height of the hood became a battlefield, with body, engine, and chassis engineers warring over millimeters. What made the conflict constructive—it ultimately led to the development of a new engine that was both compact and powerful—was the fact that all the combatants understood what the Accord had to achieve. Guided by the large product leader, who saw every argument as an opportunity to reinforce the car's basic concept, the engineers could see their work through future customers' eyes.

As Honda's experience indicates, external integration extends deeply into the development organization, and it involves much more than being "market oriented" or "customer driven." It begins with customers, to be sure, since the best concept developers invariably supplement the cooked information they get from marketing specialists with raw data they gather themselves. But strong product concepts also include a healthy measure of what we call "market imagination": they encompass what customers say they want and what the concept's creators *imagine* customers will want three or more years into the future. Remembering that customers know only existing products and existing technologies, they avoid the trap of being too close to customers—and designing products that will be out-of-date before they are even manufactured.

Interestingly, companies that are heavily driven by market data tend to slip on external integrity. As a rule, these companies have well-equipped marketing organizations with great expertise in formal research, and they are adept at using data from focus groups, product clinics, and the like to develop customer profiles. But these methods rarely lead to distinctive product concepts. In fact, to the extent that they limit or suppress the imaginations of product designers, they can actually harm a new product's future competitiveness.

How auto companies organize for external integration—and how much power they invest in their integrators—varies greatly. Some companies create an explicit role for an "external integrator" and assign it to people in a few functional units (testers in engineering, for example, and product planners in marketing). Others assign all their external integrators to a single specialized unit, which may be independent or organized by product. Similarly, the work of concept creation and concept realization may be broken up among different groups in the development organization or consolidated under one leader, as it is at Honda.

We have already seen how advantageous consolidating responsibility can be for enhancing external integration. This approach is equally successful in achieving internal integrity.

One of the thorniest issues in creating a strong product concept is when (and how) to involve functional specialists other than those who make up the product development team. As we saw with the Accord, the product concept has clear repercussions for every aspect of the development process, from design and layout to cost and manufacturability. So on the one hand, front-loading input and information from specialists downstream is highly desirable. On the other hand, broad downstream involvement can easily jeopardize the distinctiveness and clarity of a product concept if (as often happens) negotiations and battles among powerful functions lead to political compromises and patchwork solutions.

The fact that working-level engineers were involved in the concept stage of the Accord's development was essential to its product integrity. Faced with tough choices about the car's front end, the engineers had not only a clear concept to guide them but also one they felt they owned. Moreover, their solution—the new engine—enhanced the Accord's internal integrity by raising its level of technical performance. At the same time, internal demands and functional constraints never compromised the Accord's basic concept. Like many of the other product managers we spoke with, the Accord's product leader knew that democracy without clear concept leadership is the archenemy of distinctive products.

There are other ways to balance downstream expertise with strong concept leadership, of course. (One of Honda's rivals also makes early cross-functional negotiations an important part of its new product development work, for example, but gives a small group of concept creators and assistants six months or so to establish the concept first, before the negotiations begin.) The important point is that integrity depends on striking a balance between the two. Companies that trade off one for the other sacrifice both product and organizational integrity. Those that place sole responsibility for the product concept with a specialized unit (often one within marketing) end up with lots of last-minute design and engineering changes. Conversely, companies that initiate senior-level, cross-functional negotiations at the very start of every project usually find themselves with undistinguished products.

The integration that leads to product integrity does not surface in organization charts alone, nor is it synonymous with the creation of cross-functional teams, the implementation of "design for manufacturing," or any other useful organizational formula for overhauling development work. Ironically, efforts to increase integration can even undermine it if the integrating mechanisms are misconstructed or if the organization is unprepared for the change. At one U.S. auto company, we found a very coherent cross-functional project team with great spirit and purpose. But the team was made up solely of liaisons and included none of the working engineers actually responsible for drawings and prototypes. So for the most part, engineers ignored the team, whose existence only masked the lack of true integration.

What distinguishes outstanding product developers is the consistency between their formal structures and the informal organization that accomplishes the real work of development. In the case of the Honda Accord, we have seen some important characteristics of such consistency: the company's preference for firsthand information and direct (sometimes conflict-full) discussion; the way specialists are respected but never deified; the constant stream of early, informal communication (even at the risk of creating confusion or inefficiencies in the short run); and, most important, the primacy of strong concept leadership.

Integrity's Champion: The Heavyweight Product Manager

The key to product integrity is leadership. Product managers in companies whose products consistently succeed accomplish two things without fail. They focus the whole development organization on customer satisfaction. And they devise processes (both formal and informal) for creating powerful product concepts and infusing them into the details of production and design. In our lexicon, they are "heavyweight" product managers, and they differ significantly from their lighter weight counterparts in other companies.

During the 1980s, product managers began to appear at more and more of the world's auto companies. In most cases, the title means relatively little. The position adds another box to the organization chart, but the organization's basic structure is still heavily functional. Product managers in these companies coordinate development activities through liaison representatives from each of the engineering departments. They have no direct access to working-level engineers, no contact with marketing, and no concept responsibility. Their positions have less status and power than the functional managers' do, and they have little influence outside of product engineering (and only limited influence within it). Their job is to collect information on the status of work, to help functional groups resolve conflicts, and to facilitate completion of the project's overall goals. They do not actually impair a product's integrity, but neither can they contribute much to it.

The contrast with the heavyweight's job could not be more striking. In a few auto companies, product managers play a role that simply does not exist in other automakers' development organizations. Like the Accord's large product leader, they are deeply involved in creating a strong product concept. Then, as the concept's guardians, they keep the concept alive and infuse it into every aspect of the new product's design. As one heavyweight product manager told us, "We listen to process engineers. We listen to plant managers. But we make the final decisions. Above all, we cannot make any compromise on the concept. The concept is the soul of the vehicle; we cannot sell it."

Guardianship like this is crucial because the product concept can get lost so easily in the complexity of actually designing, planning, and building a new car. The problems that preoccupied the Accord's product engineers were often almost imperceptibly small: a three-millimeter gap between the window glass and the body; the tiny chips on the car's sills that come from stones kicked up on the road; a minuscule gap between the hood and the body. But problems like these are the stuff of product integrity: all the magic is in the details.

Keeping track of those details, however, is no easy matter. Nor is it easy to keep the product concept fresh and clear in many people's minds during the months (and years) that development consumes. For that reason, heavyweight product managers must be a little like evangelists, with the product concept as their Bible and the work of exhorting, preaching, and reminding as their mission. To paraphrase an assistant product manager in one of the heavyweight organizations, subtle nuances such as the car's taste and character have to be built into the design by fine-tuning. They cannot be expressed completely in planning documents, no matter how detailed those may be. So the product manager has to interact continuously with the engineers to communicate his intentions and to refresh and reinforce their understanding of the product concept.

As concept guardians, heavyweight product managers draw on both personal credibility and expertise and the organizational clout that comes with the job. Themselves engineers by training, heavyweight product managers have a broad knowledge of the product and process engineering required to develop an entire vehicle. Years of experience with their companies give their words weight and increase their influence with people over whom they have no formal authority.

Product planners and engineers working on the detailed design of specific parts typically fall into this category. Yet as we have seen, the substance of their work is vital to a new car's integrity. To track design decisions and ensure that the concept is being translated accurately, heavyweight managers communicate daily with the functional engineering departments. They also intervene directly when decisions about parts or components that are particularly problematic or central to the product concept are being made. From a functional point of view, this is clearly a breach of organizational etiquette. But in practice, this intervention is usually readily accepted, in part because it is backed by tradition but mostly because of the product manager's credibility. When heavyweights visit bench-level engineers, they come to discuss substantive issues and their input is usually welcome. They are not making courtesy calls or engaging in morale-building exercises.

Organizationally, the heavyweight manager effectively functions as the product's general manager. In addition to concept-related duties, the responsibilities that come with the job include: coordinating production and sales as well as engineering; coordinating the entire project from concept to market; signing off on specification, cost-target, layout, and major component choices; and maintaining direct contact with existing and potential customers. Some of this work occurs through liaison representatives (although the liaisons themselves are "heavier" than they are in the lightweight organizations since they also serve as local project leaders within their functional groups). But there is no mistaking the heavyweights' clout: engineering departments typically report to them (which ones depends on the internal linkages the company wishes to emphasize). Heavyweights are also well supplied with formal procedures like design review and control of prototype scheduling that give them leverage throughout the organization.

Still, probably the best measure of a product manager's weight is the amount of time that formal meetings and paperwork consume. Lightweight product managers are much like high-level clerks. They spend most of the day reading memos, writing reports, and going to meetings. Heavyweights, in contrast, are invariably "out"—with engineers, plant people, dealers, and customers. "This job can't be done without wearing out my shoes," one experienced manager commented. "Since

I'm asking other engineers for favors, I shouldn't ask them to come to me. I have to go and talk to them."

What lies behind "product managers in motion" is the central role that information plays in bringing new products to life. Take the heavyweight's interaction with customers. Talented product managers spend hours watching people on the street, observing styles, and listening to conversations. Department stores, sports arenas, museums, and discotheques are all part of their "market research" beat.

Heavyweight product managers are equally active in their relations with the test engineers. Like the product manager, test engineers stand in for the customer. When they evaluate a suspension system or test-drive a new car, they are rehearsing the experience the future customer will consume. To do this successfully, in ways that will ensure product integrity, the test engineers must know what to look for. In other words, they must be crystal clear on the product concept.

Heavyweight product managers make sure this clarity exists. They often test-drive vehicles and talk about their experiences with the test engineers. Many can and do evaluate the car's performance on the test track and show up almost daily during critical tests. They also seize every opportunity to build good communication channels and deepen their ties with younger engineers. One product manager said he welcomed disagreements among the test engineers because they gave him a good reason to go out to the proving ground and talk about product concepts with younger people with whom he would not otherwise interact.

If we reverse direction to look at how heavyweight product managers promote internal integrity, the same kind of behavior and activities come to the fore. Direct contact with product engineers and testers, for example, not only reinforces the product concept but also strengthens the links between functions, speeds up decision making and problem solving, and makes it easier to coordinate work flows. In fact, almost everything a product manager does to infuse the concept into the details makes the organization itself work better and faster. The reason is the strong customer orientation that the product concept—and product manager—convey.

The product manager's job touches every part of the new product process. Indeed, heavyweight product managers have to be "multilingual," fluent in the languages of customers, marketers, engineers, and designers. On one side, this means being able to translate an evocative concept like the pocket rocket into specific targets like "maximum speed 250 kilometers per hour" and "drag coefficient less than 0.3" that detail-oriented engineers can easily grasp. On the other side, it means being able to assess and communicate what a "0.3 drag coefficient" will mean to customers. (The fact that the translation process from customer to engineer is generally harder than that from engineer to customer explains why engineering tends to be the heavyweight product managers' native tongue.)

Because development organizations are continually involved in changing one form of information into another, face-to-face conversations and informal relationships are their life's blood. Heavyweight managers understand this and act on it. Aware that product concepts cannot be communicated in written documents alone (any more than the feel and sensibility of a new car can be captured in words alone), they travel constantly—telling stories, coining phrases, and generally making sure that nothing important gets lost in translation.

The Improvement Ethic

How a company develops new products says a great deal about what that company is and does. For most companies, the journey toward competing on integrity began during the 1980s. Quite possibly, it was inaugurated with a commitment to total quality or to reducing the lead time for developing new products. Heavyweight product management constitutes the next step on that journey. Taking it leads down one of two paths.

Some companies introduce a heavyweight product management system modestly and incrementally. A typical progression might go like this: shift from a strictly functional setup to a lightweight system, with the integrator responsible only for product engineering; expand the product manager's sphere to include new tasks such as product planning or product-process coordination; then raise the product manager's rank, appoint people with strong reputations to the job, and assign them one project rather than a few to focus their attention and expand their influence. Senior managers that face deep resistance from their functional units often choose this path.

Other companies (particularly smaller players) take a faster, more direct route. One Japanese company leapt to a strong product manager system to introduce a new model. Backed by the widespread belief that the project might well determine the company's future, senior management created an unusually heavy product manager to run it. An executive vice president with many years of experience became the product manager, with department heads from engineering, production, and planning acting as his liaisons and as project leaders within their functional groups. With these changes, management sent a clear signal that the company could no longer survive in its traditional form.

The project succeeded, and today the product is seen as the company's turnaround effort, its reentry as a competitor after years of ineffectual products. The project itself became a model for subsequent changes (including the creation of a product manager office) in the regular development organization.

How a company changes its organization and the speed with which it moves will depend on its position and the competitive threat it faces. But all successful efforts have three common themes: a unifying driver, new blood, and institutional tenacity. (See "The Case for Heavyweight Product Management," which describes Ford Motor Company's progress toward becoming a heavyweight organization.)

The Case for Heavyweight Product Management

In the early 1980s, successful products filled the Ford Motor Company's scrapbooks but not its dealers' showrooms. Its cars were widely criticized. Quality was far below competitive standards. Market share was falling. In addition, the company's financial position was woeful, and layoffs were ongoing, among white-collar staff and factory workers alike. By the end of the decade, history was repeating itself: the Ford Explorer, introduced in the spring of 1990, may prove to be Ford's most successful product introduction ever. Despite the fact that it debuted in a down market, the four-door, four-wheel-drive sport-utility vehicle has sold phenomenally well. Rugged yet refined, the Explorer gets all the important details right, from exterior styling to the components and interior design.

Behind the Explorer lay a decade of changes in Ford's management, culture, and product development organization. The changes began in the dark days of the early 1980s with the emergence of new leaders in Ford's executive offices and in design studios. Their herald was the Taurus, introduced in 1985. Designed to be a family vehicle with the styling, handling, and ride of a sophisticated European sedan, the car offered a distinctive yet integrated package in which advanced aerodynamic styling was matched with a newly developed chassis with independent rear suspension and a front-wheel-drive layout. The car's interior, which minimized the chrome and wood paneling that were traditional in American roadsters, had a definite European flavor. So did the ride and the way the car handled: the steering was much more responsive, and the ride was tighter and firmer.

The development efforts that produced the Taurus set in motion profound changes within the Ford engineering, manufacturing, and marketing organizations. Traditionally, Ford's development efforts had been driven by very strong functional managers. In developing the Taurus, however, Ford turned to the "Team Taurus," whose core included principals from all the major functions and activities involved in the creation of the new car. The team was headed by Lew Veraldi, at the time in charge of large-car programs at Ford, and it served to coordinate and integrate the development program at the senior management level.

Team Taurus was the first step on a long path of organizational, attitudinal, and procedural change. As development of the Taurus went ahead, it became clear that integrated development required more than the creation of a team and that there was more to achieving integrity than linking the functions under the direction of a single manager. So the next step in Ford's evolution was the development of the "concept to customer" process, or C to C.

The C to C process took shape during the mid-1980s, as Ford sought aggressively to cut lead time, improve quality, and continue to bring attractive products to market. Led by a handpicked group of engineers and product planners, the C to C project focused on devising a new architecture for product development: its members identified critical milestones, decision points, criteria for decision making, and patterns of responsibility and functional involvement. This architecture was then implemented step by step, in ongoing programs as well as in new efforts.

At about the same time, in 1987, Ford formalized the "program manager" structure that had evolved out of the Taurus experience. (Program manager is the term Ford uses for the position we call product manager.) As part of this structure, senior management affirmed the centrality of cross-functional teams working under the direction of a strong program manager. Moreover, cross-functional integration was reinforced at the operating level as well as the strategy level. The change in marketing's role is a good example: instead of adding their input through reports and memoranda, marketing people (led by the program manager) meet directly with designers and engineers to discuss concept development and key decisions about features, layout, and components. Similarly, program managers have been given responsibility for critical functions like product planning and layout, where many of the integrative decisions are made.

In successive programs, Ford has refined its approach and pushed integration further and further. The strength of the program managers has also increased. The results are visible in the products Ford developed during the latter part of the 1980s—and in their sales. Beginning with the Taurus, Ford has scored impressive market successes with a number of its new cars: the Lincoln Continental, which expanded Lincoln's share of the luxury market; the Thunderbird Super Coupe, which compares favorably with European high-performance sedans; the Probe, the result of a joint development project with Mazda and which enthusiasts generally rate higher than Mazda's own effort, the MX6; and the sport-utility Explorer.

Just as engineers need a vision of the overall product to guide their efforts in developing a new car, the people involved in changing an organization need an objective that captures their imaginations. Where changes have taken hold, senior managers have linked them to competition and the drive for tangible advantage in the marketplace.

During the 1980s, the quest for faster development lead time was particularly powerful in driving such efforts. But lead time is not an end in itself. Rather, its pursuit leads people to do things that improve the system overall. In this respect, lead time is like inventory in a just-in-time manufacturing system: reducing work-in-process inventory is somewhat effective, but attacking the root causes of excess inventory truly changes the system.

Companies that successfully focus on lead time generally emphasize changes in internal integration. Product integrity can drive companies to higher performance. Managed well, the drive to create products that fire the imagination gives the implementation of a heavyweight system energy and direction.

Of the many change efforts we have seen, the most successful were led by new people. Some were new to the company, but most came from within the organization. Sometimes viewed as mavericks, they saw the potential for change where others saw more of the same. A company cannot change everyone. It can, however, create new leaders and empower people who are attuned to the new direction the company has to take. It can also find nontraditional ways to identify and develop heavyweight product managers for the future, such as apprenticeship systems.

Moving to a heavier product manager structure is a process of discovery—one the U.S. auto company with the ineffectual cross-functional team we described earlier knows very well. Like many others, that company has discovered that changes in organizational structure are important but insufficient. To create a true team, greater change—particularly in the behavior of traditionally powerful functional managers—is needed.

The journey to heavyweight product management is hard, surprisingly so for many managers. Those who succeed do so because they have tenacity. Outstanding companies understand that projects end but the journey doesn't. The challenge to learn from experience and continuously improve is always there.

Yet in company after company, the same problems crop up over and over. Why do most companies learn so little from their product development projects? The explanation is simple: at the end of every project, there is pressure to move on to the next. The cost of this tunnel vision is very high. Those few companies that work at continuous improvement achieve a significant competitive edge. Moving to a more effective development organization can be the basis for instilling an ethic of continuous improvement. Companies that compete on integrity exercise that ethic every day.

PART

V

Executing Development Projects

1
The House of Quality

John R. Hauser and Don Clausing

Digital Equipment, Hewlett-Packard, AT&T, and ITT are getting started with it. Ford and General Motors use it—at Ford alone there are more than 50 applications. The "house of quality," the basic design tool of the management approach known as quality function deployment (QFD), originated in 1972 at Mitsubishi's Kobe shipyard site. Toyota and its suppliers then developed it in numerous ways. The house of quality has been used successfully by Japanese manufacturers of consumer electronics, home appliances, clothing, integrated circuits, synthetic rubber, construction equipment, and agricultural engines. Japanese designers use it for services like swimming schools and retail outlets and even for planning apartment layouts.

A set of planning and communication routines, quality function deployment focuses and coordinates skills within an organization, first to design, then to manufacture and market goods that customers want to purchase and will continue to purchase. The foundation of the house of quality is the belief that products should be designed to reflect customers' desires and tastes—so marketing people, design engineers, and manufacturing staff must work closely together from the time a product is first conceived.

The house of quality is a kind of conceptual map that provides the means for interfunctional planning and communications. People with different problems and responsibilities can thrash out design priorities while referring to patterns of evidence on the house's grid.

What's So Hard about Design

David Garvin points out that there are many dimensions to what a consumer means by quality and that it is a major challenge to design products that satisfy all of these at once.[1] Strategic quality management means more than avoiding repairs for consumers. It means that companies learn from customer experience and reconcile what they want with what engineers can reasonably build.

Before the industrial revolution, producers were close to their customers. Marketing, engineering, and manufacturing were integrated—in the same individual. If a knight wanted armor, he talked directly to the armorer, who translated the knight's desires into a product. The two might discuss the material—plate rather than chain armor—and details like fluted surfaces for greater bending strength. Then the armorer would design the production process. For strength—who knows why?—he cooled the steel plates in the urine of a black goat. As for a production plan, he arose with the cock's crow to light the forge fire so that it would be hot enough by midday.

Today's fiefdoms are mainly inside corporations. Marketing people have their domain, engineers theirs. Customer surveys will find their way onto designers' desks, and R&D plans reach manufacturing engineers. But usually, managerial functions remain disconnected, producing a costly and demoralizing environment in which product quality and the quality of the production process itself suffer.

Top executives are learning that the use of interfunctional teams benefits design. But if top management *could* get marketing, designing, and manufacturing executives to sit down together, what should these people talk about? How could they get their meeting off the ground? This is where the house of quality comes in.

Consider the location of an emergency brake lever in one American sporty car. Placing it on the left between the seat and the door solved an engineering problem. But it also guaranteed that women in skirts could not get in and out gracefully. Even if the system were to last a lifetime, would it satisfy customers?

In contrast, Toyota improved its rust prevention record from one of the worst in the world to one of the best by coordinating design and production decisions to focus on this customer concern. Using the house of quality, designers broke down "body durability" into 53 items covering everything from climate to modes of operation. They obtained customer evaluations and ran experiments on nearly every detail of production, from pump operation to temperature control and coating composition. Decisions on sheet metal details, coating materi-

Exhibit I. Startup and preproduction costs at Toyota Auto Body before and after QFD

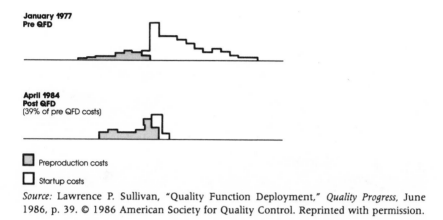

January 1977
Pre QFD

April 1984
Post QFD
(39% of pre QFD costs)

☐ Preproduction costs

☐ Startup costs

Source: Lawrence P. Sullivan, "Quality Function Deployment," *Quality Progress*, June 1986, p. 39. © 1986 American Society for Quality Control. Reprinted with permission.

als, and baking temperatures were all focused on those aspects of rust prevention most important to customers.

Today, with marketing techniques so much more sophisticated than ever before, companies can measure, track, and compare customers' perceptions of products with remarkable accuracy; all companies have opportunities to compete on quality. And costs certainly justify an emphasis on quality design. By looking first at customer needs, then designing across corporate functions, manufacturers can reduce pre-launch time and after-launch tinkering.

Exhibit I compares startup and preproduction costs at Toyota Auto Body in 1977, before QFD, to those costs in 1984, when QFD was well under way. House of quality meetings early on reduced costs by more than 60%. Exhibit II reinforces this evidence by comparing the number of design changes at a Japanese auto manufacturer using QFD with changes at a U.S. automaker. The Japanese design was essentially frozen before the first car came off the assembly line, while the U.S. company was still revamping months later.

Building the House

There is nothing mysterious about the house of quality. There is nothing particularly difficult about it either, but it does require some effort to get used to its conventions. Eventually one's eye can bounce

Exhibit II.   *Japanese automaker with QFD made fewer changes than U.S. company without QFD*

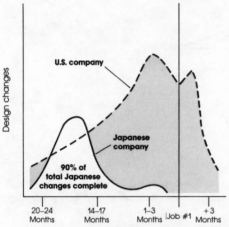

Source: Lawrence P. Sullivan, "Quality Function Deployment," *Quality Progress,* June 1986, p. 39. © 1986 American Society for Quality Control. Reprinted with permission.

knowingly around the house as it would over a roadmap or a navigation chart. We have seen some applications that started with more than 100 customer requirements and more than 130 engineering considerations. A fraction of one subchart, in this case for the door of an automobile, illustrates the house's basic concept well. We've reproduced this subchart portion in Exhibit X, "House of Quality," and we'll discuss each section step-by-step.

WHAT DO CUSTOMERS WANT?   The house of quality begins with the customer, whose requirements are called customer attributes (CAs)—phrases customers use to describe products and product characteristics (see Exhibit III). We've listed a few here; a typical application would have 30 to 100 CAs. A car door is "easy to close" or "stays open on a hill"; "doesn't leak in rain" or allows "no (or little) road noise." Some Japanese companies simply place their products in public areas and encourage potential customers to examine them, while design team members listen and note what people say. Usually, however, more formal market research is called for, via focus groups, in-depth qualitative interviews, and other techniques.

CAs are often grouped into bundles of attributes that represent an

Exhibit III.   Customer attributes and bundles of CAs for a car door

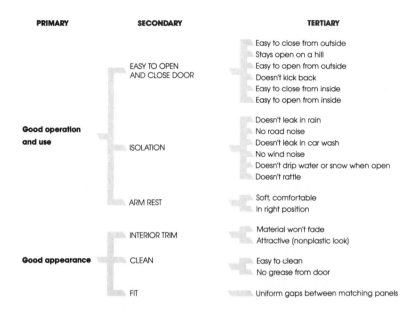

PRIMARY	SECONDARY	TERTIARY
Good operation and use	EASY TO OPEN AND CLOSE DOOR	Easy to close from outside
		Stays open on a hill
		Easy to open from outside
		Doesn't kick back
		Easy to close from inside
		Easy to open from inside
	ISOLATION	Doesn't leak in rain
		No road noise
		Doesn't leak in car wash
		No wind noise
		Doesn't drip water or snow when open
		Doesn't rattle
	ARM REST	Soft, comfortable
		In right position
Good appearance	INTERIOR TRIM	Material won't fade
		Attractive (nonplastic look)
	CLEAN	Easy to clean
		No grease from door
	FIT	Uniform gaps between matching panels

overall customer concern, like "open-close" or "isolation." The Toyota rust-prevention study used eight levels of bundles to get from the total car down to the car body. Usually the project team groups CAs by consensus, but some companies are experimenting with state-of-the-art research techniques that derive groupings directly from customers' responses (and thus avoid arguments in team meetings).

CAs are generally reproduced in the customers' own words. Experienced users of the house of quality try to preserve customers' phrases and even clichés—knowing that they will be translated simultaneously by product planners, design engineers, manufacturing engineers, and salespeople. Of course, this raises the problem of interpretation: What does a customer really mean by "quiet" or "easy"? Still, designers' words and inferences may correspond even less to customers' actual views and can therefore mislead teams into tackling problems customers consider unimportant.

Not all customers are end users, by the way. CAs can include the demands of regulators ("safe in a side collision"), the needs of retailers ("easy to display"), the requirements of vendors ("satisfy assembly and service organizations"), and so forth.

Exhibit IV.   *Relative-importance weights of customer attributes*

BUNDLES	CUSTOMER ATTRIBUTES	RELATIVE IMPORTANCE
EASY TO OPEN AND CLOSE DOOR	Easy to close from outside	7
	Stays open on a hill	5
ISOLATION	Doesn't leak in rain	3
	No road noise	2

A complete list totals 100%

ARE ALL PREFERENCES EQUALLY IMPORTANT? Imagine a good door, one that is easy to close and has power windows that operate quickly. There is a problem, however. Rapid operation calls for a bigger motor, which makes the door heavier and, possibly, harder to close. Sometimes a creative solution can be found that satisfies all needs. Usually, however, designers have to trade off one benefit against another.

To bring the customer's voice to such deliberations, house of quality measures the relative importance to the customer of all CAs. Weightings are based on team members' direct experience with customers or on surveys. Some innovative businesses are using statistical techniques that allow customers to state their preferences with respect to existing and hypothetical products. Other companies use "revealed preference techniques," which judge consumer tastes by their actions as well as by their words—an approach that is more expensive and difficult to perform but yields more accurate answers. (Consumers say that avoiding sugar in cereals is important, but do their actions reflect their claims?)

Weightings are displayed in the house next to each CA—usually in terms of percentages, a complete list totaling 100% (see Exhibit IV).

WILL DELIVERING PERCEIVED NEEDS YIELD A COMPETITIVE ADVANTAGE? Companies that want to match or exceed their competition must first know where they stand relative to it. So on the right side of the house, opposite the CAs, we list customer evaluations of competitive cars matched to "our own" (see Exhibit V).

Ideally, these evaluations are based on scientific surveys of customers. If various customer segments evaluate products differently—lux-

Exhibit V. Customers' evaluations of competitive products

BUNDLES	CUSTOMER ATTRIBUTES	RELATIVE IMPORTANCE	CUSTOMER PERCEPTIONS
EASY TO OPEN AND CLOSE DOOR	Easy to close from outside	7	
	Stays open on a hill	5	
ISOLATION	Doesn't leak in rain	3	
	No road noise	2	

Worst 1 2 3 4 5 Best

OUR CAR DOOR
COMPETITOR A'S
COMPETITOR B'S

ury vs. economy car buyers, for example—product-planning team members get assessments for each segment.

Comparison with the competition, of course, can identify opportunities for improvement. Take our car door, for example. With respect to "stays open on a hill," every car is weak, so we could gain an advantage here. But if we looked at "no road noise" for the same automobiles, we would see that we already have an advantage, which is important to maintain.

Marketing professionals will recognize the right-hand side of Exhibit V as a "perceptual map." Perceptual maps based on bundles of CAs are often used to identify strategic positioning of a product or product line. This section of the house of quality provides a natural link from product concept to a company's strategic vision.

HOW CAN WE CHANGE THE PRODUCT? The marketing domain tells us what to do; the engineering domain tells us how to do it. Now we need to describe the product in the language of the engineer. Along the top of the house of quality, the design team lists those engineering characteristics (ECs) that are likely to affect one or more of the customer attributes (see Exhibit VI). The negative sign on "energy to close door" means engineers hope to reduce the energy required. If a standard engineering characteristic affects no CA, it may be redundant to the EC list on the house, or the team may have missed a customer attribute. A CA unaffected by any EC, on the other hand, presents opportunities to expand a car's physical properties.

Exhibit VI.   *Engineering characteristics tell how to change the product*

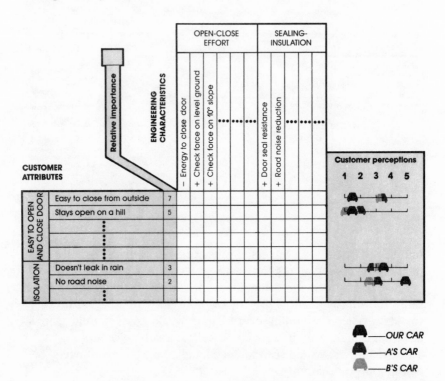

Any EC may affect more than one CA. The resistance of the door seal affects three of the four customer attributes shown in Exhibit VI—and others shown later.

Engineering characteristics should describe the product in measurable terms and should directly affect customer perceptions. The weight of the door will be *felt* by the customer and is therefore a relevant EC. By contrast, the thickness of the sheet metal is a part characteristic that the customer is unlikely to perceive directly. It affects customers only by influencing the weight of the door and other engineering characteristics, like "resistance to deformation in a crash."

In many Japanese projects, the interfunctional team begins with the CAs and generates measurable characteristics for each, like foot-pounds of energy required to close the door. Teams should avoid ambiguity in interpretation of ECs or hasty justification of current quality control measurement practices. This is a time for systematic, patient analysis

Exhibit VII.   Relationship matrix shows how engineering decisions affect customer perceptions

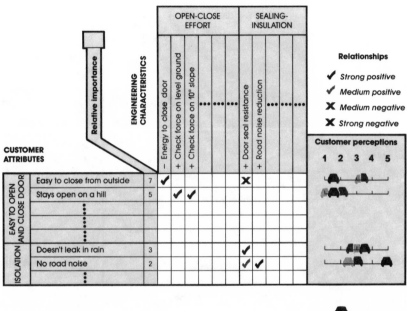

of each characteristic, for brainstorming. Vagueness will eventually yield indifference to things customers need. Characteristics that are trivial will make the team lose sight of the overall design and stifle creativity.

HOW MUCH DO ENGINEERS INFLUENCE CUSTOMER-PERCEIVED QUALI-TIES? The interfunctional team now fills in the body of the house, the "relationship matrix," indicating how much each engineering characteristic affects each customer attribute. The team seeks consensus on these evaluations, basing them on expert engineering experience, customer responses, and tabulated data from statistical studies or controlled experiments.

The team uses numbers or symbols to establish the strength of these relationships (see Exhibit VII). Any symbols will do; the idea is to choose those that work best. Some teams use red symbols for relation-

Exhibit VIII.   *Objective measures evaluate competitive products*

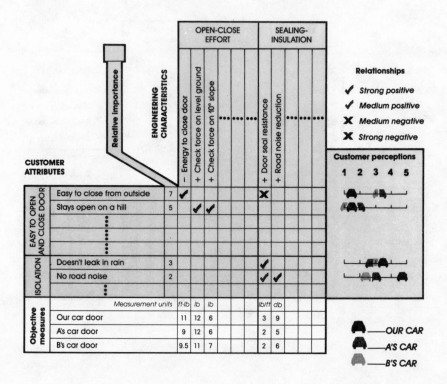

ships based on experiments and statistics and pencil marks for relationships based on judgment or intuition. Others use numbers from statistical studies. In our house, we use check marks for positive and crosses for negative relationships.

Once the team has identified the voice of the customer and linked it to engineering characteristics, it adds objective measures at the bottom of the house beneath the ECs to which they pertain (see Exhibit VIII). When objective measures are known, the team can eventually move to establish target values—ideal new measures for each EC in a redesigned product. If the team did its homework when it first identified the ECs, tests to measure benchmark values should be easy to complete. Engineers determine the relevant units of measurement—foot-pounds, decibels, etc.

Incidentally, if customer evaluations of CAs do not correspond to objective measures of related ECs—if, for example, the door requiring the least energy to open is perceived as "hardest to open"—then perhaps the measures are faulty or the car is suffering from an image problem that is skewing consumer perceptions.

HOW DOES ONE ENGINEERING CHANGE AFFECT OTHER CHARACTER-ISTICS? An engineer's change of the gear ratio on a car window may make the window motor smaller but the window go up more slowly. And if the engineer enlarges or strengthens the mechanism, the door probably will be heavier, harder to open, or may be less prone to remain open on a slope. Of course, there might be an entirely new mechanism that improves all relevant CAs. Engineering is creative solutions and a balancing of objectives.

The house of quality's distinctive roof matrix helps engineers specify the various engineering features that have to be improved collaterally (see Exhibit IX). To improve the window motor, you may have to improve the hinges, weather stripping, and a range of other ECs.

Sometimes one targeted feature impairs so many others that the team decides to leave it alone. The roof matrix also facilitates necessary engineering trade-offs. The foot-pounds of energy needed to close the door, for example, are shown in negative relation to "door seal resistance" and "road noise reduction." In many ways, the roof contains the most critical information for engineers because they use it to balance the trade-offs when addressing customer benefits.

Incidentally, we have been talking so far about the basics, but design teams often want to ruminate on other information. In other words, they custom-build their houses. To the column of CAs, teams may add other columns for histories of customer complaints. To the ECs, a team may add the costs of servicing these complaints. Some applications add data from the sales force to the CA list to represent strategic marketing decisions. Or engineers may add a row that indicates the degree of technical difficulty, showing in their own terms how hard or easy it is to make a change.

Some users of the house impute relative weights to the engineering characteristics. They'll establish that the energy needed to close the door is roughly twice as important to consider as, say, "check force on 10 degree slope." By comparing weighted characteristics to actual component costs, creative design teams set priorities for improving components. Such information is particularly important when cost cutting is a goal. (Exhibit X includes rows for technical difficulty, imputed importance of ECs, and estimated costs.)

Exhibit IX.   *Roof matrix facilitates engineering creativity*

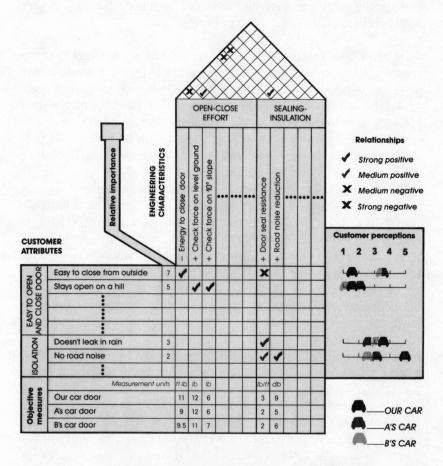

There are no hard-and-fast rules. The symbols, lines, and configurations that work for the particular team are the ones it should use.

Using the House

How does the house lead to the bottom line? There is no cookbook procedure, but the house helps the team to set targets, which are, in fact, entered on the bottom line of the house. For engineers it is a way to summarize basic data in usable form. For marketing executives it

Exhibit X. House of quality

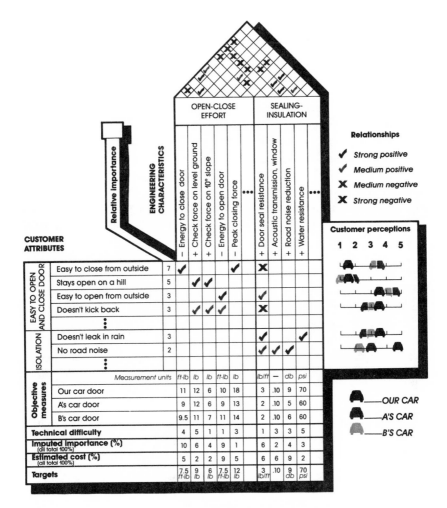

represents the customer's voice. General managers use it to discover strategic opportunities. Indeed, the house encourages all of these groups to work together to understand one another's priorities and goals.

The house relieves no one of the responsibility of making tough decisions. It does provide the means for all participants to debate priorities.

Let's run through a couple of hypothetical situations to see how a design team uses the house.

HYPOTHETICAL SITUATION 1. Look at Exhibit X. Notice that our doors are much more difficult to close from the outside than those on competitors' cars. We decide to look further because our marketing data say this customer attribute is important. From the central matrix, the body of the house, we identify the ECs that affect this customer attribute: energy to close door, peak closing force, and door seal resistance. Our engineers judge the energy to close the door and the peak closing force as good candidates for improvement together because they are strongly, positively related to the consumer's desire to close the door easily. They determine to consider all the engineering ramifications of door closing.

Next, in the roof of the house, we identify which other ECs might be affected by changing the door closing energy. Door opening energy and peak closing force are positively related, but other ECs (check force on level ground, door seals, window acoustic transmission, road noise reduction) are bound to be changed in the process and are negatively related. It is not an easy decision. But with objective measures of competitors' doors, customer perceptions, and considering information on cost and technical difficulty, we—marketing people, engineers, and top managers—decide that the benefits outweigh the costs. A new door closing target is set for our door—7.5 foot-pounds of energy. This target, noted on the very bottom of the house directly below the relevant EC, establishes the goal to have the door "easiest to close."

HYPOTHETICAL SITUATION 2. Look now at the customer attribute "no road noise" and its relationship to the acoustic transmission of the window. The "road noise" CA is only mildly important to customers, and its relationship to the specifications of the window is not strong. Window design will help only so much to keep things quiet. Decreasing the acoustic transmission usually makes the window heavier. Examining the roof of the house, we see that more weight would have a negative impact on ECs (open-close energy, check forces, etc.) that, in turn, are strongly related to CAs that are more important to the customer than quiet ("easy to close," "stays open on a hill"). Finally, marketing data show that we already do well on road noise; customers perceive our car as better than competitors'.

In this case, the team decides not to tamper with the window's transmission of sound. Our target stays equal to our current acoustic values.

In setting targets, it is worth noting that the team should emphasize customer-satisfaction values and not emphasize tolerances. Do not specify "between 6 and 8 foot-pounds," but rather say, "7.5 foot-pounds." This may seem a small matter, but it is important. The rhetoric of tolerances encourages drift toward the least costly end of the specification limit and does not reward designs and components whose engineering values closely attain a specific customer-satisfaction target.

The Houses Beyond

The principles underlying the house of quality apply to any effort to establish clear relations between manufacturing functions and customer satisfaction that are not easy to visualize. Suppose that our team decides that doors closing easily is a critical attribute and that a relevant engineering characteristic is closing energy. Setting a target value for closing energy gives us a goal, but it does not give us a door. To get a door, we need the right parts (frame, sheet metal, weather stripping, hinges, etc.), the right processes to manufacture the parts and assemble the product, and the right production plan to get it built.

If our team is truly interfunctional, we can eventually take the "hows" from our house of quality and make them the "whats" of another house, one mainly concerned with detailed product design. Engineering characteristics like foot-pounds of closing energy can become the rows in a parts deployment house, while parts characteristics—like hinge properties or the thickness of the weather stripping—become the columns (see Exhibit XI).

This process continues to a third and fourth phase as the "hows" of one stage become the "whats" of the next. Weather-stripping thickness—a "how" in the parts house—becomes a "what" in a process planning house. Important process operations, like "rpm of the extruder producing the weather stripping" become the "hows." In the last phase, production planning, the key process operations, like "rpm of the extruder," become the "whats," and production requirements—knob controls, operator training, maintenance—become the "hows."

These four linked houses implicitly convey the voice of the customer through to manufacturing. A control knob setting of 3.6 gives an extruder speed of 100 rpm; this helps give a reproducible diameter for the weather-stripping bulb, which gives good sealing without excessive door-closing force. This feature aims to satisfy the customer's need for a dry, quiet car with an easy-to-close door.

Exhibit XI. Linked houses convey the customer's voice through to manufacturing

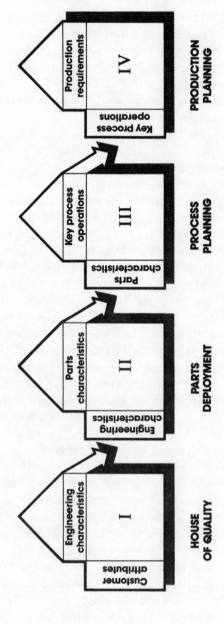

None of this is simple. An elegant idea ultimately decays into process, and processes will be confounding as long as human beings are involved. But that is no excuse to hold back. If a technique like house of quality can help break down functional barriers and encourage teamwork, serious efforts to implement it will be many times rewarded.

What is also not simple is developing an organization capable of absorbing elegant ideas. The principal benefit of the house of quality is quality in-house. It gets people thinking in the right directions and thinking together. For most U.S. companies, this alone amounts to a quiet revolution.

Note

1. David A. Garvin, "Competing on the Eight Dimensions of Quality," *Harvard Business Review*, November–December 1987, 101.

2

Manufacturing by Design

Daniel E. Whitney

In many large companies, design has become a bureaucratic tangle, a process confounded by fragmentation, overspecialization, power struggles, and delays. An engineering manager responsible for designing a single part at an automobile company told me recently that the design process mandates 350 steps—not 350 engineering calculations or experiments but 350 workups requiring 350 signatures. No wonder, he said, it takes five years to design a car; that's one signature every 3½ days.

It's not as if companies don't know better. According to General Motors executives, 70% of the cost of manufacturing truck transmissions is determined in the design stage. A study at Rolls-Royce reveals that design determines 80% of the final production costs of 2,000 components.[1] Obviously, establishing a product's design calls for crucial choices—about materials made or bought, about how parts will be assembled. When senior managers put most of their efforts into analyzing current production rather than product design, they are monitoring what accounts for only about a third of total manufacturing costs—the window dressing, not the window.

Moreover, better product design has shattered old expectations for improving cost through design or redesign. If managers used to think a 5% improvement was good, they now face competition that is reducing drastically the number of components and subassemblies for

Author's note: I am indebted to my colleagues James L. Nevins, Alexander C. Edsall, Thomas L. De Fazio, Richard E. Gustavson, Richard W. Metzinger, Jonathan M. Rourke, and Donald S. Seltzer for their contributions to this article. We have worked together for many years developing the ideas expressed here.

products and achieving a 50% or more reduction in direct cost of manufacture. And even greater reductions are coming, owing to new materials and materials-processing techniques. Direct labor, even lower cost labor, accounts for so little of the total picture that companies still focusing on this factor are misleading themselves not only about improving products but also about how foreign competitors have gained so much advantage.

In short, design is a strategic activity, whether by intention or by default. It influences flexibility of sales strategies, speed of field repair, and efficiency of manufacturing. It may well be responsible for the company's future viability. I want to focus not on the qualities of products but on development of the processes for making them.

Converting a concept into a complex, high-technology product is an involved procedure consisting of many steps of refinement. The initial idea never quite works as intended or performs as well as desired. So designers make many modifications, including increasingly subtle choices of materials, fasteners, coatings, adhesives, and electronic adjustments. Expensive analyses and experiments may be necessary to verify design choices.

In many cases, designers find that the options become more and more difficult; negotiations over technical issues, budgets, and schedules become intense. As the design evolves, the choices become interdependent, taking on the character of an interwoven, historical chain in which later decisions are conditioned by those made previously.

Imagine, then, that a production or manufacturing engineer enters such detailed negotiations late in the game and asks for changes. If the product designers accede to the requests, a large part of the design may simply unravel. Many difficult and pivotal choices will have been made for nothing. Where close calls went one way, they may now go another; new materials analyses and production experiments may be necessary.

Examples of failure abound. One research scientist I know, at a large chemical company, spent a year perfecting a new process—involving, among other things, gases—at laboratory scale. In the lab the process operated at atmospheric pressure. But when a production engineer was finally called in to scale up the process, he immediately asked for higher pressures. Atmospheric pressure is never used in production when gases are in play because maintaining it requires huge pipes, pumps, and tanks. Higher pressure reduces the volume of gases and permits the use of smaller equipment. Unfortunately, the researcher's process failed at elevated pressures, and he had to start over.

Or consider the manufacturer whose household appliance depended on close tolerances for proper operation. Edicts from the styling department prevented designs from achieving required tolerances; the designers wanted a particular shape and appearance and would not budge when they were apprised of the problems they caused to manufacturing. Nor was the machine designed in modules that could be tested before final assembly. The entire product was built from single parts on one long line. So each finished product had to be adjusted into operation—or taken apart after assembly to find out why it didn't work. No one who understood the problem had enough authority to solve it, and no one with enough authority understood the problem until it was too late. This company is no longer in business.

Finally, there was the weapon that depended for its function on an infrared detector, the first of many parts—lenses, mirrors, motors, power supplies, etc.—that were glued and soldered together into a compact unit. To save money, the purchasing department switched to a cheaper detector, which caused an increase in final test failures. Since the construction was glue and solder, bad units had to be scrapped. Someone then suggested a redesign of the unit with reversible fasteners to permit disassembly. But this time more reasonable voices prevailed. Reversible fasteners would have actually increased the weapon's cost and served no purpose other than to facilitate factory rework. Disassembly would not have been advisable because the unit was too complex for field repair. It was a single-use weapon—with a shelf life of five years and a useful life of ten seconds. It simply had to work the first time.

Manufacturers can avoid problems like this. Let's look at a success story. One company I know wanted to be able to respond in 24 hours to worldwide orders for its electronic products line—a large variety of features in small-order batches. Engineers decided to redesign the products in modules, with different features in each module. All the modules are plug compatible, electrically and mechanically. All versions of each module are identical on the outside where assembly machines handle them. The company can now make up an order for any set of features by selecting the correct modules and assembling them, all of this without any human intervention, from electronic order receipt to the boxing of final assemblies.

In another company, a high-pressure machine for supplying cutting oil to machine tools requires once-a-day cleaning. Designers recently reconfigured the machine so that normal cleanout and ordinary repairs can be accomplished without any tools, thus solving some bothersome union work-rule problems.

There are no guarantees, of course, but the experiences of these companies illustrate how design decisions should be integrated, informed, and balanced, and how important it is to involve manufacturing engineers, repair engineers, purchasing agents, and other knowledgeable people early in the process. The product designer asks, "What good is it if it doesn't work?" The salesperson asks, "What good is it if it doesn't sell?" The finance person asks, "What good is it if it isn't profitable?" The manufacturing engineer asks, "What good is it if I can't make it?" The team's success is measured by how well these questions are answered.

The Design Team and Its Task

Multifunctional teams are currently the most effective way known to cut through barriers to good design. Teams can be surprisingly small—as small as 4 members, though 20 members is typical in large projects—and they usually include every specialty in the company. Top executives should make their support and interest clear. Various names have been given to this team approach, like "simultaneous engineering" and "concurrent design." Different companies emphasize different strengths within the team. In many Japanese companies, teams like this have been functioning for so long that most of the employees cannot remember another way to design a product.

Establishing the team is only the beginning, of course. Teams need a step-by-step procedure that disciplines the discussion and takes members through the decisions that crop up in virtually every design. In traditional design procedures, assembly is one of the last things considered. My experience suggests that assembly should be considered much earlier. Assembly is inherently integrative. Weaving it into the design process is a powerful way to raise the level of integration in all aspects of product design. A design team's charter should be broad. Its chief functions include:

1. Determining the character of the product, to see what it is and thus what design and production methods are appropriate.

2. Subjecting the product to a product function analysis, so that all design decisions can be made with full knowledge of how the item is supposed to work and all team members understand it well enough to contribute optimally.

3. Carrying out a design-for-producibility-and-usability study to determine if these factors can be improved without impairing functioning.

4. Designing an assembly process appropriate to the product's particular character. This involves creating a suitable assembly sequence, identifying subassemblies, integrating quality control, and designing each part so that its quality is compatible with the assembly method.

5. Designing a factory system that fully involves workers in the production strategy, operates on minimal inventory, and is integrated with vendors' methods and capabilities.

THE PRODUCT'S CHARACTER. Clearly it is beyond the scope of this article to establish by what criteria one judges, develops, or revamps the features of products. David A. Garvin has analyzed eight fundamental dimensions of product quality; and John R. Hauser and Don Clausing have explored ways to communicate to design engineers the dimensions consumers want—in the engineers' own language.[2]

Character defines the criteria by which designers judge, develop, or revamp product features. I would only reiterate that manufacturing engineers and others should have something to say about how to ensure that the product is field repairable, how skilled users must be to employ it successfully, and whether marketability will be based on model variety or availability of future add-ons.

An essential by-product of involving manufacturing, marketing, purchasing, and other constituencies in product conception, moreover, is that diverse team members become familiar enough with the product early in order to be able to incorporate the designers' goals and constraints in their own approaches. As designers talk with manufacturing or field-service reps, for example, they can make knowledgeable corrections. ("Why not make that part out of plastic? I know a low-cost source." "Because the temperature there is 1,000°; plastic will vaporize." "Oh.")

PRODUCT FUNCTION ANALYSIS. This used to be the exclusive province of product designers. But now it is understood that to improve a product's robustness, to "design quality in" in Genichi Taguchi's good phrase, means thoroughly understanding a product's function in relation to production methods. Product designers and manufacturing engineers used to try to understand these relations by experience and intuition. Now they have software packages for modeling and designing components to guide them through process choices—software that would have been thought fantastic a generation ago. (See "Designing for Predictability: New MCAE Tools.")

Designing for Predictability: New MCAE Tools

A well-designed product is a predictable product. Managers particularly need to predict reliability, manufacturing costs, and manufacturability. In the past, engineers have dealt with these three issues only after engineering has completed the drawings, the near-final stage in the development cycle. But by then it may be too late. Moreover, when a product has hundreds, or even thousands of components, it's just not feasible to design, proto-type, and redesign slightly different versions of each.

Two new, integrated, mechanical computer-aided engineering (MCAE) systems permit engineering teams to test before they build, so they can design for total quality with reliability, performance, and manufacturing costs in mind from the start. The first of these new systems model products not just physically but analytically: a designer can not only draw a component on the screen but prompt the computer to model and test the feasibility of its features, in the manner of a business planner using an electronic spreadsheet to play "what if" games. Engineers can vary as-sumptions about materials, speeds, loads, size, and other operating condi-tions. In this way, developers can both see the effects of hypothetical stresses and estimate product costs while making design decisions.

A company making internal-combustion engines, for example, may use an integrated MCAE system to design reliability and smoothness of operation into the counterbalance for the crankshaft. The optimal coun-terbalance keeps forces from the piston's up-and-down motion and cen-trifugal forces from the unbalanced crankshaft both low and constant—to reduce vibration. The system works as follows: a desktop workstation paints an image of a cylinder with all its operating parts on the screen. The engineer then selects values for counterbalance features like angle, thickness, diameter, etc., from menus. As choices are made, the system automatically computes the merits of the design, based on about 100 engineering questions, including compression ratio and stroke. So design variations are tried, evaluated, and discarded with near instantaneous response. This puts robustness and performance optimization into the very first counterbalance designs.

The second new system is an expert system which projects probable production costs for various part or assembly configurations and provides guidance as to their manufacturability. Another parts maker might use this system to project the manufacturability of and costs for, say, its stamped carburetor parts. Typically, the PC screen has several menus listing aspects of a part's design, like materials used and manufacturing process involved. Each menu holds progressive layers of possible choices. If the engineer selects metal from the list of materials, the system offers a choice of ferrous or nonferrous. Under ferrous metals, one can pick from carbon steel, stainless, cast iron, and so on.

There are automatic default values that the engineer might not normally specify, such as surface finish and carbon content. The system also draws on its own data base for manufacturing information like material density and base unit cost. Once the designer completes the menu sequence, the system produces an approximate part cost that includes materials, processing, and tooling expenditures.

MCAE systems don't eliminate prototyping entirely, but they can drastically reduce the number of trials and help engineers address reliability, performance, and cost problems early—and thus design for total quality from the very beginning.

—PHILIPPE VILLERS

Recently I worked on a product containing delicate spinning parts that had to be dynamically balanced to high tolerances. In the original design, partial disassembly of the rotating elements after balancing was necessary before the assembly could be finished, so the final product was rarely well balanced and required a lengthy adjustment procedure. Since total redesign was not feasible, the team analyzed the reassembly procedure solely as it pertained to balance and concluded that designers needed only to tighten various tolerances and reshape mating surfaces. Simple adjustments were then sufficient to restore balance in the finished product.

Another important goal of product function analysis is to reduce the number of parts in a product. The benefits extend to purchasing (fewer vendors and transactions), manufacturing (fewer operations, material handlings, and handlers), and field service (fewer repair parts).

When a company first brings discipline to its design process, reductions in parts count are usually easy to make because the old designs are so inefficient. After catching up, though, hard, creative work is necessary to cut the parts count further. One company I know saved several million dollars a year by eliminating just one subassembly part. The product had three operating states: low, medium, and high. Analysis showed that the actions of one part in the original design always followed or imitated the actions of two others. Designers eliminated the redundant part by slightly altering the shapes of the other two parts.

This change could never have been conceived, much less executed, if the designers hadn't had deep knowledge of the product and hadn't paid attention to the actions underlying its engineering.

DESIGN FOR PRODUCIBILITY. Recently, a company bragged to a business newsweekly about saving a mere $250,000 by designing its bottles for a new line of cosmetics to fit existing machines for filling, labeling, and capping. This plan seems so obvious, and the savings were so small as compared with what is possible, that the celebration seemed misplaced. But it's a better outcome than I remember from my first job with a drug company. It spent a fortune to have a famous industrial designer create new bottles and caps for its line. They were triangular in cross section and teardrop shaped, and they would not fit either existing machines or any new ones we tried to design. The company eventually abandoned the bottles, along with the associated marketing campaign.

Obviously, nothing is more important to manufacturing strategy than designing for the production process. In the past, this has meant designing for manufacturing and assembly, and value engineering, which both strive to reduce costs. But now we have to go beyond these goals.

To take the last point first, value engineering aims chiefly to reduce manufacturing costs through astute choice of materials and methods for making parts. Does the design call for metal when a ceramic part will do? If metal, should we punch it or drill it? Value engineering usually comes into play after the design is finished, but the thoroughness we seek in design can be achieved only when decisions are made early.

Moreover, design for producibility differs from design for assembly, which typically considers parts one by one, simplifies them, combines some to reduce the parts count, or adds features like bevels around the rims of holes to make assembly easier. Valuable as it is, this process cannot achieve the most fundamental improvements because it considers the product as a collection of parts instead of something to satisfy larger goals, such as reducing costs over the product's entire life cycle.

Nippondenso's approach vividly illustrates how an overriding strategy can determine a product's parts and the production process. The Delco of Japan, Nippondenso builds such car products as generators, alternators, voltage regulators, radiators, and antiskid brake systems. Toyota is its chief customer. Nippondenso has learned to live with daily orders for thousands of items in arbitrary model mixes and quantities.

The company's response to this challenge has several components:

- The combinatorial method of meeting model-mix production requirements.
- In-house development of manufacturing technology.

- Wherever possible, manufacturing methods that don't need jigs and fixtures.

The combinatorial method, carried out by marketing and engineering team members, divides a product into generic parts or subassemblies and identifies the necessary variations of each. The product is then designed to permit any combination of variations of these basic parts to go together physically and functionally. (If there are 6 basic parts and 3 varieties of each, for example, the company can build $3^6 = 729$ different models.) The in-house manufacturing team cooperates in designing the parts, so the manufacturing system can easily handle and make each variety of each part and product.

Jigless production is an important goal at this point, for obvious reasons. Materials handling, fabrication, and assembly processes usually employ jigs, fixtures, and tools to hold parts during processing and transport; the jigs and fixtures are usually designed specifically to fit each kind of part, to hold them securely. When production shifts to a different batch or model, old jigs and tools are removed and new ones installed. In mass-production environments, this changeover occurs about once a year.

In dynamic markets, however, or with just-in-time, batches are small, and shifts in production may occur hourly—even continually. It may be impossible to achieve a timely and economical batch-size-of-one production process if separate jigs are necessary for each model. Nippondenso's in-house manufacturing team responds to this problem by showing how to design the parts with common jigging features, so that one jig can hold all varieties, or by working with designers to make the product snap or otherwise hold itself together so that no clamping jigs are needed.

By cultivating an in-house team, Nippondenso also solves three difficult institutional problems. First, the company eliminates proprietary secrecy problems. Its own people are the only ones working on the design or with strategically crucial components. Second, equipment can be delivered without payment of a vendor's markup, thus reducing costs and making financial justification easier. Third, over the years the team has learned to accommodate itself intuitively to the company's design philosophy, and individual team members have learned how to contribute to it. Designers get to know each other too, creating many informal communication networks that greatly shorten the design process. Shorter design periods mean less lead time, a clear competitive advantage. (It is worth noting that many Japanese companies

Exhibit I.   How a radiator is made—the combinatorial, jigless method

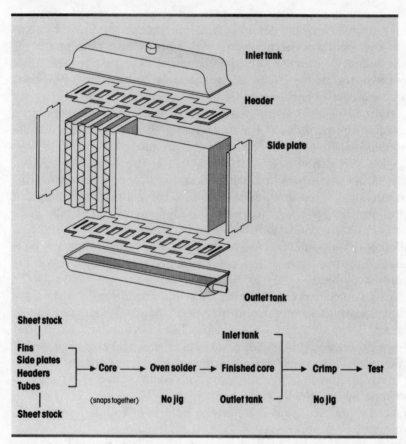

Except for final testing, this radiator is fabricated entirely without manual labor. Radiators differ by core length, width, and depth. They are available in various sizes and offer many heat-transfer capacities. Without changing part sizes, a designer can program different shapes for fins and diameters for tubes, thus allowing the same production system to achieve new heat-transfer capacities.

follow this practice of designing much of their automation in-house, while buying many product components from outside vendors. American companies usually take the opposite tack: they make many components and buy automation from vendors.)

Nippondenso uses combinatorial design and jigless manufacturing for making radiators (see Exhibit I). Tubes, fins, headers, and side plates comprise the core of the radiator. These four snap together, which obviates the need for jigs, and the complete core is oven soldered. The plastic tanks are crimped on. The crimp die can be adjusted to take any tank size while the next radiator is being put in the crimper, so radiators can be processed in any model order and in any quantity. When asked how much the factory cost, the project's chief engineer replied, "Strictly speaking, you have to include the cost of designing the product." A factory isn't just a factory, he implied. It is a carefully crafted fusion of a strategically designed product and the methods for making it.

Without a guiding strategy, there is no way to tell what suggestions for improvement really support long-range goals. Some product-design techniques depend too much on rules, including rule-based systems stemming from expert systems. These are no substitute for experienced people. Volkswagen, for example, recently violated conventional ease-of-assembly rules to capture advantages the company would not otherwise have had.

In the company's remarkable Hall 54 facility in Wolfsburg, Germany, where Golfs and Jettas go through final assembly, robots or special machines perform about 25% of the final-stage steps. (Before Hall 54 began functioning, Volkswagen never did better than 5%.)[3]

To get this level of automation, VW production management asked to examine every part. It won from the board of directors a year-long delay in introducing the new models. Several significant departures from conventional automotive design practices resulted, the first involving front-end configuration. Usually, designers try to reduce the number of parts. But VW engineers determined that at a cost of one *extra* frame part the front of the car could be temporarily left open for installation of the engine by hydraulic arms in one straight, upward push. Installing the engine used to take a minute or longer and involved several workers. VW now does it unmanned in 26 seconds.

Another important decision concerned the lowly screw. Purchasing agents usually accept the rule that low-cost fasteners are a competitive edge. VW engineers convinced the purchasing department to pay an additional 18% for screws with cone-shaped tips that go more easily into holes, even if the sheet metal or plastic parts were misaligned. Machine and robot insertion of screws thus became practical. Just two years later, so many German companies had adopted cone-pointed screws that their price had dropped to that of ordinary flat-tip screws. For once, everyone from manufacturing to purchasing was happy.

ASSEMBLY PROCESSES.   Usually assembly sequence is looked at late in the design process when industrial engineers are trying to balance the assembly line. But the choice of assembly sequence and the identification of potential subassemblies can affect or be affected by—among other factors—product-testing options, market responsiveness, and factory-floor layout. Indeed, assembly-related activities with strategic implications include: subassemblies, assembly sequence, assembly method for each step, and integration of quality control.

Imagine a product with six parts. We can build it many ways, such as bottom up, top down, or from three subassemblies of two parts each. What determines the best way? A balance of many considerations: construction needs, like access to fasteners or lubrication points; ease of assembly (some sequences may include difficult part matings that risk damage to parts); quality control matters, like the operator's ability to make crucial tests or easily replace a faulty part; process reasons, like ability to hold pieces accurately for machine assembly; and, finally, production strategy advantages, like making subassemblies to stock that will be common to many models, or that permit assembly from commonly available parts.

Again, software now exists to help the designer with the formidable problem of listing all the possible assembly sequences—and there can be a lot, as many as 500 for an item as simple as an automobile rear axle. It would be impossible for a team to attack so complex a series of choices without a computer design aid to help, according to a preestablished hierarchy of goals like that just discussed—access to lubrication points, etc. Another virtue of this software is that it forces the team to specify choices systematically and reproducibly, for team members' own edification but also in a way that helps justify design and manufacturing choices to top management.

Consider then, automatic transmissions, complex devices made up of gears, pistons, clutches, hydraulic valves, and electronic controls. Large transmission parts can scrape metal off smaller parts during assembly, and shavings can get into the control valves, causing the transmission to fail the final test or, worse, fail in the customer's car. Either failure is unacceptable and terribly expensive. It is essential to design assembly methods and test sequences to preempt them.

With respect to assembly machines and tooling, manufacturers should consider the following questions:

> Can the product be made by adding parts from one direction, or must it be turned over one or more times? Turnovers are wasted motion and costly in fixtures.

As parts are added in a stack, will the location for each subsequent part drift unpredictably? If so, automatic assembly machines will need expensive sensors to find the parts, or assembly will randomly fail, or parts will scrape on each other too hard.

Is there space for tools and grippers? If not, automatic assembly or testing aren't options.

If a manufacturing strategy based on subassemblies seems warranted, are the subassemblies designed so they do not fall apart during reorientation, handling, or transport?

There are clear advantages to combining consideration of these assembly procedures and/or quality control strategy with design. Designers who anticipate the assembly method can avoid pitfalls that would otherwise require redesign or create problems on the factory floor. They can also design better subassemblies to meet functional specifications—specifications that will be invaluable when the time comes to decide whether to take bids from outside vendors or make the part on the company's own lines, specifications that will determine how to test the subassembly before adding it to the final product.

Designers concerned about assembly must ask:

What is the best economic combination of machines and people to assemble a certain model-mix of parts for a product line (given each machine's or person's cost and time to do each operation, plus production-rate and economic-return targets)?

How much time, money, production machinery, or in-process inventory can be saved if extra effort is put into design of the product, its fabrication and assembly processes, so that there are fewer quality control failures and product repairs? A process that yields only 80% successful assemblies on the first try may need 20% extra capacity and inventory—not to mention high-cost repair personnel—to meet the original production goals.

Where in the assembly process should testing take place? Considerations include how costly and definitive the test is, whether later stages would hide flaws detectable earlier, and how much repaired or discarded assemblies would cost.

These are generic problems; they are hard to answer, and they too are stimulating the development of new software packages. This new software enhances the ability of manufacturing people to press their points in (often heated) debates about design. Hitherto, product designers, more accustomed to using computer modeling, have had somewhat of an upper hand.

FACTORY SYSTEM DESIGN. Many features of good product design presuppose that machines will do the assembly. But automation is not necessary to reap the benefits of strategic design. Indeed, sometimes good design makes automatic assembly unnecessary or uneconomic by making manual assembly so easy and reliable. Regardless of the level of automation, some people will still be involved in production processes, and their role is important to the success of manufacturing.

Kosuke Ikebuchi, general manager of the General Motors–Toyota joint venture, New United Motors Manufacturing Inc. (NUMMI), believes that success came to his plant only after careful analysis of the failures of the GM operation that had preceded it: low-quality parts from suppliers, an attitude that repair and rework were to be expected, high absenteeism resulting in poor workmanship, and damage to parts and vehicles caused by transport mechanisms.[4] The assembly line suffered from low efficiency because work methods were not standardized, people could not repair their own equipment, and equipment was underutilized. Excess inventory, caused by ineffective controls, was another problem. Work areas were crowded. Employees took too much time to respond to problems.

NUMMI's solutions focused on the Jidoka principle—quality comes first. According to NUMMI's factory system today, workers can stop the line if they spot a problem; the machinery itself can sense and warn of problems. Two well-known just-in-time methods of eliminating waste—the kanban system of production control and reductions in jig and fixture change times—are important to NUMMI's manufacturing operation.

But lots of other things also contribute to this plant's effectiveness: simplified job classifications, displays and signs showing just how to do each job and what to avoid, self-monitoring machines. NUMMI has obtained high-spirited involvement of the employees, first by choosing new hires for their willingness to cooperate, then by training them thoroughly and involving them in decisions about how to improve the operations.

Design Means Business

The five tasks of design bring us back to the original point. Strategic product design is a total approach to doing business. It can mean changes in the pace of design, the identity of the participants, and the sequence of decisions. It forces managers, designers, and engineers to cross old organizational boundaries, and it reverses some old power relationships. It creates difficulties because it teases out incipient conflict, but it is rewarding precisely because disagreements surface early, when they can be resolved constructively and with mutual understanding of the outcome's rationale.

Strategic design is a continual process, so it makes sense to keep design teams in place until well after product launching when the same team can then tackle a new project. Design—it must be obvious by now—is a companywide activity. Top management involvement and commitment are essential. The effort has its costs, but the costs of not making the effort are greater.

Notes

1. J. Corbett, "Design for Economic Manufacture," *Annals of C.I.R.P.*, 35, no. 1, 1986, 93.

2. David A. Garvin, "Competing on the Eight Dimensions of Quality," *Harvard Business Review*, November–December 1987, 101; and John R. Hauser and Don Clausing, "The House of Quality," *Harvard Business Review*, May–June 1988, 63.

3. E. H. Hartwich, "Possibilities and Trends for the Application of Automated Handling and Assembly Systems in the Automotive Industry," International Congress for Metalworking and Automation, Hannover, West Germany, 1985, 126.

4. Kosuke Ikebuchi, unpublished remarks at the Future Role of Automated Manufacturing Conference, New York University, 1986.

3
Purchasing's Role in New Product Development

David N. Burt and William R. Soukup

For all their experimentation with such new technologies as computer-aided design (CAD), computer-aided manufacturing (CAM), and robotics, many U.S. companies still follow a seriously outdated "business as usual" approach to new product development and introduction. The recent experience of Medical Technologies, Inc. (not its real name), a highly successful $100 million manufacturer of high-precision medical equipment, is all too common.

The company had compiled an impressive growth record, especially during the past several years. It was no stranger to high technology and enjoyed an enviable reputation as a supplier of high-performance, dependable, and cost-effective products for hospitals and medical research facilities. Its new product, the Unitech, a machine that combined several monitoring functions and also performed sophisticated analysis of the data, represented a technological breakthrough that would give the company a clear competitive advantage for at least three years. But the project began on a shaky note—and went steadily downhill.

At the outset, there had been two competing design configurations. One, with a key component based entirely on a new concept in buffered circuit design, was the strong favorite of the engineering and marketing departments. Manufacturing urged a somewhat more conventional approach and persisted in its arguments even after the com-

Editor's note: This article is based in part on Mr. Burt's book, *Proactive Procurement: The Key to Increased Profits, Productivity, and Quality* (New York: Prentice-Hall, Inc., 1984). The author has granted permission to use this material.

334 Executing Development Projects

pany president made a "final" decision in favor of the more advanced design.

A few months later, it became obvious that the initial cost projections had been far too optimistic. The equipment needed to perform in-house operations would come to about $600,000 rather than the $450,000 estimated. What was more serious, purchased components would exceed budget by at least 38%. Marketing protested that boosting prices to recover these higher costs would severely reduce Unitech's attractiveness to potential buyers. The compromise: minor redesign to reduce costs, an increase in price, and a decrease in projected profit margins (in the hope that margins would grow over the life of the product).

The next significant setback occurred when, during the assembly of a preproduction model, components from two important suppliers proved incompatible, although both suppliers had met reasonable interpretations of purchase order specifications. The result: further delays for design modification as well as additional expenditures for reworking tools and dies.

After a long sequence of minor problems, shipments finally began seven months after the planned date for market introduction. During the next four months, orders held up fairly well, but the company built and shipped only 52 units—not the 175 on which the budget was based. Moreover, of these 52 units, customers reported more than half as defective. Medical Technologies had 5 repaired in the field; 11 were slated to be returned to the factory for more extensive work; the company's field personnel had yet to inspect the remaining 13. Quality control and marketing both called for a halt in shipments until the company solved Unitech's reliability problems.

Overall results were discouraging, to say the least. Even so, a detailed postaudit found that:

Technical and managerial personnel were on a par with those of the competition.

Production facilities and equipment were among the best in the industry.

Hourly employees were experienced, well paid, loyal, and hard working.

Of the problems Medical Technologies had encountered when introducing new products in the past, none had even remotely approached those posed by the Unitech.

Although the Unitech represented a big step forward in technology, it was really a logical extension of the company's prior products, differing only in that it used many more purchased components and relied largely on electronic and output mechanisms that lay outside the company's design and manufacturing capabilities.

The audit concluded that the Unitech program had been plagued with unusual bad luck in addition to poor internal coordination and recommended that a new control system be developed for future new product programs.

Beyond the Traditional Approach

Sound familiar? No matter how relevant or valid the audit's individual findings, its conclusions were faulty and unproductive. Its analysis failed to see that the Unitech's long string of problems was not the result of bad luck or unexplainable misfortune but of an explicit commitment to a familiar but outmoded and dysfunctional approach to new product development. In its simplest form, this approach calls for engineering to design products to meet the price and performance criteria set by marketing—and for manufacturing to meet the resulting delivery schedules and cost targets.

Purchasing, to the extent that it figures at all in the traditional view of new product development summarized in Exhibit I, has the task of ensuring the timely availability of required supplies and services and of obtaining them at economic prices. Hidden in this allocation of effort are three dicey assumptions about the nature and role of procurement:

1. Although production can and generally should be accomplished through a combination of company-operated and independent facilities, product design should be an exclusively in-house—and a tightly centralized—process (to avoid creating a committee-designed "horse-camel").
2. Given adequate specifications for purchased items, managers ought to regard them as commodities.
3. The purchasing function consists of buying commodities and is, therefore, a clerical rather than a technical or managerial task.

These assumptions may be suited reasonably well to the environment in which many companies operated until quite recently, but that environment—as well as the traditional approach to procurement that

Exhibit I.   Traditional approach to new product development

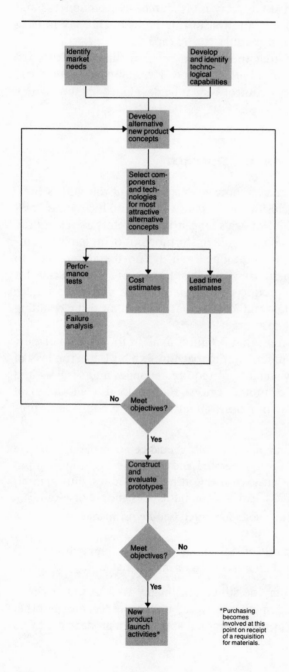

it fostered—is rapidly becoming obsolete. Thirty years ago, for example, a typical manufacturer's purchases were equal to approximately 30% of the company's total revenues; today that figure is more likely to be around 60%. The increasing rate of technological change has led to a much higher frequency of new product introductions and to much shorter lead times, both of which put additional strains on product development systems. Advancing technology has also blurred distinctions among categories of products. Electronics, largely in the form of integrated circuits, are now significant elements in such diverse products as typewriters, machine tools, and automobiles—products that little more than a decade ago were "pure" electromechanical devices.

These developments make untenable many of the assumptions underlying the traditional approach to new product development. In particular, companies will have to learn new ways to manage.

A LARGER DESIGN GROUP

The increasing variety of technologies in a given product requires a broader range of participants in the development process—especially when the product incorporates state-of-the-art technology or combines technologies that have not been used together in the past. Under these conditions, a company's engineering capability is unlikely to span the full breadth of the scientific and technical fields involved.

Medical Technologies, for instance, had some of the most competent personnel in the medical equipment field. Its marketing department did an excellent job of determining market needs. Its research and technical staffs were among the best in their own areas. They were familiar with basic electronics, of course, but they were not acquainted with the most recent developments in microprocessor design, expanded memory circuits, or high-speed, nonimpact printing devices. Thus neither the marketing nor the R&D function, on which the company's top management relied for information, could provide the full range of intelligence needed. As a result, Medical Technologies could neither take advantage of the best design concepts available nor anticipate or correct problems rooted in technologies that lay outside the company's in-house competence.

In today's environment, product development must become a cooperative venture by the primary developer and its key suppliers. This concept will horrify many executives, who fear for the security of proprietary information and materials and who nourish a desire for self-sufficiency. Yet the aerospace industry has used this cooperative approach for years, and companies in the computer and automotive industries, among others, are rapidly following.

VENDOR INVOLVEMENT

Vendor-supplied components do much to determine the quality, cost, and market availability of a product. Not only are more vendors involved today; their contributions to the total product are also more critical. Consider, for example, IBM's extraordinarily successful entry into the microprocessor (personal computer) market. In a radical departure from practice, the company elected to manufacture only a few selected items and to purchase the bulk of the system's components from specialized vendors. Similarly, General Motors has raised quality, lowered costs, and reduced investment in inventories through the timely involvement of its vendors in the design process.

General Electric's jet engine division has carried the integration of engineering and purchasing to its logical conclusion and reaped significant cost and time savings. Some 16 design teams have worked on various aspects of GE's new commercial engine. Included on each team are three members of the materials (purchasing) organization: a procurement engineer, a buyer, and a subcontract administrator. Vendors participate as appropriate throughout the design process. Normally, it takes three to four iterations through the design process to move from a clean sheet of paper on the drafting board to a workable product. Although the final results are not yet in, GE estimates that its approach to product design will reduce the required iterations by 50% to 60% and prune costs by a whopping 20%!

Including vendors in an in-house design process involves both technical and commercial issues. The technical considerations are often obvious; the commercial ones, more subtle. Traditionally, issues of production capacity, financial and managerial resources, and competitive sourcing have not received the attention they deserve. For example, the design engineering function of a computer manufacturer recently specified an advanced input-output device for a new line of computers. When purchasing attempted to establish a contract for the projected quantity requirements, it learned that the supplier did not possess adequate production capacity. The computer's introduction had to be stretched out to allow for a buildup of the vendor's capacity.

When purchasing is not involved in the design process, companies often inadvertently specify components that they can procure from only one source, but research shows that far fewer disruptions and lower prices result when competition is present during the source selection process. Indeed, studies indicate that prices tend to fall by 4% each time one additional qualified supplier submits a price. Thus an item costing $100 when only one bid has been obtained will cost $92 if three bids are available.[1] Furthermore, average savings of 12.5% result when material that previously has been purchased on a sole source basis is purchased under competitive conditions.[2]

The right purchase description can also have a great impact on product costs and availability. A San Diego manufacturer has long used its own design specifications to buy components for which suitable commercial substitutes were available. Not only have the costs of such special items averaged 10% more than those of their commercial substitutes; specification of unique items has also brought longer lead times, weaker market responsiveness, and a need for maintaining larger inventories.

Early involvement of purchasing in the design process could have avoided these problems—especially if purchasing has the expertise to deal effectively with technical personnel in vendor and in-house organizations. Recognizing this potential, some companies, Eli Lilly and Motorola among them, have begun to hire MBAs with technical backgrounds for assignments in purchasing.

The total value added by U.S. manufacturers has declined for at least two decades as companies have increasingly turned to their suppliers for complex finished parts and assemblies rather than for raw materials and commodity items. As the importance of vendors grows, maintaining satisfactory relationships with them becomes a managerial and technical operation of the greatest importance. Experience shows that long-term, collaborative arrangements mutually benefit both the customer and the supplier. Theodore Levitt compares the relationship between industrial buyers and sellers to a marriage. A courtship stage takes place during which both sides investigate technical and commercial issues; a sale consummates the courtship; and a long-lasting marriage may ensue. As Levitt notes, "The quality of the marriage determines whether there will be continued or expanded business, or troubles and divorce."[3] Both buyer and seller have a vested interest in the relationship, and both must work to make it succeed. In a manufacturing company, purchasing must establish and manage the relationship.

THE NEW ROLE FOR PURCHASING

The greatly accelerated rate of change in social, political, and economic variables as well as in technology forces companies to monitor their environments constantly. A strategic use of purchasing links a company to its environment, especially as the environment affects future procurement requirements. Sensible decisions about such requirements call for buyers and suppliers to share information. Strategic purchasing objectives grow out of a company's long-range planning process; at the same time, of course, purchasing needs and realities—critical information, say, on new products, new technology, or the likely availability of materials—may affect the choice of corporate objectives.

At a macro level, a strategic use of purchasing requires a purchasing manager to monitor the company's environment, forecast changes in that environment, share relevant information with suppliers and colleagues in other functions, and identify the company's competitive advantages and disadvantages relative to its suppliers. At a micro level, strategic purchasing involves the identification of critical materials, the evaluation of possible supply disruptions for each of them, and the development of contingency plans for all identifiable supply problems.

Thus the most vulnerable aspect of the product development system in many companies is their failure to use the full creative capabilities of potential suppliers. The biggest mistake of purchasing executives in these organizations is their failure to get involved in the requirements development process. This pattern of avoidance is a holdover from the days when purchasing was a reactive, clerical function, limited to issuing and maintaining custody of documents that confirmed other departments' decisions.

Now and in the future, however, the viability and integrity of product design, development, and production can be ensured only if purchasing steps in early in the requirements process—that is, if it has a significant role to play from the very beginning of the design process. In most organizations, purchasing is accustomed to working with manufacturing, but now it must work in tandem with R&D and engineering as well. At the heart of the new product development process, there must be room for what purchasing has to say—and do.

Purchasing and the Design Process

The model of product design outlined in Exhibit II implies that engineering and purchasing should view product design as a joint venture, which requires the same kind of early and continuing dialogue that the traditional approach demanded of engineering and marketing.

POINTS OF LINKAGE

At least six points exist in this design process where purchasing can or should provide information and advice on the services, components, and materials that the company will need to buy.

In the investigative phase, purchasing should help establish price, performance, timeliness, quality, and reliability objectives and pinpoint the trade-offs among them. Later in this stage, purchasing must inform other departments about various suppliers' abilities to meet these objectives. After engineering has developed alternative conceptual solutions to the agreed-on objectives, purchasing should determine economic and scheduling implications for necessary materials, components, and subassemblies under each option.

The several design reviews held during the laboratory phase also need the involvement of purchasing—especially in terms of deciding on the use of standard items available from, and stocked by, two or more suppliers. These reviews must carefully weigh the trade-offs between the improved performance made possible by components incorporating state-of-the-art technology and the reliability and cost advantages standard items offer.

After the design process results in a manufacturing plan that, in turn, leads to a procurement plan, purchasing has the responsibility to challenge requirements that are uneconomical or otherwise not in the company's best interests. Further, it must do so before the company commits itself to a particular design configuration. Purchasing should also encourage vendors to offer cost reduction suggestions at any time while they are supplying an item.

Exhibit II.   *The modern design process*

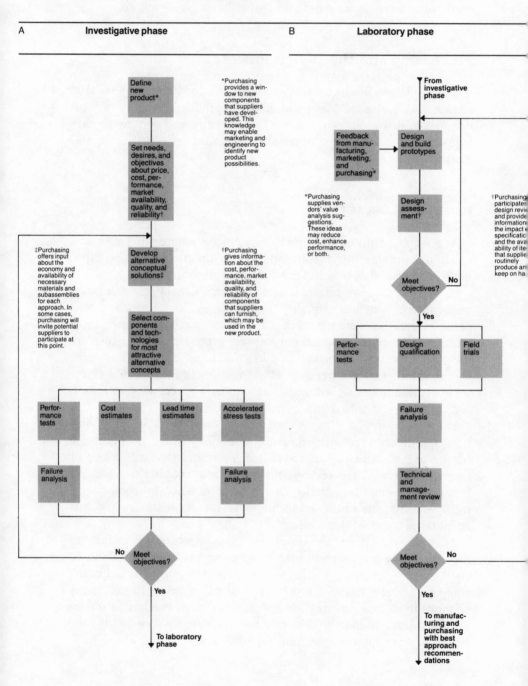

C	Manufacturing and procurement phase

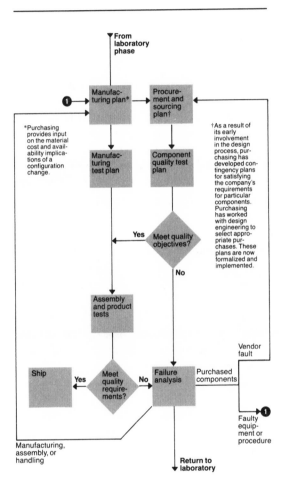

Finally, changes in an item's configuration during manufacturing may have significant cost or delivery implications. Purchasing, together with manufacturing, marketing, and inventory control, should help evaluate such engineering change requests.

CONNECTION WITH ENGINEERING

Ideally, engineering will solicit—and purchasing will aggressively seek out and disseminate—the essential information about the supply environment called for by an integrated development system. In practice, old habits and procedures are extremely resistant to change. Accordingly, senior managers must recognize the need for a new approach and put that recognition into action in the recruiting, motivating, and training of key members of both the engineering and purchasing departments. Other methods for better integrating these two functions include:

Colocation, which calls for placing purchasing staff near design engineering people. Purchasing employees with technical backgrounds can advise design engineers on the procurement implications of different components. In some organizations, these purchasing experts may have the authority to issue purchase orders; in others, they act in a liaison capacity only. For all its benefits, however, colocation is often quite expensive in that it usually requires increased personnel. Before attempting it on a large scale, companies should do thorough cost-benefit studies and perhaps undertake a pilot program.

Formal reviews, conducted through a committee consisting of representatives from engineering, marketing, manufacturing, quality control, and purchasing to review all designs prior to manufacture or purchase. One danger here is that the committee may adopt the view that its function is to veto designs rather than to provide information and ideas.

Project teams, like those established by IBM's Entry System Division (its personal computer operation) and GE's Evandale Division (developers and producers of large jet engines), among others, to develop and introduce new products. The nature of the industry and the type of product will determine the group's composition and function, team membership, and the most appropriate control system.

Recommended parts lists, which become possible when purchasing establishes and maintains a data base of recommended parts in the form of a traditional catalog or of computerized files linked to the company's CAD system. The data base includes all relevant technical information (like physical, reliability, mechanical, electrical, and thermal descriptions) and divides parts into two groups: recommended and acceptable. Engineers are free to select items with a "recommended" code. Choosing "acceptable" items or items not listed requires higher management's approval. Employing such a list sharply reduces design time and greatly assists any ongoing standardization program.

Procurement engineers, who work with design engineers on a daily basis and supply information on the commercial implications of various design approaches and on alternative materials and components.

Employee rotation, which encourages career development programs to include an assignment in the procurement department for selected technical personnel. This procedure has three big advantages: it provides an ideal transition from a technical to a management position; it brings invaluable expertise into the purchasing function; and it creates a deep appreciation of the advantages of close links between engineering and purchasing.

A Future for Purchasing

Investment in new technologies alone will not be sufficient to revitalize U.S. industry. Managers must achieve a mastery of the whole product development process—especially of such long-neglected activities as purchasing. Indeed, purchasing must develop a new relationship with engineering that reflects the importance that vendor capability plays in new product design and manufacture. Manufacturers can no longer view suppliers simply as a source for components they do not want to make themselves. Vendors can also provide ideas about new technologies, materials, and techniques, and collectively they represent a clear window through which a company can scan a number of crucial environmental variables.

Purchasing must become the conduit through which such information flows. Engineering and purchasing together must forge a partnership that incorporates that flow of information into the process of designing and developing new products.

Notes

1. "Effect of the Number of Competitors on Costs," *Journal of Purchasing & Materials Management*, November 1971, 13.

2. David N. Burt and Joseph E. Boyett, Jr., "Reduction in Selling Price after Introduction of Competition," *Journal of Marketing Research*, May 1979, 275.

3. Theodore Levitt, "After the Sale Is Over . . . ," *Harvard Business Review*, September–October 1983, 87.

4
Organizing for Manufacturable Design

James W. Dean, Jr., and Gerald I. Susman

Nowhere in a company is the need for coordination more acute than between the people who are responsible for product design and those responsible for manufacturing. As Daniel E. Whitney argues in "Manufacturing by Design," most companies have operated for years in an environment where design and manufacturing communicate infrequently, if at all. In the worst instances, product designs were just thrown "over the wall": designers felt that their job was finished when designs were released and disappeared into manufacturing's domain; manufacturing engineers struggled to build products that were dropped in their laps.

Many companies have come to appreciate the disadvantages of this sequential approach to product development. Final designs emerging from engineering may be producible only at very high cost. While design expenditures *per se* may amount to only a small part of a product's total cost, design determines a huge proportion of producing, testing, and servicing costs. Forcing manufacturing to wait to begin its work until a design is released prolongs the development time of a product and may force a company to miss a market opportunity. Often a company is forced to play catch-up by implementing numerous engineering changes long after products have been introduced.

Effective manufacturers work from designs that have as few parts as possible, as many standard parts as possible, and that can be assembled by methods within manufacturing's capabilities. Barely manufacturable designs compromise product reliability and may preclude the use of robots or computer numerically controlled machines whose purchase was justified on the assumption that they could be kept busy.

Companies that have tried to design for manufacture merely by exhorting designers to create more producible designs, that is, without changing the basic organization of product development, have run into serious trouble. There are, after all, barriers to the integration of design and manufacturing. Often engineers in the two corporate functions have had different educations and share neither a common language nor compatible goals. Design engineers tend to be more focused on the product's performance or on its aesthetics; manufacturing engineers generally concentrate on plant efficiency.

In fact, designers generally enjoy higher status and pay than manufacturing engineers. Designers are considered something akin to creative artists and may be rewarded for ingenuity that has little to do with whether or not their designs can be turned into products cheaply and easily. Manufacturing people, whatever their background, often bear the stigma of less well-educated people, managers who have worked their way up from the factory floor.

The personnel from the two functions may also be located in different buildings, cities, or even countries, and there may be no real opportunity for them to establish rapport. Budgeting practices may exacerbate rivalries, as manufacturing engineers are often not funded to work on projects until the design is released, which is precisely when funding for design ends.

Having observed numerous manufacturing organizations, we've discerned several organizational approaches to designing for manufacture that go a long way toward overcoming these barriers. They range from manufacturing sign-off on designs, to combining product and process engineering into the same department. Some are more sweeping than others, but all are quite practical, having been used by a variety of companies. Fundamental to all of the approaches is basic change in the *structure* of the organization.

MANUFACTURING SIGN-OFF. In this approach, manufacturing engineers are given veto power over product designs, which cannot be released without manufacturing's approval, though in some cases, only its final approval. It is unlikely with this approach that an unproducible or barely producible design will reach the factory floor. But the approach's biggest drawback, clearly, is its heavy-handedness: it gives a club to manufacturing without providing for creative interchange between the two functions and does not allow manufacturing to begin its work until design's work is completed.

Companies using this approach seldom let designers grope blindly for what will satisfy manufacturing. Designers can use commercially available software to assess a product's producibility. Among the best known systems are Boothroyd and Dewhurst's Design for Assembly and Hitachi's Assemblability Evaluation Method. These and other systems calculate a producibility score for nearly any product, based on the number of its parts, the number of its standardized parts, the simplicity of couplers, the motions involved in its assembly, and so on. Some programs can even generate bar charts that demonstrate the contributions of subassemblies to manufacturing cost and time.

The manufacturing sign-off is relatively simple to manage and depends little on interpersonal skills of engineers on either side of the wall. Designers' use of expert-system software permits smaller companies to benefit from the accumulated knowledge of more advanced companies and allows manufacturing engineers to focus on their principal task, namely, design of the process.

Incidentally, a number of companies have created customized software for their design engineers. Customized packages aim to give designers information about the specific constraints of the production site. Other companies use less sophisticated (and less expensive) paper versions of the same idea, that is, listings of preferred components, standard production routings, and so forth. These documents are typically distributed to the design group, so they can try to make their designs manufacturable before manufacturing approval is solicited.

One appliance manufacturer we know, with several billion dollars in annual sales, has its product designers use a number of self-checking software modules to monitor such qualities as moldability (for plastics), formability (for metal drawings), and ease of automated assembly. The company wants products to achieve acceptable scores on manufacturability before manufacturing even sees the designs. This allows designers to see these programs as a tool to help them, rather than something that manufacturing uses to frustrate them. Approval must be granted by a producibility-feasibility group, however, at as many as ten phases in the design process. If approval is withheld, the design cannot pass to the final phases, when designers would ordinarily order equipment to build prototypes.

Senior managers at this appliance company believe that their software programs have educated designers and that they've helped the company make major strides in cost and quality. Again, however, the system's greatest weakness is the lack of day-to-day communication between designers and manufacturing people. As a manager who helped to design the current system put it, designers still "work in a vacuum." He wishes there were more interaction "when the paper is clean."

The company has considered bringing design and manufacturing into the same building, though the cost is currently prohibitive. Plans for shifting responsibility for building prototypes from design to manufacturing are underway. Executives are also contemplating letting manufacturing contract for toolmaking by outside vendors before the design is finalized so vendors can be "partners" in the process. However, such an approach may lead to complex (and possibly costly) negotiations with these vendors whenever a design is changed, and managers in finance are resisting it.

THE INTEGRATOR. Integrators work with designers on producibility issues, serving as liaisons to the manufacturing group. Naturally, such a role requires individuals who can keep design and manufacturing perspectives in balance. An integrator who leans too heavily toward manufacturing will lose credibility with designers, and someone who leans too heavily toward design will simply not get the job done.

Given the way engineers are currently educated and promoted, integrator candidates may be hard to find. Manufacturing and design engineers are the products of separate and distinct degree programs. And once working for a company, they tend to be promoted within their respective hierarchies. There is usually little opportunity to broaden their provincial outlook to include the other group's concerns.

The integrator approach has been used by the electronics division of a multibillion dollar company we know, a company that sells advanced avionics and communications equipment to the military. Now that the Defense Department insists that its contractors make provision for the producibility, serviceability, and maintainability of weapons systems, the division must pursue design for manufacture even more carefully. Moreover, since it recently spent tens of millions of dollars on an advanced electronics assembly plant, the company wants to see its products designed to take advantage of this new facility.

Company executives originally hired as integrator an industrial engineer with a background in design. He began by preparing a manual for the design engineers to use and by securing top-management support for manufacturing sign-off on product designs. The manual, planned as a collaboration between design and industrial engineering, was to be divided into five volumes, covering such things as lists of standard components and circuit-board mountings to the more obscure cost implications of producibility mistakes in complex, low-rate products.

Company executives also assigned a test engineer to make sure components were manufactured in a way that allowed for systematic inspection, and they issued a directive that the producibility coordinators were to approve all designs before release. As one supervisor put it, "The preachers became auditors."

This division has already seen substantial payoffs from these efforts. Boards on which automated component placement techniques can be used have increased from 40% to about 55%; for newly designed boards, almost 90%. Plans include designating a third producibility coordinator, as well as hiring a number of scientists to develop new production methods for the advanced designs that it will soon have to produce. The company also plans to involve its subcontractors in future efforts to improve producibility.

Clearly, the integrator approach is reasonably flexible. A single individual (or a small team) can easily keep track of new capabilities in manufacturing. Manufacturing engineers don't have to become more knowledgeable about design or designers become more expert in manufacturing. Rather, the approach develops an "expert" in producibility, who can become the focal point for companywide efforts.

There are some disadvantages, however. One problem is the downside of the integrator's virtue, what one integrator we spoke with called the "guru syndrome." Since the integrator is there to worry about producibility, no one else does. The integrator approach makes the organization very dependent on one (or only a few) individuals. It does not facilitate simultaneous engineering—that is, manufacturing cannot begin its work before design's work has been completed.

CROSS-FUNCTIONAL TEAMS.   Another step away from the traditional approach is cross-functional teams. At a minimum these consist of a designer and a manufacturing engineer, who work together throughout the whole process. The team meets regularly or may even be located in the same office.

This is the first approach that facilitates simultaneous engineering: the manufacturing engineer becomes familiar with the design well before it is released and may even have had a hand in creating it. The manufacturing process can be partially if not completely planned before the design is finalized.

Perhaps the best example we know of the cross-functional team is a process-control company with annual sales of about $100 million. It became interested in producibility about two years ago, when, like the military contractor we just discussed, it began to utilize autoinsertion equipment for circuit-board production. The company was also discouraged by the failure of one of its recent products whose poor quality was attributed to a barely producible design.

Initially, individuals from manufacturing engineering and quality assurance were formally assigned to the design team, and from the first day of a new product program, the entire group met once or twice a week. A program manager, who acted as a mediator, determined the meeting schedule. Eventually people from test engineering, purchasing, and marketing joined the team.

The new approach created some frictions. Designers felt that quality assurance and manufacturing were preempting them and wondered why the company didn't trust them to create good designs independently. They also felt manufacturing's demands were often unrealistic, particularly concerning clearances among the various components. They were upset that the new system undermined their creativity.

These sentiments have all dissipated over time, largely because the company took the trouble to calculate the relative cost of various designs at the circuit-board level and proved beyond doubt the importance of using autoinsertable components. Costs are so much lower now with automated assembly that the team recently set a goal of using autoinsertable components 97% of the time. Incidentally, while conflicts between design and manufacturing have generally been settled in team meetings, final authority over design rests with the engineering manager.

The team approach has also been used successfully by a multibillion dollar aerospace company we've studied that produces for both military and commercial markets. The company wanted to decrease its development time for major products from 36 to 24 months, to reduce the number of engineering changes necessary to meet production standards, and to fully utilize its advanced manufacturing capabilities.

The producibility effort began in 1983 with a series of seminars for designers. By 1985, the company was ready to experiment with what it called product centers. It formed design teams with representatives from engineering, manufacturing, quality assurance, and product support (documentation, etc.), with either design or manufacturing providing leadership.

The product-center concept has continued to evolve. There are six now working on a single big project, organized around major subcomponents. Each product center has a manager and deputy manager and, whenever possible, people working on the project are located in the same room. Manufacturing begins process planning as soon as a week or two after design begins its work. Traditionally, manufacturing engineers would not begin to work until designs were released; today they *finish* almost simultaneously with design release.

The possibility of simultaneous engineering is one benefit of the team approach. Also, the frequent interaction involved (especially when product and process designers are located in the same place) permits people from the two functions to educate one another, thus enhancing capability for future efforts. Perhaps the most attractive feature of this team approach is the way it substitutes collaboration for auditing. Yet team members report through separate hierarchies, which helps them to hold to their respective missions. There are tensions, but these often stimulate greater creativity.

The team concept is expensive because it means assigning people to a development effort not only during the time when their special expertise is crucial but before and after as well. The approach requires members to gain broad expertise in producibility, since there is no longer a single producibility expert, and it demands excellent interpersonal skills. There are probably some engineers on both sides of the wall who would do more harm than good on such teams. Finally, the team approach runs the risk associated with any method that allows simultaneous engineering: process planning done before the final design is released may have to be scrapped as the design evolves.

THE PRODUCT-PROCESS DESIGN DEPARTMENT.   Our fourth approach to design for producibility involves the greatest degree of structural change. It entails creating a single department responsible for both product and process both. A number of variations of this approach are possible, including:

- A senior manager with responsibility for both product and process design, but separate subunits for each function.
- Product and process engineers combined into a single department with one manager having responsibility for both groups.
- One department composed of product-process engineers, that is, individuals with responsibility for both aspects of the design, a rarely found ideal, since very few people have the skills necessary to straddle both worlds.

One $100 million defense technology company we know learned the virtues of a product-process department the hard way. At first it subjected products to nonbinding manufacturability reviews; this worked fairly well until the value engineering group came up with an idea for reducing the cost of a critical component by substituting a die casting for a machined blank. Manufacturing liked the concept but contended that vendor-supplied components would not perform as promised without costly rework. The value engineers dismissed manufacturing's objections, and manufacturing didn't press the issue.

Unfortunately, the protests were justified. Reprocessing increased the cost of the component by almost 100%, as much as $300,000 over the life of the program. Ironically, the company had already intended to move to the product-process department approach and had even begun giving the head of value engineering the added responsibility of managing the manufacturing engineering department. As it happened, unfortunately, this person was not comfortable with the manufacturing group and spent very little time there.

Now the company is operating with an interim structure. In the absence of an organization that supports manufacturable designs, producibility depends heavily on the personal inclinations of the designers. The company's computer-aided design system is networked between design and manufacturing, and designers can discuss the implications of designs with manufacturing while both view the drawings on their screens. Unfortunately, this happens far less often than management would like.

An automobile components company, a subsidiary of one of the big three, has the second type of product-process department; design and process engineers report to the same manager at the first level. Product-process teams share software systems and offices, and members are encouraged to decide on a design among themselves. If they don't, their manager resolves the issue. The company adopted this approach in order to reduce development time and cost, and these goals have been achieved, in addition to a reduction in engineering changes after products are in production.

The one-department approach permits simultaneous engineering and leads to mutual education through day-to-day contact. It also places a high premium on the technical and interpersonal skills of department members. The department head must strike a balance between engineering functions and bring a great deal of expertise to the table.

The one-department approach creates the greatest degree of structural change of the four approaches. It may also create the greatest resistance, as people are torn from the comfortable surroundings of their professional and departmental loyalties. Perhaps the greatest danger of the one-department approach is that, as the design and manufacturing communities work more closely together, they may find it too easy to compromise on designs that are merely acceptable to both sides—rather than insisting on functional excellence from their own disciplinary standpoint.

It is clear from our examples that a number of different approaches can lead to producible designs. How can managers choose among the alternatives? The approaches range in impact on the organization from manufacturing sign-off (relatively low) to the product-process department (quite high). Higher impact approaches allow for collaboration and simultaneous engineering, while lower impact approaches do not. On the other hand, higher impact approaches place much greater demands on people, in terms of absorbing change and developing new skills, both technical and interpersonal.

Companies that enjoy substantial freedom in product and process design, and that have the organizational ability to rapidly absorb change, are well positioned to take advantage of the higher impact approaches. Such companies can profit from the collaboration and simultaneous engineering that such methods afford.

Companies whose products and/or processes are relatively fixed, or whose capacity for absorbing change is limited, would be better advised to begin with manufacturing sign-off or the integrator approach. When products or processes are fixed, there is little to be gained by the intense interaction that the higher impact approaches feature. And organizations slow to change would take so long to implement the higher impact designs that they would get greater benefit by using one of the simpler approaches. Of course, such companies could always move to higher impact designs at a later date.

These approaches are not cast in concrete or meant to seem exclusive of one another. Structures for organizations ought to accommodate the messy dilemmas managers face, so each organization should customize its own approach, using the four identified here as building blocks. Whatever the chosen method, change in organization structure will be necessary in a program to achieve manufacturable design.

PART

VI

Creating a Competitive Advantage

1
Mastering Chaos at the High-Tech Frontier: An Interview with Silicon Graphics' Ed McCracken

Steven E. Prokesch

Edward R. McCracken listens with amusement to those who say that low costs are what competing in the 1990s is all about, that even high-tech products are becoming commodities. He passionately believes that staying on the cutting edge of innovation is the only real source of competitive advantage.

McCracken's views might be unconventional, but he can make a boast that few other CEOs of computer companies can: his company, Silicon Graphics, Inc., is not only coping with the rapid change and chaos that has upset everyone from IBM to Apple to Digital, it is thriving. At a time when the profit margins of many computer hardware and software companies have become razor thin or disappeared, fast-growing Silicon Graphics earned a record $95.2 million on revenues of $1.09 billion in its fiscal year, which ended June 30.

James H. Clark, who founded the company in 1982, believed that the "visual computing" capabilities he had developed as a professor at Stanford University were the wave of the future. Until then, the world of computer graphics was two-dimensional. Clark's innovation enabled people to create moving, three-dimensional graphics on computer screens. His goal in creating realistic images that were easy to manipulate was to enable people who relied on computers to be more productive, whether they were scientists concocting molecules for a new drug, engineers designing jets or cars, or moviemakers creating special effects. (Industrial Light & Magic used Silicon Graphics machines to create the cyborg from liquid metal in *Terminator 2*, the dinosaurs in *Jurassic Park*, and the sea creature in *The Abyss*.)

The belief that visual computing's time is at hand has propelled

Silicon Graphics to add digital audio and video capabilities to its array of brightly colored machines. A digital video camera that makes teleconferencing a snap comes standard with its newest desktop computer, the Indy. These audio and video capabilities require the crunching of enormously complex algorithms. One of Clark's innovations to enable computers to do this faster was putting the graphics code right on the silicon chips, hence the company's name.

Silicon Graphics' chief products are still workstations used mainly by scientists and engineers. But its quest to make graphics run ever-faster has led it into supercomputers. In January, the company unveiled its Power Challenge machines, whose prices begin below $120,000. Silicon Graphics has also expanded into the other end of the computing spectrum with the Indy, introduced in July. The company's first machine priced below $5,000, the Indy puts Silicon Graphics into competition with high-end Macintoshes and PCs. And alliances with Time Warner in interactive digital TV and Nintendo in home video games will push the company's technology into the mass market.

If Chairman Jim Clark is Silicon Graphics' visionary, President Ed McCracken, who joined the company in 1984 after 16 years at Hewlett-Packard Company, is the architect of its strategy and structure. In this interview, McCracken, 49, shares his views on what it takes to prosper in the high-tech—or any fast-moving—market. He talked to *Harvard Business Review* senior editor Steven E. Prokesch at company headquarters in Mountain View, California, and in San Diego.

HBR: *As many industries, including high-tech industries, have seen, time-based competition—doing everything faster, more efficiently, and therefore with lower costs—does not necessarily translate into higher profits. What has gone wrong?*

Edward R. McCracken: The conventional wisdom is that many industries, including computers, have become commodity businesses and that the way to compete is to compress the time it takes to develop a new product and get it to market. Companies subscribing to this view believe that the mass market is more important than the high end, because large volume creates economies of scale. And since these companies think that price is the key to competing in the mass market, they strive to be the leader in low costs, rather than in innovation.

These companies are reacting to chaos in the rapidly changing marketplace by trying to keep up with or stay just ahead of the pack. Our philosophy is that the key to achieving competitive advantage isn't reacting to chaos; it's producing that chaos. And the key to being a chaos producer is being an innovation leader.

A case in point is the computer industry. Those who think that computers are turning into commodities believe that products will become cheaper and cheaper, that competitiveness will depend more on manufacturing costs and distribution than on innovation, and that they can cut their R&D as well as their relationships with customers.

But I think the key to obtaining competitive advantage in the 1990s is making your customers feel like you designed a product specifically for them, that your product has special features or capabilities for which they would pay a premium. It's difficult to add value if you're removed from your customers. This is especially true in an industry like computers, which I don't think actually is a commodity business.

There has never been a commodity market with the rate of technological change that exists in the computer industry. The performance, or computing power relative to price, is now increasing tenfold every 3½ years. That compares with a tenfold increase every 7 years in the 1980s and every 10 years in the 1970s.

When there are two tenfold increases, the paradigm shifts because everything changes: the software, the design and packaging, the way customers use the product. If you're not out there trying to shift paradigms, then your products become commodity-like very quickly, which is what happened to the PC market.

What happens when a company that had been a leader in innovation allows itself to slip?

Once a company is no longer on the leading edge of technological change, its gross margins shrink. Then the company must reduce its sales costs to practically nothing, so it can't spend enough to know its customers very well. And it can't make enough money to spend more than 4% or 5% of revenues on R&D. In contrast, we spend about 12%. In the computer industry, 4% or 5% is not enough to retain a position on the cutting edge of technology. It's a one-way ticket that doesn't allow a company to switch back into an innovation strategy. And over the long term, it's hard enough to survive, let alone prosper.

PCs and Macintoshes, for example, are old technology. The fundamental way that those products were originally defined is all wrong for today's marketplace, which increasingly demands digital audio and video capabilities and moving, three-dimensional graphics in the user interface. Pretty soon, $300 cable TV boxes will have all these capabilities. There's so much software out there that the PC and Macintosh will carry on for a long time. But companies that are dependent on the old technology have to work especially hard to bring their products into the future.

How can companies avoid falling irrevocably behind in technology?

Here's how we do it: we don't use yesterday's technology. In other words, we don't try to make old technology do something it was not intended to do. We only use the latest technology, which makes it easier to embed powerful digital-media capabilities in our products. We're convinced that the computer of the future will be able not only to process all different types of data—numbers, text, objects, photographs, audio, and video—but also to integrate them. We believe we're leading in this area.

Our feeling is that this rapid, chaotic rate of change will continue forever and will continue to accelerate. The capabilities that everyone will consider routine ten years from now will require extreme amounts of performance—supercomputing performance.

For example, you're going to want to keep your photo album in your little portable computer. And you're going to want to combine parts of two or three photos, or change the exposures and sharpen the images, or play around with the colors to create a piece of art. You're going to want to use image-processing routines that today are used only by the intelligence community and require supercomputers. You're going to want to do these things because they'll be easy and fun; you won't know you're using complex algorithms.

If a company is in an industry marked by rapid technological change, how should it approach time-based competition?

Those who are just reacting to chaos use short cycle times to lower costs by squeezing the waste out of their systems, by getting rid of inefficient processes and reducing defects. In general, that's great. But where many companies are going wrong is in how they get new products to market faster.

Many companies compartmentalize product development. They do market research to determine what customers want and then come up with a product concept. That concept is handed to engineers, who figure out how to make the product. Then it is manufactured. The reason for accelerating the cycle is to get new ideas from engineering into the marketplace rapidly. We have the opposite reason: we have short cycle times so that we can start our development cycles later. By doing so, we can get the latest input from customers and use the latest technologies to give them what they want.

When we finish one product-development program, we raise our heads and look around to see what to invent next. We try to get a sense of what customers might want and what is happening with changing technologies. Then we put our heads down, engineer like mad, and get the product into the marketplace. Once we've done that, we do it all over again. That's our planning cycle. If we can do that in nine months or a year rather than three years, we will have a tremendous advantage.

We did our IRIS Crimson, a mid-range graphics workstation introduced in January 1992, in six months. The Indy, our new desktop computer, took about two years. I'm convinced that if we had started the Indy three months before we did, we would not have included a digital camera. Our customers were telling us that they wanted video conferencing capabilities, and the technology became available just in time.

So what does this say about the way many corporations practice long-term planning?

Long-term product planning is dangerous in our industry and many others because it forces companies to make wild guesses about what customers might want. We don't believe in planting flags way out ahead and then trying to reach them. Long-term planning weds companies to approaches and technologies too early, which is deadly in our marketplace and many others. No one can plan the future. Three years is long-term. Even two years may be. Five years is laughable.

What is top management's role in deciding which products to develop?

At Silicon Graphics, top management's role is to make sure that the company's organizational structure encourages our brightest technologists to maintain close working relationships with customers. Top management's role is to divide customers into segments determined by their needs and the technology required to satisfy them. Then we put a project team in each segment and let those teams decide what to design in cooperation with their customers. As long as the teams have bright ideas and are really excited about them, our top managers stay out of the way.

Isn't there the danger that a team might develop a product that will cannibalize one in the market that still has some life left?

We don't pay a lot of attention to whether or not a product is still gaining market share when we decide to launch a new product. This approach is the only way to ensure that no one gets to the market first with a faster, better, cheaper product. When someone beats us to the market, which has happened only a very few times, we are embarrassed.

So if an existing product is still selling like hotcakes, and we've got a new product that works twice as well, that new product goes right into the marketplace. For example, the fact that our Indigo workstation was still gaining market share didn't stop us from coming out with our Indy system. The Indigo, introduced in July 1991, is currently priced between $7,000 and $30,000. The Indy is priced below $5,000, comes with a standard digital video camera, which the Indigo doesn't have, and is just as fast.

You said that many companies are making a mistake in focusing on the low end rather than the high end of the market. Why is this a mistake?

I don't think it should be an either/or situation. In this rapidly changing environment, a broad product line is very important. By owning the high end, we get access to new technology and capabilities first, which we can then drive down to the mass market.

It would have been disastrous for our stockholders to have restricted Silicon Graphics to being a $200 million company competing only in a high-end niche, which might have happened had we not learned to take the paradigm down ourselves. If you're only in niche markets, you're constantly scrambling to react to the new paradigms, and you never get the payoff.

For years, people told us that three-dimensional graphics were going to be a little niche; now people are starting to understand that this technology represents a fundamental human interface. For a few years, we were way ahead in integrating video into our systems; now people are starting to say that the new paradigm involves digital video.

Our average system prices were around $50,000 until 1986, when we had to make a major decision: Should we remain a high-end niche player? Should we take the technology into the lower end? Or should we try to do both? We chewed on these questions a long time. Of course, we decided to do both. Driving that decision was our philosophy that there's no place to hide in the computer market.

With our $50,000 to $100,000 systems, we're out there learning about developments in image processing, virtual reality, and so on. We stay close to our best and brightest customers and learn how their changing technical demands should fundamentally change the computers we produce.

A company can't use traditional market research to pick up on paradigm shifts. Its best technologists, its most creative R&D people, must be out there to see or sense firsthand what its most creative customers—what we call our "lighthouse" customers—might want in the future. These technologists aren't getting customer input on the current product line; they're getting some feeling about how they might define a brand-new product that would do things differently. A company can't accomplish this very well with marketing or salespeople. Such innovation requires engineers talking to customers.

How do you ensure that this interaction occurs?

We encourage our first- and second-level engineering managers to spend time with customers. We rate our key managers every six months. I remember sitting in on an evaluation for engineering managers at which we lowered the rating of two or three because we thought that they and their teams hadn't spent enough time with customers.

Our division managers aren't there to manage our financial performance. Their job is to manage a special relationship between the technology and the customer's requirements. We have segmented our market rigorously. We have added about one market segment a year and have created a new operating division to serve each segment, to focus on a certain class of customer and technology in a boutique-like way.

Our objective in each segment is to develop partnerships with both the software companies that write applications programs for that segment and with lighthouse customers and to design the right technology into our general-purpose products. We use the same hardware in all our segments, but the specialized applications software for each segment is provided by a variety of third-party developers. This strategy enabled us to build a market share of over 50% in many of these segments.

This approach dates back to our early days as a workstation company. Our machines, which were sold to just a few of the best and brightest engineers and scientists at places like Industrial Light & Magic, NASA, and the military, were the best but were difficult to use and quite expensive. By working with these lighthouse customers, who also now include Boeing, Disney, and Merck, we learn what they are trying to do with our machines or what they want to do with them, and we try to put that capability in an easy-to-use form in our next generation of products.

The workstation market for moviemaking, for example, represents only 5% to 10% of our business, but our engineers spend an unusual amount of time talking to moviemakers. They always have long lists of things we don't do right. Of course, they're trying to make movies with lots of special effects, on no budget, in a very short time. So they run into everything that's wrong with the system, and this pushes us to stay on the leading edge.

For instance, we have been working with Industrial Light & Magic and Pacific Data Images on texture mapping, the capability that enables you to create realistic images. This technology allows you to put a texture onto a graphic image, like putting painted sheet metal onto a three-dimensional image of a car, so that the design looks like the real thing. Today texture mapping is embedded in all our systems.

What are your criteria for choosing lighthouse customers? How do you know which customers can best help you learn the new paradigms?

Let me give an example. About three years ago, when I was visiting Nissan, I asked a senior manager in the engineering organization what we could do to serve the company's needs better. He sat on the edge of his chair and said, "We need you to make your computers run ten times faster than they do in both computing and graphics. And let me tell you how we could change our design process if you could do that."

He then spent an hour explaining how they could change the way they designed a car's engine compartment if their computers were that powerful. The mechanical designers would have a system that included not only the parts each one was designing but also the parts others were designing. And they would have a complete range of tools that would enable them to analyze how vibrations in one part would affect other parts, how the thermal air would flow through the engine compartment, and so on. All this information would be kept electronically on a very complicated database. With systems that powerful, he thought that they could cut significantly the time required to design a car.

The products we had on the market at the time didn't have that kind of capability; he really was asking for at least ten times more power, maybe a hundred times. Since then, we've designed the capabilities they wanted into our product line. This is the kind of customer we're looking for.

I visited another car company about three weeks after visiting Nissan and asked the same question. The answer was: "We need your computers to be cheaper." We don't send engineers to work with such companies because we won't learn anything.

This brings up pricing. You said your approach is to offer capabilities for which customers would pay a premium. How does this fit into your strategy of taking new capabilities from the high end of the market to the low end?

More accurately, our strategy is to be in a position to charge a premium but then not to do so. We want to expand and change the nature of the market. Supercomputers are a good example. We could have priced our supercomputers at $600,000, rather than $200,000 to $300,000. Maybe we could have made more money in the short run. But we're not interested in getting into the old-fashioned supercomputer market.

Customers are used to dealing with supercomputer companies that charge $5 million to $20 million for their products. In return, these companies give their customers lots of support, such as training and maintenance. Instead, we say, "You can have this kind of performance from Silicon Graphics, and it's going to cost you $300,000, but we're not going to hold your hand." Our goal is eventually to put a supercomputer on the desktop of every scientist and engineer for $5,000. At that price, you're not going to get a lot of support.

Of course, such a supercomputer would still be outside the mass market. For that matter, so is the Indy. But with the Time Warner and Nintendo alliances, you will enter the mass market. Isn't this a radical departure fraught with risks?

There are ways of moving into radically new markets that minimize the demands on or risks to the organization. For example, our relationships with Time Warner and Nintendo are not the radical departures they might seem. We want to provide the technology that will be used in cable boxes for interactive digital TV and in electronic virtual-reality games. We see ourselves providing the supercomputer digital video servers that will store and dish out the programming for interactive TV. And we hope that both projects will increase sales of our workstations to those who develop programming for games and interactive TV.

But interactive TV and electronic games are not the mass market for us. When you sell to cable companies, you sell to one of 10 or 20 companies. We're providing cable companies with the technology, not actually making the boxes ourselves. Our technology will either be embedded in the TVs or leased to consumers by cable companies.

Whatever market we're in, we want to manufacture only the products that give us a 50% gross margin, which we think we need to stay on the leading edge of innovation. That box on your TV won't have a 50% gross margin, so it will be made by someone else. But playing in this market will build our capabilities and improve the ease with which our workstations can be used. Volume also helps broaden our application software market and gives us more customer relationships on which to build.

Emerging markets such as interactive TV will also enable us to expand the market for our microprocessor architecture, a capability that we gained through our merger with MIPS Technologies last year. The chip manufacturers that use our designs and from whom we buy our microprocessors will achieve economies of scale that drive down their costs, thereby driving down the prices of our components. This expansion will also enable us to spend more on R&D to improve the performance and broaden the applications for MIPS-architecture-based microprocessors.

You've talked a lot about the importance of a company being the leader in innovation so it can be the one producing chaos in the market. But how does a CEO create an organization that can cope with, let alone thrive on, rapid change?

In a way, it's simple: by having the guts to place bold bets. We place bold bets on the strategic portions of our business and then subcontract everything else. We place bold bets on the people we hire and then give them the freedom, indeed push them, to make bold bets too. The result is a $1.1 billion company with only 3,800 people. The result is agility, low costs, and the ability to innovate.

We evaluate every element of our business to decide which technologies we must invest in to stay on the cutting edge of innovation. We commit to being world-class at these core technologies.

One core technology that helps define what we're all about is our talent for putting functions directly on chips. We have extended that original capability in high-performance, moving, three-dimensional graphics to include video and audio and the ability to integrate and manipulate all three. Altogether, these technologies have given us a powerful position in the emerging digital-media market.

So have our intuitive interfaces, which enable people to relate to a computer in ways that are more fun, more stimulating, and require less training. One example of an intuitive interface is in *Jurassic Park*. Toward the end of the movie, the young girl goes into the computer room, walks up to a system, which is actually ours, and says, "Oh, this is UNIX. I know UNIX." She then calls up a user interface of ours that lets you fly through a lot of data presented in visual form. She was trying to find the program that controlled the security on one of the doors to keep out the dinosaurs. She was able to fly through thousands of data items to find the one she wanted in about 20 seconds.

When you're doing home shopping, essentially going into different virtual-reality stores, you'd better be able to do that in an intuitive way that's easier than setting the clock on your VCR. We think that intuitive interfaces that make it easier to interact with computers will be one of our core competencies. Another is symmetric multiprocessing, the technology we use in our supercomputers to harness the collective power of an array of microprocessors. Yet another is the design of high-performance microprocessors.

If we gave Intel responsibility for designing and manufacturing our microprocessors, our innovation rate would slow because Intel is designing its microprocessors for the middle of the marketplace. We wouldn't be able to include an additional capability in the microprocessor. The same would be true if we used an industry standard operating system like Microsoft's. But this does not mean that we need to manufacture microprocessors. Instead, we have partnerships with companies that are world-class at manufacturing and marketing them.

We're constantly evaluating whether or not something is strategic. For example, we manufactured printed circuit boards and loaded components on them for our first six or seven years. But then we decided this process wasn't strategic and subcontracted the job to companies like Solectron, which won the Malcolm Baldrige National Quality Award. If you do your subcontracting and alliances right, you can be world-class at everything you do.

How have you been able to stay small, in terms of employees, when so many companies seem unable to avoid becoming large and bureaucratic?

Our approach to subcontracting is one reason we can run this company with so few people. But even more important is our practice of hiring highly talented people and then trusting them. In 1976, when Hewlett-Packard was our size in terms of sales, it had about 18,000 people. We have 3,800 and are more focused. We have always been obsessed with managing our size. We don't have job descriptions that include a required number of subordinates (see "Battling Bigness").

Battling Bigness

With revenues of over $1 billion and nearly 4,000 employees, Silicon Graphics is dealing with the fact that it is no longer a start-up. Having built Silicon Graphics on an entrepreneurial, "make-it-happen" spirit, the company's leaders are determined to preserve its climate of urgency. But how does a company do that when it is no longer a cash-starved start-up?

"Push each team and/or manager to identify critical issues—whether they are changes in technology or a competitor's new products—and treat them as crises," says Edward R. McCracken, Silicon Graphics's CEO. "This mind-set has enabled us time and again to spot emerging threats and to mobilize ourselves to attack them before they become serious problems. In other words, I want our managers pulling the fire alarm before other companies would have pulled it. This is a great way to create goals that everyone believes in. Some of our best systems, including our IRIS Crimson workstation, are the result of this approach."

But crises and the intensity they generate must be balanced. "High morale is just as critical as a sense of urgency," McCracken says.

How does Silicon Graphics maintain high morale? By encouraging teams to celebrate their successes. Every employee is a stockholder; every person receives stock options when he or she joins the company. Options are also used to reward employees throughout the company, not just senior management. And Silicon Graphics provides a six-week sabbatical to each employee after every four years of service.

These programs are hardly unique in Silicon Valley. But Silicon Graphics is obviously doing something other companies are not: its turnover rate of about 10% is one-third the rate typical in the valley.

Another element of its start-up culture that Silicon Graphics is determined to preserve is the attitude that organizational boundaries should never prevent someone from offering an idea or a helping hand. The company has a cadre of "chief engineers" without product responsibility whose job is to make sure that those developing new products are using the hottest, latest technology. And rather than being chastised or resented, those who breach organizational boundaries are extolled—as long as generating the best idea or solution, not ego gratification, was their motivation.

Every year, 35 to 40 people like these are nominated by their colleagues as the employees who best represent the spirit of Silicon Graphics. "Our spirit is one of caring, dealing with people in an upfront way, having fun, and getting on with the job," McCracken says. "We announce the finalists of the 'Spirit of Silicon Graphics' and the winner at our Christmas party. Then we take all of them and their significant others to Hawaii not only to celebrate but also to help plan how to keep our spirit growing as we get larger."

While Silicon Graphics employees take pride in belonging to such "an intense, elite group," they admit that it is not always easy. "We're very well compensated financially, and there is a camaraderie that comes from being part of a company so successful and intense, but I don't have a lot of time to date," one 31-year-old manager confides.

Eva Manolis, an engineering manager in the digital-media software group, talks about how exciting it is to work in a company packed with bright, creative people who are "always trying to do something that no one else is doing." But Manolis, who joined Silicon Graphics shortly after receiving her master's degree from Brown University in 1986, also wonders, "Is the whole world as wild as Silicon Graphics?"

Others seem worried that Silicon Graphics is not as crazy as it once was. "Of course, there's more bureaucracy and more paperwork," laments Kurt Akeley, a chief engineer who was one of the company's original employees. "I remember the day they locked up the parts inventories. It used to be that when you were working on a new product, you could just walk back and grab whatever you needed."

He also misses the days when everybody knew everyone else. "It's harder and harder to know who to talk to in order to get something done," he says. But given the kind of place Silicon Graphics still is, Akeley did not have to get formal approval to pursue a solution to that problem. With the help of others, including a summer intern, he has been creating a database that will contain the names, expertises, locations, and even the faces of all employees.

"It took me longer than it would have ten years ago to get the ball rolling," Akeley says. "Then again, the only way to have done it ten years ago would have been to do it myself."

Another way we have managed to keep employment growth to a minimum is by focusing on productivity. I mentioned that some of our financial targets, from which all else flows, are maintaining a 50% gross margin and being able to spend 12% of revenues on R&D. Another is increasing revenues per person by 15% every year. We finished our last fiscal year with revenues of $307,000 per employee. That's high for our industry.

We often put one or two people on a project that would involve as many as 50 people at other companies—like designing an ASIC chip or an application-specific integrated circuit. The Indy was developed by a team of 50 to 100 people. This computer could account for half of our volume within a year or two; it could be the biggest seller in our history. A lot of companies would have used 500 to 1,000 people to design this computer.

Unlike IBM and many other companies, we don't have two competing teams working to develop a product. I think that this tactic wastes many people and is one of IBM's main problems. Internal competition is anathema to us. We do one project and really bet on it. We have only one approach to parallel processing. We have only one microprocessor family. All our graphics systems use the same fundamental architecture. We want our people focused on real competition, not on internal competition.

What are the advantages of operating a company with fewer people?

It's much easier to manage fewer people. We can be faster on our feet, we can concentrate, and we can rely on our intuition, which is extremely important in an industry where the pace of technological change is so rapid. We don't have time to plan and say, "This is step one. This is step two. This is step three." We depend on having bright employees and bright customers. We decide what to do, we do it, and then we hope it works.

One way to create a work force capable of operating in this fashion is to hire people who know themselves well enough not to be threatened by a changing environment and who are willing to grab something and run with it. We say to job candidates, "If you mind having your desk moved three times a year, you shouldn't work here." That really happens. Our organizational structure is very fluid.

We have a poster that shows one of our employees with a chainsaw cutting right down the middle of a maze of hedges. That is how we view things around here: we want to break the rules to make things simple. We've had a tremendous string of capabilities in our computers out there a year or two before our competitors. One of the main reasons is that we approached product development in a more straight-forward manner.

Despite all the preaching about empowerment, many managers fear that it will cause their companies to lose focus, to degenerate into chaos. How can managers prevent that?

If people are going to think for themselves, managers must create a vision and convince everyone to buy in. Otherwise, there will be anarchy.

It's very difficult for a big company to have a consistent vision. Most small companies do, but as U.S. companies have grown, they've delegated responsibility for the vision to people lower in the organization. As a result, many companies have lost their focus.

We haven't. We feel very strongly that all computing will move toward our vision that the screen is a window onto a virtual world. We believe that this paradigm will affect everything from TV to computing to all kinds of electronic devices.

Another constant is our architecture and operating-system software, which are shared by all our products. That means an application-software package written by one of our third-party developers will run across all our platforms.

In a rapidly changing environment, people also need to be able to talk to each other. We don't keep a lot of secrets. We have frequent "All Hands" meetings where we talk to our people not only about what's going on but also about why it's going on. If we're not succeeding at something, we talk about why and what we think it will take to succeed. It becomes a dialogue.

I try to be approachable and visible. This means wandering through the R&D labs talking to people. It means going out with our people on sales calls. I do these sorts of things a lot, and the top managers who work for me do too. A lot of people leave me voice mail, and we have an active e-mail network.

Many Silicon Graphics employees talk about the importance of having fun. How important is fun?

Very important. We've always said that Silicon Graphics is all about making technology fun and usable, and that means that working here should be fun. Too many companies in the United States and Japan have cut the fun out of their businesses. We think that if people are enjoying themselves, they will come up with better products in a shorter time. When people have fun, they bring more of themselves to the work environment. Irreverence is also important in a highly creative environment. If you're too reverent, your productivity decreases.

Fun and irreverence also make change less scary. For example, we recently replaced two old divisions with five new ones. We brought in a New Orleans band and held a wake on our Mountain View campus. We filled two coffins with paraphernalia from each division and then buried them. This ceremony reinforced our philosophy that we must view life as it is and how it might be rather than how it was.

Another element you've mentioned is trust.

I believe that my job is to help set an overall vision, to communicate our situation, and to challenge our people. But I don't view my job as a control job. Many CEOs think that they actually control what's going on in a company of thousands of people. That's silly.

If there's a difference between common sense and company policy, or if people get beaten down, they can't trust their instincts. If they are constantly second-guessed by management, then a job becomes just a job rather than a passionate commitment.

We try not to let that happen. There's a great story we tell around here about Kurt Akeley, one of our chief engineers, who was one of the seven original employees and has been involved in inventing seven generations of products.

In the mid-1980s, Kurt came up with a new graphics design that violated one of the fundamental design principles in the company. We had founded the company on the notion of putting a certain kind of mathematics for graphics right onto the chips as opposed to doing it with software. But Kurt's design used a combination of chips based on someone else's architecture.

Jim Clark, our chairman, was vehemently opposed to this design. For a week, the two did battle in a conference room outside my office. Every morning, they came in and presented technical papers to each other. There were about ten people in the room, and they'd argue and debate the papers, break in the afternoon, go home and write another set of technical papers, come in the next morning, and start all over again. Kurt, who at 23 was one of the youngest people in the company, ultimately won. Jim let him use his design on the product, the

IRIS/4D GT workstation, and the product succeeded in the market-place.

The moral isn't that you can do whatever you want to do. It's that if you've got a great idea and have the technical ability, decisions will be based on the technical merits of your idea, not where you happen to be in the organization.

Another way we have built trust is by not going on hiring and firing binges. Except for about 225 MIPS people let go after the merger, we haven't had layoffs. That doesn't mean that we will never reduce our employment. But we've tried to minimize the likelihood by being very careful about the number of people we employ and their productivity.

It sounds like your approach allows you to operate in a relatively uncomplicated fashion. Is simplicity an important part of remaining competitive?

Many companies are too complex, which has undermined their agility. We're always trying to find a simple solution. In addition to our organizational approach, our technological approach is driven by our passion for simplicity. Our decision in 1987 to go with reduced instruction set computing fits in with this belief. RISC allows you to accelerate processing speed by eliminating less frequently used in-structions and circuits on a microprocessor. We were the first work-station company to commit to RISC architecture. It was an obvious move for us because a RISC system is three to four times faster than a non-RISC system.

Intel boasts about this R&D miracle that they performed by putting 3.2 million transistors on the Pentium, its new microprocessor. We don't have to do that. We can get more performance with 900,000 transistors on a chip. It's cheaper to design, which permits our partners who manufacture it to charge less. And it requires one-tenth of the power in terms of wattage.

You've stressed how much you think your success has been the result of staying and acting small. How can you preserve that? Despite efforts to keep the increase in your number of employees to a minimum, the number is still bound to be much bigger in five to ten years.

We can increase the number of divisions and sales regions, but the environment within those divisions and regions will remain very en-trepreneurial. The issue will be managing that larger number. There aren't many examples of companies larger than we are that have mastered this management challenge. So we all have to learn how.

Do you think you can pull it off?

I think we have as good a shot as anyone. There must be a way to become large, have a large impact, and still be vital. I don't think we have to accept the rule that being bigger means being boring.

2
Commercializing Technology: What the Best Companies Do

T. Michael Nevens, Gregory L. Summe, and Bro Uttal

Just as quality and manufacturing excellence were key to competitiveness in the 1980s, superior commercialization of technology will be crucial in the 1990s. In the coming decade, businesses will rise and fall depending on whether they discipline their commercialization efforts. Some companies—like Canon, Philips, and Merck—already have the capability to bring sophisticated technology-based products to market faster and more often than competitors that treat commercialization as a purely intuitive, creative process. Most other companies will be compelled to develop this capability if they are to thrive.

Over the past year, we have examined the difference between leaders and laggards in commercialization in the United States, Japan, and Europe. Our study found that leading companies . . .

commercialize two to three times the number of new products and processes as do their competitors of comparable size

incorporate two to three times as many technologies in their products

bring their products to market in less than half the time and

compete in twice as many product and geographic markets.

These differences are not one-time occurrences that reflect specific product introductions, nor are they limited to certain nations. The study found that the critical differences between high-performing companies and low-performing companies . . .

were sustained over multiyear periods and

were as great in Japan as in America or Europe.

As part of the study, managers were asked to describe their commercialization processes. An interesting pattern emerged. Companies that are good at commercialization did not describe processes that are idiosyncratic to their organizations. Rather . . .

> high performers explained their success in strikingly similar terms and low performers did not describe their businesses in the terms high performers used.

In short, the study found large differences among companies' abilities to commercialize technology, and the good companies seemed to be doing certain things that the poor companies were not. While many businesses treat the commercialization process as a series of separate steps or an inherently creative task that should not be tightly managed, the good companies view commercialization as a highly disciplined system. They apply to the total commercialization process the basic principles for improving manufacturing quality: they establish it as a top priority, set measurable goals for ongoing improvement, develop the necessary organizational skills, and encourage managers to take aggressive action. They see it as management's job to ensure that handoffs and communication are rapid and smooth, and they pay relentless attention to improving the process (see "The Commercialization Process").

The Commercialization Process

Commercialization begins when a business identifies a way to use scientific or engineering advances to meet a market need. The process continues through design, development, manufacturing ramp-up, and marketing, and includes later efforts to improve the product. While it is often viewed as a linear process—a series of steps performed by people in different functions—companies with strong commercialization capability see the process as a series of overlapping phases that involve many business functions simultaneously.

Take Hewlett-Packard's development of the DeskJet printer. In the mid-1980s, HP's Vancouver, Washington division, which specializes in printers for personal computers, needed a blockbuster. Market research had shown that PC users would welcome a relatively slow-speed device that printed as clearly as a laser printer but sold for less than half the $2,000 price. In late 1985, a team of researchers, engineers, and marketers formed to explore the feasibility of such a product.

In conceptualizing the product, the team defined customer's needs precisely and clarified the drawbacks of existing low-cost printers. It sized up the proposed product's technical feasibility by reviewing HP's thermal-ink-jet technology, which uses electrical current to vaporize ink and shoot it onto paper in patterns of microscopic dots. Although earlier printers using that technology required specially coated paper and created narrow, blurred characters, the DeskJet team concluded that given sufficient resources, HP's InkJet Components Operation in Corvallis, Oregon could refine the technology enough to produce patterns as dense and clear as those from a laser printer.

Still in the concept-generation phase, the team brought manufacturing engineers into the process to verify that the company could produce the print head and the printer. Then the team submitted a formal plan, which Vancouver management approved.

Next, the team had to design a manufacturing prototype that could be tested for performance, reliability, producibility, and product cost. It started with a breadboard prototype, an assemblage of components handwired to printed circuit boards that represented the technical core of the printer. As soon as the breadboard proved technically feasible and appropriate for the market, HP augmented its project team with specialists in component sourcing, mechanical design, and control software. Six months later, the expanded group released several working prototypes, complete with cabinet, control software and panel, and paper-handling mechanism, and let consumers try them. The team improved print quality based on feedback from the trials, and the DeskJet was ready for manufacture.

While the DeskJet team was designing and developing the product, the printer factory in Vancouver and the print-head factory in Corvallis had been constructing pilot production lines. At the same time, marketing had developed distribution, promotion, sales, and service plans and had primed the sales force and scheduled an advertising blitz.

HP officially launched the DeskJet in February 1988—just 26 months after the Vancouver division first explored the idea. It rang up strong sales almost immediately.

Most DeskJet team members transferred to other projects after the launch, but several key engineers and marketers stayed on to oversee ongoing improvements. As customers asked for greater printing speed and more typefaces, the team went back to the concept-generation stage and executed a short version of the commercialization effort. In April 1989, they launched a faster, more flexible, less expensive version of the original printer, and in July 1989, a model that would work with Apple's Macintosh.

Further, the study found a strong linkage between an organization's competitiveness and its ability to commercialize technology. In many markets—such as copiers, facsimile machines, computers, automobiles, semiconductor production equipment, and pharmaceuticals—industry leadership clearly depends on superior commercialization skill. In these and a growing number of industries, companies that are first to market with products based on advanced technologies command higher margins and gain share. Companies that spin out variants more rapidly and leverage their core technologies across more markets earn higher returns. Superior commercialization skill is, then, among the most important competitive challenges managers will face in the coming decade.

The Commercialization Imperative

The ability to commercialize technology, to move a product from concept to market quickly and efficiently, is crucial in light of changes in the business environment. First among these now-familiar trends is the increasing proliferation of new technologies and the speed with which they render previous technologies obsolete. Empirical evidence of this trend is abundant and includes the shrinking life cycles of many products.

Typewriters are one example. The first modern generation of typewriters was mechanical and dominated the market for some 25 years, but subsequent generations of typewriters have had progressively short lives: 15, 7, and 5 years. That is, it took 25 years for sales of mechanical typewriters to fall below sales of electromechanical ones; 15 years for electromechanical models to give way to entirely electric ones; 7 years for sales of electric models to be overtaken by sales of microprocessor-controlled machines; and 5 years for sales of first-generation, microprocessor-controlled models to be exceeded by sales of second-generation machines.

Injectable cephalosporins—drugs that are prescribed for various bacterial infections—followed the same pattern in the West German hospital market. The first generation of these drugs was introduced there in 1965. Not until 1977 did sales of second-generation cephalosporins surpass those of the original products. But a fourth generation began to overtake the third in only one year.

Technological innovations also are spreading very rapidly, a result in part of the growth of research consortia and international suppliers. Indeed, it is difficult to point to an important technology breakthrough in recent years that was—and remained—truly proprietary.

And technology is increasingly expensive. Perhaps the most powerful and familiar example of the rapid cost inflation of developing base technologies is the silicon process technology used in DRAM production. The process technology for a 256K DRAM, which was state-of-the-art in 1985, cost about $100 million to develop and required a $100 million capital investment in the production facility. The next generation of DRAMs had a 1Mb capacity, cost about $250 million, and required a $200 million capital investment. The generation after that, 4Mb DRAMs, will end up costing close to $500 million and requiring a manufacturing investment of nearly half a billion dollars.

Another factor driving the increased importance of commercialization capability is the fragmentation of markets—the result of higher real per capita incomes and more sophisticated consumers. In the U.S. automobile market, for instance, the number of segments rose by one-third in seven years—from 18 in 1978 to 24 in 1985 (see Exhibit I). Many of these market segments remain untapped until a company introduces a product offering that is tailored to that niche.

These competitive realities make the capability to commercialize technology at least as important as traditional sources of advantage such as scale, skilled labor, possession of proprietary technology, and access to capital. Companies that possess the capability to bring technology to the market can often drive out competitors. Companies that lack it may see even prominent market positions quickly erode. Xerox and certain Japanese microcomputer printer manufacturers learned this lesson the hard way.

Xerox dominated the copier market for many years, but in the mid-1970s, its four- to seven-year development cycle cost it that lead. In 1976, competitors like Canon began introducing mid-range plain-paper copiers in quick succession. Between 1976 and 1982, more than 90 new models reached the market, most of them mid-range machines, and Xerox's 82% share of the total market fell by half. Since Xerox had no competitive mid-range model of its own, it embarked on a crash program to develop one. But the company's commercialization process faltered under extreme pressure. The resulting prod-

Exhibit I.

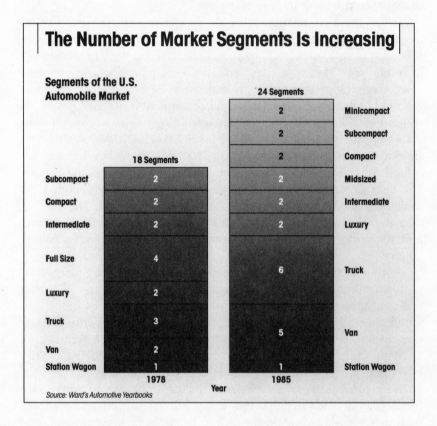

The Number of Market Segments Is Increasing

Segments of the U.S. Automobile Market

uct—the 3300 model—was unreliable and too expensive. Moreover, Xerox was unable to introduce variants quickly enough to position the 3300 as part of a product family covering several segments of the mid-range market.

Canon, on the other hand, had developed great skill at commercializing technology. It produced a number of technology innovations and launched four low-end and mid-range copiers in quick succession with speeds, respectively, of 12, 20, 30, and 40 copies per minute. It gained a solid position in the mid-range market, mostly at Xerox's expense.

Xerox has since strengthened its commercialization skills. During its turnaround in the early 1980s, the company cut development cycles from seven to as little as two years, and it introduced more than six major technical innovations in the five models that comprise its "10 series." It achieved a three-year lead over competitors in these technologies and began to reverse its decline in market share.

Just as Xerox dominated the copier market in the early 1970s, Japanese companies practically owned the microcomputer-printer business in the early 1980s. But in the mid-1980s, Hewlett-Packard used its ability to commercialize technology to take share away from the entrenched players. In quick succession, HP introduced a broad line of printers based on innovative laser, ink-jet, and software technologies. Over the past six years, it has seized a significant share of the market, including nearly 60% of the U.S. market for desktop laser printers.

Measuring Commercialization Capability

Companies like Hewlett-Packard that have the capability to manage the commercialization process differ from other organizations in four respects. They get products or processes to market faster, use those technologies in products across a wider range of markets, introduce more products, and incorporate a greater breadth of technologies in them. Thus time to market, range of markets, number of products, and breadth of technologies are good measures of a company's ability to commercialize—and to compete.

TIME TO MARKET. When base technologies are widely available and product life cycles are short, getting to market quickly is essential. For one thing, the company that is first to market often can command premium pricing because of its de facto monopoly. In the European market for car radios, for example, the first to market typically can charge 20% more than a competitor that introduces a comparable product a year later.

Those early premiums are important since prices decline rapidly as soon as competition arrives. Companies typically try to offset the price declines by improving production efficiency, but the resulting savings are not necessarily enough to compensate for sliding prices and to recover high development costs.

Early entrants also achieve volume break points in purchasing and production sooner than laggards, and they gain market share. In some industries, like prescription pharmaceuticals, the market-share rewards for being first are especially great. In that industry, the regulatory process imposes irreducible delays, and physicians' prescribing habits

Exhibit II.

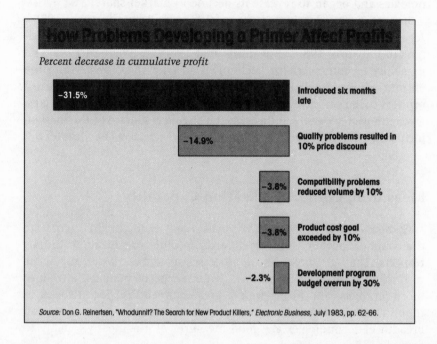

How Problems Developing a Printer Affect Profits

Percent decrease in cumulative profit

-31.5% **Introduced six months late**

-14.9% **Quality problems resulted in 10% price discount**

-3.8% **Compatibility problems reduced volume by 10%**

-3.8% **Product cost goal exceeded by 10%**

-2.3% **Development program budget overrun by 30%**

Source: Don G. Reinertsen, "Whodunnit? The Search for New Product Killers," *Electronic Business,* July 1983, pp. 62-66.

tend to be slow to change, which makes it difficult for later entrants to catch up.

Many managers fail to acknowledge the benefits of getting to the market first. The same program managers who know to the penny what an additional engineer will cost and what profits will be lost if the company misses manufacturing cost targets seldom can quantify the losses associated with a six-month slip in the development process. They willingly slow down the development process to contain the project budget or to hit their cost targets. What they don't know is the overall economics: assuming that the market grows 20% a year, that prices drop 12% a year, and that the product life cycle is five years, launching a laser printer six months behind schedule can reduce the product's cumulative profits by one-third. In contrast, under the same set of assumptions, a development cost overrun of 30% will trim cumulative profits by only 2.3% (see Exhibit II).

RANGE OF MARKETS. The cost of developing technologies is high— and rising. Companies that incur these costs must spread them across as many product and geographic markets as possible. Otherwise, they will be unable to recover costs, maintain price parity, and renew development efforts—all of which are essential to competitiveness. For example, the telecommunications industry spent a total of $1.2 billion on R&D for telephone switches in 1983 and $1.9 billion in 1988. That represents a 10% compound yearly increase over the five-year period. The increases reflect existing companies' attempts to add new features to their software systems—not new entrants to the market. At the same time, prices for central office switches declined about 8% a year. Obviously, there was intense pressure to find ways to recover that spending.

One way to spread costs is to leverage core technologies across multiple product and geographic markets. In the late 1970s, Northern Telecom anticipated that developing the software for its digital switch was going to be expensive, so it made an aggressive drive to spread the technology across many markets at the same time. To compensate for limited marketing resources, it formed international alliances with partners that could tailor the switch to national markets where Northern Telecom's own distribution networks were relatively weak. Northern Telecom also used part of the software in several product areas like PBXs, hybrid analog-digital switches, and fully configured central-office switches.

Honda, too, spreads the costs of innovation over several product markets. When it invested heavily to develop multivalve cylinder heads with self-adjusting valves, for example, it applied the technology to motorcycles, cars, lawn mowers, and power-generation equipment. Similarly, Canon exploits its basic investments in optics and lens grinding across the markets for photolithography, cameras, and copiers. It has used the miniaturized motors from its photolithography equipment in its cameras and is now incorporating them in copiers. Hewlett-Packard uses technology from its instrumentation business in half a dozen highly differentiated markets, from oscilloscopes to cardiac analyzers.

Joint ventures, technology cross-licensing, and marketing relationships are effective solutions for companies that lack the ability to spread technology costs. International marketing alliances have worked well for drug companies.

NUMBER OF PRODUCTS. Market fragmentation creates opportunities for companies that can easily adapt products to appeal to market niches. As long as the models have meaningful differences and the boundaries around the niches are real and sustainable, total sales volume correlates with the number of models produced.

The market segments of the automobile industry are widely discussed, but even in mature industrial markets like machine tools there is the opportunity to gain share by developing models offering different trade-offs among ease of setup, throughput, flexibility, and price. Making products aimed at these niches means going through the commercialization process not just once but three and four times and incorporating incremental changes—not necessarily big breakthroughs—in each new release.

Leading companies serve many more market segments than do followers. Over a ten-year period, Casio, the industry leader in the Japanese market for hand-held calculators, introduced 2.5 times as many products as Sharp, the follower. In the world market for point-and-shoot 35mm cameras, the gap between leader and follower is now two times. In mid-range UNIX computer systems, the gap is nearly four times.

BREADTH OF TECHNOLOGIES. In many markets, products incorporate an increasing number of technologies, and companies must be able to master—or to acquire and integrate—all of them if they are to compete. The copier market illustrates the point.

Ten years ago, copiers simply coordinated the light source and a toner system with a moving piece of paper, requiring technology for three things: to mechanically move the paper, to coordinate and focus the lens and the light source, and to apply and fuse toner. Competing in that market meant pushing for innovation in mechanical paper movement, optics, and fusing systems. Competence in those technologies is still needed but is no longer enough. Companies also need to be at the cutting edge of other technology areas: control hardware and software, organic photoreceptors, and panel displays. Companies that fall behind in any one area risk producing an uncompetitive product.

The situation is the same in many industries. Automobiles now include a range of new control electronics, braking systems, structural materials, and engine materials. Semiconductors involve innovations not just in process technology but also in packaging, testing, and interconnect technologies. Manufacturers of DRAMs have had to keep up with ever more complex production processes. The number of process steps needed to manufacture state-of-the-art DRAMs has increased from 230 in 1985 to 550 today, and the variety of equipment needed for manufacture has risen 20%. Even in pharmaceuticals, which has always been interdisciplinary, the need to stay current in chemical, biological, and biomedical technologies has grown over the past ten years as understanding of disease mechanisms and genetic engineering has grown.

Building Commercialization Capability

The best commercializers do more than understand the importance of getting the right product to the market repeatedly and quickly. They take steps to ensure that the organization can achieve that result reliably and quickly, even if it means changing the way they do business. Canon's efforts typify the manner in which high-performing companies strengthen their commercialization capability.

Canon is widely recognized as a leader in optical and imaging technologies, electronics assembly, software, and high-precision assembly of small parts. It has used this leadership to build and grow successful businesses in cameras, copiers, office automation, and medical equipment. The company's revenues have grown as a result, from ¥200 billion in 1981 to ¥1 trillion in 1988. In 1981, Canon was about the same size as Nikon. It is now four times as large.

Canon had always valued its ability to bring technology to the market, but as competition intensified in the mid-1980s, company president Ryuzaburo Kaku decided to act. Shrinking product life cycles and an increasing dependence on suppliers for key subsystems, which competitors could buy as well, led him to conclude that Canon's future lay in becoming a market leader with its own unique technologies. Kaku established superior commercialization as a high priority and expressed that priority in two clear objectives: "winning with our own technology" in optics, electronics, and precision manufacturing and "50% down" (cutting product development cost and time in half). To reinforce these goals, the company built a highly automated lens-grinding plant and created a central lab to feed improved optical technologies to the plant. Management also supported the objective of "50% down" by encouraging divisional managers to be readily accessible to project managers. Everyone in the company learned that delays caused by waiting for management approval were acceptable no longer.

The focus on commercialization capability had different but important effects on the ways Canon's managers thought and acted. The semiconductor-equipment division, which produces photolithographic systems, was already skilled at commercialization. It had been staffing new project teams with experienced members who could transfer learning from previous projects, organizing primarily around products rather than functions to ease coordination and involving customers in subsystem testing to discover problems early. But the division saw the president's message as a challenge to be even more aggressive. It set the ambitious goal of cutting six months off the development time for new equipment. To achieve that goal, it used computer-aided-design tools to eliminate some phases of project management, and it overlapped other phases.

The streamlined commercialization process cut development costs by 30% and time to market by 50% and enabled the division to launch two generations of equipment in the time it took competitors to introduce one. Canon could also offer upgraded versions of each generation every one-and-a-half years, while its toughest competitor took three years. Canon's share of the world market for photolithographic equipment rose from 16% in 1978 to 25% in 1988. One of its main competitors, which made little effort to strengthen commercialization capability, saw its share drop from 51% to 23% in the same period.

Canon's camera division also revitalized its commercialization processes. In 1985, Minolta challenged Canon's top standing in the market for 35mm single-lens-reflex cameras by launching the first autofocus model, which incorporated novel electronic controls and a miniaturized motor. The model opened a whole new market of consumers who wanted the sharpness of 35mm photographs without having to master complex focus controls. Minolta quickly followed up the original autofocus model with two different models aimed at smaller segments of the new market. And by 1986, with 36% of the market, Minolta eclipsed Canon as the 35mm market leader.

Spurred by top management's call for aggressive action and drawing on the company's research in optics, Canon's camera division retaliated by introducing two products that exploited a breakthrough in lens technology: sonically driven motors mounted in the lens to allow 50% faster focusing. By the end of 1986, Canon had pulled even with Minolta, and over the next 15 months it battled to remain at the top by hammering out three other models that covered additional segments.

To strengthen their commercialization capability, high-performers like Canon do the following: make commercialization capability a top-management priority; set goals to focus the effort; develop skills; and get managers directly involved in the commercialization process to speed actions and decisions.

MAKE COMMERCIALIZATION A PRIORITY. However obvious it seems, top managers at successful companies explicitly put commercializing technology high on the corporate agenda. Average performers fail to make this simple effort, sometimes because they equate commercialization with R&D and think they can improve it by spending more money. But consider the fate of one high-technology company whose top managers recognized the importance of commercialization but failed to make it an explicit priority.

In the mid-1980s, this U.S. semiconductor company was performing well. Its revenues and profits had been growing steadily. In several of its markets, it controlled nearly 50% of the business, and it had excellent relationships with its leading customers. By 1986, however, the U.S. semiconductor industry was in a worldwide competitive struggle, and this company was in the thick of it. After much thought and debate, top management promulgated a set of initiatives designed to maintain the company's leadership position.

The initiatives emphasized improved quality, world-class manufacturing, and excellent customer service. The managers consciously decided not to include commercialization, innovation, or technological leadership on the list of corporate priorities. They thought those objectives were obvious. As the CEO explained, "We felt that better use of technology and more effective product development was the essence of our business. We're a high-tech company, after all. We didn't need to put those priorities on the list."

Over the next three years, though, the company began to slip. Margins declined, and market shares fell in several businesses the company had once dominated. Top management assigned task forces to study the failing businesses, and in each case, the findings were the same: the competition was "outcommercializing" them. Competitors were marketing more products in a shorter time, developing a lead in new product and process technology, gaining share, increasing their margins, and feeding money back into their commercialization efforts.

In 1989, the besieged semiconductor company amended its corporate priorities and put leadership in technology commercialization at the top of the list. In retrospect, the CEO says that overlooking that priority in 1986 was the worst decision he had made in his 25-year career. He now emphasizes whatever is fundamental to the business, not just what needs the most improvement.

This company's problems are understandable, given the way organizations work. People at lower levels of the organization are not privy to discussions among top executives and have no way of knowing why things are or are not on the priority list. They naturally direct their resources toward studying, training for, and measuring progress against top management's explicit objectives.

If commercialization is truly important, business leaders must send clear signals. Canon's corporate goal of "winning through our own technology" and Hewlett-Packard's objective of "making a needed and profitable contribution" sound innocuous but are actually important drivers of behavior at all levels of these organizations.

SET GOALS AND BENCHMARKS.   Simply identifying superior commercialization capability as a priority does not suffice. Leaders of successful commercializers also translate this priority into objectives others can act on, and they create incentives for them to do so. For instance, they specify key technologies in which the company must lead or set targets for price or product features, and they spur action by making those goals aggressive.

When Canon was developing its personal copier, it aimed for copy quality as good as that of IBM's office copiers, a price of less than $1,500—as opposed to $3,000 for the lowest priced model on the market—and a weight below 20 kilograms—versus 35 kilograms for the lightest competing model. Because the goals were so specific, the project team knew exactly what it had to accomplish. Because the goals were aggressive, managers were forced to find novel ways to reach them. They looked everywhere for opportunities: product and process design, manufacturing, marketing, and service. The management team achieved the quality, price, and weight goals in part by developing a replaceable module that combined critical parts of the image-transfer and fusing systems and by going outside Canon and the copier industry for technology to manufacture the module.

Establishing benchmarks based on competitors' products is another good way to encourage managers to improve the commercialization process. Information about competitors is widely available, and companies that are good at commercializing technology routinely use it to advantage. Customers, suppliers, employees hired from competitors, and joint-venture partners can provide valuable insight into how other companies are performing. Companies should track data on the four dimensions that measure commercialization capability—time to market, range of markets, number of products, and breadth of technologies—as well as cost, delivery time, and service.

When a company that makes a filtering device for radio-transmission equipment wanted to know how it compared with competitors, it went directly to its suppliers and asked, "How are we as a client?"

The vendor responded, "You guys are hard to do business with. You overspecify and overconstrain us, so it costs us more." The company subsequently improved its relationship with the supplier and cut its costs by allowing the supplier to do more of the component-design work.

Several Xerox managers credit competitive benchmarking with producing the shock that created the will and energy the company needed to overhaul its copier business in the early 1980s. The analysis forced Xerox to realize that, compared with competitors, its design cycles were long, its technologies old, and its product line limited.

Hewlett-Packard's use of competitive benchmarks saved it in at least one product market. Its radio-frequency analyzer dominated the market, but when HP engineers tore down a competing Japanese product, they discovered that it was superior to their own design. While HP used separate wires to connect components, the Japanese company had redesigned the chassis to allow the use of a wire harness to replace separate connections. This difference in design made the Japanese product cheaper and more reliable than HP's own, more popular, product. HP quickly turned its attention to improving its design and was able to preserve its market position.

While successful commercializers use goals and benchmarks, they are careful to select only a handful and to use the same ones for several years. In a turnaround effort, one troubled company set 25 challenging goals, but because managers down the line could not follow up on all of them, they made little progress on any one of them. The company abandoned all 25 within a year. Honda, on the other hand, set a single goal for the team that developed the City car for the Japanese market—"Do something different enough to capture the youth market"—and stuck with it for three years, frequently sending the project team back to its drawing boards. This demanding, enduring goal eventually drove the team to develop the "tall boy" concept: a car shorter, taller, and lighter than most, a packaging concept that promised a roomy interior, superior acceleration, and miserly fuel consumption. Both the initial City car and a follow-on turbo-charged model were big hits.

BUILD CROSS-FUNCTIONAL SKILLS. People cannot improve the commercialization process without the necessary skills. High-performing companies emphasize a set of skills notably different from their less successful counterparts. They value cross-functional skills, while other companies pride themselves on their functional strengths. High performers boast, "We've got the best project managers in the world." Low performers say, "We've got the best circuit designers."

Building excellent cross-functional skills is a challenge, especially because structures and habits work against them. People identify with their profession and usually want to get better at what they do. And most day-to-day work is function specific.

But functional excellence alone does not ensure that a company will be competitive. Compare the testing procedures of a European pharmaceuticals company with that of its U.S. partner. The two companies had entered a joint venture to develop and market a particular drug, but the European company kept falling behind in the development cycle. The drug required two tests—one chemical, one biomedical. The European company was effective in both areas, but separate groups of people in buildings three miles apart conducted the tests. There was little communication between them, and no one took responsibility for coordinating their efforts.

The U.S. company, on the other hand, organized its activity not by scientific discipline but by development phase. It had one manager assigned to oversee the development process, and it performed the testing in one lab with one group of researchers. While the slower company needed six weeks to complete the chemical analysis, the faster company took just three days. The European partner had so much trouble changing its testing procedures that it actually found it more expedient to send samples to the United States and get results shipped back to Europe.

Many companies try to smooth the transitions between separate functions through programs like "design for manufacturability," which links R&D and manufacturing, or "quality function deployment," which links marketing and manufacturing. Superior commercializers also use these programs, but they go far beyond them. They strive to build an extensive network connecting R&D, manufacturing, sales, distribution, and service, and they organize around products, markets, or development phases rather than functions. For them, cross-functional teams are standard practice.

Training can go a long way in blurring functional lines and easing coordination. When Epson, the Torrance, California high-tech manufacturer, was preparing to develop its first personal copier, it sent the mechanical engineer assigned to lead the project back to school for two years of electrical engineering courses.

Job rotation is another way to cross-train. Companies that transfer design engineers to the factory floor during production ramp-up find that it lessens the finger-pointing between them and the manufacturing engineers. Other companies rotate engineers throughout their careers. At NEC, another good commercializer, fewer than half the engineers who start in the research department remain there after ten years. The rest are scattered across various functions within the same business unit.

PROMOTE HANDS-ON MANAGEMENT TO SPEED ACTIONS AND DECISIONS. Priorities tend to fade if high-level managers don't act on them. At high-performing companies, top managers maintain a visible presence to reinforce the importance of commercialization. Regardless of the company's management style, executives must be interventionist if the rest of the organization is to take commercialization seriously. Even at companies like 3M and Hewlett-Packard that are known for being decentralized and divisionalized, management feels free to go in and meddle in issues crucial to the commercialization process.

It is impossible to guarantee that the organization will always do the right things, but asking hard questions and demanding honest answers about technical performance, cost, and alternative technologies can help prevent big mistakes. Managers at one successful European electronics company ask questions throughout the development cycle: When will the proposed product's price-performance ratio make it competitive with existing technologies? How far down the road is the technology, and how much money do we need to push it into the market? Where could we go wrong? What's the evidence for that conclusion?

Senior managers at high-performing companies promote commercialization in other ways as well—by acting as tiebreakers for disputes at the project level, keeping up to date on the progress of key commercialization efforts, clearing their calendars when serious problems arise, speeding decision making, and making sure the right people and the right information come together. When comparing two quite similar office equipment companies, we observed that senior managers at the company that demonstrated stronger commercialization capability were able to resolve project-level disputes in as little as one day. Senior managers at the other company took up to six weeks to make such decisions.

Inspired genius and scientific breakthroughs will remain essential elements in competitive success. But they are not enough. Increasingly, competitive success hinges on the coordinated efforts of scientists, engineers, manufacturing staff, and marketers building on breakthroughs with ongoing improvements in products and processes. This might mean redesigning a machine tool to incorporate a new motor to serve a new application and doing so faster than competitors, even when the motor was not developed in-house.

Consistently outexecuting competition on this dimension—being better at commercializing technology—requires a disciplined approach. Improvement starts with top management setting the right priorities along with ambitious goals. Then management throughout the company must follow through with initiatives to build cross-functional skills and to remove obstacles to quick decisions and actions on commercialization projects. Those companies that take this approach will prosper. Those that do not will fall by the wayside.

Appendix

About the Study

This study of commercialization was conceived and conducted by McKinsey & Company to better understand the difference between leaders and laggards in commercializing technology and the links between improved commercialization and competitive success.

To formulate hypotheses to test, McKinsey commissioned a survey of the academic and management literature and reviewed its client work in this area. Then, between December 1988 and April 1989, McKinsey interviewed managers at 19 companies in the United States, Europe, and Japan to find out how they commercialize technology. The number of interviews at each company ranged from as many as 50 to as few as 5, and interviews were conducted with managers at all organizational levels, from chairman to first-line supervisor. The companies were selected to include leaders and laggards in commercialization in industries where commercialization is important, where many companies compete, and where competitive leadership has changed hands in the last decade.

The authors would like to acknowledge the assistance of their colleagues Lorraine Harrington and Roland Wolfram, who conducted many of the interviews and contributed to the analysis; Richard Foster, who guided the effort with his experience and advice and helped shape the conclusions; and Charles Ferguson of MIT's Center for Technology, Policy, and Industrial Development, who conducted the literature search. The authors also appreciate the cooperation and advice throughout this project of the Council on Competitiveness and its chairman, John Young.

3
Make Projects the School for Leaders

H. Kent Bowen, Kim B. Clark, Charles A. Holloway, and Steven C. Wheelwright

Leadership is the key to developing great products. What's a great product? One that surprises and delights its customers. To achieve that goal, all the technical elements of the product must work well together as a system, the manufacturing process must produce everything that the design requires, and the product must be delivered to customers in an outstanding fashion. And if the development of a great product is not an isolated case—if one great product is followed by another and another—the result is a great enterprise. Leadership is the key to achieving this kind of consistency.

Two development efforts that created great products—Eastman Kodak's FunSaver project and Hewlett-Packard's DeskJet printer project—exemplified such consistency and, not coincidentally, exceptional leadership. The initial FunSaver "single-use" camera became the basis for a whole family of products that has created a significant business for Kodak. In a similar way, HP's DeskJet project, which created a new segment in the printer market by bringing to customers a relatively low-cost yet very high-quality desktop printer, has been the basis for several generations of a line of products that now constitutes a major business for HP.

The plain fact of the matter is that creating a great product on time and within budget is very difficult. And having to do that while building effective long-term capabilities is a daunting challenge indeed. But the result—the ability to create a stream of great products consistently over time—is certainly worth the effort.

Developing a new product is relatively easy in a stable environment, one in which what customers want and what competitors offer today are similar to what they'll want and offer three years from now. But when markets are dynamic or turbulent, anticipating how customers will perceive and evaluate products in two to three years can be extremely difficult, considering that it is the myriad details of a product and the way they come together that determine how customers perceive and evaluate that product. These important details are in the product's design, aesthetics, and specific functions as well as in the manufacturing processes that will determine its quality and reliability, and in the way it will be sold and serviced. In other words, achieving greatness means pulling all the details together today in a coherent package that will surprise and delight customers tomorrow.

The DeskJet printer is a superb illustration. Like all great products, it achieved excellence in three dimensions:

1. **Functionality.** The printer supplied superior print quality (based on HP's proprietary ink-jet technology) at an unprecedented price point for that quality.
2. **Coherence.** All elements of the total system—including the product's design, its manufacturing process, and the way it was marketed and positioned in customers' minds—worked together to achieve the cost and quality image that HP sought.
3. **Fit.** The details of the printer's design as well as the nuances of its form and features reflected a deep understanding of the targeted customer and his or her expectations of what a superior printer meant.

To be really great, a new product must be the fruit of a project that also builds the capabilities critical to the success of future products that are in turn critical to the future success of the business. Seen in this light, a development project is the way the business both probes and creates the future. This was the case in the FunSaver project, which, in addition to the product, developed a customized computer-aided-design and computer-aided-manufacturing (CAD/CAM) system to design the camera's plastic parts and the molds that would be used to make them. By enabling the members of the team to integrate their work and to give one another immediate feedback, the CAD/CAM system gave Kodak the capability to develop both quickly and at a low cost not just one camera but a stream of FunSaver products. The first offering in the product line was important, but what made the Fun-Saver a great business was all the products in the family.

Thus a great product and the project that creates it must be linked to a strategy for the business that utilizes and in turn supports the power inherent in both. There must be a consistency of purpose and action at the level of the product, the project, and the business. All this takes leadership.

Great Products and Patterns of Leadership

Of course, there are many ways to organize and lead development projects. The Manufacturing Vision Group found it helpful to use a four-category framework originally developed in studies of the automobile industry.[1] Each mode of organization and leadership differs in terms of who exercises leadership, where responsibility for specific aspects of the project resides, and how decisions are made.

In *functionally organized projects*, technical problem solving, not integrating the work of different functions, is the challenge, which is why development work is divided among functional disciplines and no one person has overall responsibility for the total project. Leadership occurs primarily within the specialized groups or disciplines. While relatively narrow in scope, this type of leadership is substantive because the leaders within the functions are technical specialists who are overseeing work on critical, functional problems.

In projects with "lightweight" organizational structures, where it is more important to coordinate the work of functions and to help them spot problems that cross functional lines, a coordinator and a team of representatives from the functions operate as a support group. They pull together information, spot emerging problems of coherence, and facilitate interaction and problem resolution. But functional leaders continue to hold the real power. The project coordinator is not responsible for the overall project, has much less status than the functional managers, has no responsibility for the people actually doing the work, and has no direct contact with targeted customers. This is not to suggest, however, that such a coordinator cannot have an important impact on the coherence of the product or process and the speed and efficiency of the project; *lightweight* does not necessarily mean ineffective or unimportant. Indeed, in playing the coordinating role exceptionally well, a lightweight-project coordinator can exercise a form of diplomatic leadership that facilitates integration. Of course, if the organization works against that kind of leadership—if the coordinator becomes nothing more than a de facto clerk who tracks events, schedules meetings, and publishes minutes—then lightweight can mean ineffective.

In heavyweight projects, integrating work is both crucial and the most important responsibility of the project leader. The project leader, ideally an influential manager with experience in more than one function, is responsible for the project's overall success. He or she acts like a general manager and wields considerable power over the details of the program and the way in which those details, including customer expectations, are orchestrated and integrated into an effective whole. In other words, the heavyweight-project leader, unlike leaders of functionally organized or lightweight projects, oversees both the way that all critical work is performed and how it is integrated into the whole. The project leader is supported by a core team of functional leaders who command significant authority within their respective disciplines. But the team members' loyalty is to the project, not to their individual functions. Their paramount goal is achieving an outstanding system solution, not just a technically elegant part. Thus the team provides leadership within the functions as well as across the entire project effort.

In a project conducted by a *dedicated, autonomous team,* breaking new ground or taking thinking "out of the box" is the mission. This is why a dedicated team is smaller and more self-contained than a heavyweight-project team and why its leader acts like an entrepreneur starting up a new business. As in heavyweight projects, the leader has responsibility for the overall project's success and for all the work critical to that success. But unlike the heavyweight-project leader, the leader of a dedicated team does not prosper by exercising leadership within the context of established structures and methods (and with the support of the established functions). Individuals working on such a project are removed from their respective functions and dedicated to the team. Compared with people on other kinds of project teams, these individuals have to be broader, take on more work, and get things done without the resources or the constraints of the functional organization. When outside help is needed, the team typically subcontracts the job to organizations independent of the parent company. So leading such a team means finding new ways to get work done, inventing new procedures, and defining new roles.

When is each of the four modes of organization and leadership the most appropriate? The functional structure is best suited for situations in which the environment is relatively stable and success depends on the application of relatively narrow areas of expertise. The lightweight system is best for situations in which coordination is somewhat more critical, or in smaller projects. Those include projects for developing incremental extensions or derivatives of existing products. The heavyweight approach is often best for carrying out major complex projects in which time is critical. Those projects are typically charged with developing products that must satisfy an existing set of customers and be produced, sold, and serviced by an existing operating system. Good examples include a new automobile or a new family of computers. The dedicated, autonomous team should be used when the goal is to make a technical leap (like developing a radically new process), to invent or enter a new market segment, or to create a new business. This approach makes sense when a project does not have to draw or rely on the organization's existing resources and systems.

Guiding Visions

In the turbulent 1990s, creating great products and building enduring capabilities linked to business strategy often requires the type of strong, integrative leadership evident in the heavyweight and dedicated-team approaches. It requires forceful leadership to integrate the business strategy, the product concept, and the project. But what is it that successful leaders do to integrate these three levels? What sets them and their teams apart from the usual, the traditional, the average?

In the successful efforts it studied, the Manufacturing Vision Group found a distinctive, consistent pattern operating at each level. Effective leaders are those who see a future that does not yet exist. Moreover, they must connect that vision to specific actions that need to be integrated. Because many other people have to be involved, that integration is a process of articulating, communicating, and implementing, which we call "the guiding vision." And it is a *process*. Effective leaders do not just lay out a scenario for the future. They have an ability to see the future, to frame it in compelling terms, and to translate it into action-oriented missions both for the members of the project team and for people in specialized areas who support the team. This is the essence of development leadership.

All the outstanding projects studied by the group had powerful guiding visions for the business, the project, and the product. In addition, the three visions were mutually reinforcing, energizing the people on the teams, focusing attention and effort on the right things, and getting them done in the right way. HP's DeskJet project illustrates how powerful leadership can be when it operates in an integrative fashion at the business, project, and product-concept levels.

The DeskJet project was launched at Hewlett-Packard's Vancouver division in 1985. The division had been formed in 1979 to develop and market impact printers. But by the mid-1980s, its market share was declining and its fortunes were at risk because of two main challenges. The first was performance based: the emergence of laser printers, which, while more expensive, offered much higher-quality print. The second and more immediate threat was price based: the emergence of dot-matrix printers at the low end of the market. The effect was to squeeze the Vancouver division's market position, imperiling its future.

In November 1985, after a full review of HP's printer line, Vancouver received and endorsed a new charter from group management: concentrate on developing a printer for the low-end personal and office market. The project that emerged from that charter was designed to take HP's ink-jet technology and develop it into a much lower-cost platform that could serve as the basis for a whole family of high-quality products. The targeted initial product that became the focus of a substantial effort was the DeskJet printer.

Here, then, was a business in need of a new strategy, a project designed to build new capability, and a new product headed for a specific market. At each level, Vancouver's leaders developed a vision of what the future could hold. It was this set of guiding visions and the leadership behind them that provided focus and brought new energy and resolve to the people performing the actual work.

THE VISION OF THE BUSINESS. The vision for the business that emerged at Vancouver was to create a new market segment. The idea was to build a family of products with print quality close to that of laser printers but at a price so much lower that they would largely replace low-price, low-quality impact and dot-matrix printers in the general computer market. At that time, Epson virtually owned the low end of the market, with an 80% market share. The future Vancouver's leaders envisioned, therefore, was one in which HP (with its proprietary technology) would emerge as a formidable player in the retail end of the computer-printer market. This was not going to be a one- or two-year effort. Success would require sustained activity over the course of a decade.

All in all, this was not a modification of an established approach. It was a vision of the future that would position HP at the center of a very different world. But for Vancouver, the alternative was oblivion. Thus it was not hard for senior managers in the division to articulate, communicate, and sell this new future to the people working there.

THE VISION OF THE PROJECT. It is one thing to articulate and lay out a vision for the future of the business. It is quite another to realize that vision by executing a series of projects consistently over a period of time. This was the challenge that the Vancouver division faced in the mid-1980s. The DeskJet project was much more than simply delivering one product to the market. The project had to deliver a product to the market and begin to build a range of capabilities that would allow the division to execute a series of projects successfully.

In effect, the guiding vision of the business defined the agenda for the DeskJet project. Creating three critical capabilities dominated it. First, to be successful in realizing the business vision, the Vancouver division had to learn how to produce large numbers of a sophisticated consumer product at a very low cost. Low-cost manufacturing capability was therefore crucial. Some of that capability involved creating production systems capable of high volume and high yields. Some lay in getting HP design engineers to create a manufacturable design. As a result, a central thrust of the DeskJet project became the integration of design and manufacturing to create designs that were easy to make in volume and manufacturing processes that delivered efficiently everything the design required.

A second critical capability was establishing ink-jet technology in the retail market. As it existed in the mid-1980s, ink-jet technology offered very high print quality. But the designs were sophisticated and expensive, and products using the technology were sold to professional customers. What was needed was the capability to simplify the ink-jet mechanism to make it less expensive without hurting its ability to deliver a high-quality image—high quality, that is, as perceived and experienced by the *retail* customer. At the outset of the project, Vancouver's R&D people knew of many ways to lower the cost of the printhead while reducing quality. But achieving lower cost and high quality would require new solutions and new design capabilities.

Finally, because the division was moving into the high-volume, dealer-oriented retail market in which it had little experience, the project needed to build the capability to serve that market well. This meant the product had to be easy to sell, hook up, and operate without hand-holding by a field service organization. HP also needed to understand the retail customer as well as service and support dealers and to manage the retail order-delivery pipeline.

The vision for the project was to create specific capabilities that would lay the foundation for a family of products that would emerge over time. It called for designers, manufacturers, and marketers to work together to create the segment and then systematically realize its potential. Framed in these terms, the business guiding vision defined the broad objectives, and the project guiding vision was a plan for obtaining the capabilities needed to make the business vision a reality.

THE VISION OF THE PRODUCT.   The challenge for the product also was clear. The first offering in this new line of products had to signal to the market the emergence of something new and exciting from HP. It had to be sufficiently compelling that it would attract customers and dealers not used to thinking of HP as an alternative when they chose printers. It had to pave the way for other offerings that would follow. It had to plant a stake in the ground and help define the new market segment.

The power of a product concept lies in its ability to communicate to the people on the project team what the customer's experience with the product will be. In the case of the DeskJet, the concept could be framed quite simply: a laser-quality printer under $1,000. One thousand dollars was a psychological breakpoint in the marketplace in the mid-to late 1980s. A printer that offered the resolution of a much more expensive laser printer, ease of use, attractive features, and a price close to that of dot-matrix printers could have a dramatic effect on the market. It was a compelling concept for the project team and the targeted customers.

The DeskJet concept had a number of crucial characteristics often found in projects where strong leadership delivered an outstanding product to the market. In the first place, the concept was evocative: it evoked in different parts of the organization and in different kinds of people a common understanding of the overall project goal. This enabled designers, marketers, and manufacturing people to align their individual daily decisions with the objectives of the project as a whole.

In addition to evoking appropriate responses, the concept was also enduring. The project leaders owned the concept. They sustained it and made it real in the minds of all the people involved in the project. Particularly in light of the need to do things that HP had not done before, it was important that the concept be stable and enduring so people working on the project could move with confidence to achieve things that required significant change and investment on their part.

Finally, the concept was simple and easy to grasp. Everyone understood and related to the concept of an extraordinarily high-quality printer that could be sold at an unbelievably low price. Moreover, as the product concept took shape, team members took an unusual step:

they brought prototypes to shopping malls. These mall studies, unprecedented at HP, offered unique insights into how potential customers would evaluate the product. These studies were later supplemented by face-to-face meetings between engineers and targeted customers. The net effect was a concept that clearly identified who the customers were, how they would experience the product, and what a truly compelling product would look like to them.

Like the business vision and the project vision, the product concept was not an exercise. It was something the project leaders used to shape and guide the creation of the DeskJet. The way they handled the development of the printhead and persuaded the design engineers to reverse themselves and incorporate changes recommended by targeted customers are two cases in point.

THE PRINTHEAD. The DeskJet's printhead would be crucial to the printer's success. But developing a low-cost printhead with a near-laser-quality image involved making technical advances in both the product and the production system. It quickly became apparent that the printhead device, whose development would require advanced knowledge of electronics, mechanics, fluid dynamics, and heat transfer, would need to be disposable. That requirement was governed by factors as mundane as the volume of ink that could be stored on the moving head and the durability of microcomponents designed to throw tiny droplets of ink onto paper.

For the printhead to be disposable meant that it had to be produced at a very low cost and in high volume—an untraditional approach for the HP organization. Moreover, the project was under significant cost and time constraints given the pace and rhythms of the market. (The project had to be concluded within 22 months.) But thanks to the clarity of the product concept, team leaders recognized early on the crucial nature of the printhead and assigned the development work to a dedicated subteam. The leaders also structured the subteam's objectives in creative ways. For example, they relaxed the target for the operating speed of the printhead so that the subteam would not compromise print quality in its quest for speed. Then they assigned groups working on other parts to figure out ways to make the printer fast. These efforts enabled the printhead subteam to make even greater advances in image sharpness than it had originally set out to make.

LISTENING TO CUSTOMERS. Had the powerful product concept not led the project leaders to question traditional HP ways, the design engineers would not have made crucial visits to malls to listen to targeted customers. Early in the project, marketing's interactions with shoppers in malls resulted in 24 suggestions for modifying specific features of the printer. But when marketing brought those suggestions back, R&D engineers accepted only 5.

In most HP projects, that would have been the end of it. But the DeskJet project leaders had known from the outset that this would be an unusual project for HP. While the company's customers had traditionally been engineers, a large portion of the targeted customers this time around were mass-market retail consumers who would buy the printer for use in their homes and small businesses. So from the outset, the project's leaders were sensitive to the need to be on the lookout for traditional HP approaches that would hinder the team from achieving its goals. They included the tendency of design engineers to base design decisions on what they and other HP engineers liked themselves and to pay marketing little heed.

For this reason, the project leaders made sure that the marketing people on the team, who would have been second-class citizens in the typical HP project, were treated as true equals. When the marketing people suggested that the team conduct the market tests in malls, the project leaders encouraged them to do so. And when the design engineers initially dismissed most of the findings, it set off an alarm for the project leaders. Moreover, the marketing people did not meekly bow to the design engineers this time around. With both the project leaders and marketing pressuring them, the design engineers (and, eventually, other functions as well) made the trek to the malls to hear for themselves what their future customers wanted and discovered that they really did want 17 more changes. Those features, including faster-drying ink and easier ways to load or feed paper into the machine, were incorporated into the product. Without them, the DeskJet printer would have fallen far short of its potential.

Linking the Visions

The effectiveness of the DeskJet project's leadership stemmed both from its articulation and application of a distinctive product concept and from its ability to link that concept to the project and business visions. Beyond the excitement generated by the concept, what was energizing to team members was the realization that they were laying the foundation for a family of HP products.

In situation after situation, the leaders of the project took actions that met both short-term product requirements and longer-term strategic goals. Here are two illustrations.

EARLY MANUFACTURING INVOLVEMENT. It was evident from the outset that close involvement of manufacturing in the design of the product was essential to achieving a high-quality ink-jet printer that could be sold profitably at a retail price of less than $1,000. Other than a successful foray into handheld calculators that began in the 1970s, HP had only limited experience in selling to retail customers and engaging in high-volume production. To achieve these objectives, the project leaders moved aggressively. For example, the project leader (who was also the R&D manager) established within the R&D organization a manufacturing-engineering group assigned solely to the DeskJet project. These engineers significantly influenced the design engineers.

At a very early stage of design, they compiled a materials checklist, which helped designers better understand cost issues. Later, the manufacturing engineers got ahead of the game and had tooling designed and released to build early test units. The traditional approach at HP was to have design engineers use temporary tooling and let manufacturing catch up once the product was further developed. All this work not only had a positive impact on the DeskJet project but also began to build a capability for high-volume, low-cost, high-quality manufacturing within the Vancouver division.

PROTOTYPES. Traditionally, HP design engineers used the scheduling of prototypes to allow themselves as much time as possible for last-minute changes, many of which created subsequent manufacturing problems and often led to delays and poor quality. To blaze a new path, DeskJet project leaders put manufacturing in charge of prototypes, and each month, regardless of whether the R&D group was ready, manufacturing built 50 prototypes. This helped the team maintain a fast pace and was crucial in testing performance and proving out the ability of the system to deliver a printer that could be sold for less than $1,000. Building prototypes on a regular schedule made the state of readiness of each function and subsystem apparent to all. It gave manufacturing and marketing a view into the design work and provided the discipline for the integration that was crucial in meeting the project's goals. And it played an important role in creating new ways of working. The DeskJet team leaders used prototypes and colocation (having R&D, manufacturing, and marketing people share the same workplace) as tools to get team members to communicate and to integrate their work.

This approach to using prototypes was not something the team did just to meet all the objectives for the DeskJet printer; they realized they were pioneering a whole new way of working that would be crucial in future HP projects when time, cost, and quality pressures would intensify. Thus managing with a guiding project vision as well as a clear business strategy gave leaders in Vancouver a framework for linking action on the product to the long-term health of the enterprise. They not only launched a product, they built a business.

The success of leadership in the DeskJet project (and in the Vancouver division) is evident in the market results. The team got the initial product to market in the planned 22 months. When the product was introduced in September 1987, HP's market share rose dramatically. Subsequent products—improved variants of the basic DeskJet, including a high-end color version and a portable version—have also been highly successful. HP has leveraged its investment in the DeskJet project many times over.

Leadership and Leaders

We began this article with a recognition that consistently creating great products is difficult but powerful when achieved. To use a mountain-climbing analogy, the path is not easy, the climb is steep, but the view is breathtaking and very few can follow those who make it. Without in any way slighting the role of good, sturdy hiking boots, strong ropes, or a good backpack, we have emphasized the importance of leaders who know how to pick the right mountain, to chart the course, to build climbing skills, and to lead the team so that it overcomes a series of obstacles and achieves key objectives on the trail to the top.

We are now beginning to understand what effective leadership of development projects means and how it can be achieved. The notion of guiding visions at multiple levels of the enterprise has proven particularly useful in understanding what leaders do.

The Perils of Inadequate Leadership

Eastman Kodak's "Factory-of-the-Future" project demonstrates how and why a project to develop a product or a process can flounder when it lacks sufficient leadership and compelling guiding visions. In 1984, managers of film manufacturing (a functional division) and of central engineering and design (a corporate functional group) agreed that substantial new capacity would be needed by 1990 for 35mm film finishing (cutting, perforating, winding, and packaging)—a process involving sophisticated, high-speed, automated equipment. They also agreed that competitive pressures dictated that the company create new approaches to finishing to improve performance in terms of cost and quality.

The engineering and design group saw this as an opportunity to make a quantum leap in finishing technology. The project that emerged was dubbed the Factory of the Future. Eventually, the project had a staff of more than 100 full-time representatives from five Kodak functional groups: manufacturing, engineering and design (from which the majority came), maintenance, quality assurance, and marketing. There was no overall project leader with heavyweight responsibility, and each group had its own perspective on what the project was intended to do.

The people from engineering were determined to push the process-technology envelope as much as possible. They saw the project as an opportunity (perhaps one of the last) to incorporate advanced technology into finishing. In their eyes, the key was speed and quality—developing a process that could finish film at a high speed without compromising quality.

The team members from manufacturing saw the project as a chance to turn the company into a "world-class manufacturer" by improving materials handling, work flows, employment practices, and systems. For them, the project was a broad-gauged improvement effort in which new equipment played an important but not central role.

For the marketing people, the project was an opportunity to reduce the need to repackage millions of rolls of film for specialty markets. They saw a growing need for different packaging for different channels and customers. For them, variety and flexibility were key.

At the senior level, the overarching mission of the project was to add capacity to meet the growing demand for 35mm film. While improvements in the process would be desirable, senior managers considered them secondary.

With a leadership vacuum and no vision at the level of the business, the project, or the process, the Factory-of-the-Future effort went off in several directions. As conflicts and inconsistencies surfaced, the team focused its efforts on redesigning the technical elements of the process to try to come up with a total system that could meet the complex interests and needs of the various functional groups. And, as the project grew in complexity, the original budget and lead time ballooned. What had started out as an 18-month project was turning into a five-year effort.

While the project was struggling to find coherence, Kodak reorganized its operations into business units. In 1987, the managers of the new film line of business took a hard look at the Factory-of-the-Future project. They realized it would be another two years before capacity would be on-line, and they canceled the project.

Not all the work was abandoned, however. Senior managers of the film business mounted a new finishing project. This time around, they made sure that the new initiative was guided by a coherent strategy for the business and by a much more focused, consistent vision for the project and the sought-after process. Demand for film was growing, so capacity was crucial. The market was increasingly fragmented, requiring an increasing variety of packaging and the ability to respond quickly to shifts in the needed product mix. The new finishing process had to supply the required total capacity and had to be able to produce a high volume at a low cost. It also had to be fast and flexible so that it could cope with a much higher level of variety.

Armed with a much clearer sense of purpose and much stronger overall leadership, the Factory-of-the-Future project was launched again. Led by a business-unit team, the project utilized improvements in conventional technology and many new ideas in operational flexibility, materials handling, work flow, and systems to achieve its objectives. In the end, Factory of the Future II was a significant success.

Invariably, however, senior executives arrive at this point with some fundamental questions: "What we've seen here makes sense. But look at what you are asking these leaders of heavyweight projects and dedicated, autonomous teams to do. You want them to be influential across a range of disciplines. Yet they have to be able to integrate and see the whole. You want them to have a down-to-earth business sense. Yet they need imagination: their crystal ball must anticipate customers' unarticulated needs, preempt competitors' moves, and spot technological trends. It's not that we don't have any people like that, but where are we going to find enough of them?"

The problem is actually much worse. Companies not only need project leaders of substantial quality. They also need people who can do two things effectively: serve as team members and lead the effort within their respective functions. What is more, they need senior executives (heads of businesses and heads of functions) who are capable of a very different kind of leadership than they have exercised in the past.

The challenge is both to find and develop the right kind of people and to expand significantly their capacity for leadership. The challenge is to understand what leadership requires of people and to create a process and a system in which leaders develop naturally as part of the life of the business. In all the companies that we have studied where leadership thrives, senior managers consistently do three things.

1. **They expect leadership.** Leaders will not and cannot lead unless that role has been defined and that expectation established. Part of this involves simply setting up something like a heavyweight structure (or a dedicated team) with formal roles for the project leader and the core functional leaders. But it also means setting expectations for what senior managers want those leaders to do. Expectations define not only the responsibilities but also the attitudes, behaviors, and patterns of action required to carry them out.

2. **They support leaders.** In some of the five companies studied, the job of project leader was not an attractive assignment. One engineering manager at Digital Equipment spoke disdainfully about his role as a project leader. "It's not my real job," he said. He derived satisfaction and respect only from his engineering work and his role as an engineering manager. In such settings, project leaders are little more than clerks. So part of what support means is to redefine the status of the role.

   Project leaders also need supporting processes and systems that give them what they need to lead. They need a project charter that defines the project's link to the business strategy. They need a contract with senior managers that defines the boundaries of the project, its vision, its objectives, and its access to resources. They need information critical to the project. They need a senior-executive sponsor who counsels and coaches, advises and consults, and provides air cover for the project, protecting it from meddling. They need meaningful control and influence over critical resources. They need a license to challenge what needs to be challenged in order for the project to achieve its objectives. And, above all else, they need an organization that has provided them with the right experience, training, and personal development. This is what outstanding companies do.

3. **They reward leaders.** To be consistent, companies must reward good leaders for substance: actions taken, not just form. There is much to learn here from the small, hungry entrepreneurial companies, where the rewards for leading a great project and for building the business are clear. The coin of the realm is equity, promotions, and the chance to

take on the next really great project. Too often, big companies offer too few rewards. Especially where the functions control the rewards, leading a project can be a big negative—out of sight, out of mind. It is almost impossible to attract the best people to project leadership if the job is not valued enough or means missed promotions or lower compensation. Outstanding companies value and reward leadership.

Taken together, these three actions define a distinctive pattern of senior-executive leadership in product development. At its heart is the notion that the way to grow and attract leaders and make them effective in a heavyweight or a dedicated team is to make projects the engines that power the enterprise. In most companies, but especially those with a strong functional orientation, projects are too often an exception to the standard way of getting things done. The functions are at the center of the business.

But to make heavyweight and dedicated teams work, to build great leaders capable of creating great products, projects must be central. Indeed, in organizations where the concept of teams and leadership takes hold, projects become the way the business gets anything complex and significant done on time, on target, and within budget. And we mean *anything*: entering a new market, opening a new store, building a new information system, starting up a new channel of distribution, or introducing a new class of service. Anything that is complex, confronts an uncertain future, involves multiple functions or disciplines, and must happen under rigorous time, budget, and quality constraints is an opportunity for a heavyweight or dedicated team and heavyweight leadership.

It should be clear from this perspective that where projects are central, where leaders thrive, the values, concepts, and practices that we have sketched permeate the organization. In an important way, leadership in product development and leadership in carrying out major projects is like a fractal: no matter how far down in the organization one goes, one sees the same pattern.

Once that happens, the question the senior executive posed earlier—where to find enough leaders—finds a ready answer. As that pattern of getting work done and as that kind of leadership begins to take hold, experience in the business attracts and creates a new kind of leader. Not everyone will be a leader, but leaders will emerge naturally as part of normal growth and development within the company. Leading projects will become the way one develops as a general manager. Over time, the ranks of the senior executives will be filled by people capable of integrative leadership with a rich background of getting things done through projects. For them, building capabilities, using projects to change the company, and fostering leadership throughout the organization will be second nature. And it is that capacity that will be crucial in the turbulent years ahead. It is the capacity for perpetually renewing the enterprise—the ability to see a different future, to seize opportunities, to marshal resources, and to take action to build that future—that will be the touchstone of the future.

Note

1. Kim B. Clark and Takahiro Fujimoto, *Product Development Performance: Strategy, Organization, and Management in the World Auto Industry* (Boston: Harvard Business School Press, 1991), 247–285.

About the Contributors

H. Kent Bowen, formerly at the Massachusetts Institute of Technology, is the William Barclay Harding Professor of Business Administration at the Harvard Business School, where he teaches a technology and operations course. He has carried out research and lectured extensively on materials development, manufacturing, and technology transfer.

Joseph L. Bower is the Donald Kirk David Professor of Business Administration, chair of doctoral programs, and director of research at the Harvard Business School. He is the author of *When Markets Quake: The Management and Challenge of Restructuring Industry,* and editor of *The Craft of Management* (both Harvard Business School Press).

David N. Burt is the National Association of Purchasing Management Professor of Marketing and Procurement at The University of San Diego. He has been a consultant for numerous manufacturing, service, health care, and government clients, and is the co-author of *Zero Base Pricing: Achieving World Class Competitiveness Through Reduced All-in-Costs* and *Purchasing and Materials Management: Text and Cases,* and the author of *Proactive Procurement: The Key to Increased Profits, Productivity and Quality.*

Kim B. Clark is the Harry E. Figgie, Jr., Professor of Business Administration at the Harvard Business School, where he serves as chair of the technology and operations management area and heads the Science and Technology Interest Group. Specializing in issues of product development and technology, and operations strategy, he is a frequent contributor to the *Harvard Business Review* and other management journals, and is the co-author with Steven Wheelwright of *Revolutionizing Product Development, Managing New Product and Process Development,* and *Leading Product Development.* He is also the co-author with Takahiro Fujimoto of *Product Development Performance: Strategy, Organization, and Management in the World Auto Industry* (Harvard Business School Press), which received the 1992 Nikkei Culture Award for economics publications.

Don Clausing is the Bernard M. Gordon Adjunct Professor of Engineering Innovation and Practice at the Massachusetts Institute of Technology, where he has integrated the principles of quality function development, low-cost quality engineering, and other international practices designed to improve product development and manufacturing. Formerly principal engineer at Xerox, Dr. Clausing served on the MIT Commission of Industrial Productivity and the Defense Science Board, and is the author of *Total Quality Development.*

James W. Dean, Jr., is an associate professor of management in the College of Business Administration at the University of Cincinnati. He conducts research on total quality management, advanced manufacturing, concurrent engineering, and strategic decision making. He is the author of *Total Quality: Management, Organization, and Strategy* and *Deciding to Innovate: How Firms Justify Advanced Technology.* Professor Dean also serves on the editorial boards of *Academy of Management Review* and *Journal of Engineering and Technology Management.*

Richard N. Foster is a director in McKinsey & Company's New York office. He works primarily with multinational, multibusiness, technology-based companies on issues of strategy, organization, operations, and mergers and acquisitions. He has written on technology and innovation for *Business Week, The Wall Street Journal,* and the *Harvard Business Review.* In 1986 he published *Innovation: The Attacker's Advantage,* which has sold over 180,000 copies in 18 languages.

Takahiro Fujimoto is an associate professor of business administration at Tokyo University. He is the co-author with Kim Clark of *Product Development Performance: Strategy, Organization, and Management in the World Auto Industry* (Harvard Business School Press), which won the 1992 Nikkei Culture Award for economics publications.

Frederick W. Gluck is a director in McKinsey & Company's New York office. In July 1994 he completed two three-year terms as the firm's managing director. He has advised companies throughout the world in telecommunications and electronics, as well as broadcasting, health care, and machinery, on issues of corporate and business-unit strategy and technology. Mr. Gluck has written on the topics of strategy and technology in the *Journal of Business Strategy, The McKinsey Quarterly, The Wall Street Journal,* and the *Harvard Business Review.*

Ralph E. Gomory has been president of the Alfred P. Sloan Foundation since 1989. He is also a director of The Bank of New York, The Washington Post Company, Ashland Oil, Inc., Lexmark International, Inc., and the Polaroid Corporation. In recent years he has written on the nature of technology and product development, research in industry, industrial competitiveness, and economic models involving economies of scale.

John R. Hauser is the Kirin Professor of Marketing, head of the marketing group, and co-director of the International Center for Research on the Management of Technology at MIT's Sloan School of Management. He was editor-in-chief of *Marketing Science* from 1988 to 1994. His primary research interest is the integration of customer perspectives into product and service management. He is the co-author of two textbooks, *Design and Marketing of New Products* and *Essentials of New Product Management,* and two computer-based texts/software packages, *Applying Marketing Management* and *Enterprise: An Integrating Management Exercise.*

Rebecca Henderson is the Robert N. Noyce Career Development Associate Professor of Strategic Management at the Massachusetts Institute of Technology and a research fellow at the National Bureau of Economic Research. She specializes in technology strategy and product and process management.

James E. Hodder is the Charles and Laura Albright Professor of Finance and a Wisconsin Distinguished Professor of Business at University of Wisconsin, Madison. His research interests include international and domestic finance, as well as international plant location decisions. Professor Hodder has published articles in a wide variety of finance and economics journals, including *Journal of Finance, Harvard Business Review,* and *European Journal of Operational Research.*

Charles A. Holloway is the Kleiner, Perkins, Caufield and Byers Professor of Management at the Stanford University Graduate School of Business, where he is co-director of the Stanford Integrated Manufacturing Association.

Charles H. House was general manager of the Software Engineering Systems Division of Hewlett-Packard in Palo Alto at the time of his article's publication. For five years, he had been HP's corporate engineering director.

Thomas M. Hout is a vice president of The Boston Consulting Group and head of the firm's worldwide operational effectiveness practice. Hout is co-author, with his colleague George Stalk, Jr., of *Competing Against Time*, published in 1990 and now available internationally in eight languages. Hout and Stalk first coined the term "time based competition," and are featured in the Harvard Business School Management Productions video series "Time Based Competition." Hout speaks and writes widely on reengineering strategic issues in business competition.

Marco Iansiti is an associate professor at the Harvard Business School, and is the faculty chairman of Leading Product Development, a summer executive program. Specializing in issues of technology management and product development, he has also consulted to several major Fortune 500 companies, and is currently researching technology and product development in the microelectronics, computer, and automobile industries. Some of Professor Iansiti's most recent written work is included in *The Perpetual Enterprise Machine: High Performance Product Development in the 1990s*.

Jon R. Katzenbach has been with McKinsey & Company, Inc. for more than three decades, and since the mid-1980s has led the firm's worldwide organization performance and change practice. During his years with McKinsey, Mr. Katzenbach's primary areas of interest have been strategy, organization, and leadership/managing issues of large institutions. He has served the top executives of leading companies in forest products, energy, electronics, industrial products, consumer products, medical products, and financial services. He is the co-author with Douglas Smith of *The Wisdom of Teams: Creating the High-Performance Organization* (Harvard Business School Press), and has also authored several articles and papers on teams.

Fumio Kodama is a professor of science, technology, and industry at the University of Tokyo, Research Center for Advanced Science and Technology. Previously a visiting professor at Stanford University and Harvard University's Kennedy School of Government, he conducts research and lectures worldwide on issues of innovation and technology policy. He is the co-author, with Lewis Branscomb, of *Japanese*

Innovation Strategy and author of *Emerging Patterns of Innovation: Sources of Japan's Technological Edge* (Harvard Business School Press).

Dorothy Leonard-Barton is a professor at the Harvard Business School, where she served for three years as faculty chair for the Harvard course on building development capabilities, and is a faculty member of Harvard programs in managing global opportunities and managing international collaboration. Professor Leonard-Barton's major research interests and consulting expertise are in technology strategy and commercialization. Her more than 25 publications appear in academic journals, practitioner journals, and books on technology management, and she is currently writing *The Knowledge Renaissance: Creating Core Technological Capabilities* (Harvard Business School Press).

Christopher Meyer is managing director of the Strategic Alignment Group, a consulting firm in Portola Valley, California, that specializes in helping companies reduce time in knowledge-based work, such as product development, and design and implement multifunctional teams. He is the author of *Fast Cycle Time: How to Align Purpose, Strategy, and Structure for Speed.*

T. Michael Nevens is a director in McKinsey & Company's San Jose office. He works with companies in the computer, semiconductor, telecommunications, and defense/aerospace industries on sales and marketing, R&D, and organization and strategy issues, and is leader of the firm's electronics practice. Mr. Nevens is co-author of McKinsey's annual report on the computer industry, and has written for the *Harvard Business Review, Electronic Business, The Wall Street Journal,* and the *Financial Times.*

Ikujiro Nonaka is a professor of management at the Institute for Business Research, Hitotsubashi University in Tokyo. He has published several articles in the *Harvard Business Review,* including "The Knowledge-Creating Company."

Raymond L. Price is director of employee training and development at Boeing Commercial Airplane Group, where he has introduced and improved alternative learning methods, and established a standard of performance-based training that focuses on the accomplishment of business goals. His articles on organizational development have appeared in *Organizational Dynamics,* and he contributed a chapter entitled "A Customer's View of Organizational Literature" to *Publishing in the Organizational Sciences.*

418   *About the Contributors*

Steven E. Prokesch is a senior editor at the *Harvard Business Review.* He previously served as an editor and reporter at *The New York Times* and *Business Week* magazine.

Henry E. Riggs is president and professor of engineering at Harvey Mudd College in Claremont, California. His academic interests focus on management of technology, technical strategy, new venture management, and financial analysis and control. His most recent book is *Understanding the Financial Score,* and he has published articles in a wide variety of finance, engineering, and business journals. He is currently a director of Income Fund of America, Growth Fund of America, American Balanced Fund, Fundamental Investors, Inc., AMCAP, and Sera Solar Corporation.

W. Earl Sasser, Jr., is the UPS Foundation Professor of Service Management at the Harvard Business School, where he serves as faculty Chair of the advanced management program. He has co-authored several publications in the field of service management; his most recent book is *Service Breakthroughs: Changing the Rules of the Game,* and he is featured in the Harvard Business School Management Productions video series "People, Service, Success."

Douglas K. Smith is a leading commentator on organizational performance and change and a former McKinsey & Company, Inc. consultant. He was most recently the co-author with Jon Katzenbach of *The Wisdom of Teams: Creating the High-Performance Organization* (Harvard Business School Press), and previously published *Sources of the African Past* and *Fumbling the Future: How Xerox Invented and Then Ignored the First Personal Computer.*

William R. Soukup is an associate professor of management at the University of San Diego, where his teaching focuses primarily on entrepreneurship and strategic management. He has also conducted seminars and presentations in Taiwan and Moscow, and has taught international management in Paris and international negotiations in London. Dr. Soukup has had extensive industrial experience in new product development, strategic planning, and production management for several leading companies, including ITT, Colt Industries, and Cummins Engine Company. He is a winner of the A.T. Kearney Award for outstanding research in the field of general management.

Gregory L. Summe is the vice president and general manager of AlliedSignal's General Aviation Avionics Division. Prior to joining

AlliedSignal in 1993, he was the general manager of commercial motors at General Electric and a partner at McKinsey & Company, Inc. He is also the co-author of "Keep Your Customers Coming Back," included in the *Harvard Business Review* collection *Keeping Customers* (Harvard Business School Press).

Gerald I. Susman is the Robert and Judith Klein Professor of Management at The Pennsylvania State University, director of the University's Center for the Management of Technological and Organizational Change, and chairman of the department of management and organization. Professor Susman has been a consultant to many public and private organizations, including the Office of Personnel Management, the National Center for Productivity and Quality of Working Life, U.S. Department of Labor, and the cities of Baltimore and San Antonio. His books and monographs include *Autonomy at Work: A Sociotechnical Analysis of Participative Management*, *A Guide to Labor-Management Committees in State and Local Government*, *The Roles of Third Parties in Labor-Management Cooperative Endeavors*, and *Integrating Design and Manufacturing for Competitive Advantage*.

Hirotaka Takeuchi is a professor at the Institute for Business Research, Hitotsubashi University in Tokyo. At the time of his article's publication, Professor Takeuchi's research focused on marketing and global competition.

Bro Uttal is a consultant in McKinsey & Company's New York office. He has written more than 60 articles on innovation, technology management, and new product development. He is also the co-author of another *Harvard Business Review* article, "Service Companies: Focus or Falter," included in the *Harvard Business Review* collection *Command Performance* (Harvard Business School Press), and of the book, *Total Customer Service: The Ultimate Weapon*.

Steven C. Wheelwright is the Class of 1949 Professor of Business Administration at the Harvard Business School, having previously been the Kleiner, Perkins, Caufield and Byers Professor of Management at Stanford University's Graduate School of Business, where he directed the strategic management program. His research and writing focuses on product and process development, manufacturing strategy, and competing through manufacturing, especially related to commercializing new product and manufacturing process technologies. Dr. Wheelwright is the author or co-author of numerous articles and thirteen books, including *Revolutionizing Product Development, Managing*

New Product and Process Development, and *Leading Product Development,* with Kim Clark; *Restoring Our Competitive Edge,* with Robert Hayes; and *Dynamic Manufacturing,* with professors Clark and Hayes.

Daniel F. Whitney is a senior research scientist at the Center for Technology, Policy, and Industrial Development at the Massachusetts Institute of Technology. His research interests are in design and manufacturing strategy, technical core competencies, and worldwide benchmarking of design and manufacturing capabilities. He is an authority on Japanese methods for using product design to achieve manufacturing strategies.

INDEX